P9-CLS-285

LONGSTREET HIGHROAD GUIDE
TO THE

MAINE
COAST

BY ELIZABETH EDWARDSEN

LONGSTREET
ATLANTA, GEORGIA

Published by
LONGSTREET PRESS, INC.
a subsidiary of Cox Newspapers,
a subsidiary of Cox Enterprises, Inc.
2140 Newmarket Parkway
Suite 122
Marietta, Georgia 30067

Great efforts have been made to make the information in this book as accurate as possible. However, over time, trails are rerouted and signs and landmarks may change. If you find a change has occurred to a trail in the book, please let us know so we can correct future editions.
A word of caution: Outdoor recreation by its nature is potentially hazardous. All participants in such activities must assume all responsibility for their own actions and safety. The scope of this book does not cover all potential hazards and risks involved in outdoor recreation activities.

Printed by RR Donnelley & Sons, Harrisonburg, VA

1st printing 1999

Library of Congress Catalog Number 99-61769

ISBN: 1-56352-545-3

Book editing, design, and cartography
by Lenz Design & Communications, Inc., Decatur, Georgia

Cover illustration by J. Douglas Woodward, *Picturesque America*, 1872

Cover design by Richard J. Lenz, Decatur, Georgia

Illustrations by Danny Woodard, Loganville, Georgia

Photographs courtesy of the Maine Office of Tourism

The edge of the sea is a strange and beautiful place.
All through the long history of Earth it has been an area of unrest where waves have
broken heavily against the land, where the tides have pressed forward over the
continents, receded, and then returned.
For no two successive days is the shore line precisely the same.
Not only do the tides advance and retreat in their eternal rhythms,
but the level of the sea itself is never at rest.
It rises or falls as the glaciers melt or grow, as the floor of the deep ocean basins shifts
under its increasing load of sediments, or as the earth's crust along the continental
margins warps up or down in adjustment to strain and tension.
Today a little more land may belong to the sea, tomorrow a little less.
Always the edge of the sea remains an elusive and indefinable boundary.

—Rachel Carson, *The Edge of the Sea*

Contents

Maine

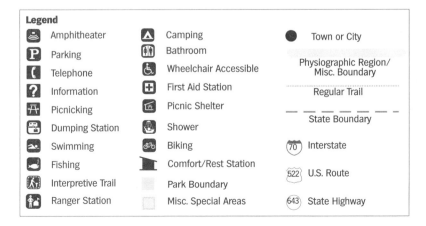

Legend

Amphitheater		Camping		Town or City	
Parking		Bathroom		Physiographic Region/ Misc. Boundary	
Telephone		Wheelchair Accessible			
Information		First Aid Station		Regular Trail	
Picnicking		Picnic Shelter		State Boundary	
Dumping Station		Shower			
Swimming		Biking		Interstate	
Fishing		Comfort/Rest Station		U.S. Route	
Interpretive Trail		Park Boundary		State Highway	
Ranger Station		Misc. Special Areas			

How Your Highroad Guide Is Organized

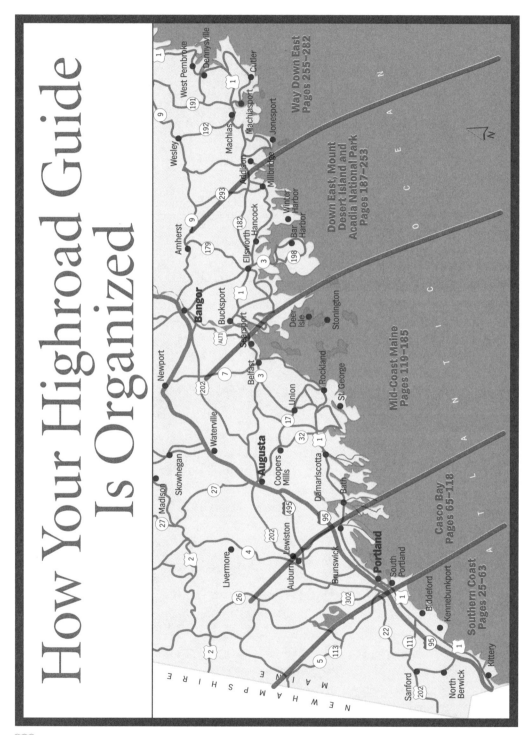

How to Use Your Longstreet Highroad Guide

The *Longstreet Highroad Guide to the Maine Coast* offers detailed information about the best places on the Maine coast to pursue your favorite outdoor activities, including hiking, camping, fishing, boating, biking, wildlife watching, and touring of historic sites. The book also includes restaurant, lodging, and night life information. These attractions are known to change over time, altering their operating hours, ownership, or style, so it is wise to call ahead before making a long drive to visit an establishment listed here.

The book includes detailed descriptions of the flora and fauna you may encounter on your travels along the Maine coast, as well as information on the natural and human history of most areas, which can add dimension and depth to any outdoor pursuit.

The book is divided into six sections: the Southern Coast, Casco Bay, Mid-Coast Maine, Down East Maine, Mount Desert Island and Acadia National Park, and Way Down East Maine. An additional chapter covers the coast's natural history.

The maps in the book are keyed by figure number and referenced in the text. They should help both casual and seasoned coastal travelers get oriented. While some Maine trails have remained unchanged for decades, others may be rerouted or closed. In Acadia National Park, trails and carriage roads are sometimes closed for renovations or because peregrine falcons are nesting nearby. Many island nature preserves are closed for the seabird nesting season.

A word of caution: The Maine coast can be a dangerous place. The weather can change quickly and unexpectedly, and even at the height of summer, hikers would do well to carry a fleece jacket or other warm clothing with them. The rocks along the coast can also be hazardous. Rockweed and algae can make the rocky coast very slippery, and rogue waves have washed many a sightseer into the surf at scenic points. The water along the Maine coast is extremely cold. Sea kayakers and others venturing out onto the sea here should wear adequate clothing, which may include a drysuit or wetsuit, and carry safety equipment including a personal flotation device. Several of the island hikes described in this book require you to consult a tide calendar and keep an eye on your watch; stay too long on these islands and an incoming tide will strand you until the next low tide. Most local newspapers include the area's high and low tides. Many of the trails described here do not have access to fresh water, so make sure to carry it with you. Use common sense when exploring the Maine coast to ensure your memories are all happy ones.

Preface

Many an amateur naturalist has been born along the Maine coast. The conversion you undergo on the rocky coast sneaks up, as the forces of nature beguile unsuspecting tourists. You arrive, intent simply on escaping the heat of your hometown, ready to enjoy some scenery, shop in a harbor village straight out of *Murder, She Wrote*, and eat a lobster or two.

But it doesn't take long for the Maine coast's natural wonders to work their magic. Coastal birds, standing stone still on the shore or torpedoing into the sea, catch your eye. As you eat your lobster and admire the view in one of Maine's scenic harbors, you notice a harbor seal, curiously looking back at you. Your gaze stays on geologic features—dramatic, wave-beaten points, pink granite cliffs, and simple round boulders that appear to have been dropped out of nowhere along roads and trails.

A visit to the beach gets more interesting as you take a minute to inspect the tide pools among the rocks, where you can watch tiny snails, starfish, crabs, barnacles, and other sea life up close.

Along the Maine coast's famous and lovely rocky shore, pine trees grow in just a few inches of soil at the water's edge. Deep in the forests and on the many peat bogs found here, orchids and other flowers grow in surprising pockets of color.

How did all this get here? Where and when can I find more wildlife, plants, and scenery? Those are the questions I hope curious explorers will keep in mind as they walk, paddle, pedal, and otherwise travel along this unique coastline with their *Highroad Guide to the Maine Coast* in hand.

LOBSTER
(Homarus americanus)
Lobsters are decapods (ten-legged crustaceans) that can grow to 40 pounds and more than a yard in length.

The natural and historic sites you will find in these pages will entice you off the heavily worn tourist track along this coast. Many of these parks, preserves, and historic sites are pockets of calm very close to the busy tourist towns. Some can be explored as part of a day trip, while others would take days, weeks, or longer to fully explore.

I've included tips on what to look for while you're here. Please use this guide as a starting point. Bring a pencil along and mark the margins up, keep notes on what you saw, and make this book your own.

I've also included attractions, restaurants, and lodging that I believe are worth a visit. Our tastes may differ, or these businesses may undergo a change of ownership. (And please always call ahead to check on pricing and hours, which can fluctuate wildly over the course of a year.)

Please walk lightly along the Maine coast. Many of the sites in these pages are very fragile. Stay on the trails and the boardwalks and help preserve the Maine coast's natural resources.

Finally, many of these special places wouldn't be here but for the organizations that have protected them, like The Nature Conservancy, the Maine Audubon Society, the Maine Coast Heritage Trust, and the Maine Island Trail Association. Anyone who loves the Maine coast should consider joining these organizations and supporting their work.

—Elizabeth Edwardsen

CARDINAL FLOWER
(Lobelia cardinalis) This wildflower gets its name from its bright red flowers. It is found in damp areas, especially along streams.

Acknowledgments

The Maine coast has long attracted naturalists, scientists, conservationists, and others interested in studying and preserving its habitats and natural beauty. I owe many of these people a huge debt for taking the time to share some of their expertise with me as I compiled the information for what I hope is an accurate and comprehensive guide to this ecologically rich region.

I'm especially grateful to Judy Walker, staff naturalist at Maine Audubon Society, for her sharp eye and good advice. And I owe a big thank you to Ranger Wanda Moran at Acadia National Park and to Stephen M. Dickson, Ph.D., marine geologist at the Maine Geological Survey.

The Maine Chapter of the Nature Conservancy does invaluable work preserving important natural areas along the Maine Coast. Many Conservancy staffers and preserve stewards were helpful in the preparation of this book. The Conservancy's Kyle Stockwell and Bruce Kidman were extremely generous with their time and knowledge.

Several employees of the Maine Bureau of Parks and Lands were also a big help. Thank you to the Bureau of Parks and Lands Deputy Director Herb Hartman, Andy Hutchinson at Wolfe Neck Woods State Park, Stuart Wagner at Cobscook Bay State Park, Philip Farr at Holbrook Island Sanctuary, Gordon Bell at Camden Hills State Park, John Smith at Quoddy Head State Park, and Jim Davis at Fort Edgecomb.

Also offering valuable assistance were Dennis Brown at Colonial Pemaquid, Harold L. Bailey at Campobello, Eugene Dumont of the Department of Inland Fisheries and Wildlife at Swan Island, Kent Kirkpatrick and Laura Stone at the Wells National Estuarine Research Reserve, Tom Bradbury at Kennebunkport Conservation Trust, John Andrews at Saco Trails, Laura Newman and Alix Hopkins at Portland Trails, Robert Peyton, Maurice Mills Jr., and Lauri Munroe at Moosehorn National

BOREAL CHICKADEE
(Parus hudsonicus)
Common in boreal forests, these "brown caps" sometimes travel hundreds of miles south of their normal range in search of food.

COMMON RAVEN
(Corvus corax)
Ravens are large birds with long heavy bills and long wedge-shaped tails. They are sometimes mistaken for their smaller cousins, the crows.

Wildlife Refuge, Stan Skutek at Petit Manan National Wildlife Refuge, Dawn Kidd at Boothbay Region Land Trust, Eliza Bailey at the Georges River Land Trust, Susan Bloomfield at Rachel Carson National Wildlife Refuge, Mike Kempner at Native Trails, and Karen Stimpson at the Maine Island Trail Association. Thanks, too, to Nancy Marshall and Ann Gordon of Nancy Marshall Communications. The staffs at the Southworth Planetarium, Two Lights State Park, Lake Saint George State Park, and Reid State Park were also helpful.

Thanks to Kathryn Buxton, Rick Ackermann, Victoria Brett, Pat Wellenbach, Jerry Harkavy, Glenn Adams, Martha Englert, Tim Queeney, Ann Kocher, Ruth Ayers, Deb Dalfonso, Marsha Donahue, and Cynthia Hacinli for sharing their coastal knowledge and recommendations. Thanks to Dee Dee Blake, Darien Brahms, Linda Beidel, and Wendy Keeler for keeping the decks clear while I wrote.

And thank you to Marge McDonald, project director of the Highroad series at Longstreet Press, for hiring me, and to Pam Holliday and Richard Lenz of Lenz Design and Communications Inc., two very patient and meticulous editors. Thanks, too, to Phil Brown, writer of the impressive *Longstreet Highroad Guide to the New York Adirondacks*, who got me started on this book.

Finally, a big thank you to my husband, Tim Beidel, for being an enthusiastic traveling companion during the research phase of this guide. Thanks, too, to my daughter, Harriet, for behaving her 2-year-old self in countless nature preserves, parks, and sanctuaries, and for displaying what Rachel Carson would call a sense of wonder—something we all should have as we explore the Maine coast.

—Elizabeth Edwardsen

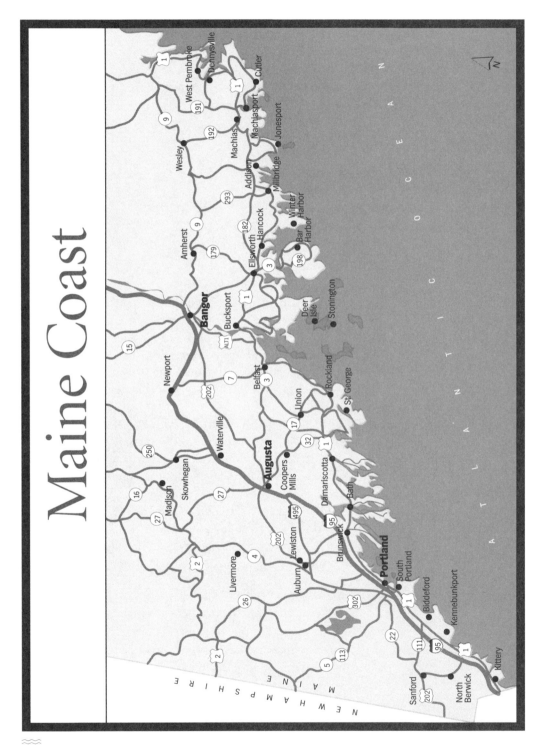

Maine Coast

The Natural History
of the Maine Coast

I t is about 230 miles from one end of Maine's coast to the other. But the coastline takes a meandering route from Kittery northeast to Eastport. There are more than 3,500 miles of coast when tracing Maine's many peninsulas, bays, and islands. This jagged continental border is rich with ecological variety. Sand beaches and salt marshes make up much of the southern coast. A relatively straight stretch of sandy coastline comes to an end at Casco Bay and Mid-Coast Maine, where rocky peninsulas point into the sea between dozens of tidal rivers and streams. Maine's famous windswept rocky coastline is most evident in Down East Maine, beginning in Penobscot Bay and heading to the farthest reaches of the state. More than 4,000 islands, from rocky ledges to year-round communities, speckle the waters off the coast.

The Maine coast is a place of transition. It is here that the gentle, sandy seashore more typical of the Mid-Atlantic coast gives way to the rocky headlands of the North

[*Above: A view from Acadia National Park*]

Geologic Time Scale

Era	System & Period	Series & Epoch	Some Distinctive Features	Years Before Present
CENOZOIC	**Quaternary**	Recent	Modern man.	11,000
		Pleistocene	Early man; northern glaciation.	1/2 to 2 million
	Tertiary	Pliocene	Large carnivores.	13 ± 1 million
		Miocene	First abundant grazing mammals.	25 ± 1 million
		Oligocene	Large running mammals.	36 ± 2 million
		Eocene	Many modern types of mammals.	58 ± 2 million
		Paleocene	First placental mammals.	63 ± 2 million
MESOZOIC	**Cretaceous**		First flowering plants; climax of dinosaurs and ammonites, followed by Cretaceous-Tertiary extinction.	135 ± 5 million
	Jurassic		First birds, first mammals dinosaurs and ammonites abundant.	181 ± 5 million
	Triassic		First dinosaurs. Abundant cycads and conifers.	230 ± 10 million
PALEOZOIC	**Permian**		Extinction of most kinds of marine animals, including trilobites. Southern glaciation.	280 ± 10 million
	Carboniferous	Pennsylvanian	Great coal forests, conifers. First reptiles.	310 ± 10 million
		Mississippian	Sharks and amphibians abundant. Large and numerous scale trees and seed ferns.	345 ± 10 million
	Devonian		First amphibians; ammonites; fishes abundant.	405 ± 10 million
	Silurian		First terrestrial plants and animals.	425 ± 10 million
	Ordovician		First fishes; invertebrates dominant.	500 ± 10 million
	Cambrian		First abundant record of marine life; trilobites dominant.	600 ± 50 million
	Precambrian		Fossils extremely rare, consisting of primitive aquatic plants. Evidence of glaciation. Oldest dated algae, over 2,600 million years; oldest dated meteorites 4,500 million years.	

Atlantic coast. The northern hardwood forest mingles with the northern boreal forest along the Maine coast, and many plants and birds are at the northern or southern reaches of their ranges here. Just offshore, the cool Eastern Maine Coastal Current can chill humid summer air, creating a wall of fog that can swiftly enshroud the coast and its islands. The Maine coast's climate, which is influenced by latitude, altitude, and the ocean waters of the Gulf of Maine, is also quite varied.

This immense variety in terrain and climate contributes to the beauty of the Maine coast. It also provides many different habitats that help support diverse communities of plants and animals.

Coastal Maine Geology

Much of the story behind the Maine coast can be read in the rocks that make up its shoreline and traced to a few geological events that took place over hundreds of millions of years.

Geologically, most of the rocks on the Maine coast can be traced to the Paleozoic Era, between 245 million and 545 million years ago, when most of its bedrock was formed.

Over the course of hundreds of millions of years, a series of processes occurred and reoccurred: Silt and mud were deposited on the floor of an ancient sea, piling up until titanic forces of pressure and heat transformed them into bedrock.

As this long period of bedrock-building was continuing, the face of the earth was being shaped by a series of larger geologic occurrences. According to the Plate Tectonics theory, large sections of the earth's crust, or plates, are constantly moving apart, colliding, or grinding by each other. Collisions of the plates can cause major, mountain-building upheavals called orogenies, while rifts in the crust can create oceans. Geologists believe the earth's continents have drifted apart and merged together several times. As this continental drift progresses, at the rate of a few inches per year, powerful forces of heat and pressure are created, metamorphosing sediments and lava into hard rock.

A series of orogenies, or mountain-building events, shaped the surface of North America. During the Acadian orogeny, about 400 million years ago, the landmasses that would eventually become Europe and North America collided. It was that event and the heat it generated that geologists believe formed much of the granite found on the Maine coast. Maine then lay in the middle of an ancient supercontinent geologists call Pangea. Most of the earth's continental crust stayed together in Pangea for 200 million years. This supercontinent eventually broke apart, creating the continents and oceans we know today. A later episode of igneous activity, during early continental rifting, sent eruptions of molten rock into cracks in the granite. Some of the solidified molten rock can be seen today at Schoodic Point (*see* page 259), where black diabase dikes run through the pink granite cliffs.

The plates of the earth's crust continue to move at an imperceptible rate. Earthquakes and volcanoes tend to occur at the boundaries between active plates, now far from the Maine coast.

Bedrock is the outer portion of the earth's crust. Maine's bedrock is typically covered with a thin layer of soil and vegetation—often just a few inches thick. There are several places to see Maine's bedrock exposed—at the dramatic, wave-pummeled shores of Pemaquid Point or Portland Head Light, or at the top of the glacially rounded coastal summits at Cadillac Mountain or the Camden Hills.

Much of the bedrock along the Maine coast is granite, which contributes to the acidic nature of the soil above it. This relatively thin layer of acidic soil has an impact on what kind of vegetation will grow here. Trees or plants that have shallow roots and thrive in low-nutrient soil are well suited for much of the Maine coast.

GLACIERS AND THE DROWNED COAST

The most recent Ice Age was a blip in the geologic time scale, but its impact on the landscape of the Maine coast was profound.

Geologists believe that glaciers covered Maine several times during the Pleistocene Epoch, which lasted from about 2 million years ago to about 10,000 years ago. The most recent glacier to cover most of North America, including Maine, was the Laurentide ice sheet, a massive layer of ice that spread over New England about 25,000 years ago and is thought to have been 1 mile or more thick. As the sheet of ice moved, it rounded the summits of the mountaintops. Rocks, stone, and grit that were embedded in its base abraded the bedrock over which it passed. The grooves and scratches it left can still be seen on bedrock around the state.

The glacier also picked up debris and deposited it miles from its original location. The erratic boulders that sit obtrusively along several coastal trails are evidence of this. Mount Desert Island is one of the best places in Maine to find evidence of the Ice Age. Scrapes, or chattermarks, left by the moving ice can be seen on rounded mountain summits and exposed bedrock. Nearly every mountain on Mount Desert Island has a north-to-south ridge. The lakes, ponds, and Somes Sound fjord, too, bear witness to the southerly route the ice mass followed.

About 18,000 years ago, a warming trend stopped the final glacier. The thick ice had been weighing the coast down. As it melted, the water it shed caused the sea level to rise by as much as 400 feet, and the Maine coastline was miles inland from its present location. The coastal land, freed from the weight of the ice, sprang slowly back up, which had the effect of dropping sea level back some 150 feet below the modern coastline. In the last 10,000 years, the sea has risen again, creating the "drowned coast" of Maine, where what were once mountaintops are now islands, and what were ridges and river valleys are now peninsulas and the tidal rivers and bays between them. This historic look shows that the Maine coastline is not a permanent line between sea and land. Indeed, the coastline today is being affected by a continuing, slow rise in the sea level.

NATIVE MAINERS

While European explorers may have been the first to record their impressions of Maine's coastal bounties, they weren't the first to appreciate it. Historians say the first human residents of the coast were Paleo-Indians, wandering hunters who followed big game—wooly mammoth, bison, and other mammals—toward the coast as the last glacier was receding. These early Native Americans are believed to have died off as a result of the environmental changes that followed the Ice Age.

One of the exciting archeological finds in Maine in the early twentieth century was the discovery of ancient burial grounds of Native Americans now called the Red Paint People because of the dusting of red ochre found in their burial sites. Judging from the tools and carvings of marine animals found buried with these 4,000-year-old remains, the Red Paint People relied on the sea as well as the land for their food.

The next known inhabitants of the fertile Maine Coast are now referred to as the Oyster Shell People, after the shell heaps they left along the shoreline 2,400 years ago. These shell heaps or "middens," which are federally protected and shouldn't be disturbed, can still be seen along riverfronts and island shores. The most famous is probably the 30-foot-tall Glidden Midden in Damariscotta.

Habitats of the Maine Coast

SAND BEACHES

Just 75 miles, or about 2 percent, of the Maine coast is beach. About half of that is sandy beach, while the rest is made up of coarser gravel, cobblestones, or rocks.

Most of the large sandy beaches are along the southern coast, with some of the more popular sunbathing and swimming beaches in the towns between Kittery and Scarborough. A few more sandy beaches, including Reid State Park and Popham Beach, are near the mouth of the Kennebec River in Maine's mid-coast region. The state's coast also has many small beaches nestled between headlands or at the heads of bays. These small beaches play an important role in the ecology of the Maine coast, as they are less likely than the long, wide beaches to be overrun with sunbathers in July and August.

With few exceptions, Maine beaches are made up of glacial outwash left by the last Ice Age. (One such exception is Sand Beach on Mount Desert, where the sand contains a percentage of ground seashells more typical of tropical beaches.)

Wind, waves, and tides are continually wearing away at the Maine coast. The work of these natural forces on the landscape is most obvious at the beach, where the sand

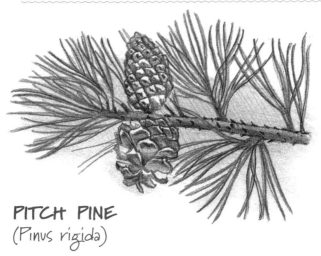

PITCH PINE
(Pinus rigida)

shifts every day and a big storm can make dramatic changes in a matter of hours. During storms, winds and large waves pull sand off the beach. After a storm has passed, small waves replace the sand on the beach, and the wind drives some of the sand into dunes that separate the beach from the marshes or uplands behind it.

Maine's beaches typically undergo a huge transformation every year, with tons of sand eroded each winter and replaced every summer.

At the rear of the beach, dunes play an important role in protecting inland areas from the sea. These dunes are built by the wind, and they are held in place by a small but powerful plant. Dune grass (*Ammophilla breviligulata*) sends long roots deep into the sand, stabilizing the dunes. The dune grass also serves as a stabilizing force atop the dunes, catching and trapping sand as it blows in the wind. Once the dune grass, also known as beach grass, has done its work, plants that are tolerant of salt spray often grow nearby. Beach heather (*Hudsonia tomentosa*) and beach pea (*Lathyrus japonicus*) can often be found growing on the sand dunes. Pitch pine (*pinus rigida*), a tree that is also tolerant of salty air and sandy soil, often grows behind the dunes.

Dunes are a fragile part of the coastal environment, and visitors should take care not to walk on them or otherwise disturb them. The open sand near the front of the dunes is a nesting area for two federally endangered species, the least tern (*Sterna antillarum*) and piping plover (*Charadrius melodus*). Their nests, which are monitored by the Maine Audubon Society, should be given a wide berth. Most dune areas that lead to popular beaches have boardwalks or paths to prevent damage to the dunes and the plants and birds that live in them.

The big Maine beaches —including Ogunquit Beach, Scarborough Beach, Popham Beach State Park, and Reid State Park—are wildly popular with locals and tourists in the summer months. The rest of the year, bird watchers often have the beaches to themselves. (Some beaches also allow leashed dogs in the off-season.) During the migration seasons—usually early May to June in the spring and mid-July to October in the fall—land birds and a wide variety of shorebirds can often be seen following the coast on their migration. In the coldest months, wintering birds, like buffleheads (*Bucephala albeola*), oldsquaws (*Clangula hyemalis*), common mergansers (*Mergus merganser*), red breasted mergansers (*Mergus serrator*), and scoters can sometimes be seen offshore.

NORTHERN HARDWOOD FOREST

Much of the environment of the southern Maine coast is similar to that found in the Mid-Atlantic or southern New England regions. Many trees, such as tupelo (*Nyssa sylvatica*) and sassafras (*Sassafras albidum*), that are common south of Maine reach their northern range and are sparsely distributed here.

The northern hardwood forest, which contains much of its original assemblage of trees, is dominated by red oak (*Quercus rubra*), sugar maple (*Acer saccharum*), American beech (*Fagus grandifolia*) and white birch (*Betula papyrifera*), with a broad scattering of Eastern white pine (*Pinus strobus*). These trees all grow in the sandy and typically deep and well-drained soil of the southern coast, where the climate is warm enough to support trees that grow new leaves every year. This forest puts on quite a display in the fall, when the blaze of red, yellow, and orange foliage attracts another seasonal wave of tourists to the Maine coast. The trees of the hardwood forest let a good bit of sun reach the forest floor in the spring, allowing for a healthy understory of tree seedlings and wildflowers. Star flowers (*Trientalis americana*) are a common sight in late spring and early summer in this forest.

AMERICAN BEECH
(*Fagus grandifolia*)

Many bird species breed in the Maine coast's deciduous woodlands. They include several types of thrush, red-eyed vireo (*Vireo olivaceus*), and ovenbirds (*Seiurus aurocapillus*). White-tailed deer (*Odocoileus virginianus*), raccoons (*Procyon lotor*), and Eastern gray squirrels (*Sciurus carolinensis*) are among the mammals that live in this hardwood forest. Some black bears (*Ursus americanus*) may also be found here, although they are much more common inland. Amphibians in these woods include Eastern red-backed salamanders (*Plethodon cinereus*) and Eastern newts (*Notophthalmus viridescens*). Common garter snakes (*Thamnophis sirtalis*) are resident reptiles.

NORTHERN BOREAL FOREST

The northern boreal forest dips south into Maine from Canada, covering much of inland northern Maine and a swath of the Down East Coast.

The mostly coniferous trees of the northern boreal forest represent a climax forest and are well equipped to deal with the region's cold winters. Evergreen trees, including red and white spruces and balsam firs found along the boreal coast, are built to withstand the region's cold temperatures and short growing season. Thick sap prevents them from freezing, and a waxy coating on their needles preserves moisture. The trees' flexible boughs are able to hold loads of heavy snow without snapping. Evergreen trees keep their needles year-round, so they don't have to expend energy growing new ones in a short growing season each year.

The soil along the coast tends to be thin, which is suitable for the shallow root systems of spruces and firs. Because of the cool temperatures and short growing season, the needles that drop from trees in this forest decompose very slowly, so the floor of the boreal forest is typically heavily strewn with brown needles. The soil here is nutrient-poor and acidic. Not much grows below the boreal forest trees. An exception is the bunchberry (*Cornus canadensis*), a small wildflower that blooms among the brown needles in the spring. It's a member of the dogwood family, and its little white flower resembles those found on dogwood trees. In the late summer, its flower is replaced with red berries. Another wildflower that blooms in the boreal forest is the Canada mayflower or wild lily of the valley (*Maianthemum canadense*), which looks like a more feathery version of the classic lily of the valley.

The coast's boreal forests attract a remarkable variety of migrating land birds and can be a rewarding place to bird watch. Several kinds of northern warblers, as well as Swainson's thrush (*Catharus ustulatus*), golden-crowned kinglet (*Regulus satrapa*), and blue-headed vireo (*Vireo solitarius*) nest in this forest. Several other species, including the boreal chickadee (*Parus hudsonicus*), gray jay (*Perisoreus canadensis*), and spruce grouse (*Canachites canadensis*), which eats the brown spruce needles, can be found here year-round.

Red squirrels (*Tamiasciurus hudsonicus*) scurry through the coniferous trees in the boreal forest. Porcupines (*Erethizon dorsatum*) and snowshoe hare (*Lepus americanus*), which are brown in summer and white in the winter, also live here. Moose (*Alces alces*) live in the boreal forest, although they are much more common in inland Maine than along the coast. As in the hardwood forest, the most common amphibian found in the coastal boreal forest is the Eastern red-backed salamander (*Plethodon cinereus*), which lives under fallen logs.

SNOWSHOE HARE
(*Lepus americanus*)
This rabbit changes its coat from brown in summer to white in winter.

SALT MARSHES

Salt marshes, an often unappreciated habitat on the coast, are more likely to attract the attention of oceanfront property developers than tourists. Fortunately, thousands of acres of Maine salt marshes have been protected by conservationists, for these soggy fields of tall grasses play an important role in the coast's ecosystem and provide essential feeding and resting spots for migrating waterfowl.

Maine's salt marshes are flooded by the tides twice a day, and the plants that live in them have to be able to tolerate fluctuating salinity, water levels, and temperature. There are two zones in a salt marsh: the lower zone, which is flooded twice a day by the incoming tide, and the upper zone, which is flooded by very high tides as infrequently as once a month. Ponds found in the upper zone are called salt pans.

Salt marsh cordgrass (*Spartina alternifolia*) is the predominant plant in the lower zone of Maine's coastal salt marshes. This 7-foot-tall plant thrives in the salt marsh because it is able to excrete excess salt through glands on its stem and leaves. Salt marsh cordgrass has deep roots that help it colonize marshes by trapping sediments. The cordgrass also stabilizes the marsh, filters the sea water that washes through its web of thin stems, and sits near the bottom of a long and vital food chain that begins here. As the cordgrass deteriorates, it feeds a multitude of micro-organisms, which are eaten by small fish and shellfish, which in turn are eaten by larger fish. Much of the detritus created in a salt marsh is washed out to sea, where it nourishes still more organisms. The salt marsh also serves as a nursery for many ocean fishes and shellfish, making it one of the most productive habitats on the coast.

The upper zone of a salt marsh is hospitable to more plants, typically salt meadow cordgrass (*Spartina patens*), sea lavender (*Limonium carolinianum*), and black grass (*Juncuss* sp.).

Many kinds of birds feed in the nutrient-rich salt marshes, making the

Great Blue Heron

Great blue herons (*Ardea herodias*) can frequently be seen standing in Maine's coastal salt marshes and mud flats. They stalk their prey in shallow water, using the strong muscles in their long necks to quickly stab fish, frogs, crabs, and occasionally small mammals. In flight, a heron will tuck its head in and trail its feet behind it.

At 4 feet tall, the great blue heron is the tallest bird on the Maine coast. Great blue herons nest in trees in colonies called heronries, typically located on islands. The birds will return to their huge nests of sticks each spring.

When watching a great blue heron or any other shorebird, keep your distance and take care not to flush the bird. These birds need to conserve their energy and fuel for migrating.

GREAT BLUE HERON
(*Ardea herodias*)

ROSEATE TERN
(*Sterna dougallii*)

marshes very rewarding bird-watching spots, especially during migration times. The salt pans are great places to look for migrating shorebirds and peregrine falcons (*Falco peregrinus*), which are attracted by the large concentrations of other birds.

Most of Maine's salt marshes are along its southern coast. The largest salt marsh is the 3,100-acre Scarborough Marsh, which can be explored by a canoe or on foot from the Maine Audubon Nature Center there (*see* page 60). The scenic Salt Bay Preserve Heritage Trail in Damariscotta (*see* page 145) skirts a salt marsh that often attracts a wide variety of birds.

Many salt marshes in Maine used to be farms where cordgrass was harvested for fodder. It's not surprising to see a farmhouse dating back to the eighteenth or nineteenth century sitting in a meadow near a large salt marsh. At the Salt Bay Farm in Damariscotta (*see* page 145) and at Laudholm Farm at the Wells National Estuarine Research Reserve (*see* page 41), the old farmhouses are used by the organizations that protect the salt marshes.

ISLANDS

How many islands are there off the Maine coast? It depends on your definition of an island. A survey in the mid-1990s by a state geography office increased the number of islands off the Maine coast by more than 1,000—to 4,617. That includes many rocky ledges that remain exposed at high tide.

Fifteen Maine islands have year-round communities, while another 29 have summer colonies.

Many of Maine's islands serve as nesting habitats for seabirds. Some nesting birds like Atlantic puffins (*Fratercula arctica*) and Leach's storm petrels (*Oceanodroma leucorhoa*) keep their eggs in burrows dug on island shores. Common and arctic terns nest directly on the shore, while roseate terns (*Sterna dougallii*) tend to hide their eggs under vegetation or driftwood. Great blue herons (*Ardea herodias*) and osprey (*Pandion haliaetus*) build huge nests high in island trees.

These islands are typically closed to visitors, at least for the mid-March to mid-August nesting season. Visitors should take care not to disturb nesting birds by lingering offshore.

THE ROCKY COAST

From its cobblestone beaches and boulder-strewn shores to its wave-pummeled points and granite cliffs, Maine is famous for its rocky coast. This dramatic shoreline presents a challenging and ever-changing set of conditions for flora and fauna.

While the conditions on the rocks may seem inhospitable, a variety of organisms can be found living between or on top of the rocks. These are plants and animals well suited to survive in a habitat where moisture and temperature conditions can change dramatically over the course of a few hours.

The plants and animals that live on or between the rocks of the Maine coast occupy different zones of coast land, depending on how much dry air they can tolerate. Look at a strip of coast as a series of six horizontal bands, each providing a habitat for the organisms that can withstand conditions there. The top zone is constantly exposed to air and varying amounts of sea spray and surf, while the lowest zone remains underwater. Between them is the intertidal zone, a fascinating area of the coast that is exposed twice a day by the tides. The plants and animals here can tolerate varying degrees of air and water.

THE SPLASH ZONE

The top layer of the rocky coast is the splash zone, or black zone, which gets most of its moisture from sea spray. The splash zone is often marked with a slippery black smudge of microscopic algae. The algae are covered with a slick, gel-like substance that prevents them from drying out. Rough periwinkles (*Littorina saxatalis*), small snails that can survive long periods in the air, crawl across the rocks here, grazing on the algae.

THE HIGH INTERTIDAL ZONE

The high intertidal zone is submerged by only the highest tides. It is also home to the rough periwinkle, a tough species of snail that can withstand the changing conditions here. While this zone and the others in the rocky coast habitat offer a challenging array of moisture and temperature, there are benefits to life in the intertidal zone. The sea delivers a fresh supply of nutrients with each incoming tide. Also, some predators can't cope with the conditions here.

THE BARNACLE ZONE

This zone is in an almost constant state of flux as the tides move in and out twice daily. The animals that can survive here are equipped to adapt to the ever-changing state of submersion and exposure wrought by the tides.

Typically, they can seal moisture in when exposed to prolonged periods of dry air. Most of the inhabitants of this stretch of the intertidal zone also are able to stay put, by using suction or some other means to attach themselves to the rocks.

Northern rock barnacles (*Balanus balanoides*) are often the most prolific species in this zone, and they are permanently affixed to rocks or other hard objects. When the tide is out, barnacles appear to be small hard

NORTHERN ROCK
BARNACLES
(Balanus balanoides)

bumps on rocks and other surfaces. This bump is really a series of plates the barnacle uses to shut out the dry air. When covered with water, the barnacle opens a series of plates in its cone-shaped exterior shell and dangles its legs into the water, filtering food brought in by the new tide. Common periwinkles (*Littorina littorea*) are a common sight in Maine's intertidal zone and seal themselves to rocks to retain moisture during low tide.

THE ROCKWEED ZONE

The next layer of the intertidal zone is the rockweed zone, which is exposed to less air than the zones above it. Rockweed (*Fucus vesiculosus*) and knotted wrack (*Ascophyllum nodosum*) are species of seaweed that thrive on the shoreline here. Both plants have air bladders along their fronds that allow them to float when the tide is in to ensure they get enough sunlight. The rockweed provides a hiding place for mollusks that need to stay submerged for part of the day. Blue mussels (*Mytilus edulis*) attach themselves to rocks here with thin strands secreted from a gland. They filter food from the water when the tide is in, and they seal themselves tightly closed and lie exposed on the rocks or sand when the tide is out.

THE IRISH MOSS ZONE

The next layer of rocky coast habitat is the Irish moss or chondrus zone, where red-brown Irish moss (*Chondrus crispus*) is exposed during only the lowest monthly tides. This zone is submerged most of the time, and northern sea stars (*Asterias vulgaris*) and green crabs (*Carcinus maenas*) can sometimes be seen in the curly Irish moss.

SUBTIDAL ZONE

The subtidal zone remains underwater even at low tide and is home to organisms that aren't equipped to tolerate dry air, including smooth periwinkles (*Littorina obtusata*) and northern sea stars. Sometimes small fish, sea urchins (*Strongylocentrotus droebachiensis*), or other animals become trapped in this zone at the bottom of a tide pool for the duration of a low tide. The next high tide will deliver the species back to freedom in the sea.

TIDE POOLS

From 1-mile-wide Biddeford Pool to small crevices between the rocks at Cobscook Bay, the Maine coast has countless tide pools. These ever-changing pools offer an opportunity to get an up-close look at the rocky coast habitat and are home to many species of sea plants and animals.

Tide pools are also good places to see the coastal food chain in action. Gulls and other birds, attracted by the newly exposed bounty at each retreating tide, will snatch up shellfish and smash them on the rocks. Starfish will latch on to mussels, slowly prying them open. When barnacles are covered with water, they will open their shells and

ROSE
POGONIA
(*Pogonia
ophoglossoide*)

reach feeding legs out to filter organisms delivered by the new tide.

Periwinkles creep across the rocks above and below the water line, scraping off algae as they go. Dog whelks or dogwinkles (*Thais lapillus*), a type of carnivorous snail, will eat periwinkles, barnacles, and mussels by breaking into their shells with a tooth.

ROCKY SHORE CONDITIONS

The generally thin soil and cool, moist climate of the rocky coast lends itself to spruce trees. Red spruce (*Picea rubens*) and white spruce (*Picea glauca*) share this coast with balsam fir (*Abies balsamea*) trees, often growing just inches from bare rock and sea spray.

On the farthest reaches of the Down East coast, conditions can be quite harsh. On the points that stretch farthest out to sea, the climate is similar to that found in Maritime Canada. Some of the subarctic plant species found here are at the southern limit of their range. This is the only place in the United States where the beachhead iris (*Iris hookeri*) is known to grow. Other subarctic species found in the far reaches of Maine include marsh felwort (*Lomatagonium rotatum*) and bird's eye primrose (*Primula laurentiana*). All three of these plants thrive in the cool, moist conditions found, for example, at the shore of Great Wass Island (*see* page 267).

While conditions may seem particularly brutal in the winter, several species of seabird are well equipped to weather the cold water. Harlequin ducks (*Histrionicus histrionicus*), for example, migrate south to Maine for the winter from even colder climes.

Rose Pogonia

Orchids may have a reputation as hothouse flowers, but nearly 50 species of orchid grow wild in Maine. The rose pogonia (*Pogonia ophoglossoide*) is one that can be found in bogs and other acidic, damp spots along the coast.

Rose pogonias come in several shades of pink, from a near-white pastel to a bright rose. Their bottom "lip," or lowest petal, is covered with fine yellow bristles. (*Pogonia* is Latin for "bearded," in reference to this hairy lower lip.) These 12-inch flowers bloom from May to July in Maine and tend to grow in large colonies. They are easy to identify when in bloom, but hard to spot otherwise.

PEATLANDS

The Maine coast has several peatlands, freshwater bogs that are full of stagnant water and peat, typically formed by layers of old sphagnum moss. Because there is little or no moving water in a peat bog, the bacteria that would break down organic matter like plants in other wetlands is missing. The partially decomposed sphagnum and other plants accumulate to form peat. The peat can hold many times its weight in water, and the ground in a peat bog tends to be very spongy.

Most of Maine's coastal peat bogs, including the 4,000-acre Great Heath in Columbia (*see* page 265) and the Big Heath, or Seawall Bog (*see* page 250), on Mount

Desert, are Down East. One exception is the Saco Heath Preserve on the southern Maine coast (*see* page 55).

Peat bogs are highly acidic, and only certain plants and trees will flourish in them. Black spruce (*Picea mariana*) is the most common tree found near a peatland. Tamarack (*Larix laricina*) and white cedar (*Chamaecyparis thyoides*) can also be seen growing in or near peat bogs.

Despite a lack of nutrients, peat bogs can be very colorful places in the summer. Several species of orchid, including pink lady's slipper (*Cypripedium acaule*) and rose pogonia (*Pogonia ophioglossoides*), grow in peat bogs, as do the insectivorous northern pitcher plant (*Sarracenia purpurea*) and round-leaved sundew (*Drosera rotundifolia*), both of which get nitrogen missing in the soil from the insects they trap and digest. Sheep laurel (*Kalmia angustifolia*) and Labrador tea (*Ledum groenlandicum*) are flowering shrubs typical of Maine peat bogs.

While the big attraction here is the interesting flora, peatlands can also be interesting bird-watching spots, especially in northeastern Maine, where boreal species like the gray jay (*Perisoreus canadensis*) and boreal chickadee (*Parus husonicus*) can be seen

ROUND-LEAVED SUNDEW

nearby. Other characteristic peatland birds include the palm warbler (*Dendroica palmarum*), olive sided flycatcher (*Nuttallornis borealis*), and Cape May warbler (*Dendroica tigrina*). It's best to view a bog from the edges, taking care to stay on roadways and paths. Peatland plants are very fragile and very wet. Expect to encounter many bugs if visiting in the summer.

▓ THE CONTINENTAL SHELF

Given the varied topography of the Maine coast, it should come as no surprise that the ocean floor off the coast of Maine is far from a smooth, flat surface. The Gulf of Maine contains a series of ledges and banks that make up a varied submarine topography. Off the coast is the continental shelf, a gentle slope made of sediment washed out to sea from the coast. About 180 miles east of the New England coast is Georges Bank, a portion of the continental shelf that fishermen and scientists have long considered one of the most productive and biologically diverse in the Atlantic.

This region was historically a rich fishing ground, thanks to natural processes that allow large numbers of plankton, diatoms, and other small organisms to flourish. The patterns of currents along the North Atlantic Coast are responsible for this rich marine environment. Warm water from the tropics flows north near the surface of the sea into the North Atlantic, becoming chilled and enriched with oxygen as it moves. As the water becomes very cold in the North Atlantic, it sinks, flowing south again near the ocean's bottom, where it collects silica, a primary component of diatoms, a microscopic plant or phytoplankton that begins the marine food chain. These little plants float, or "bloom," at the ocean's surface, where they can photosynthesize and where zooplankton and small fish will feed on them. This is the beginning of a food chain that will support a wide variety of marine life, from bottom-dwelling lobsters and groundfish like cod and haddock to big migrating fish like tuna.

LIFE OFFSHORE

The complex marine food chain that begins with diatoms, zooplankton, and phytoplankton involves a rich mix of organisms, including unicellular microorganisms, resident and migrating finfish, crustaceans, and marine mammals.

While dozens of species live in Maine's coastal waters, it is the lobster that is most often identified with this region. The adult lobster (*Homarus americanus*) typically

Lobster

Lobster is one of Maine's most popular entrées and its leading fishery. In 1997, more than 46 million pounds of lobster worth $136 million were trapped off the Maine coast.

Because it is typically sold alive or served whole, the northern lobster (*Homarus americanus*) is an easy species to examine.

The lobster has five sets of legs—four sets of smaller walking legs and a larger front set with big pinchers or claws. The lobster has eyes atop moveable stalks and two sets of antennae. Its front claws are not symmetrical. One claw is larger and has rounded teeth. That's the crushing claw, used to crush clamshells and other food. The other pincer is more pointed and sharp and is used to tear food apart. If a lobster loses one of its claws, it can grow a new one. Lobsters are usually sold with rubber bands around their front pinchers. Those bands go on as soon as the lobster is removed from the trap to protect lobsters from each other.

The lobster's shell is an external skeleton, which the animal must shed, or molt, as it grows. Young lobsters molt several times a year. Adult lobsters usually molt once a year until they grow old, when they may shed their shells less frequently. A 1.25-pound lobster has molted about seven times. After it sheds its shell, a lobster hides from predators until its new shell has hardened.

Maine has size regulations governing which trapped lobsters may be kept and which must be returned to the sea. Lobsters that are too small, too big, or bearing eggs must be thrown back in. While eating a lobster tail, diners often notice a firm red substance and a slippery green substance inside the tail and body. The red substance is called coral, and it is immature lobster eggs. Some people consider this a delicacy. The "green stuff" is tomalley, the lobster's liver. Do not eat the tomalley, as it may contain mercury or other impurities that the liver has filtered.

spends summers close to shore and migrates to deeper, offshore waters in the winter. While the lobster is ubiquitous in harbor side restaurants and coastal souvenir shops, it's just one of the crustaceans found in Maine waters. Several varieties of crab, including Jonah crabs (*Cancer borealis*), Atlantic rock crabs (*Cancer irroratus*), and green crabs (*Carcinus maenas*) also live here. Another crustacean, the northern shrimp (*Pandalus borealis*), often referred to here as Maine shrimp, is at the southern edge of its range in Maine. These shrimp are noted for their midlife transformation from sperm-producing male to egg-producing female.

Crustaceans have exoskeletons that they must shed as they grow. Another class of marine invertebrate in Maine are echinoderms, or spiny-skinned organisms, which include northern sea stars (*Asterias vulgaris*), sea urchins (*Strongylocentrotus droebachiensis*), sand dollars (*Echinarachnius parma*), and sea cucumbers (*Cucumaria frondosa*).

Among the fish found offshore are the Atlantic sturgeon (*Acipenser oxyrhynchus*), alewife (*Alosa pseudoharengus*), striped bass (*Marone saxatilis*), and bluefish (*Pomatomus saltarix*), as well as bottom-dwelling groundfish, including Atlantic cod (*Gadus morhua*), pollock (*Pollachius virens*), yellowtail flounder (*Pleuronectes ferrugineus*), and Atlantic halibut (*Hippoglossus hippoglossus*).

Several species of Maine coastal fish spend part of their lives in fresh water. Anadromous fish, such as alewives and sturgeon, live in salt water but enter freshwater estuaries to spawn. Catadromous fish, such as elvers (*see* page 151) spend most of their lives in fresh water but migrate to salt water to spawn.

The Eastern White Pine

Maine is nicknamed "The Pine Tree State" after the Eastern white pine, a towering tree that played a part in Maine's colonial history and its economy. The Eastern white pine still grows widely across the state and can be found in all of the coast's forest communities.

The white pine (*Pinus strobus*) is the largest and fastest-growing coniferous tree in Maine. The trees, many of them more than 100 feet tall, caught the eye of earlier settlers who arrived at the Maine coast in the 1600s. Before long, the British government was staking claim to every white pine more than 74 feet tall for use as naval masts. Colonists valued the trees as masts, but they also admired the clear, straight-grained timber white pines produced. Many historic Maine homes have wide-plank pine floors made from this beautiful wood. Resentment over the British claim on the tall white pines added to a building colonial discontent that culminated in the American Revolution.

The white pine was also harvested by paper makers. Today, while white pines continue to grow throughout Maine, few stands of old-growth white pine forests remain. One stand that is easily accessible and shows just how impressive these old trees can be is on the campus of Bowdoin College in Brunswick, where a 33-acre lot of century-old Eastern white pines towers over a quiet footpath (*see* page 112).

Bird Migration

Almost 400 species of birds have been spotted in Maine. Most of those bird species could not withstand Maine's cold winters and do not stay year-round. They participate in twice-yearly migrations when flock after flock follows the Atlantic flyway. Along the Maine coast, the spring migration typically occurs from early May to early June. The longer fall migration can begin in July with shorebirds and run into October with songbirds. These migrating times can bring unforgettable bird-watching experiences, as very large flocks of shorebirds and land birds follow the coast. Mixed flocks of raptors, shorebirds, and waterfowl can sometimes be seen on shore as they stop to rest and feed at salt marshes, mud flats, or other open habitats. Many of these resting spots are in sanctuaries, refuges, or nature preserves accessible to the public. In the fall, bird watchers often take to the mountains, especially Cadillac Mountain on Mount Desert (*see* page 233) and Mount Agamenticus in York (*see* page 33), to see and count migrating raptors.

EASTERN WHITE PINE
(Pinus strobus)
White pines were prized by colonists and the British for use in shipbuilding. The straight tall trees made excellent masts.

Marine Mammals

Maine waters are feeding grounds for several species of marine mammals, notably seals, whales, and porpoises.

Visitors are most likely to encounter harbor seals (*Phoca vitulina*), 5-foot-long gray seals with doglike faces that often haul out at low tide to sun on ledges and shorelines. Harbor seals have been known to travel several miles up tidal rivers in pursuit of fish. Harbor seals are shy, so don't approach them or you will frighten them from a ledge and possibly force a seal to abandon her pup.

Less common in near coastal waters is the gray seal (*Halichoerus grypus*), which is about 8 feet long and much bulkier than the harbor seal. Gray seals tend to stay farther out to sea. The Gulf of Maine is a summer feeding ground for several species of whale, all of them federally endangered, including the huge finback whale (*Balaenoptera physalus*), at 70 feet long and 50 tons the second largest mammal on earth. Humpback whales (*Megaptera novaeangliae*) are a favorite of passengers on whale-watching cruises because of their playful jumps, rolls, and splashes. The Minke whale (*Balaenoptera acutorostrata*) also summers in Maine waters, as does the northern right whale (*Balaena glacialis*), the most endangered whale off the U.S. coast.

NORTHERN RIGHT WHALE (Balaena glacialis)

The northern right whale species, which once was plentiful enough to supply enough oil to power public street lights in New England and lighthouses along the Atlantic coast, has been reduced to a few hundred individuals.

It got its name because it was the "right" whale to hunt: It was slow-moving and floated after being killed. Scientists estimated that in 1999 there were only 325 right whales in the world.

Four out of 10 right whales that die are killed by fishing gear or hit by ships, and new regulations require whale-watching ships and other craft to stay at least 500 yards away from them. The National Marine Fisheries Service maintains hotlines for right whale sightings and sightings of entangled or dead whales.

Whale-watching cruises often see another marine mammal, the harbor porpoise (*Phocoena phocoena*). Many of these porpoises, which are about 5 feet long, have drowned off the New England coast after becoming entangled in commercial fishing nets. Under new regulations aimed at protecting harbor porpoises, some fishermen are required to equip their nets with pingers, small devices that make a sound detectable by the porpoises.

Tides

A good bit of man's daily life on the Maine coast is determined by the coming and going of the tides. Some waterways can only be sailed at high tide, some paths only walked at low tide. Spots on the coast that are very nice swimming spots at high tide become mucky mud flats at low tide. Boats beached too close to the water at low tide can drift away as the tide returns.

Low tide can be a fascinating time to explore the coast and the intertidal zone, the strip of coast that is underwater at high tide and exposed at low tide. In some places, the retreating tide leaves behind massive mud flats—an ideal feeding spot for birds but an uninviting swimming spot for vacationers. In other spots, low tide is the time to explore tide pools, where periwinkles, mussels, barnacles, and even the occasional trapped fish can be examined up close.

The comings and goings of the sea also dictate the lives of the Maine coast's wildlife. The tide delivers fresh nutrients to salt marshes, tide pools, and estuaries. Each retreating tide exposes a variety of organisms, leaving them easy prey to birds and other predators. Organisms that live in the tidal zone of the rocky coast (*see* page 10) are equipped to deal with submersion in sea water and exposure to air brought by the tides. The Maine coast's many estuaries and bays, which may be full of water at high tide, can become wide mud flats at low tide. Each high tide leaves small shellfish and other detritus on the newly exposed shore, making this a prime feeding area for many birds, including great blue herons (*Ardea herodias*), and glossy ibis (*Plegadis falcinellus*).

Maine has a wide tidal range. In Kittery, tides reach about 9 feet. In Eastport, high tide can be more than 20 feet.

Two forces are at work as the tides rise and fall: the gravitational pull of the moon and sun, and the centrifugal pull of the revolving earth. As the moon rotates around the earth, its gravitational force pulls the earth's surface. This causes a bulge in the ocean beneath the moon. A second bulge occurs on the other side of the earth. These two bulges are the high tide. A low tide occurs between each two high tides. High and low tides occur 50 minutes later each day because it takes the moon 24 hours and 50 minutes to circle around the earth.

A few factors contribute to the extreme tidal range along the Maine coast. One is the increasing latitude, or distance from the equator. At the equator, the tides are very slight because the water is spread over a much greater distance than in the North

Atlantic. Another great factor is the Bay of Fundy, a funnel-like bay just to the north of the Gulf of Maine, where water rushes in dramatic tides of 40 feet or more. The tidal range in the Bay of Fundy, off the Canadian coast, is the greatest on earth.

The moon is much closer to earth than the sun, so its gravitational pull on the ocean is much stronger. During the full moon and the new moon, the moon and the sun are aligned and their gravitational forces combine to bring the twice-monthly "spring tides," which are 1 foot to 2 feet higher than usual. During the quarter phases of the moon, the moon and the sun are at right angles, bringing the smaller "neap tides" twice a month.

Every few years, a "proxigean tide"—which produces unusually low and unusually high tides—occurs. The proxigean tide occurs when the moon, which travels an elliptical path around the earth, reaches its closest point to the earth at the same time that it aligns with the sun. In some places along the Maine coast, a proxigean tide can be 4 feet higher than a usual high tide.

Maine Coastal Climate and Weather

The Maine coast has a maritime climate that is heavily influenced by the Atlantic Ocean. The sheer size of the Atlantic protects it from quick temperature changes. It helps keep the Maine coast warmer in the winter and cooler in the summer than areas just 20 miles inland. The region receives about 40 inches of rain and 70 inches of snow annually. That's a little more rain than inland areas and much less snow than northern Maine.

The climate has some impact on what vegetation grows on the coast. In the farthest Down East coast, the boreal forest (*see* page 7) dominates, in part because of the cool temperatures, sun-blocking fog, and shorter growing season.

The Maine Coast's Natural Resources and Economy

The Maine coast's natural resources, including its trees, fish, and scenery, have always played a significant role in the region's economy.

The first European explorers to see the Maine coast were struck by the towering pines and other trees growing near the shore. These trees fueled a shipbuilding and shipping industry that was a mainstay of the region's economy for more than a century. Maine's deep-water harbors and a network of rivers to deliver timber from the vast Maine woods made the coast an ideal place to build schooners, clippers, and other ocean-sailing vessels. By the midnineteenth century, Maine was the shipbuilding capital of the nation. The prosperity delivered by wooden ships didn't last forever. The invention of steamships clad in iron or steel in the later 1800s brought an end to the need for canvas sails and wooden ships. That wasn't an end to Maine's timber days, however. Most of the state's commercial timberland is now owned by paper companies that produce pulp and paper products at several Maine mills.

While the days of schooners and clippers are long gone, Maine still is a shipbuilding state. Now a defense contractor, General Dynamics, takes advantage of the deep, sheltered port at Bath to build giant Aegis destroyers at Bath Iron Works. The Navy repairs nuclear-powered submarines at its shipyard in Kittery. And some of the nation's finest boat builders still ply their trade in Maine harbors, building everything from luxury yachts to working lobster boats.

Shortnose Sturgeon

Instead of scales, shortnose sturgeon (*Acipenser brevirostrum*) have five rows of armorlike bony plates growing along their heads and bodies. These plates, along with the fish's shark-type tail and the thick whisker "barbels" growing from its nose, give the shortnose sturgeon a prehistoric look. Indeed, the sturgeon is an ancient species of fish that has been found in fossils dating back 60 million years. These 3-foot long fish are fast-moving bottom feeders and use those "barbels" to find worms and other foods.

The shortnose sturgeon is a federally endangered fish whose population was threatened by pollution and overfishing. While its never been in much demand as a commercial fish, it was likely caught incidentally in nets cast for other species, especially the larger Atlantic sturgeon, which are fished for their eggs, or roe. Shortnose sturgeon have also lost much of their spawning grounds to dam construction.

The shortnose sturgeon usually lives in the salt water but travels up rivers to spawn in fresh water. Maine's Kennebec and Androscoggin rivers contain up to 10,000 adult shortnose sturgeon, one of the largest populations on the East Coast.

Shortnose sturgeon can be found from Maine to Florida. They mature at a different rate in different regions. In southern rivers, females mature and can reproduce after about 6 years. In Maine, they mature at about age 12.

The first Europeans to explore the Maine coast region weren't interested in getting on land. They came to fish in the Gulf of Maine and the Georges Bank, where a mix of cold and warm currents creates ideal conditions for many species of fish. The Maine coast had a thriving fishing industry that pulled millions of pounds of fish—cod, haddock, mackerel, pollock, herring, sardines, and lobster among them—from the seas. While the popularity of some species, like sardines, fell, the public's taste for others, like lobster, rose, and the state maintained a healthy commercial fishing fleet for generations.

Men started harvesting fish from the Gulf of Maine as early as the 1500s, and the fishing industry continued to prosper through most of the twentieth century. For centuries, it seemed like the sea had a limitless bounty of fish. But that view changed in recent years, when more boats and better fishing technology led to a record depletion of some fish stocks. Hardest hit were the groundfish—cod, haddock, yellowtail flounder, and other fish from the ocean bottom—that had been a core of the fishing industry here. Federal regulators have enacted restrictions on gear, cuts in allowable catch and number of days at sea, and closures of vast offshore fishing grounds in an effort to let the groundfish stocks rebuild. Some Maine fishermen left the business through a program in which the government paid them to destroy their fishing vessels. Others diversified,

ATLANTIC COD

(Gladus morhua) Cod was historically one of the most common fish in the North Atlantic. Overfishing has resulted in a crash in numbers.

opting to fish for lobster or other fish when they can't go after cod and haddock. Maine's seafood industry has also been working to create markets for previously unused "garbage fish" by promoting recipes for dog fish and other seafood not traditionally found on menus or dinner tables.

While groundfishing is on the decline, another type of fishery is flourishing along the Maine coast—aquaculture, or fish farming. Successful aquaculture operations in the Mid-Coast and Down East regions raise and sell fin fish and shellfish, mostly salmon and mussels, in pens offshore. The coast off Washington County is particularly suited for salmon farming because of its extremely cold water, good water quality, and strong tides and currents. Another new fish farming "crop" is nori, a type of algae that is dried, pressed flat, and sold in sheets for use in wrapping sushi rolls. Seaweed is grown and harvested for use in fertilizers and other products.

In the seventeenth century, Maine had a healthy whaling industry. New England's whaling industry flourished until the mid-1800s, when several factors—notably the discovery of petroleum oil, which burned better than whale oil, and the Civil War's toll on whaling ships—resulted in the demise of the whaling fleet.

Maine's scenery is another of its valuable natural resources. Millions of people travel to Maine every year, most of them to the coast. In 1997 alone, out-of-state tourists generated $7.7 billion in sales of goods and services and more than $300 million in tax revenues statewide. The top single destination in Maine is Acadia

National Park, followed by L.L. Bean in Freeport. The most popular time to visit is late July and early August.

This modern tourism trend began 150 years ago, when a group of artists, including Thomas Cole and Frederick Church, became enamored of the Maine coast, especially Mount Desert Island, as a painting subject. Their work attracted the attention of wealthy urbanites looking to escape the heat of Philadelphia, Boston, New York, and other East Coast cities. These "rusticators" made the coast of Maine their summer home, building shingled and clapboard mansions they called cottages on Mount Desert Island and in several coastal towns. All that old money attracted other tourists, and by the 1870s, the Maine coast was well on its way to being a top tourist destination. The Great Depression, the imposition of a federal income tax, and a huge fire on Mount Desert Island took their toll on the wealthiest summer people. Some of those huge summer cottages have stayed in their original families, but many others now house historic inns and bed and breakfasts.

Loon

Common loons (*Gavia immer*) typically nest in freshwater ponds and lakes for the summer, but they can often be spotted swimming and fishing in Maine harbors, especially in the fall and winter.

Loons are easiest to identify in their summer plumage, when their backs are checkered black and white. In the winter, their backs are a more solid, slate color.

The birds spend most of their time in the water and are very good swimmers. Watch a loon's swift dive from the surface. You'll be surprised how far they can travel underwater before surfacing again.

Loons' legs are placed far back on their bodies, so they are awkward walkers at best. But they are fast fliers and can be identified by their feet, which trail back behind their tails in flight.

COMMON LOON
(Gavia immer)
Loons are famous for their distinctive calls that are considered among the most extraordinary sounds in nature.

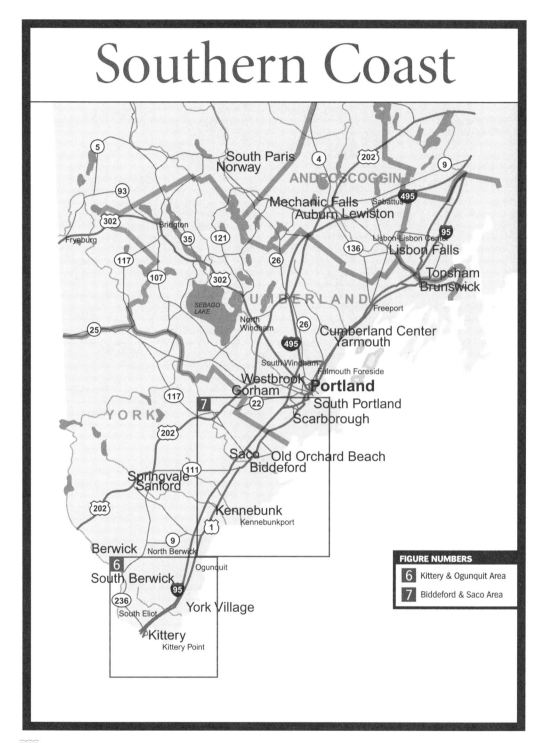

Southern Coast

FIGURE NUMBERS

6 Kittery & Ogunquit Area

7 Biddeford & Saco Area

The Southern Coast

For many visitors, the big attraction on the southern coast of Maine is the beach. The shoreline here is a series of gentle sweeps of sand, divided by rocky out-croppings and salt marshes. But don't confine your visit to the southern coast to sunbathing. This region is teeming with history and blessed with many natural sites. There are museums and historic homes that provide a lively illustration of life in Maine over the centuries. Historic forts are open for exploration as well.

Development is going strong along this swath of coast, and conservationists have worked to preserve many wonderful natural areas here. There's a grassland plains that is home to endangered plants, a vast peat bog where an endangered butterfly has been spotted, and the region's only mountain, where bird watchers spend fall mornings scanning the sky for migrating hawks and other birds.

Some of the Northeast's finest bird-watching can be found on Maine's southern

[*Above: Lobster boats on the southern coast*]

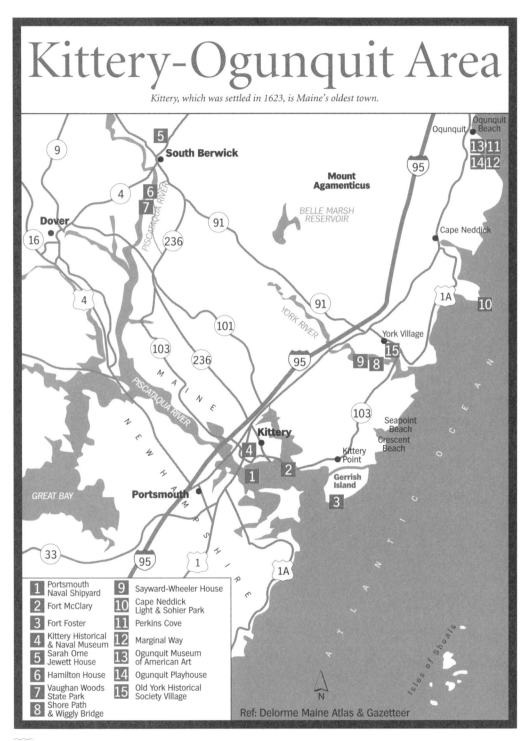

Kittery-Ogunquit Area

Kittery, which was settled in 1623, is Maine's oldest town.

9

5

South Berwick

Ogunquit
Ogunquit Beach

95

13 **11**
14 **12**

4

6
7

PISCATAQUA RIVER

91

Mount Agamenticus

BELLE MARSH RESERVOIR

Dover

16

236

Cape Neddick

4

91

YORK RIVER

1A

10

101

103

236

95

York Village

9 **8**

15

M A I N E

PISCATAQUA RIVER

103

Seapoint Beach
Crescent Beach

Kittery

4

N E W   H A M P S H I R E

Kittery Point

1

2

Gerrish Island

A T L A N T I C   O C E A N

GREAT BAY

Portsmouth

3

33

95

1

1A

Isles of Shoals

1	Portsmouth Naval Shipyard	**9**	Sayward-Wheeler House
2	Fort McClary	**10**	Cape Neddick Light & Sohier Park
3	Fort Foster	**11**	Perkins Cove
4	Kittery Historical & Naval Museum	**12**	Marginal Way
5	Sarah Orne Jewett House	**13**	Ogunquit Museum of American Art
6	Hamilton House	**14**	Ogunquit Playhouse
7	Vaughan Woods State Park	**15**	Old York Historical Society Village
8	Shore Path & Wiggly Bridge		

N

Ref: Delorme Maine Atlas & Gazetteer

coast at a 1-mile wide tide pool and in a 3,000-acre salt marsh, both of which attract serious birders from across the country.

There are also many towns and villages, seaside communities that look like movie sets of quaint New England.

Kittery

Settled in 1623, Kittery is Maine's oldest town. It's also the first Maine locale most visitors see because of its location at the Maine end of the I-95 bridge over the Piscataqua River from New Hampshire.

For the millions of tourists that spill over the border each summer, it's probably most famous for its outlets, which fill strip malls on either side of Route 1. Shoppers can buy china, designer clothes, athletic gear, luggage, cookware, and other consumer goods at a discount. For outdoor gear, check out the sprawling Kittery Trading Post, which is an L.L. Bean of the southern coast.

Don't limit a stop in Kittery to shopping. There are two historic forts here, both of which are fine spots for picnics and bird-watching. The town is dominated by a working defense institution, the Portsmouth Naval Shipyard, where nuclear submarines are overhauled.

Every first-time visitor to the coast should stop in Kittery at the Maine Information Center, a highly informative visitor center and rest stop on I-95.

PORTSMOUTH NAVAL SHIPYARD

[Fig. 6(1)] The Portsmouth Naval Shipyard is the nation's oldest military shipyard. Today, nuclear submarines are repaired at this yard. A shipyard museum with displays detailing 200 years of history at this historic military facility is open by appointment only.

The shipyard has been the subject of a long, not always neighborly, dispute between the states of New Hampshire and Maine. Since the shipyard is on an island in the Piscataqua River, New Hampshire lawmakers say the shipyard is in their state, not Maine. New Hampshire officials hope the U.S. Supreme Court will one day decide the winner of this two-century-old tug of war.

Directions: From the Kittery traffic circle, take Route 1 south to the first light, then turn left on Walker Street. Follow Walker Street to the Portsmouth Naval Shipyard.

Dates: The museum is open Thursdays, by appointment only.

Fees: None.

Closest town: Kittery.

For more information: Portsmouth Naval Shipyard, Kittery, ME 03903. Phone (207) 438-1000.

FORT MCCLARY

[Fig. 6(2)] Like most of the historic forts along the Maine coast, Fort McClary saw little military action. But it protected the mouth of the Piscataqua River during the Revolutionary War, War of 1812, Civil War, and Spanish-American War, and was manned as an observation post during World War I. It is named for Maj. Andrew McClary, who died during the Battle of Bunker Hill.

Today, there are a handful of buildings and some groundworks and foundations at the 27-acre site on Kittery Point. Fort McClary's granite and log blockhouse was the last blockhouse built in Maine. The area is now operated as a state historic site.

The beautiful ocean views, well-kept grounds, and picnic areas at Fort McClary encourage lingering, so bring lunch along.

Directions: From the Kittery traffic circle, follow Kittery Point Road, or ME 103, east for 2.5 miles.

Activities: Exploring the ruins, sight-seeing, picnicking.

Facilities: Picnic areas.

Dates: Open from Memorial Day through Sept.

Fees: There is a charge for admission.

Closest town: Kittery.

For more information: Fort McClary State Historic Site, c/o Maine Bureau of Parks and Land, 22 State House Station, Augusta, ME 04333. Phone (207) 384-5160 in summer; (207) 624-6075, off-season.

FORT FOSTER

[Fig. 6(3)] Cross a small bridge from Kittery Point to Gerrish Island to reach a popular local park on the grounds of Fort Foster. This early 1900s fort did duty as recently as World War II, although all that remains these days are earthworks, towers, and walls.

The big attractions at Fort Foster are its recreational facilities. Visitors fish from its long pier, walk its nature paths and explore tide pools, and use the park's three beaches to swim, kayak, sailboard, and scuba dive. Please note there are no lifeguards at the park.

The park is very popular on warm summer days. Bird watchers love it during the spring and fall, when it's a frequent stop for many species of migrating land birds. The park has a forest, a marsh, and three beaches, so it's a good place to spot a variety of birds in one afternoon.

Looking offshore, the lighthouse visible from Fort Foster is the Whaleback Light off Portsmouth, New Hampshire. On a clear day, the islands that may be seen farther offshore are the Isles of Shoals, which are jointly owned by Maine and New Hampshire.

Directions: From the Kittery traffic circle, follow ME 103 east for 3.5 miles. Look for signs for Gerrish Island just north of the village of Kittery Point and turn right onto Chauncy Creek Road to the bridge. Follow Pocahontas Road to the park.

Activities: Fishing (no license required), swimming, kayaking, sailboarding, walking, bird-watching, picnicking, scuba diving.

Facilities: Pier, restrooms, picnic areas, pavilion.

Dates: Open daily from Memorial Day weekend through Labor Day and weekends in May and Sept.

Fees: There is a charge for admission and a parking fee.

Closest town: Kittery.

For more information: Fort Foster, Route 103, Kittery, ME 03905. Phone (207) 439-2182 (in season). Kittery Recreation Department. Phone (207) 439-3800 (off-season.)

SEAPOINT BEACH AND CRESCENT BEACH

[Fig. 6] These two small, sandy beaches on the northern side of Gerrish Island are separated by a small peninsula and backed by a salt marsh. Do not enter the marsh, which is posted by the town of Kittery to protect fragile vegetation and wildlife. These beaches have no lifeguard and no facilities.

Both are popular with bird watchers. In the summer, watch for wading birds, including great blue herons (*Ardea herodias*), in the salt marsh. During the fall, the headland separating the beaches is a prime spot to scan for migrants, including sparrows. In the winter, hardy purple sandpipers (*Calidris maritima*) and sanderlings (*Calidris alba*) are sometimes spotted on the beach here. Watch for sanderlings chasing the surf to feed on the small shellfish left on the sand.

Directions: From the Kittery Traffic Circle, follow ME 103 east 3.5 miles and turn right on Chauncey Creek Road. Follow it nearly 2 miles to Seapoint Beach. A parking area next to the beach is reserved for Kittery residents. Another parking area up the road is open to nonresidents.

Activities: Bird-watching, swimming, (there is no lifeguard).

Facilities: None.

Fees: None.

Closest town: Kittery.

For more information: Kittery Recreation Department, 200 Rogers Road, PO Box 808, Kittery, ME 03904. Phone (207) 439-3800.

KITTERY HISTORICAL AND NAVAL MUSEUM

[Fig. 6(4)] This small museum is loaded with maritime history. There are several boat models, including a 10-foot replica of the USS *Ranger*, John Paul Jones's ship that was launched near here in 1777. Other displays illustrate the early shipbuilding industry at the Portsmouth Shipyard and in the region.

Directions: The Kittery Historical and Naval Museum is on Route 1 in Kittery, just north of the ME 236 rotary.

Dates: Open May through Oct.

Fees: There is a charge for admission.

Closest town: Kittery.

For more information: Kittery Historical and Naval Museum, Rogers Road, PO Box 546, Kittery, ME 03904. Phone (207) 439-3080.

ISLES OF SHOALS

[Fig. 6] The nine islands and ledges that make up the Isles of Shoals straddle the border between New Hampshire and Maine about 6 miles offshore. In the 1600s, their owners split them between the two territories. Today, five of the islands are in Maine and four are in New Hampshire. There's no public access to most of the Isles of Shoals, but there are a few opportunities to get a close look at these rocky islands.

Maine's Appledore Island was once the home of the poet Celia Thaxter. Her 1894 book *An Island Garden* is still a cult favorite among seacoast gardeners and her garden is open on a very limited basis for tours. These days, the Shoals Marine Laboratory, a Cornell University lab run in conjunction with the University of New Hampshire, occupies the island. The Shoals Marine Lab conducts tours of the Thaxter garden and also holds multiday adult courses on topics like island birds, marine mammals, and celestial navigation.

The only island readily accessible to the public is Star Island, which is the site of religious and educational conferences. The island's owners allow visitors for three hours each day. Bring your own lunch along.

It's hard to imagine that one of these beautiful, windswept outposts was the scene of a bloody, headline-filling killing. But in 1873, Smuttynose Island was the scene of a terrible double murder. Two young women, both Norwegian immigrants, were battered to death with an axe. A third woman hid in the freezing cold to survive and finger the murderer, a fisherman who proclaimed his innocence. Perhaps it was the unusual locale or the viciousness of the crime, but at the time the murders were big news around the country (Celia Thaxer wrote a detailed account for *Atlantic Monthly*). The murders had been forgotten until 1997, when Anita Shreve's fictionalized account, *The Weight of Water,* hit the best-sellers' list. Rumor has is that a movie about the Smuttynose double murder may put the Isles of Shoals back in the public consciousness.

Directions: The Isles of Shoals Steamship Company in Portsmouth, New Hampshire, operates ferries to Star Island. Visitors to Appledore need to take a ferry to Star Island and then wait for a research vessel from the Shoals Marine Lab.

Activities: Nature walks.

Facilities: The ferries have restrooms and snack bars.

Dates: Tours of Celia Thaxter's gardens are by advance arrangement only on Wednesdays during the summer. Visits to Star Island are allowed only in the summer months.

Fees: There is a charge for the garden tours and for ferry rides.

Closest town: Kittery, 6 miles.

For more information: To visit the Thaxter Garden on Appledore Island, contact the Shoals Marine Laboratory, G-14 Stimson Hall, Cornell University, Ithaca, NY 14853. Phone (607) 254-2900.

The Isles of Shoals Steamship Company, 315 Market Street PO Box 311, Portsmouth, NH 03802. Phone (603) 431-5500 or (800) 441-4620.

DINING IN KITTERY

There's fast food aplenty along the strip of outlet malls on Route 1. For a little more atmosphere, try lobster on a dock. If you're looking for gourmet food, head a little farther up the coast to York or Ogunquit.

CHAUNCEY CREEK LOBSTER PIER. Chauncey Creek Road, Kittery Point. The lobster rolls are a specialty at this creekfront, casual spot. *Inexpensive. (207) 439-1030.*

FRISBEE'S SUPERMARKET. Route 103, Kittery Point. This 1828 market claims to be the oldest family-run store in the country. It's a good spot to pick up lunch fixings for a picnic on the beach. *(207) 439-0014.*

LODGING IN KITTERY

Kittery has chain motels, tourist cottages, and several bed and breakfast inns.

ENCHANTED NIGHTS BED & BREAKFAST. 29 Wentworth Street, Kittery. This Victorian inn is open year-round. *Moderate to expensive. (207) 439-1489.*

MELFAIR FARM BED & BREAKFAST. 11 Wilson Road, Kittery. This farmhouse on 9 acres has four rooms, some with shared baths. *Moderate. (207) 439-0320.*

SALMON FALLS RIVER VALLEY

A few miles up the Piscataqua River from Kittery, the tidal waterway becomes the Salmon Falls River. The historic riverfront town of South Berwick is home to some beautifully preserved historic homes and a state park.

SARAH ORNE JEWETT HOUSE

[Fig. 6(5)] With her vivid depictions of New England small-town life, the writer Sarah Orne Jewett (1849-1909) was a popular regional writer in the late nineteenth century. Several of her works, including the 1896 Maine classic *Country of the Pointed Firs*, were set on the Maine coast. Among her most famous works are the novel *A Country Doctor* and the short story *A White Heron*.

Jewett was born in South Berwick and spent most of her life here in a Georgian home built in 1774 and owned by her family since 1819. The home has been nicely restored to reflect the time that Jewett lived and wrote here. The desk where she penned many of her books sits near a window in a second floor hallway. A gift shop sells books by and about Sarah Orne Jewett. *Country of the Pointed Firs* is available in most Maine bookstores. The Sarah Orne Jewett House is now owned by the Society for the Preservation of New England Antiquities.

Directions: Take I-95 to Exit 3 and follow ME 236 north 10 miles to South Berwick. The Sarah Orne Jewett House is in the center of town, where Routes 236 and 4 divide.

Dates: Open June 1 through Oct. 15, Wednesday through Sunday.

Fees: There is a fee for admission.

Closest town: South Berwick.

For more information: Sarah Orne Jewett House, 5 Portland Street, South Berwick, ME 03908. Phone (603) 436-3205.

HAMILTON HOUSE

[Fig. 6(6)] This beautiful Georgian manor home is filled with antiques and surrounded by meticulously kept grounds, including a formal garden that is the site of a summer concert series. Now owned by the Society for the Preservation of New England Antiquities, this commanding home was built in 1785 by a West Indies sea trader. The writer Sarah Orne Jewett, who lived nearby (*see* page 31) set her book *The Tory Lover* at Hamilton House.

Directions: Take I-95 to Exit 3 and follow ME 236 north for 9 miles. After the junction with ME 91, take the first left onto Brattle Street and then the second right onto Vaughan's Lane. Follow Vaughan's Lane to the end.

Dates: Open June 1 through Oct. 15, Wednesday through Sunday.

Fees: There is an admission charge.

Closest town: South Berwick.

For more information: Hamilton House, 40 Vaughan's Lane, South Berwick, ME 03908. Phone (603) 436-3205.

VAUGHAN WOODS STATE PARK

[Fig. 6(7)] This 250-acre state park used to be part of the grounds of nearby Hamilton House (see above), a 1785 Georgian manor home that can be seen from the park. The park has 3 miles of short trails that loop through stands of towering hemlock and pine trees and pass by the Salmon Falls River. Bring lunch along on a nice day. There's a picnic area near the parking lot, as well as several quiet trailside benches.

Directions: From South Berwick, head south on ME 236 about 0.5 mile and turn right opposite the junior high school onto Vine Street. In about 1 mile, turn right onto Old Fields Road and watch for the Vaughan Woods entrance on your right.

Activities: Hiking, picnicking.

Facilities: Trails, picnic areas, restrooms.

Dates: Open Memorial Day weekend through Labor Day.

Fees: There is a charge for admission.

Closest town: South Berwick, 1.5 miles.

For more information: Vaughan Woods State Park, Old Fields Road, South Berwick, ME 03908. Phone (207) 384-5160 (in season), (207) 624-6075 (off-season).

The Yorks

Four villages—York Harbor, York Village, York Beach, and Cape Neddick—make up the town of York, known locally as "the Yorks." The town is known for its miles of sandy beaches and its dedication to preserving the region's history in some of Maine's most imaginative history museums.

History buffs will find plenty to do here, especially at Historic York, a collection of Colonial-era buildings. Lighthouse lovers won't want to miss the much-photographed Nubble Light, and bird watchers, horseback riders, and mountain bikers should all head to Mount Agamenticus, an old ski mountain that is now a town recreation area.

BEACHES IN THE YORKS

There are three popular beaches in the town of York—Harbor Beach, Short Sands Beach, and Long Sands Beach. All have fine sand and gentle surf. All have restrooms and lifeguards in the summer. There is limited, metered parking at each beach, but many of the local campgrounds and inns are within walking distance to the sand and surf.

Directions: To reach Harbor Beach, take Route 1A to Harbor Beach Road in York Harbor. Head north on Route 1A to reach Long Sands Beach and Short Sands Beach.

Activities: Sunbathing, swimming.

Facilities: Restrooms, lifeguards.

Dates: Lifeguards are on duty from mid-June through Labor Day.

Fees: There is a charge to park at all three beaches.

Closest town: York

For more information: York Parks and Recreation Department, 186 York Street, York, ME 03905. Phone (207) 363-1040.

OLD YORK HISTORICAL SOCIETY VILLAGE

[Fig. 6(15)] Several Colonial-era buildings make up this historic museum village on the banks of the York River. One is the Old Gaol, a 1719 jail with walls 2 feet thick that is described as the oldest government building in America. There's also an old schoolhouse, a warehouse and wharf that once belonged to John Hancock, the Jefferds Tavern, the Old Burying Ground cemetery, and two historic homes.

Visitors can wander between the buildings and the cemetery at their own pace; costumed tour guides can answer questions in the buildings. Begin your tour at the Jefferds Tavern, where tickets are sold.

Directions: Old York Village sits along the riverfront in York Village. From Route 1, follow Route 1A east into the village.

Dates: Open from mid-June through September. Also open Columbus Day weekend. The Old Burying Ground is accessible year-round.

Fees: There is a charge for admission.

Closest town: York

For more information: Old York Historical Society. PO Box 312, York, ME 03909. Phone (207) 363-4974.

SHORE PATH AND WIGGLY BRIDGE

[Fig. 6(8)] The Shore Path is an easy walk along York Harbor, which offers pretty views and the chance to walk over the unique Wiggly Bridge suspension footbridge. (You'll soon figure out where it gets its name!) The bridge leads into a preserve owned by the Old York Historical Society called the Steedman Woods Preserve, where a 1-mile trail loops through the woods and along the water.

Shore Path: 0.5 mile, one way, easy.

Steedman Woods Trail: 1 mile loop, easy.

Directions: The path begins at the waterfront at Stageneck Road.

Activities: Walking, sight-seeing.

Closest town: York.

For more information: Old York Historical Society, PO Box 312, York, ME 03909. Phone (207) 363-4974.

SAYWARD-WHEELER HOUSE

[Fig. 6(9)] This 1718 home overlooks York Harbor and is beautifully furnished with period antiques. It's a nice stop when exploring the Shore Path and Wiggly Bridge. The house is owned by the Society for the Preservation of New England Antiquities.

Directions: From Route 1A in York Harbor, take Lilac Lane to Barrell Lane and the Barrell Lane Extension. The Sayward-Wheeler House is 79 Barrell Lane Extension.

Dates: The house is open weekends from June through Oct.

Fees: There is a charge for admission.

For more information: Society for the Preservation of New England Antiquities, Sayward-Wheeler House. 79 Barrell Lane Extension, York Harbor, ME 03911. Phone (603) 436-3205.

MOUNT AGAMENTICUS

[Fig. 6] The summit of this old ski mountain is only 692 feet above sea level, but it's the highest point in York County and offers splendid views of miles of coastline. Visitors can walk or drive 0.5 mile to the summit, where there's a choice of activities. The Agamenticus Riding Stables offers horseback riding lessons and trail rides. The Summit Cycle Shop rents mountain bikes for use on the mountain's miles of groomed bike trails. For a more peaceful experience, head off on a hiking trail, keeping an eye out for deer, pheasant, and other wildlife that live in these shady woods. Or climb the fire tower for an even better view.

The summit of Mount Agamenticus is worth a visit in the fall, when miles of colorful foliage can be scanned. Bird watchers also flock to Mount Agamenticus in the fall when they can spot thousands of hawks. Bring binoculars and a field guide.

Directions: From Route 1 in Cape Neddick, take Mountain Road west for 4.2 miles to the Mount Agamenticus access road.

Activities: Hiking, biking, horseback riding, bird-watching.

Dates: The mountain is accessible year-round. The businesses are open in the summer.

Fees: None.

Closest town: York.

For more information: York Parks and Recreation Department. 186 York Street, York ME 03905. Phone (207) 363-1040. Summit Cycle Shop, phone (207) 363-0470. Agamenticus Riding Stables, phone (207) 361-2840.

CAPE NEDDICK LIGHT AND SOHIER PARK

[Fig. 6(10)] This picturesque lighthouse, which sits on its own tiny island just offshore of Cape Neddick, is popularly known as the Nubble Light and is one of the most photographed spots on the coast. The island isn't accessible, but visitors can get a great view of the lighthouse and its outbuildings from the town's Sohier Park, directly across the channel. The 1879 lighthouse is only 44 feet tall, but its beacon is 80 feet above sea level because the island is so high. Lighthouse keepers lived on the island with their families until 1987, when the Nubble Light became the last light in Maine to be automated.

The lighthouse is a scenic spot any time of year, but it may be at its prettiest in winter, when the lighthouse, keeper's house, oil house, and other buildings are covered in Christmas lights. Winter is also a good time to bird watch from Sohier Park. Birders occasionally report seeing flocks of harlequin ducks riding the surf here in the winter.

Directions: From Route 1A in Cape Neddick, head east on Nubble Road to Sohier Park.

Activities: Sight-seeing, bird-watching.

Facilities: Restrooms, gift shop, welcome center.

Dates: Sohier Park is open year-round. The welcome center and gift shop are open seasonally.

Fees: None.

Closest town: York.

For more information: Friends of Nubble Light, PO Box 9, York, ME 03909.

CAMPING IN THE YORKS

There are several commercial campgrounds where you can hook up an RV or pitch a tent in the Yorks, including some within walking distance to the beach.

DIXON'S CAMPGROUND. 1740 Route 1, Cape Neddick. This campground is geared toward tents and small RVs. It has electrical hookups and shower rooms and provides transportation to Ogunquit Beach. *(207) 363-2131.*

CAPE NEDDICK CAMPGROUND. PO Box 1, Cape Neddick. This oceanside campground has sites for RVs with hookups plus a tenting area. *(207) 363-4366.*

FLAGG'S TRAILER PARK. Webber Road, York Beach. This campground is 500 feet from the beach. *(207) 363-5050.*

DINING IN THE YORKS

The Yorks have restaurants to meet every taste, from hot dogs and fried fish to vegetarian fare.

FLO'S. Route 1, Cape Neddick. Hot dogs and potato chips are the only things served at this wildly popular local institution. *Inexpensive.*

FRANKIE & JOHNNY'S NATURAL FOODS. 1594 Route 1 North, Cape Neddick. Inventive vegetarian and other entrées make this a popular summer dinner spot. *Moderate. (207) 363-1909.*

THE LOBSTER BARN. Route 1, York. Eat lobster and other seafood inside or out. *Inexpensive. (207) 363-4721.*

LODGING IN THE YORKS

DOCKSIDE GUEST QUARTERS. Harris Island, York. This hotel and cottage complex sits on Harris Island in York Harbor. *Moderate to expensive. (207) 363-2868.*

THE ANCHORAGE INN. 265 Long Beach Avenue, York Beach. This big, modern motel is across the street from Long Sands Beach. *Moderate to expensive. (207) 363-5112.*

Ogunquit

Ogunquit has a beautiful sandy beach, a long tradition as an artists' colony, a fishing harbor ringed with boutiques, and some of the best restaurants on the coast. None of this is a secret, however, so Ogunquit is hopping with tourists and seasonal residents in the summer months.

Artists, attracted by the beautiful landscapes and seascapes and the numerous galleries where they can show their work, have been spending summers in Ogunquit since the 1920s. Ogunquit also has a first-rate American art museum and an impressive summer theater.

HARBOR SEAL
(Phoca vitulina)

Ogunquit's most popular attractions—the beach, Perkins Cove, and Marginal Way—are short of parking. It's a good idea to park on the outskirts of the village and catch a trolley. These trolleys (buses, actually) stop frequently at dozens of posted trolley stops around Ogunquit. You can pay a small fare for each trip or buy a day pass when you board.

OGUNQUIT BEACH

[Fig. 6] Many Mainers and visitors list this broad expanse of silky sand as the nicest beach on the Maine coast. The 3.5-mile strip of sand and warm, gentle surf attract lots of sunbathers on nice days. Take a stroll along the beach and watch some expert sand castle builders at work. Head north and cross a small footbridge to reach Footbridge Beach, a section of Ogunquit Beach. Both beaches are on a large sand bar between the ocean and the Ogunquit River. You can swim in either the river or the ocean. There are lifeguards on duty in the summer. While there are parking lots at two entrances to the beach, the lots fill early in the summer. Your best bet is to leave your car elsewhere and take a trolley to the beach.

Directions: From Route 1 in Ogunquit, follow Beach Street to the main beach entrance. Or enter at Footbridge Beach by taking Ocean Street from Route 1 north of the village.

Seals On The Beach

With their huge wet eyes and mournful little cries, baby seals are irresistibly cute. If you find one crying on the beach, it's very tempting to want to rescue it, or at least comfort it. Resist the temptation. While it's true that some orphaned or sick seals are in need of rescuing, seal cows often leave their pups on the beach while they go in search of food. Those pitiful cries help the mother seal keep track of her pup's location. Human interference—even standing too close to the seal—can scare off the mother.

If you do find a seal or other sea mammal that appears to be stranded on the beach, keep your distance. (This is for your own protection too, as seals can bite). Do not attempt to move the seal or return it to the water. Note the animal's condition, size, and color and determine its exact location. Then call the Marine Animal Lifeline rescue hotline at (207) 851-6625. This nonprofit, volunteer-driven organization responds to stranded mammals on the coast, assessing whether they need help, then rescuing, rehabilitating, and, releasing them into the sea.

While most stranded mammals on Maine's beaches are seals, whales and dolphins also need to be rescued occasionally. If you find a beached whale or dolphin, call the hotline for help immediately.

Federal law prohibits handling or harassing marine mammals.

For more information: Marine Animal Lifeline, PO Box 453, Biddeford, ME 04005. Phone (207) 773-7377. The 24-hour Lifeline hotline number is (207) 851-6625.

Activities: Sunbathing, swimming.

Facilities: Changing rooms, restrooms, snack bars, lifeguards.

Dates: The beach is open year-round, although the services are open only in the summer months.

Fees: There is a charge for parking.

Closest town: Ogunquit.

For more information: Ogunquit Chamber of Commerce Visitor Information Center, PO Box 2289, Ogunquit, ME 03907. Phone (207) 646-5533.

PERKINS COVE

[Fig. 6(11)] Perkins Cove started out as a little waterside fishing enclave in the nineteenth century. The weathered gray fishing shacks are still there, but now they house pricey boutiques, restaurants, gift shops, and galleries. The fishermen are still here, too. This is the home port for many lobster boats. It's also the spot to hook up with a charter fishing boat or whale watching cruise. Some lobstermen take tourists on lobster cruises to show them how Maine's most famous entrée is caught.

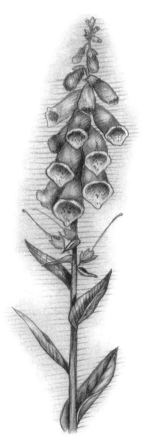

COMMON FOXGLOVE
(Digitalis purpurea)

Directions: Perkins Cove is on the water in the middle of town and has very little parking. It is best approached either on foot or aboard a trolley.

MARGINAL WAY

[Fig. 6(12)] Marginal Way is a winding 1-mile footpath along the rocky shoreline. It runs between Perkins Cove and the Shore Road. It's an easy walk that takes in crashing surf and tide pools, depending on the tide. There are benches from which to admire the view or look for birds. In the winter, it's a good spot to look for sea ducks and loons.

Expect to run into many other strollers on this path in the summer.

Trail: 1 mile, one-way.

Directions: In the summer, take a trolley to the path or enter it from Perkins Cove. The Shore Road entrance is about 1 mile south of Route 1 in Ogunquit.

For more information: Ogunquit Chamber of Commerce Visitor Information Center. PO Box 2289, Ogunquit, ME 03907. Phone (207) 646-5533.

OGUNQUIT MUSEUM OF AMERICAN ART

[Fig. 6(13)] This waterfront museum has an impressive permanent display of twentieth-century American artists, including Rockwell Kent and Marsden Hartley. It also puts on a wide range of interesting seasonal shows. Once you're done admiring the work inside the museum, spend some time admiring its grounds.

Directions: The museum is on Shore Road, about 1.5 miles south of downtown Ogunquit.

Dates: The museum is open from July 1 through Sept. It is closed when new exhibits are being hung, so call ahead.

Fees: There is a charge for admission.

Closest town: Ogunquit.

For more information: The Ogunquit Museum of American Art, 183 Shore Road, Ogunquit, ME 03907. Phone (207) 646-4909.

OGUNQUIT PLAYHOUSE

[Fig. 6(14)] This summer theater has been putting on musicals, mysteries, and comedies for more than 60 years. There are five different pieces each summer, usually starring famous performers. Evening and matinee performances often sell out, so visit the box office early.

Directions: The playhouse is on Route 1 in Ogunquit.

For more information: Ogunquit Playhouse, PO Box 915, Ogunquit, ME 03907. Phone (207) 646-2402. For tickets, phone (207) 646-5511.

NIGHT LIFE IN OGUNQUIT

Ogunquit doesn't roll up the sidewalk at sundown. There are plenty of night spots where you can listen to live music or enjoy the view.

JONATHAN'S. 2 Bourne Lane, Ogunquit. Jonathan's serves dinner and attracts many national acts, especially folk and blues musicians. *(207) 646-4777.*

SIR FRANCIS DRAKE. Route 1, Moody. This English-style pub has a variety of British beers and live jazz on weekends. *(207) 646-1800.*

DINING IN OGUNQUIT

Ogunquit has some wonderful restaurants, especially if money is no object. Wander down Perkins Cove if you're in the mood for lobster on the waterfront.

ARROWS. Berwick Road, Ogunquit. No detail is left to chance at this elegant restaurant, which is considered one of the best in Maine. The menu is innovative and includes many items grown in the restaurant's kitchen garden. *Expensive. (207) 361-1100.*

THE HURRICANE. Perkins Cove, Ogunquit. This waterfront restaurant is known for its creative seafood dishes and spectacular view. *Expensive. (207) 361-1000.*

LODGING IN OGUNQUIT

THE CLIFF HOUSE. Shore Road, Ogunquit. This cliff-top resort has been in the same family since 1872. Bird watchers scan the ocean here in the winter for harlequin ducks, and amateur geologists love to check out Bald Head Cliff. The dining room is open to the public. *Expensive. (207) 361-1000.*

SPARHAWK OCEANFRONT RESORT. Shore Road, Ogunquit. Near the entrance to the Marginal Way footpath, this sprawling resort has more than 80 rooms in a variety of buildings. *Expensive. (207) 646-5562.*

Wells

Wells has the same fine, sandy beaches found in neighboring towns, but it's also the site of a sprawling estuarine habitat, where the Webhannet River runs into the Atlantic Ocean. Much of this is preserved at the Wells National Estuarine Research Center and Rachel Carson National Wildlife Refuge, two spots that should be on the itinerary of any birder or naturalist.

Wells also has a high concentration of antique shops and used bookstores. Lighthouse buffs won't want to miss the Lighthouse Depot, a store devoted entirely to lighthouses.

▨ WELLS BEACHES

[Fig. 7] Wells has about 7 miles of fine sand beaches. Wells Beach sits between the Atlantic and the Webhannet River. The beach is pretty much overrun by sunbathers on sunny, summer days, but the rest of the year it is a fine bird-watching spot, with shorebirds, sea birds, and wading birds all in evidence. There are restrooms and lifeguards on duty in the summer.

Drake's Island Beach, farther up the shore, is a little less crowded than Wells Beach. There are restrooms and lifeguards on duty in the summer. Drake's Island Beach borders Laudholm Beach, part of the Wells National Estuarine Reserve.

Directions: To reach Wells Beach, turn east from Route 1 onto Mile Road and follow it to the end. To reach Drake's Island Beach, turn east from Route 1 onto Drake's Island Road and follow it to the end.

Activities: Sunbathing, swimming, bird-watching.

Facilities: Restrooms, lifeguards.

Dates: The beaches are open year-round. Lifeguards are on duty during the summer.

Fees: There is a charge for parking.

For more information: Wells Town Office, 208 Sanford Road, PO Box 398, Wells, ME 04090. Phone (207) 646-5113.

WELLS NATIONAL ESTUARINE RESEARCH RESERVE

[Fig. 7(18)] Known locally as Laudholm Farm, this reserve includes 1,600 acres of forest, field, salt marsh, freshwater wetlands, and sandy beaches. This variety of habitats makes it a wonderful place to look for interesting plants and birds. There are 7 miles of interpretive trails that loop through historic and natural highlights of the reserve. Pamphlets at the visitor center will point to interesting features along the way.

The 1.3-mile Salt Marsh Loop is an easy loop that includes a salt marsh overlook. The 1.4-mile Barrier Beach Walk trail crosses several habitats on its way to sandy Laudholm Beach. The 1.8 mile River Loop crosses a swamp and ends at a river overlook. The 1.6-mile Salt Hay Loop winds around a glacial delta. It's easy to spend a day walking these trails, stopping to look at flora and fauna.

Laudholm Farm is a frequent stopover for birds migrating on the Atlantic Corridor. More than 200 species of birds have been seen over the course of a year. Endangered or rare species seen here include the least tern (*Sterna albifrons*), piping plover (*Charadrius melodus*), bald eagle (*Haliaeetus leucocephalus*), and peregrine falcon (*Falco peregrinus*). Other birds that use the reserve, either as a nesting spot or a stopover, include egrets, ducks, geese, falcons, hawks, gulls, warblers, owls, woodpeckers, kinglets, waxlets, sparrows, finches, loons, cormorants, bitterns,

BALD EAGLE
(Haliaeetus leucocephalus)

and herons. The presence of thousands of birds here illustrates the importance of the estuarine habitat, especially the salt marshes formed where the Webhannet and Little rivers head toward the Atlantic Ocean. These nutrient-rich marshes are fed by the tides, which wash organisms in and out of the marsh. As salt marsh grasses rot, the tide spreads the decaying organic matter across the marsh, enriching the mix even more. The marshes support a wide array of wildlife, including birds and small mammals that feed here and fish that spawn here.

This land was farmed for centuries, and its old mowed fields, lined with apple trees and being overtaken by trees and shrubs, can still be seen. An old Greek Revival farmhouse and other outbuildings house a visitor center, exhibits, a research lab, classrooms, and an auditorium. Guided tours, a lecture series, and children's programs are offered.

The Wells Reserve, an interesting and informative spot for day visitors, but it is also a research center for students and scientists studying estuaries, the impact of land use on the estuary, and how marshes support Gulf of Maine fisheries.

In the early 1980s, developers began eyeing this land as prime coastal real estate. A group of concerned citizens joined together to help save Laudholm Farm, which is now managed by representatives of the local, state, and federal governments that serve on the Wells Reserve Management Authority.

Directions: Heading north on Route 1 in Wells, look for the reserve sign on the right at a blinking light just beyond the Lighthouse Depot.

Activities: Walking, bird-watching, nature watching.

Facilities: Visitor center, restrooms, trails, exhibits on estuaries.

Dates: The reserve trails and visitor center are open year-round. The visitor center is open daily from May through Oct. and weekends from Nov. through Apr.

Fees: There is a parking fee on weekends in June and Sept. and daily in July and Aug.

Closest town: Wells.

For more information: Wells National Estuarine Research Reserve, 342 Laudholm Farm Road, PO Box 1007, Wells, ME 04090. Phone (207) 646-1555.

RACHEL CARSON NATIONAL WILDLIFE REFUGE

[Fig. 7(17)] The Rachel Carson National Wildlife Refuge is actually 10 parcels of coastal land between Kittery and Cape Elizabeth that were acquired to protect coastal wetlands and habitats for migrating birds. The only portion of the refuge developed for public use is at the refuge headquarters. A 1-mile interpretive trail, the Carson Trail, heads through a forest of white pine (*Pinus strobus*), red pine (*Pinus resinosa*), and hemlock (*Tsuga canadensis*) and wanders along the edge of a huge salt marsh.

The path, which is wheelchair accessible, has several spots to stop and watch the birds in the marsh. Great blue herons (*Ardea herodias*) and snowy egrets (*Egretta thula*) can be seen stalking in the marsh for food in the summer. In the spring and fall, migrating birds, including ducks and shorebirds, often stop here. Fall visitors should be aware that some hunting is permitted in the refuge. In the winter, try the Carson Trail on showshoes or cross-country skis and look for resident woodpeckers in the woods and black ducks (*Anas rubripes*) in the coastal salt marshes. The path is a lovely walk and a fitting tribute to Rachel Carson, who helped spark the modern environmental movement with her 1962 book, *Silent Spring.*

The refuge was created in 1966 as the Coastal Maine National Wildlife Refuge. On June 27, 1990, it was renamed to honor Rachel Carson.

Directions: Heading north on Route 1 in Wells, turn right on Route 9. The Rachel Carson National Wildlife Refuge is about 0.5 mile down the road on the right and is marked with a large sign.

Activities: Walking, bird-watching, cross-country skiing, hunting (with a permit).

Facilities: Refuge headquarters, nature trail, restrooms..

Dates: The refuge is open year-round.

Fees: None. Donations are accepted.

Closest town: Wells.

For more information: Refuge Manager, Rachel Carson National Wildlife Refuge, 321 Port Road, Wells, ME 04090. Phone (207) 646-9226.

LIGHTHOUSE DEPOT

[Fig. 7(16)] It's easy to believe the Lighthouse Depot's claim that it's "The World's Largest Lighthouse Gift Store." This store has two stories full of lighthouse merchandise, from models, clothing, and puzzles to calendars, books, and videos. It's something of a mecca for lighthouse buffs, so feel free to ask around for advice on the best lighthouses to visit along the coast.

Directions: The Lighthouse Depot is on Route 1 in Wells, about 0.5 mile south of the Route 9 intersection.

Dates: Open daily, year-round.

Closest town: Wells.

For more information: The Lighthouse Depot, PO Box 1690, Wells, ME 04090. Phone (800) 758-1444.

WELLS AUTO MUSEUM

[Fig. 7(15)] This museum's exhibits include more than 70 vehicles, dating back to 1894, including automobiles powered by steam, electricity, and gas. Highlights include some Stanley Steamers, an 1894 Wolfmuler motorcycle, and a 1963 Studebaker Avanti. There are also antique arcade games and nickelodeons on display.

Directions: The Wells Auto Museum is on Route 1 in Wells, 1 mile south of the ME 109 intersection.

Dates: Open Memorial Day weekend through Columbus Day.

Fees: There is a charge for admission.

Closest town: Wells.

For more information: Wells Auto Museum, Route 1, Wells, ME 04090. Phone (207) 646-9064.

SNOWY EGRET
(Egretta thula)

CAMPING IN WELLS

Wells has several campgrounds for RVs and tents.

BEACH ACRES CAMPGROUND. 563 Post Road, Wells. Beach Acres has 380 sites, RV hookups, and a pool and is close to the beaches and other Wells attractions. *(207) 646-5612.*

PINEDEROSA CAMPGROUND. 128 North Village Road, Wells. Pinederosa has 162 sites scattered on 35 acres, with hookups, a pool, and laundry. *(207) 646-2492.*

DINING IN WELLS

Seafood is the specialty at most Wells restaurants, many of which are family-style spots.

MAINE DINER. Route 1, Wells. This diner serves breakfast all day, plus great chowder. *Inexpensive. (207) 646-4441.*

THE GREY GULL. 321 Webhannet Drive, Wells. The window side tables at The Grey Gull may have the best view in town. *Moderate. (207) 646-7501.*

LODGING IN WELLS

Motels and tourist cottages line Route 1 in Wells, but make sure you've got reservations if you are arriving in July or August.

WATER CREST COTTAGES. Route 109, Wells. This complex of 50-some cottages is on land bordering the Rachel Carson National Wildlife Refuge. *Moderate. (207) 646-2202.*

CHRISTMAS TIDE INN. 1820 Post Road, Wells. This comfortable inn in an old sea captain's house is open year-round. *Moderate to expensive. (207) 646-5498.*

The Kennebunks

Kennebunkport achieved some notoriety as the summer home of former President George Bush. Even years after Bush was voted out of the White House, busloads of tourists come to town to admire his family's oceanfront estate at Walker's Point. But Kennebunkport and neighboring Kennebunk (known collectively as the Kennebunks) have been summer vacations spots for the well-heeled since sea captains built beautiful mansions and settled here in the nineteenth century.

While many tourists come to Kennebunkport to gawk at the Bush estate, even more come to relax on the sand at the area's beaches and window shop at the boutiques along Dock Square. Most of these visitors don't stop to see some of the area's most interesting natural features, including a glacial marine delta that is home to a colony of rare grasshopper sparrows and a meadow of threatened wildflowers, an island nature preserve that you can reach on foot when the tide is right, and a small sea cave where the mist sometimes spouts high in the air.

BEACHES IN THE KENNEBUNKS

[Fig. 7] The beaches in the Kennebunks are known for their powdery-soft sand and their lack of parking places. Beach parking stickers are required and can be purchased at Town Hall or, on weekends, the police station. If you're staying nearby, it's easiest to walk or grab a trolley bus to the beach.

Kennebunk's main beach, Kennebunk Beach, has three sections—Middle Beach, which is somewhat rocky, Mothers Beach, which is popular with families and has lifeguards and toilets, and Gooches Beach, which is most popular and also has lifeguards and toilets. All three can attract a good-sized crowd on sunny summer days.

The longest strip of sand nearby is Goose Rocks Beach, on the eastern end of Kennebunkport. An adjacent salt marsh can be a productive spot to bird watch.

Directions: To reach all three sections of Kennebunk Beach: From Route 9 take Sea Road, which becomes Beach Avenue. To reach Goose Rocks Beach from Route 9, take Dyke Street and then turn left on King's Highway.

Activities: Swimming, bird-watching.

Facilities: Restrooms, lifeguards.

Dates: Beaches are open year-round. Lifeguards and restrooms are seasonal.

Fees: There is no charge for admission but a permit is required to park.

Closest town: Kennebunkport.

For more information: Kennebunk Kennebunkport Chamber of Commerce, PO Box 740, Kennebunk, ME 04043. Phone (207) 967-0857.

WALKER'S POINT

[Fig. 7(14)] The summer estate of George and Barbara Bush continues to be one of the biggest tourist draws in Kennebunkport. The estate is on a peninsula that juts out into the surf. It's easily seen from the roadside, but no parking is allowed. Leave your car on the outskirts of town and walk along Ocean Avenue, passing the pretty, seaside St. Ann's Church and Blowing Cave before reaching Walker's Point. Tourists with binoculars often spot the former president heading out to fish in his boat or walking around the grounds of the compound. The Bushes try to blend into the regular Kennebunkport summer crowd, so don't be surprised if you bump into them shopping or walking through town.

Directions: From downtown Kennebunkport, follow Ocean Avenue south and then east along the coast. Walker's Point is quite prominent and will be on your right. The local tourist trolley buses also drive by Walker's Point. Tour boats routinely pass it, as well.

Closest town: Kennebunkport.

BLOWING CAVE

[Fig. 7(13)] Visit this sea cave at high tide to see how it got its name. When waves cover the mouth of this cave at high tide, air compressed inside the cave builds up. The water is then forced through a small hole in the roof of the cave, sending spray up to 30 feet in the air.

Directions: Blowing Cave is on Ocean Avenue on Sand Cove, about half way between Walker's Point and Arundel.

Closest town: Kennebunkport.

VAUGHN'S ISLAND PRESERVE

[Fig. 7(12)] Consult a tide calendar and keep an eye on your watch when visiting this island preserve. Vaughn's Island is just a few hundred feet off the shore of Kennebunkport, and you can walk there at low tide. If you don't want to get stranded, limit your visit to Vaughn's Island to about an hour. That's plenty of time to walk to the ocean side of the island and enjoy the beach and the view. Low tide is also a good time to scan the area for shorebirds looking for food left by the outgoing tide.

Directions: From downtown Kennebunkport, follow Ocean Avenue to Turbat's Creek Road. There's a small parking area across the street from the Shawmut Ocean Resort.

Activities: Walking, bird-watching.

Closest town: Kennebunkport.

For more information: Kennebunkport Conservation Trust, PO Box 7028, Cape Porpoise, ME 04014.

KENNEBUNK PLAINS

[Fig. 7(11)] This 1,041-acre wildlife management area on a glacial marine delta is the only place in Maine to see several rare bird and plant species. It is also one of only a few sandplain grasslands in New England to escape development pressure. The Nature Conservancy manages the grassland to protect rare and endangered species. The state Department of Inland Fisheries and Wildlife manages the forests and streams, which are open for hunting, trapping, and fishing.

The 450-acre sandplain sits atop about 70 feet of sand and gravel left by a glacier 12,000 years ago. The dry, well-drained, and nutrient-poor conditions are perfect for the grasses and woody shrubs growing here. The plain is home to a number of grassland-nesting birds, including what is thought to be one of the largest populations of grasshopper sparrows (*Ammodramus savannarum*) in New England. The vesper sparrow (*Pooecetes gramineus*), Eastern meadowlark (*Sturnella magna*), and horned lark (*Eremophila alpestris*) can also be found here. All these birds nest in the grass, so please follow the preserve restrictions governing foot traffic, vehicles, and pets, especially during the May to September nesting season. Any time of year, it is important to stay on the roadways that cross the plains and to not disturb the grassland. Many other birds can be seen here as well. The Nature Conservancy says some 87 species of birds nest at Kennebunk Plains, and another 50 have been spotted during migration times.

In mid- to late-August, the plains are ablaze with purple wildflowers called northern blazing stars (*Liatris scariosas*). The million-plus stems growing here make up the largest population of this species in the world. Two other rare wildflowers, the toothed white-topped aster (*Sericocarpus asteroides*) and the upright bindweed (*Calystegia spithamaca*) grow here in smaller numbers.

This plain used to be home to a commercial blueberry operation, and there are still many berries to be found. Picking for personal consumption is still allowed in posted areas. Look for signs in July and August.

The sandplain is surrounded by forests of pitch pine (*Pinus rigida*) and scrub oak (*Quercus ilicifolia*). A forest of mixed hardwoods and white pine lies at the moister southern edge of the preserve. The cool forests and the brooks that run through them are home to white-tailed deer (*Odocoileus virginianus*), beaver (*Castor canadensis*), red fox (*Vulpes vulpes*), mink (*Mustela vison*), and coyote (*Canus latrans*). Visitors should be aware that hunting, trapping, and fishing are allowed here.

The surrounding forests would overtake the grasslands, robbing the birds and plants of their habitat, if the grasslands were not periodically burned. About every five years, each section of the plains is set afire by Nature Conservancy fire leaders. The fire gets rid of invading shrubs, creates nesting habitat and stimulates the growth of some of the plain's vegetation.

The species that live in sandplain grasslands like this one have lost much of their habitat, mostly to developers who value the flat, well-drained land for construction. Kennebunk Plains was the site of commercial blueberry operations from the 1920s to 1988. Between 1983 and 1988, the herbicide Velpar, which killed most vegetation other than the blueberry shrubs, was used here. Many of the plants growing here are recovering from Velpar use. Some plants appear to grow in rows on the plains. According to The Nature Conservancy, these rows are strips that were missed by the herbicide applicators. In 1987, a majority of Maine voters approved a $35 million bond issue to create a Land for Maine's Future fund to buy natural lands. Kennebunk Plains was the first purchase under that program.

Recently, Nature Conservancy workers and volunteers devoted a great deal of time and effort trying to minimize the impact of a natural gas line that was dug through the plains. The soil was carefully preserved so that the top layer of soil that contains seed would be placed on top again. Many plant plugs were pulled from the earth and replaced after the gas line trench was filled in, and many plants were dug up and stored in a nursery during the project.

Directions: From Kennebunk, take ME 99 west for 3.5 miles past the interstate. Kennebunk Plains is on both the left and the right. Parking and an interpretive sign are on the right.

Activities: Bird-watching, nature walking, blueberry picking, hunting, trapping, fishing.

Dates: The preserve is accessible year-round. Due to the presence of grassland nesting birds, there are restrictions during the May to September nesting season.

Closest town: Kennebunk.

For more information: The Nature Conservancy, Maine Chapter, Fort Andross, 14 Maine Street, Suite 401, Brunswick, ME 04011. Phone (207) 729-5181. For hunting and fishing information, Maine Department of Inland Fisheries and Wildlife, 284 State Street, 41 State House Station, Augusta, ME 04333-0041. Phone (207) 287-8003.

THE BUTLER AND MARSHALL PRESERVES

[Fig. 7(10)] The 14-acre Butler Preserve and 181-acre Marshall Preserve sit on either side of the Kennebunk River. The Butler Preserve is mostly shoreline, while the Marshall Preserve includes a forest of pine, hemlock and balsam fir trees.

The highlight of the Butler Preserve is Picnic Rock, a large glacial boulder on the shore that is popular with picnickers and swimmers. A short trail leads from Picnic Rock into the forest, where an old logging road loops through the woods. There are no trails on the river section of the Marshall Preserve, but it's possible to walk on shore.

Directions: By land, from Kennebunkport take the Old Port Road 1.7 miles to a woods road on the right just before the Kennebunk River comes into view. Park along the road and walk in. By water, Picnic Rock is 1.5 miles upstream from Kennebunkport. Do not land a canoe in front of the house on the Marshall Preserve. This is private property.

Activities: Swimming, paddling, picnicking.

Closest town: Kennebunk.

For more information: Kennebunk Land Trust, PO Box 1164, Kennebunk, ME 04043.

TOM'S OF MAINE

[Fig. 7(9)] Tom's of Maine is known for its natural toothpaste, deodorant, and other personal care products. The Kennebunk-based company also prides itself on its progressive workplace and environmental policies. The Tom's of Maine Natural Living Store sells the company's products (including some steeply discounted factory seconds) plus other all-natural merchandise, gardening supplies, books, toys, and organic cotton clothing. If you wonder how all these natural products are manufactured, go for a tour of the Tom's of Maine factory. The tour will show you how Tom's gets the toothpaste into the tube—at a rate of 80 tubes per minute. Reservations are necessary for factory tours.

Directions: The Tom's of Maine Natural Living Store is in Lafayette Center, a restored old mill building on Storer Street off Main Street in Kennebunk. To reach the factory, take Route 35 in Kennebunk to Railroad Avenue and turn right.

Dates: The factory tours are held Monday through Thursday in the summer and on Wednesdays the remainder of the year. Reservations are required.

Fees: No charge for factory tours.

Closest town: Kennebunk.

For more information: Tom's of Maine, PO Box 710, Kennebunk, ME 04043. Phone (207) 775-2388.

SEASHORE TROLLEY MUSEUM

[Fig. 7(8)] This museum has close to 300 trolleys from around the world. Many of these historic old cars make runs on a 2-mile track that runs through the woods around this museum. Visitors can also check out the trolley workshop, where old streetcars undergo restoration and maintenance.

Directions: From the intersection of Routes 1 and 35 in Kennebunk, head north 2.8 miles on Route 1. Turn right on Log Cabin Road and drive 1.7 miles south.

Dates: The museum is open daily from June to mid-Oct. and weekends in May and late Oct.

Fees: There is a charge for admission.

Closest town: Kennebunk.

For more information: Seashore Trolley Museum, PO Box A, 195 Log Cabin Road, Kennebunk, ME 04046. Phone (207) 967-2712.

THE BRICK STORE MUSEUM

[Fig. 7(7)] The Brick Store Museum is a row of four restored historic buildings from the early 1800s, including the 1825 William Lord Store. The museum has an impressive array of changing exhibits that can include historic clothing and decorative arts, maritime items, and paintings. The Brick Store Museum also offers tours of nearby historic homes and an architectural walking tour.

Directions: The Brick Store Museum is located at 117 Main Street in Kennebunk.

Activities: Sight-seeing.

Facilities: Museum.

Dates: Open year-round.

Fees: There is a charge for admission.

Closest town: Kennebunk.

For more information: The Brick Store Museum, 117 Main Street, Kennebunk, ME 04043. Phone (207) 985-4802.

GOLFING IN THE KENNEBUNKS

There are three 18-hole golf courses in the area. Call ahead to each to inquire about tee times.

Webhannet Golf Club in Kennebunk and Cape Arundel Golf Club in Kennebunkport are both semiprivate clubs that allow nonmembers to play. In Arundel, the Dutch Elm Golf Course is a public course.

For more information: Webhannet Golf Club, Old River Road, Kennebunk, ME

04046. Phone (207) 967-2061. Cape Arundel Golf Club, 19 River Road, Kennebunkport, ME 04046. Phone (207) 967-3494. Dutch Elm Golf Course, 5 Brimstone Road, Arundel, ME 04005. Phone (207) 282-9850.

WHALE-WATCHING FROM THE KENNEBUNKS

Starting around Memorial Day, a handful of whale-watching boats head out of the Kennebunks daily. Reservations are recommended. Remember to take along a hat, sunscreen, a jacket, and a camera.

Several whale species have been sighted off the Maine coast. The humpback whale (*Megaptera novaeangliae*), which can reach 40 feet long, puts on the best show, jumping into the air and crashing back into the sea. The fin whale (*Balaenoptera physalus*) is the second largest mammal on earth growing to 70 feet long. Whale watchers are least likely to see the northern right whale (*Balaena glacialis*), the most endangered whale off the U.S. coast. It got its name because it was the "right" whale to hunt—it was slow moving and floated after being killed. Scientists estimated that in 1999 there were only 325 right whales in the world. Four out of 10 right whales that die are killed by fishing gear or hit by ships.

The whale-watching boats in the Kennebunks leave from various wharves. The Indian Whale Watch leaves from the Arundel Wharf Restaurant. First Chance leaves from Doane's Wharf in Kennebunk. The Nautilus departs from the Kennebunk Marina.

For more information: Indian Whale Watch, PO Box 2672, Ocean Avenue, Kennebunkport, ME, 04046. Phone (207) 967-5912. First Chance Whale Watch, 217 Atlantic Avenue, North Hampton, NH 03862. Phone (207) 967-5507. Nautilus Whale Watch, PO Box 2775, Kennebunkport, ME 04046. Phone (207) 967-0707.

CAMPING IN THE KENNEBUNKS

There are several campgrounds in and around the Kennebunks.

SALTY ACRES CAMPGROUND. 272 Mills Road, Kennebunkport. Salty Acres is 1 mile from Goose Rocks Beach and has a pool, full RV hookups, and a pool. *(207) 967-2483.*

KENNEBUNKPORT CAMPING. 117 Old Cape Road, Kennebunkport. This wooded campground has RV sites with hookups and a tenting area. *(207) 967-2732.*

NIGHT LIFE IN THE KENNEBUNKS

The Kennebunks can be lively on warm summer evenings, when music spills out open windows onto the sidewalks.

FEDERAL JACK'S RESTAURANT AND BREWPUB. 8 Western Avenue, Kennebunk. This brewpub serves lunch and dinner and has music on weekends. *(207) 967-4322.*

THE KENNEBUNKPORT INN. 1 Dock Square, Kennebunkport. This Dock Square inn has a piano bar. *(207) 967-2621.*

⬚ DINING IN THE KENNEBUNKS

Whether you want to eat off a picnic table or white linen, there's a table for you in the Kennebunks, a region loaded with restaurants.

THE WHITE BARN INN. 37 Beach Street, Kennebunk. Reservations and jackets are a must at this gourmet restaurant in an elegant barn. An adjoining inn is just as nice and expensive. *Expensive. (207) 967-2321.*

ARUNDEL WHARF. 43 Ocean Avenue, Kennebunkport. Watch the lobster boats come in while you eat your lobster at this riverfront spot. *Moderate. (207) 967-3444.*

⬚ LODGING IN THE KENNEBUNKS

This is a popular tourist destination and has many inns, B&Bs, resort hotels, motels, and cottages. Make your reservations well in advance if you're planning a summer visit.

ST. ANTHONY'S MONASTERY. Beach Street, Kennebunk. For a unique vacation experience, try staying in the guest house at this monastery. Monks live in the main house, and the riverfront grounds are beautiful and open for strolling. No credit cards. *Moderate. (207) 967-2011.*

THE COLONY. Ocean Avenue, PO Box 511, Kennebunkport. This big, beautiful, old-style resort sits on the water and has a heated saltwater swimming pool, a beach, and a reputation of being environmentally responsible. *Expensive. (207) 967-3331.*

Biddeford and Saco

Biddeford and Saco—two cities that sit on either side of the Saco River—aren't among the major tourist destinations on the Maine coast. But they are a worthy addition to the itinerary of any traveler set on exploring Maine's natural and cultural history. The contrast between these cities is striking. Biddeford is an old mill town. The sprawling brick textile mills have been idle for decades, but the impact of the Canadians who worked here remains in a strong Franco-American heritage. This French heritage is celebrated the last full weekend in June each summer at *La Kermesse,* a huge festival with French food, dancing, and entertainment. Across the river, Saco looks like a picture-perfect New England town, with beautiful and large clapboard homes once occupied by mill owners and managers.

Birders from around the country come to Biddeford Pool, a section of Biddeford, for its extraordinary bird-watching potential. Biddeford Pool features a huge tidal basin, mud flats, and a rocky headland that juts into the Atlantic, attracting migratory birds and seabirds. Bird watchers will also want to visit Saco Heath, the southernmost raised peat bog in Maine and the Maine Audubon Society's East Point Sanctuary.

Ferry Beach State Park, a popular beach in the summer, provides good examples of the variety of habitats found in this region.

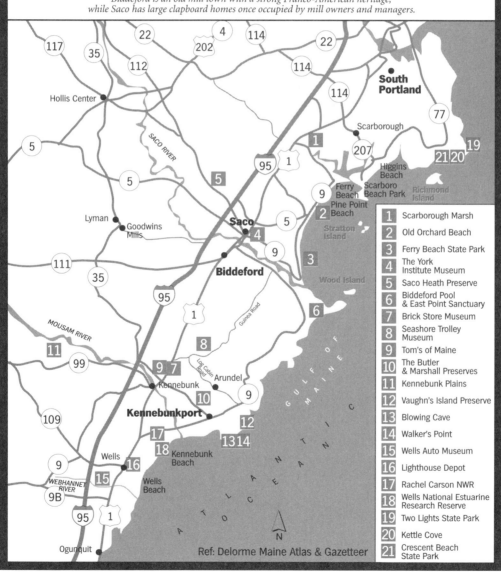

Biddeford and Saco Area

Biddeford is an old mill town with a strong Franco-American heritage, while Saco has large clapboard homes once occupied by mill owners and managers.

1. Scarborough Marsh
2. Old Orchard Beach
3. Ferry Beach State Park
4. The York Institute Museum
5. Saco Heath Preserve
6. Biddeford Pool & East Point Sanctuary
7. Brick Store Museum
8. Seashore Trolley Museum
9. Tom's of Maine
10. The Butler & Marshall Preserves
11. Kennebunk Plains
12. Vaughn's Island Preserve
13. Blowing Cave
14. Walker's Point
15. Wells Auto Museum
16. Lighthouse Depot
17. Rachel Carson NWR
18. Wells National Estuarine Research Reserve
19. Two Lights State Park
20. Kettle Cove
21. Crescent Beach State Park

Ref: Delorme Maine Atlas & Gazetteer

BIDDEFORD POOL AND EAST POINT SANCTUARY

[Fig. 7(6)] Biddeford Pool is an enormous tide pool, about 1 mile across, that attracts an astonishing number of birds and a very large number of bird watchers, especially in the spring and fall.

The pool itself is a great place to watch for wading birds, including great blue herons (*Ardea herodias*), green herons (*Butorides striatus*), and snowy egrets (*Egretta thula*), that stalk for food after a high tide. Several species of shorebirds frequent the pool as well, and are most visible close to high tide. (At low tide, the birds are spread across a large area, making them hard to see.) Warblers and sparrows can be seen in the grasses around the pool. Common terns (*Sterna hirundo*) and several species of gulls can be spotted feeding here.

In the winter, look for lapland longspurs (*Calcarius lapponicus*), snow buntings (*Plectrophenax nivalis*), and wintering waterfowl like black ducks and goldeneyes.

There is little public access to the shore of the pool. The best place to enter is next to Hattie's Deli, which sits on the southern edge of the pool on Route 208. Go inside and ask permission first. You'll also want to sample some of the great muffins, soups, or sandwiches and make use of one of Hattie's outside picnic tables.

The southern and eastern borders of the pool are created by an arm of land that sticks far east into the Atlantic, where it attracts many migrating birds in the spring and fall. Thirty acres at the tip of this arm make up the East Point Sanctuary, a Maine Audubon Society sanctuary.

A 1-mile trail loops through the sanctuary, heading through thickets of rugosa roses (*Rosa rugosa*) and other shrubs to a rocky point. The variety of habitats here— mud flats, forest, meadow, thickets, beach, and rocky shore—makes this a wonderful place to look for birds. During the spring and fall, watch for raptors like hawks and peregrine falcons, which may be attracted by the large population of other birds as prey.

In the summer, glossy ibis, snowy egrets, and black-crowned night herons can sometimes be seen flying to nearby Wood Island, a nesting island. In the winter months, this is a good spot to scan for rafts of ducks.

Directions: From Biddeford, take ME 9/208 south for 5 miles and you will see the pool to your left. Turn left at the T intersection, and look for Hattie's Deli on your left in less than 1 mile. To reach the East Point Sanctuary, continue on Main Street, bearing right at two forks, until it runs into the oceanfront and Ocean Avenue. The entrance to the sanctuary is back about 20 yards and is marked with a chain link gate and small sign. There is limited parking on Main Street. Do not block the gate or park on Ocean Avenue.

Activities: Walking, bird-watching.

Facilities: Trails.

Dates: Open year-round.

Fees: None.

Closest town: Biddeford.

For more information: Maine Audubon Society, Gilsland Farm, 118 US Route 1, PO Box 6009, Falmouth, ME 04105. Phone (207) 781-2330.

BIDDEFORD BEACHES

Biddeford has two beaches in the Biddeford Pool section of town. A city parking sticker is required in the summer months. Parking permits can be purchased at City Hall, but they are very pricey for nonresidents.

Fortunes Rocks Beach is a long, narrow strip of sand on the southern side of the point south of Biddeford Pool. It has lifeguards and restrooms in the summer.

Hills Beach is a small beach on the northern side of the pool and has no lifeguards or restrooms.

Sunbathers, swimmers, and surfers congregate here in the summer months. The remainder of the year, the beaches are popular with bird watchers.

Directions: To reach Fortunes Rocks Beach, take ME 208 south from the center of Biddeford to Biddeford Pool. Turn left at the T in the road. The entrance to the beach is on the right, across the road from Hattie's Deli. A parking permit is required during the summer. To reach Hills Beach, from ME 9 and 208, turn at the University of New England onto Hills Beach Road.

Activities: Swimming, surfing, sunbathing, bird-watching.

Fees: None. There is a charge for parking stickers, which are required in the summer.

Closest town: Biddeford.

For more information: Biddeford Parks and Recreation Department, 284 Hill Street, Biddeford, ME 04005. Phone (207) 283-0841.

WOOD ISLAND

[Fig. 7] Just off the coast of Biddeford, Wood Island Light has guarded Wood Island Harbor and the mouth of the Saco River since it was built in 1808. It is easily seen from the East Point Sanctuary (*see* page 53) in Biddeford Pool and can also be seen from the beach at Old Orchard Beach.

Local legends hold that many Maine lighthouses are haunted. According to the ghost story that swirls around this beacon, a local lobsterman killed a deputy sheriff near here in 1858, then came out to the lighthouse and took his own life. The lobsterman is said to have haunted the lighthouse ever since.

Maine Audubon owns Wood Island and nearby Stage Island. They may be reached by boat, but are important nesting islands. Maine Audubon asks that visitors remain below the high tide line during the nesting season, March through August.

Visitors to Wood Island should be forewarned that there is an abundance of poison ivy here. If it's not nesting season, stay on the boardwalk that leads to the lighthouse.

Directions: Follow ME 208 and ME 9 south from Biddeford staying on ME 208 when the highways split. About 0.5 mile after the split you will see Biddeford Pool to your left. Turn left at the T intersection. Bear right through two forks, following the road to the sanctuary. Walk along the path to the point for a good view of Wood Island.

Activities: Bird-watching, walking, lighthouse viewing.

Closest town: Biddeford.

For more information: Maine Audubon Society, Gilsland Farm, 118 US Route 1, PO Box 6009, Falmouth, ME 04105. Phone (207) 781-2330.

SACO HEATH PRESERVE

[Fig. 7(5)] This 1,000-acre domed peat bog is a vast ecological gem in the city of Saco. The coast of Maine has a few other raised peat bogs farther up the coast, most notably the Big Heath, or Seawall Bog, on Mount Desert Island (*see* page 250) and the Great Heath in Washington County (*see* page 265.) Saco Heath is the southernmost bog. It is also the site of the largest stand of Atlantic white cedar (*Chamaecyparis thyoides*) in Maine, and it's the only known spot in Maine where there are Hessel's hairstreak butterflies (*Mitoura hesseli*), a globally threatened butterfly whose larvae feed on the cedar.

Saco Heath is a raised coalesced bog, meaning its domed surface has grown above the water table (and is therefore *raised*) and it was formed when two domes that began as separate bogs grew together (or *coalesced*). Because the peat bog is above the water table, the plants in the bog get all their nutrients from precipitation.

In the bog, plants grow in peat, or saturated sphagnum mosses that can hold many times their weight in moisture. Several plants can thrive in the nutrient poor, acidic conditions of a peat bog. In the spring, the bog is colorful with pink and purple sheep laurel (*Kalmia angustifolia*) and rhodora (*Rhododendron canadense*). Also look for leatherleaf (*Chamaedaphne calyculata*), an evergreen with small white flowers in the spring.

Along with the Atlantic white cedars, which grow most densely in the higher and drier center portion of the bog, look for tamarack or larch trees (*Larix laricina*)—the only conifer that drops its needles in the fall— and pitch pines (*Pinus rigida*) in the bog.

For bird watchers, the highlight of the Saco Heath is the nesting palm warblers (*Dendroica coronata*) and other species that nest in peat lands, including black-capped chickadees (*Parus atricapillus*) and swamp sparrows (*Melospiza georgiana*).

The heath and the forest around it are also home to white-tailed deer (*Odocoileus virginianus*) and moose (*Alces alces*). The deer are more plentiful, but there

WHITE-TAILED DEER

have been plenty sightings of moose here, too.

The Saco Heath has a 1-mile nature trail that begins in a forest of maple and white pine (*Pinus strobus*) before heading off into the bog on a boardwalk. The peat bog is a fragile environment, and visitors should remain on the trail or boardwalk. An old all-terrain vehicle trail that crosses under the boardwalk has compacted the peat and damaged the hydrology of the immediate area. The disruption will likely last for decades.

Directions: From Saco, take ME 112 north. About 2 miles past I-95, the parking lot for the Saco Heath Preserve will be on your right.

Activities: Nature walking, wildlife watching, and bird-watching.

Facilities: Trail and boardwalk.

Dates: Open year-round.

Fees: None.

Closest town: Saco.

For more information: The Nature Conservancy, Maine Chapter. Fort Andross, 14 Maine Street, Suite 401, Brunswick ME 04011. Phone (207) 729-5181.

THE YORK INSTITUTE MUSEUM

[Fig. 7(4)] This Saco museum has an impressive collection of early American paintings, decorative arts, and other items. One of its more rare exhibits is the 850-foot-long *Panorama of Pilgrim's Progress*, painted in 1851 by a group of artists in New York City. There's also a nineteenth century display on the birds of New England.

Directions: The York Institute Museum is at 371 Main Street in Saco.

Dates: Open year-round.

Fees: Donations are accepted.

Closest town: Saco.

For more information: The York Institute Museum, 371 Main Street, Saco, ME 04072. Phone (207) 282-3031.

FERRY BEACH STATE PARK

[Fig. 7(3)] Most locals know Ferry Beach as a great swimming beach, but that's just the beginning of the story. This 117-acre state park also has nature trails through a forest and over a swamp for visitors interested in looking for plants and birds.

The centerpiece of the natural area at Ferry Beach is Tupelo Swamp, named for the black tupelo trees (*Nyssa sylvatica*) that grow here. These trees can be found in much of the eastern United States, but are very uncommon in Maine and are at the northernmost point of their range here. They are easily identified in the swamp by their deeply fissured bark and their branches, which grow horizontally from their trunks. The swamp is very wet and impenetrable, but a boardwalk crossing it gives a good view of the vegetation and birds found here. The swamp is very buggy, so many kinds of small birds and frogs can be seen and heard here.

Other trails wander through woodlands of maple, birch, beech, pine, and hemlock trees. The trails are well marked, but signs are removed from the late fall through early spring.

A boardwalk also takes visitors through the dunes to the beach. As is the case at all the beaches in Maine, visitors should stay off the dunes. The grasses growing here are very fragile and the ecosystem is easily disturbed. Dune grasses stabilize the dunes by sending roots deep down through the sand. Without these plants, the dunes would disappear. Also, endangered piping plovers (*Charadrius melodus*) and other shorebirds sometimes nest in the dunes here and should not be disturbed.

AMERICAN TOAD
(*Bufo americanus*) A primarily nocturnal amphibian, this toad is a prodigious insect eater.

Directions: From Saco, follow ME 9 to Bay View Road.

Activities: Swimming, nature walks, picnicking.

Facilities: Lifeguards, changing rooms, restrooms, picnic area, nature trails.

Dates: Open Memorial Day through Sept., but accessible year-round. Trail signs are down from late fall through early spring.

Fees: There is a charge for admission during the summer.

Closest town: Saco.

For more information: Ferry Beach State Park, 95 Bay View Road, Saco, ME 04072. Phone (207) 283-0067 (in season). Phone (207) 624-6075 (off-season). Maine Bureau of Parks and Lands, 22 State House Station, Augusta, ME 04333.

SACO TRAILS

Take a Hike—in the Saco Bay Area is a guide of several trails in the Saco, Biddeford, and Old Orchard Beach. It's the work of Saco Trails, a nonprofit land trust that works to get public access to hiking trails and footpaths around Saco Bay. Most of the hikes are on private land. The guide is available for sale at several area businesses, including Bookland in Saco and Biddeford. One of the trails described is the Cascade Falls Trail, which begins behind the Cascade Restaurant on Route 1 in Saco. (The restaurant prepares trail lunches for picnics at the falls.) This 1.2-mile round-trip trail follows a brook to a beautiful waterfall.

For more information: Saco Bay Trails, PO Box 852, Saco, ME 04072.

WATER PARKS

If it's hot and you're traveling with kids, you may want to visit one of Saco's two water parks. Funtown/Splashtown USA has an amusement park with rides (Funtown) and a water park with water slides (Splashtown). Aquaboggan Water Park has water slides, miniature golf, and other attractions.

Directions: Funtown/Splashtown and Aquaboggan Water Park are both on Route 1 in Saco.

Dates: Funtown opens in May. Splashtown and Aquaboggan Water Park open in June.

Fees: There is a charge for admission.

Closest town: Saco.

For more information: Funtown/Splashtown USA, PO Box 29, Saco, ME 04072. Phone (800) 878-2900. Aquaboggan Water Park, Route 1, Saco, ME 04072. Phone (207) 282-3112.

CAMPING IN BIDDEFORD AND SACO

The large campgrounds along Route 1 can fill up at peak summer season, so it's best to call ahead.

SILVER SPRINGS CAMPGROUND. 705 Portland Road (Route 1), Saco. This campground has full hookups, a pool, a store, and other recreational facilities. It also has cottages and a motel. *(207) 283-3880.*

DINING IN BIDDEFORD AND SACO

Biddeford and Saco have a wide variety of eateries. Think about taking a cooked lobster to the beach for a real Maine picnic.

HATTIE'S DELI. Biddeford Pool, Biddeford. The location on one of Maine's best bird-watching spots can't be beat. The pie, sandwiches, and soups are good, too. *Inexpensive. (207) 282-3435.*

NEW MORNING NATURAL FOODS. 230 Main Street, Biddeford. This natural food store and lunch spot has delicious organic foods to eat there or to go. *Inexpensive. (207) 282-1434.*

CORNFORTH HOUSE. 893 Portland Road (Route 1), Saco. This elegant restaurant serves gourmet seafood, veal, and other entrées for dinner. Its Sunday brunch is famous. *Moderate. (207) 284-2006.*

LODGING IN BIDDEFORD AND SACO

This region has several B&Bs and motels, depending on whether you want to stay in Victorian splendor or modern convenience.

HODSON HOUSE. 398 Main Street, Saco. This antique-filled inn is a restored, 1820, Greek Revival mansion in the middle of Saco. *Moderate. (207) 284-4113.*

CLASSIC MOTEL. 21 Ocean Park Road, Saco. This motel has several efficiency units and an indoor pool. *Moderate. (207) 282-5569.*

SALT MARSH HAY
(Spartina patens)

Old Orchard Beach is popular with families from New England and Canada.

Old Orchard Beach

[Fig. 7(2)] Old Orchard Beach—or O.O.B. as it's often called in Maine—is probably the most touristy of the tourist towns on the Maine coast. If you want to ride a Ferris wheel, play arcade games, and eat fried dough while having your weight guessed on the boardwalk, this is the place for you. It's a popular spot. In the summer, Old Orchard Beach's population explodes from about 10,000 to 100,000 sun-loving souls.

Old Orchard Beach has beautiful white sand beaches that are big enough to hold a crowd on sunny days. Don't be surprised if you hear a lot of French on the beach. This is traditionally a summer destination for Canadians. When the exchange rate favored the Canadian dollar, more than half the people spending summers in Old Orchard Beach were thought to be Canadian. That has slowed since the Canadian dollar has declined in recent years, but French-speaking tourists are still very much in evidence.

LODGING IN OLD ORCHARD BEACH

Old Orchard Beach has thousands of campsites and hundreds of motel rooms and tourist cottages.

BEAU RIVAGE MOTEL. 54 East Grand Avenue, Old Orchard Beach. This big motel has a pool and hot tubs and is within walking distance of the beach and the amusement parks. *Moderate. (207) 934-4668.*

KEBEK 3 MOTEL. 53 West Grand Avenue, Old Orchard Beach. This motel sits practically on the beach. *Moderate. (207) 934-5253.*

Scarborough

The sandy beaches of southern Maine meet the rocky coast of the Mid-Coast in Scarborough. Stand at Prout's Neck, where Winslow Homer painted pictures of the rocks and the surf, then explore the sandy beaches on either side of this famous point.

Scarborough is a fast-developing coastal town. Fortunately, much of the land here, including the largest salt marsh in Maine, some lovely strips of beach, and an island being used for seabird restoration projects by the National Audubon Society, has been preserved for public or conservation uses.

One of Scarborough's most scenic spots is also a hard one to visit. Prout's Neck, where Winslow Homer had a studio and where wealthy people from Philadelphia and other East Coast cities have summered for generations, has dramatic granite cliffs, a beach, and a bird sanctuary. But there is virtually no parking for visitors unless they are staying at the elegant Black Point Inn (*see* page 63) or have been invited by a resident of this exclusive summer colony with an electric gate.

SCARBOROUGH MARSH

[Fig. 7(1)] The best way to explore this 3,100-acre salt marsh—the largest in the state—is from a canoe. If you don't have a canoe, you can rent one during the summer at the Scarborough Marsh Nature Center, operated by the Maine Audubon Society.

The marsh is a wildlife management area overseen by the state Department of Inland Fisheries and Wildlife. But Maine Audubon maintains an active presence here in the summer, operating a nature center with displays, renting canoes, conducting guided nature walks and paddles, and holding a wide variety of nature programs for children and adults.

This sprawling coastal marsh is a critical habitat for many birds. Wading birds, waterfowl, and shorebirds can be spotted here in abundance, especially during the spring and fall migrations. Canada and snow geese stop in the marsh's meadows by the thousands, and a variety of ducks rest and nest in its ponds and streams.

Look for herons, egrets, ibis and shorebirds in the salt marsh in the summer. Keep your distance and be careful not to flush the birds from their feeding grounds. Some of these birds likely nest offshore on Stratton Island (*see* page 61) so keep an eye on the sky, as well. If you plan on exploring the salt marsh from a canoe, check tide tables ahead of time and make sure you're paddling with the tide. You can put your canoe in right behind the nature center. Maine Audubon conducts full moon canoe tours that offer a beautiful and unique way to explore the marsh.

The marsh also can be explored on foot. There's a nature trail and boardwalk at the nature center. Also, Eastern Road, a 2.2-mile road that runs through the middle of the marsh, is within walking distance of the nature center. Other roads approach the marsh from different directions. There's a board at the nature center where recent bird sightings are posted. Look at that and talk to the Maine Audubon workers to pick a good route for the day.

Visitors should keep in mind that this is a wildlife management area. Hunting, trapping, and fishing are permitted in season.

Directions: The main access to the Scarborough Marsh is from the Scarborough Marsh Nature Center. From Route 1 in Scarborough, head east on ME 9. You will soon see the Scarborough Marsh Nature Center on your left.

Activities: Bird-watching, canoeing, walking, fishing, hunting.

Facilities: Trails. The nature center has restrooms accessible only in the summer.

Dates: The marsh is accessible year-round. The nature center is open from mid-June to Labor Day.

Fees: None. There is a canoe rental charge.

Closest town: Scarborough.

For more information: For hunting and fishing information, Maine Department of Inland Fisheries and Wildlife, 284 State Street, 41 State House Station, Augusta, ME 04333-0041. Phone (207) 287-8003. For nature center information, Maine Audubon Society, Gilsland Farm, PO Box 6009, Falmouth, ME 04105. Phone (207) 883-5100 (in season). Phone (207) 781-2330 (off-season).

GREAT EGRET
(Casmerodius albus)

STRATTON ISLAND

[Fig. 7] Just 1.5 miles off the shore of some of Maine's most crowded beaches, Stratton Island is a valuable seabird nesting site. Researchers from the National Audubon Society's seabird restoration team camp out on this rocky island during the nesting season, protecting the nests of endangered roseate terns (*Sterna dougallii*) from gulls and conducting the occasional tour for avid bird watchers. Maine Audubon Society typically brings bird watchers out on organized trips a few times each summer.

Stratton Island sees a wide variety of birds. In the spring and fall, migrants and storm-swept vagrants land here to rest. In the summer, terns, herons, egrets, glossy ibises, and other birds nest here. Many of these birds can be seen in some of the coastal bird-watching hotspots—Biddeford Pool and Scarborough Marsh.

One victorious bird species has been the roseate tern (*Sterna dougallii*), whose population on Stratton and other seabird restoration islands has soared in the past decade. Common terns (*Sterna hirundo*) and arctic terns (*Sterna paradisaea*) can also be seen. Common and arctic terns nest on the island's beaches, while the roseate terns tend to hide their eggs under some vegetation or driftwood. Roseate terns almost always nest with common terns. The roseate tern can be distinguished by its lighter gray back, its longer tail feathers, and its bill, which is predominantly black with a small amount of red at the base during the breeding season.

The island has also been home to Maine's only known pair of breeding American oystercatchers, a 19-inch shorebird recognizable by its black head, white chest, brown back, and long orange beak. In a typical Maine mingling of species, the arctic terns here are at the southern end of their range, while the American oystercatchers are at the northern limits of their range.

Seabird restoration volunteers and naturalists are trying to repair damage done to seabird populations by humans a century ago. In the early 1900s, several species of seabirds became nearly extinct because their feathers were fashionable adornments for hats and their eggs were considered a delicacy.

Stratton Island is an important seabird nesting island, and most of its shore is off-limits to boat landings. Maine Audubon Society holds occasional bird-watching trips to Stratton Island.

Directions: Stratton Island is 1.5 miles off the coast of Scarborough. Maine Audubon Society conducts periodic tours of the island.

Activities: Bird-watching.

Facilities: None.

Dates: Occasional tours of Stratton Island are offered.

For more information: For information on the National Audubon Society's seabird restoration projects, write Project Puffin, 159 Sapsucker Woods Road, Ithaca, NY 14850. To ask about Stratton Island, write or call National Audubon's Maine office, P.O. Box 524, Dover-Foxcroft, ME 04426. Phone (207) 564-7946. For information on tours of the island, Maine Audubon Society, Gilsland Farm, 118 US Route 1, PO Box 6009, Falmouth, ME 03105. Phone (207) 781-2330.

SCARBOROUGH BEACHES

[Fig. 7] Scarborough has four sandy beaches that are popular for swimming and sunning in the summer. The southernmost is Pine Point Beach, which is a continuation of Old Orchard Beach. It has nice, white sand, restrooms, a snack bar, and some parking. Ferry Beach, also known as Western Beach, is on the western shore of Prout's Neck, at the mouth of the Scarborough River. Scarboro Beach Park is a former state park now owned by the town of Scarborough. It is popular with families, swimmers, and surfers in the summer. It is the only Scarborough beach with lifeguards. Behind the beach is a freshwater marsh called Massacre Pond. In the early 1700s, 20 settlers were slain here by Indians.

Higgins Beach is at the mouth of the Spurwink River and is a popular beach for swimming and exploring. Parking here is very limited. If you've got your heart set on swimming at Higgins Beach, check into one of the many guest houses or inns in the area.

Directions: To reach Pine Point Beach, from Route 1 in West Scarborough, follow Pine Point Road or ME 9 to Pine Point.

To reach Ferry Beach or Scarboro Beach Park, from Route 1 in Scarborough, follow Black Point Road about 4 miles to the beaches, which are well marked.

To reach Higgins Beach, from Route 1 in Scarborough, follow Black Point Road to Spurwink Road, or ME 77. Turn left and drive about 2 miles to the beach.

Activities: Swimming, surfing, picnicking.

Facilities: Pine Point Beach has a snack bar and restrooms. Scarboro Beach Park has picnic areas, restrooms, a snack bar, and lifeguards.

Closest town: Scarborough.

For more information: Scarboro Beach Park, Black Point Road, Scarborough, ME 04074. Phone (207) 883-2416. Visitor Information Center, Convention and Visitors Bureau of Greater Portland, 305 Commercial Street, Portland, ME 04101. Phone (207) 772-5800.

CAMPING IN SCARBOROUGH

BAYLEY'S CAMPING RESORT. 27 Ross Road, Scarborough. Bayley's has more than 400 sites for everything from tents up to the largest RVs with hookups. It has three swimming pools, two ponds for fishing or paddle-boating, a double-decker bus to take campers to area attractions, miniature golf, and an outdoor theater, among other features. *(207) 883-6043.*

THE WILD DUCK CAMPGROUND. 39 Dunstan Landing Road, Scarborough. This 70-site campground is next to the Scarborough Marsh and offers canoe rentals and hookups. *(207) 883-4432.*

DINING IN SCARBOROUGH

For a big night out, head to nearby Portland, which is loaded with restaurants. But you'll find great lunches and down-home food near the beach in Scarborough.

SPURWINK COUNTRY KITCHEN. 150 Spurwink Road, Scarborough. This casual spot specializes in homey dishes like macaroni and cheese and meatloaf and is a family favorite. *Inexpensive. (207) 774-6652.*

LODGING IN SCARBOROUGH

Scarborough has some nice beachfront hotels and many motels. If you're staying a week or more, look into renting one of the many beachfront cottages available.

BLACK POINT INN. Black Point Road, Prout's Neck. Arguably Maine's most elegant inn. This shingled, 1878 oceanfront inn on exclusive Prout's Neck has two pools, two beaches, gourmet dining, and access to golf and tennis at a nearby country club. *Expensive. (207) 883-4126.*

HIGGINS BEACH INN. 34 Ocean Avenue, Scarborough. This oceanfront inn is across the street from Higgins Beach. Its Italian and seafood restaurant, Garofalo's, is open to the public. *Moderate. (207) 883-6684.*

Casco Bay

Mexico (2)
Rumford Dixfield
(108)
Chisholm
Livermore Falls
(133)
KENNEBEC
(26)

(27)
Oakland
Waterville
Winslow
(201)
(202)
(104)
Augusta
Winthrop Hallowell
Farmingdale
(17)
Randolph
Gardiner
(3)
KNOX
(17)
(32)

South Paris (4)
(202)
(9)
Norway
ANDROSCOGGIN
Mechanic Falls Sabattu
Auburn Lewiston
(495)

Richmond
LINCOLN
Waldoboro
(1)
Damariscotta-Newcastle

Bridgton
(35) (121)
(26)
(136)
Lisbon-Lisbon Center
(95)
Lisbon Falls SAHOO
(1)
(27)
(302)
CUMBERLAND
SEBAGO LAKE
Topsham Bath
Brunswick
Boothbay Harbor

Freeport
(26)
Cumberland Center
Yarmouth
(495)
10 Falmouth Foreside
Westbrook
Gorham
(117)
(22)
Portland
South Portland
Scarborough
9
(202)
Saco Old Orchard Beach
(111)
Biddeford

11

Kennebunk
Kennebunkport
(1)

Ogunquit
(95)
York Village

FIGURE NUMBERS	
9	South Portland
10	Portland
11	Falmouth & Yarmouth Area

Casco Bay

The communities of Casco Bay run the gamut, from an island with a population in the dozens to Portland, Maine's largest city with 65,000 residents. Ecologically, this is a region where many plant and bird species reach their northern borders and others reach their southern borders. The beaches and salt marshes typical of the Mid-Atlantic coast creep into this region of Maine, rubbing elbows with the boreal forest and peat lands found farther north, creating a unique mix of plant and animal species.

Many a bird watcher has been born along the shores of Casco Bay. The geography of the region, with its undulating coastline, protected harbors, and uncountable islands makes this a wonderfully accessible place to look for birds. Migrating shorebirds and land birds follow the coastline here every spring and fall. Expert and novice bird watchers can find many species in a single morning in some of the Casco Bay's

[*Above: Portland Head Light is the oldest lighthouse in Maine*]

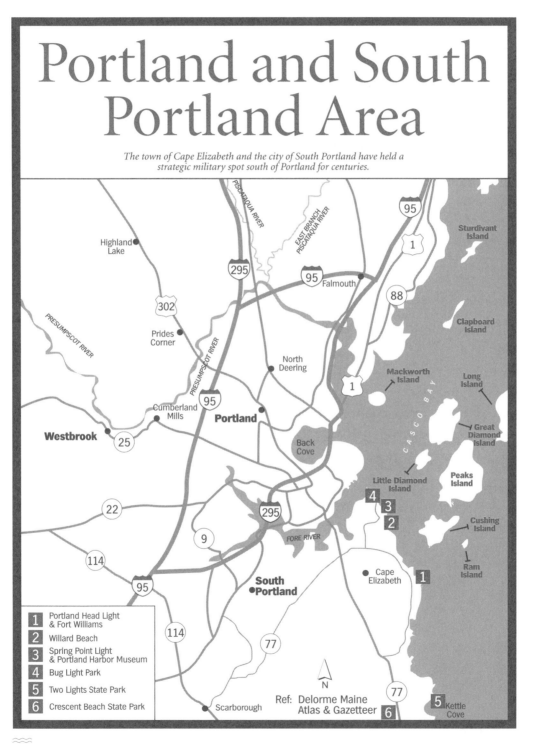

Portland and South Portland Area

The town of Cape Elizabeth and the city of South Portland have held a strategic military spot south of Portland for centuries.

Highland Lake

Sturdivant Island

95

1

295

95 Falmouth

88

302

PRESUMPSCOT RIVER

Clapboard Island

Prides Corner

North Deering

1

Mackworth Island

Long Island

CASCO BAY

Cumberland Mills

95

Portland

Back Cove

Great Diamond Island

Westbrook

25

Little Diamond Island

Peaks Island

4
3
2

22

295

FORE RIVER

Cushing Island

9

114

Ram Island

95

South Portland

Cape Elizabeth

1

1	Portland Head Light & Fort Williams
2	Willard Beach
3	Spring Point Light & Portland Harbor Museum
4	Bug Light Park
5	Two Lights State Park
6	Crescent Beach State Park

114

77

N

Ref: Delorme Maine Atlas & Gazetteer

77

Scarborough

6

5 Kettle Cove

PRESUMPSCOT RIVER

PISCATAQUA RIVER

EAST BRANCH PISCATAQUA RIVER

reliable resting and feeding spots. Don't limit your naturalist explorations to the rich bird life found along the shores of Casco Bay. There are also interesting plants and trees to be easily viewed. One of Maine's last surviving old-growth forests grows on a college campus here, and New England's largest community of linden trees grows along a public path in Portland. Nature preserves protect the habitats of rare plants, butterflies, and birds. Harbor seals are often visible sunning on ledges or island shores during boat trips in the bay.

All this variety makes the Casco Bay region an interesting one to explore. Visitors can spend a day wandering the beach and exploring an old fort or museum, then watch the sun set from the deck of a passenger ferry before heading to a lobster wharf for supper.

Cape Elizabeth and South Portland

The town of Cape Elizabeth and the city of South Portland have held a strategic spot south of Portland Harbor for centuries.

Two historic forts here guarded the entrance to Portland Harbor through World War II and now serve as parks. A handful of lighthouses continue to protect mariners from the rocky shores, and there are now museums—and plenty of Maine photo opportunities—at two of these lighthouses.

Cape Elizabeth has some popular, sandy beaches where the locals swim when it's warm and walk in the cooler months.

South Portland is home to some marinas and waterfront restaurants. It's also home to the Maine Mall and a surrounding commercial strip, should the need for fast food, a multiplex, or department store shopping strike.

PORTLAND HEAD LIGHT AND FORT WILLIAMS PARK

[Fig. 9(1)] This beautiful white lighthouse was commissioned by President George Washington and has been guarding the entrance to Portland Harbor since 1791. Its stunning location on a rocky, windswept promontory and its easy accessibility make this one of Maine's most visited lighthouses. It's also the oldest lighthouse in the state. Portland native and nineteenth century poet Henry Wadsworth Longfellow is said to have visited this lighthouse often in his youth, and the lighthouse appears in some of his poems.

The lighthouse is off limits, but the old keeper's house is now the Museum at Portland Head Light. The museum has a collection of lighthouse lenses and displays on lighthouses and local history. There's also a gift shop with lighthouse and Maine souvenirs.

Portland Head Light sits on the shore of Fort Williams Park, a 90-acre town park great for walking, bicycling, and, when the snow falls, sledding. The strong breeze here makes it a very popular spot for kite flying. There are acres of neatly mowed lawns, tennis courts, and a small beach. Kids love to explore the ruins of an old stone mansion that overlooks the bay.

The Portland Symphony Orchestra holds a few nighttime pop concerts here in the summer. The music, the sea air, and the scenery make for a stunning display.

Directions: From Broadway in South Portland, head south on Cottage Road, which will turn into Shore Road. Fort Williams Park will be on your left.

Activities: Sight-seeing, walking, cycling, kite flying.

Facilities: Museum, walkways, tennis courts, picnic areas.

Dates: The park is open year-round. The museum is open daily from June through Oct. and weekends off-season.

Fees: There is no charge for admission to the park. There is a charge for admission to the museum.

Closest town: Cape Elizabeth.

For more information: Museum at Portland Head Light, 1000 Shore Road, Cape Elizabeth, ME 04107. Phone (207) 799-2661.

TWO LIGHTS STATE PARK

[Fig. 9(5)] This 40-acre oceanfront state park is relatively small, but it overflows with scenery. There are trails along the rocky headlands, incredible views across Casco Bay from atop an old gun battery, rocks to scramble over, and countless spots to sit quietly with a picnic or just your thoughts.

There are also plenty of tide pools to explore at low tide at Two Lights. Look for green crabs, sea urchins, and other creatures trapped in the pools. They'll likely return to the sea as the next tide comes in.

The rocks at Two Lights are continually battered by the surf and have a grained texture that makes them look almost like petrified wood. These lines in the rocks are really thin layers of sparkly metamorphic material called schist.

Despite its name, there is only one light near Two Lights park, the Cape Elizabeth Light (a second beacon was removed in 1924). That lighthouse and its keeper's house, a private residence, are not within the park boundaries. The attractive lighthouse and keeper's cottage were immortalized in a famous painting by Edward Hopper in the 1920s. But the keeper's cottage was at the center of a major local controversy in 1999 when a new owner decided to renovate it and changed its appearance substantially. (The painting, which hangs in the Metropolitan Museum of Art in New York, also served as a stamp in 1970 noting Maine's sesquicentennial as a state.) With no law outlawing changes to historic structures, townspeople were powerless to prevent the renovations.

Two Lights is a great place to bring a picnic. If you didn't pack any food, there is a lobster shack right down the road (*see* The Lobster Shack, page 71).

Directions: From Broadway in South Portland, take ME 77 south and follow the signs to Two Lights.

Activities: Walking, bird-watching, picnicking.

Facilities: Trails, picnic tables and grills, restrooms.

Fees: There is a charge for admission.

Closest town: Cape Elizabeth

For more information: Two Lights State Park, 66 Two Lights Road, Cape Elizabeth ME 04107. Phone (207) 799-5871. State Bureau of Parks and Lands, 22 State House Station, Augusta, ME 04333. Phone (207) 287-3821.

KETTLE COVE

[Fig. 9] This small cove between Two Lights and Crescent Beach state parks has a town beach that is easily overlooked. Parking is very limited; it's hard to snag one of the few places on a sunny summer day. But you'll have little company here if you come to enjoy the scenery in the off-season.

In the winter, rafts of common eiders (*Somateria mollissima*) can occasionally be seen off the coast. In the spring, birds heading to northern breeding areas sometimes stop here.

Directions: From Broadway in South Portland, follow ME 77 south, past the Two Lights State Park. Take a left on Ocean House Road. Look for the small sign for the Kettle Cove parking area.

Activities: Walking, bird-watching, swimming.

Facilities: Restrooms.

Fees: None.

Closest town: Cape Elizabeth.

For more information: Cape Elizabeth Parks, PO Box 6260, Cape Elizabeth, ME 04107. Phone (207) 767-2273.

CRESCENT BEACH STATE PARK

[Fig. 9(6)] This Cape Elizabeth beach is a popular spot on sunny summer days. The sand is kind of coarse near the water, but the gentle surf makes this a favorite family beach. There are lifeguards, a playground, and a snack bar. There are also picnic areas and cold showers.

Directions: From Broadway in South Portland, head south on ME 77. Crescent Beach will be on the left, shortly after Two Lights State Park.

Activities: Swimming, picnicking.

Facilities: Restrooms, snack bar, cold showers, playground, lifeguards.

Dates: The park is open Memorial Day through Sept. The beach is accessible year-round.

Fees: There is a charge for admission.

Closest town: Cape Elizabeth.

For more information: State Bureau of Parks and Lands, 22 State House Station, Augusta, ME 04333. Phone (207) 287-3821. Crescent Beach State Park, phone (207) 799-5871.

▓ WILLARD BEACH

[Fig. 9(2)] This little beach in South Portland forms a sandy crescent between two rocky headlands. It's considered a good family beach because of its typically calm water and its facilities, which include lifeguards, a playground, restrooms, and a snack bar. It also has a beautiful view of some of the Casco Bay islands. The campus of the Southern Maine Technical Institute sits near the top of this beach.

For a quick, easy walk with wonderful views, follow the 0.5-mile Spring Point Shore Path from the beach along the shore to the Spring Point Light.

Directions: Heading east on Broadway in South Portland, turn right on Preble Street, then left on Willow Street and into the beach parking area.

Activities: Swimming, picnicking.

Facilities: Restrooms, snack bar, changing rooms, playground, lifeguards.

Dates: The beach is accessible year-round, although the facilities are only open in the summer.

Fees: None.

Closest town: South Portland.

For more information: South Portland Parks and Recreation Department, 21 Nelson Road, South Portland, ME 04106. Phone (207) 767-7651.

▓ SPRING POINT LIGHT AND PORTLAND HARBOR MUSEUM

[Fig. 9(3)] If the weather is calm, walk the 900-foot breakwater out to the Spring Point Light. This lighthouse, which marks a dangerous ledge near the harbor mouth, was built in 1897. It was surrounded by water until 1951, when the granite breakwater was built. Spring Point is adjacent to the campus of the Southern Maine Technical College. This is also the site of the Portland Harbor Museum, which has exhibits on the development of the harbor, commercial fishing, and recreational boating.

The ruins of old Fort Preble, built during the Revolutionary War, offer beautiful panoramic views, from Portland Harbor to Casco Bay. The original fort here was built in 1808. The fort was manned until 1950, when the newer buildings became the campus of Southern Maine Technical College.

For a short, easy walk with some of the best views in town, take the Spring Point Shore Trail from the Spring Point Light to Willard Beach. It's a paved, 0.5-mile path that looks out at the islands and several lighthouses.

This is a popular fishing and picnicking spot, especially on warm summer evenings, when parking is plentiful. It's hard to find a spot when the college is in session.

Directions: Head east on Broadway in South Portland until the road ends, turn right and head into the Southern Maine Technical College campus.

Activities: Picnicking, sight-seeing.

Facilities: Museum, trail.

Dates: Accessible year-round.

Fees: There is a charge for admission to the museum.

Closest town: South Portland.
Spring Point Shore Trail: 1 mile, one-way. Easy.
For more information: Portland Harbor Museum, Fort Road, South Portland, ME 04106. Phone (207) 799-6337.

BUG LIGHT PARK

[Fig. 9(4)] South Portland's newest park is built on the grounds of an old shipyard, where World War II Liberty Ships were built. It's named for the little lighthouse at its tip. The 13-acre waterfront park has stunning views of Portland, Portland Harbor, and Casco Bay. It has a paved path popular with walkers, cyclists, and in-line skaters. There's also a public boat launch into Portland Harbor here.

Directions: Head east on Broadway in South Portland until the road ends. Turn left and head into the park.
Activities: Picnicking, bicycling, walking, sight-seeing.
Facilities: Path, public boat launch.
Dates: Open year-round.
Fees: None.
Closest town: South Portland.
For more information: City of South Portland, Parks and Recreation Department, 21 Nelson Road, South Portland, ME 04106. Phone (207) 767-7651.

DINING IN CAPE ELIZABETH AND SOUTH PORTLAND

Head towards the Maine Mall area if the food court or other fast food is going to fill the bill. Otherwise, try lobster on the rocks at Two Lights or a dinner overlooking Portland's skyline.

THE LOBSTER SHACK. 225 Two Lights Road, Cape Elizabeth. Pick out your own lobster, or other entrée, at this oceanside lobster shack and enjoy the view. *Inexpensive. (207) 799-1677.*

THE GOOD TABLE. 527 Ocean House Road, Cape Elizabeth. This relaxed spot on Route 77 near Two Lights State Park serves fish, chicken, and beef and is known for its baked goods and inspired brunch offerings. *Moderate. (207) 799-4663.*

SEA DOG TAVERN AND GRILLE. 231 Front Street, South Portland. The best views of Portland are from the other side of the harbor, like from the deck of this brewpub-affiliated lunch and dinner spot. *Moderate. (207) 799-6055.*

LODGING IN CAPE ELIZABETH AND SOUTH PORTLAND

South Portland has many national chain hotels, most of them in the vicinity of the airport. But there are also a few waterfront spots in this area.

INN BY THE SEA. 40 Bowery Beach Road, Cape Elizabeth. Inn By The Sea is a modern and luxurious shingled complex of suites and cottages. It has a boardwalk to Crescent Beach, as well as a pool and tennis. *Expensive. (207) 799-3134.*

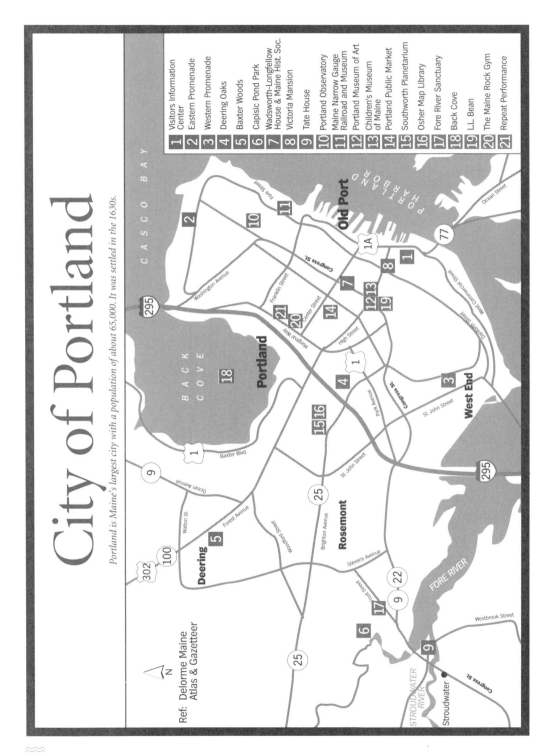

City of Portland

Portland is Maine's largest city with a population of about 65,000. It was settled in the 1630s.

Ref: Delorme Maine
Atlas & Gazetteer

1	Visitors Information Center
2	Eastern Promenade
3	Western Promenade
4	Deering Oaks
5	Baxter Woods
6	Capisic Pond Park
7	Wadsworth-Longfellow House & Maine Hist. Soc.
8	Victoria Mansion
9	Tate House
10	Portland Observatory
11	Maine Narrow Gauge Railroad and Museum
12	Portland Museum of Art
13	Children's Museum of Maine
14	Portland Public Market
15	Southworth Planetarium
16	Osher Map Library
17	Fore River Sanctuary
18	Back Cove
19	LL Bean
20	The Maine Rock Gym
21	Repeat Performance

PETER A. MCKERNAN HOSPITALITY CENTER. Fort Road, South Portland. Eight elegant rooms with wonderful water views in the old Fort Preble's Officers' Quarters serve as a laboratory for students in the Hotel, Motel, and Restaurant Program at Southern Maine Technical College. *Expensive. (207) 767-9672.*

Portland

With a population of about 65,000, Portland is Maine's largest city. But much of this peninsula city, which was first settled in the 1630s, is decidedly nonurban. There are trails along the water, through forests, and beside salt marshes. There are islands ripe for exploring on foot, bike, or kayak. And there are the historic neighborhoods, the Old Port, and a working waterfront—all perfect for wandering.

Portland also has a thriving arts community, an impressive art museum and children's museum, historic homes faithfully preserved, a local symphony, an opera company, and several theater companies. Visitors also flock to the city's Public Market and to the many galleries here.

Portland is more of a year-round destination than other coastal towns in Maine, but summertime is when the city really comes alive. Bands play aboard ferries cruising the harbor, large cruise ships spill passengers from around the world into the Old Port, and concerts are regularly held in several city parks.

SEASTAR (Henrica sp.)

Outside magazine recently named Portland one of its 10 best places to live, because of its proximity to outdoor adventures along with its somewhat urban conveniences. Many Portland residents apparently agree. Cars all over the city have bikes and kayaks strapped to their roofs and local outings clubs have many members.

The city of Portland is resilient. The people here have rebuilt their community several times since English settlers arrived in 1632. An early British settlement was destroyed twice by Indians. After Colonial sentiments grew, the British bombarded Portland (then called Falmouth Neck) from the harbor in 1775, burning nearly every building here. The city was rebuilt and was again a thriving shipping center when a fire destroyed much of the port area on July 4, 1866. The Victorian buildings built after that fire can still be seen today.

Portland is on a peninsula that runs northeast to southwest between the Eastern Promenade and the Western Promenade. Two major streets that can be helpful when orienting yourself are Commercial Street on the waterfront and Congress Street, which runs through the middle of the downtown and then west off the peninsula. The peninsula is only 2.5 miles long by 1 mile wide, so it's not too hard to find your way if you get lost.

VISITORS INFORMATION CENTER

[Fig. 10(1)] A good first stop in Portland is the Visitors Information Center of the Convention and Visitors Bureau of Greater Portland.

The information center is loaded with maps and brochures on area sights and is staffed by helpful employees who always have great ideas of ways to spend your time here. Ask for some of the Portland walking or cycling tour maps.

The information center, which sits across the street from the Portland waterfront, also sells souvenirs and postcards and has public restrooms.

Directions: The Visitors Information Center is at 305 Commercial Street, the main road along Portland Harbor.

Facilities: Information center, restrooms.

Dates: Open year-round.

Closest town: Portland.

For more information: Visitors Information Center, Convention and Visitors Bureau of Greater Portland, 305 Commercial Street, Portland, ME 04101. Phone (207) 772-5800.

HISTORIC WALKING TOURS

Learn about the history of Portland and its architecture by taking a self-guided tour of some of its historic neighborhoods. The preservation group Greater Portland Landmarks has prepared maps for walking tours of four areas of the city: the Old Port, the Western Promenade, State Street, and Congress Street.

These brochures, which are sold at the Visitors Information Center and some bookstores, include drawings and the history of the city's historic buildings. Historic homes, businesses, churches, graveyards, and monuments are highlighted.

Greater Portland Landmarks also offers tours of historic places, including some islands ordinarily not open to the public. Call for a schedule.

The Women's Studies Program at the University of Southern Maine has prepared a series of four walks that take in sites of particular importance to women's history in Portland. The Women's History Walking Trail begins at an old chewing gum factory, where young women toiled long days for half the salary of their male counterparts in the late 1800s and early 1900s. It takes in dozens of other landmarks in Portland women's history.

Directions: Purchase the walking tour maps at the Visitors Information Center, 305 Commercial Street, or in Portland bookstores.

Activities: Walking, sight-seeing.

For more information: Greater Portland Landmarks, Inc., 165 State Street, Portland, ME 04101. Phone (207) 774-5561. Portland Women's History Trail, c/o Women's Studies Program, University of Southern Maine, 96 Falmouth Street, PO Box 9300 Portland, ME 04104. Phone (207) 780-4289.

HISTORIC BICYCLE TOUR OF PORTLAND

The Bicycle Transportation Alliance of Portland has prepared a bicycle tour of the city. The brochure, available for a fee at the Visitors Information Center, is based on an 1896 bike tour published by the League of American Wheelmen.

The tour begins at Monument Square, named for the 1891 monument for Maine soldiers who fought in the Civil War, and makes 19 stops at historic sites. The bike tour, which has a few hills, is about 7 miles long.

Directions: Purchase the bicycle tour map at the Visitors Information Center, 305 Commercial Street.

Activities: Bicycling, sight-seeing.

Fees: There is a charge for the guide.

For more information: Bicycle Transportation Alliance of Portland, PO Box 4506, Portland, ME 04112. Phone (207) 773-3053.

Downtown Guides

As you walk through Portland during the summer months, you may bump into some friendly, helpful people wearing purple shirts, shorts, and "outback" hats. These are the Downtown Guides sponsored by the Portland Downtown District, and they're there to help.

The guides are equipped with maps and brochures and lots of advice on everything from where to eat or get your film processed to the closest bathroom or nature cruise. If you look lost, don't be surprised if one of these guides approaches you.

PORTLAND TRAILS

The city of Portland has an abundance of walking and cycling trails, thanks in part to Portland Trails, a nonprofit land trust organization dedicated to promoting trail building and use. Portland Trails is working to create a 30-mile network of trails in Greater Portland. This plan, which would connect city parks, neighborhood open spaces, rivers, and the shoreline, is based on a plan first envisioned by Frederick Law Olmsted Jr. in 1900. The network includes trails along Portland's Eastern Promenade, through the Maine Audubon Society's Fore River Sanctuary, across Baxter Woods, around Back Cove, along the commercial waterfront, and through other scenic and natural areas in Portland. Pick up a copy of *A Trail Guide to Portland Maine* at the Visitors' and Convention Bureau on Commercial Street and contact Portland Trails for the latest on this ever-expanding trail network.

Activities: Walking, hiking, biking.

Facilities: Miles of trails in Greater Portland.

Dates: Open year-round.

Fees: None.

Closest town: Portland.

For more information: Portland Trails, 1 India Street, Portland, ME 04101. Phone (207) 775-2411.

THE OLD PORT

[Fig. 10] With its historic buildings, cobblestone streets, and dozens of interesting shops, galleries, and restaurants, the Old Port district is a neighborhood worth exploring.

NORTHERN GANNET
(Morus bassanus)

This is a vibrant commercial district. On sunny days, there are concerts in the parks and street musicians on the corners. Portland police ride through on horseback and bicycles, and office workers mingle with sightseers and shoppers on the bumpy sidewalks. There are dozens of places to eat, from pizza-by-the-slice parlors and hot dog vendors to pricey gourmet restaurants and interesting sandwich shops. There are also several coffee shops, most of which display local artists' work.

At night, the Old Port's many bars and taverns make this a center of Portland night life, especially for the under-30 crowd.

The Old Port runs down to the harbor and Portland's working waterfront. Fishing boats can be seen coming and going from a series of wharves. Commuter ferries pull out of the Maine State Pier, carrying passengers and freight to the Casco Bay islands. Excursion boats depart from the harbor, taking passengers on seal-watching trips, lighthouse cruises, and other trips.

Most of the buildings in the Old Port were built after an 1866 fire destroyed the commercial district. The Old Port fell on hard times in the 1950s and 1960s, but the run-down neighborhood had another resurgence in the 1970s when a revitalization effort cleaned it up and the artists and shopkeepers moved in.

Directions: The Old Port district is bordered roughly by Commercial, Exchange, Federal, and Pearl streets.

Activities: Walking, shopping.

THE EASTERN PROMENADE

[Fig. 10(2)] The Eastern Prom, as it's known locally, runs along the eastern end of the Portland Peninsula, atop a hill of homes and business called Munjoy Hill.

From a grassy spot at the top of the hill here, look out at Casco Bay and the islands. Markers can help you identify which you are looking at. The easiest to identify is the island fort of Fort Gorges, an 1858 structure that was armed during the Civil War and Spanish-American War. The large island behind it is Peaks Island, the most populated of Portland's commuter islands.

This grassy open space on the Eastern Prom is Fort Allen Park, built on the earthworks of a fort built during the war of 1812. Paved walking trails lead past gardens and to East End Beach, where it's possible to swim or launch a kayak.

The 2.1-mile Eastern Promenade Trail is an easy, paved path that runs between the beach and the Old Port.

Directions: Follow Congress Street east to the end of the peninsula.

Activities: Walking, swimming, boating, picnicking.

Facilities: Trails, beach (no lifeguard), boat launch, playground, bandstand, restrooms, changing area, picnic areas.

Dates: Open year-round.

Fees: None.

Closest town: Portland.

For more information: Portland Parks Department, 17 Arbor Street, Portland, ME 04103. Phone (207) 756-8383.

Northern Gannet

From a distance, it's easy to mistake a northern gannet (*Morus bassanus*) for a gull, until it spots a fish. Then the northern gannet is easy to mistake for a rocket. While feeding, northern gannets dive from as high as 100 feet, head first and wings back, to catch dinner. The sight of a flock of northern gannets diving into the Atlantic after a school of fish is breathtaking. Northern gannets are big white birds with long, black-tipped wings. They spend most of their lives in the open sea, coming onshore only to nest. They can be seen offshore, where their distinctive plunges into the sea make them easy to identify.

THE WESTERN PROMENADE

[Fig. 10(3)] The Western Prom as the locals call it, is at the western end of the Portland Peninsula. The West End neighborhood is full of beautiful historic homes, including several stately mansions.

There's a short footpath along the end of the promenade with views of some beautiful homes and over the Fore River to South Portland.

Visit the Western Promenade on a nice summer night and you'll see many Portland residents taking advantage of this green space. The city sponsors a series of evening acoustic concerts here.

Directions: From Commercial Street, drive up the hill (east) on State Street. Just before the Congress Street intersection, turn left on Pine Street and follow it to the end and the Western Promenade.

Activities: Walking.

Facilities: Footpaths.

Dates: Open year-round.

Fees: None.

Closest town: Portland.

For more information: Portland Parks Department, 17 Arbor Street, Portland, ME 04103. Phone (207) 756-8383.

DEERING OAKS

[Fig. 10(4)] Portland is called the Forest City, and a crew of city arborists makes sure it will stay that way. Among their responsibilities is looking after the 200-year-old oaks in Deering Oaks park.

The 51-acre Deering Oaks is probably the most used park in Portland. On sunny days its big lawns are full of activity, including dog walking, Frisbee throwing, and sun soaking. On weekends there is a farmers' market. A Shakespeare troupe performs here on summer night. In the winter, ice skaters take to its pond and cross-country skiers cross the grounds.

There are walkways all around the park, and it's possible to rent a paddleboat for trips around the duck pond. The park's recreational facilities include tennis, badminton, and volleyball courts, softball fields, and horseshoe pits.

The Castle, a beautiful building next to the pond, has a restaurant, The Barking Squirrel.

Deering Oaks is a peaceful spot these days, but it was anything but peaceful during the French and Indian wars. In 1689, British soldiers defeated the Indians in a fierce and bloody battle. The next year, the Indians and the French delivered retribution, destroying the British settlement here.

Directions: From Congress Street, head north on Forest Avenue or High Street for three blocks. There is free parking next to the Castle.

Activities: Walking, paddle boating, tennis, and other sports.

Facilities: Paths, duck pond, restaurant, restrooms, athletic fields and courts, playground.

Dates: Open year-round.

Fees: None.

Closest town: Portland.

For more information: Portland Parks Department, 17 Arbor Street, Portland, ME 04103. Phone (207) 756-8383.

BAXTER WOODS

[Fig. 10(5)] Former Gov. Percival Baxter gave Baxter Woods Park to the city of Portland in honor of his father, a former Portland mayor who was an early park builder in Portland.

It's a peaceful, 30-acre nature preserve with a century-old pine forest and a series of looped footpaths.

Directions: Baxter Woods is between Forest Avenue and Stevens Avenue. From Congress Street, take Forest Avenue northwest. Look for the park on your left after the intersection with Hartley Street. Park along Forest Avenue or Stevens Avenue.

Activities: Walking, bird-watching.

Facilities: Trails.

Dates: Open year-round.

Fees: None.

Closest town: Portland.

For more information: Portland Parks Department, 17 Arbor Street, Portland, ME 04103. Phone (207) 756-8383.

CAPISIC POND PARK

[Fig. 10(6)] The pond in this 18-acre city park and nature preserve is actually a dammed portion of the Fore River. But between this pond, a marsh, and a field, there's a nice variety of bird life here to watch. Look for ducks in the pond and sparrows around the marsh and field.

Directions: From outer Congress Street (ME 22), head east on Stevens Avenue, turning left on Frost Street in 0.2 mile and then bearing right on Capisic Street. Capisic Street will cross the pond at the park. Park on Capisic Street.

Activities: Walking, bird-watching, picnicking.

Facilities: Trails.

Dates: Open year-round.

Fees: None.

Closest town: Portland.

For more information: Portland Parks Department, 17 Arbor Street, Portland, ME 04103. Phone (207) 756-8383

WADSWORTH-LONGFELLOW HOUSE AND MAINE HISTORICAL SOCIETY

[Fig. 10(7)] Portland's most famous native may well be the poet Henry Wadsworth Longfellow, who was born here in 1807. Longfellow spent his boyhood years in this 1785 brick home built by his grandfather, Gen. Peleg Wadsworth, a Revolutionary War officer.

The house is full of belongings of the Wadsworth and Longfellow families, and gives visitors an interesting glimpse at life in Portland in the nineteenth century. Don't miss the well-kept, quiet garden behind the house.

Wadsworth left Portland to attend Bowdoin College in Brunswick. He taught at Bowdoin for five years, then moved to Cambridge, Massachusetts, to teach at Harvard. He was a beloved and famous poet in the nineteenth century. His most famous poems may be *Hiawatha*, *The Children's Hour*, and *The Courtship of Miles Standish*.

Longfellow's sister was the last to live here, and she left the house to the Maine Historical Society, which has an office, gallery, library, and gift shop behind the home.

Directions: The Wadsworth-Longfellow House is at 485 Congress Street, one of Portland's major streets.

Activities: Sight-seeing.

Facilities: Museum, history gallery, library, gift shop.

Dates: The Wadsworth-Longfellow House is open June to mid-Oct. The Maine Historical Society is open year-round.

Henry Wadsworth Longfellow

Henry Wadsworth Longfellow, one of America's most beloved and famous poets, was born in Portland, Maine, in 1807. After graduation from Bowdoin College in 1825, he studied languages in Europe and returned to become a professor and librarian at Bowdoin from 1829 to 1835. He then taught at Harvard from 1836 to 1854, and wrote many classics of American poetry, including *Evangeline, The Song of Hiawatha, the Courtship of Miles Standish*, and *Paul Revere's Ride*. Longfellow died in 1882.

The Lighthouse

The rocky ledge runs far into the sea,
and on its outer point, some miles away,
the lighthouse lifts its massive masonry,
A pillar of fire by night, of cloud by day.

Even at this distance I can see the tides,
Upheaving, break unheard along its base,
A speechless wrath, that rises and subsides
in the white tip and tremor of the face.

And as the evening darkens, lo! how bright,
through the deep purple of the twilight air,
Beams forth the sudden radiance of its light,
with strange, unearthly splendor in the glare!

No one alone: from each projecting cape
And perilous reef along the ocean's verge,
Starts into life a dim, gigantic shape,
Holding its lantern o'er the restless surge.

Like the great giant Christopher it stands
Upon the brink of the tempestuous wave,
Wading far out among the rocks and sands,
The night o'er taken mariner to save.

And the great ships sail outward and return
Bending and bowing o'er the billowy swells,
And ever joyful, as they see it burn
They wave their silent welcome and farewells.

They come forth from the darkness, and their sails
Gleam for a moment only in the blaze,
And eager faces, as the light unveils
Gaze at the tower, and vanish while they gaze.

The mariner remembers when a child,
on his first voyage, he saw it fade and sink
And when returning from adventures wild,
He saw it rise again o'er ocean's brink.

Steadfast, serene, immovable, the same,
Year after year, through all the silent night
Burns on forevermore that quenchless flame,
Shines on that inextinguishable light!

It sees the ocean to its bosum clasp
The rocks and sea-sand with the kiss of peace:
It sees the wild winds lift it in their grasp,
And hold it up, and shake it like a fleece.

The startled waves leap over it; the storm
Smites it with all the scourges of the rain,
And steadily against its solid form
press the great shoulders of the hurricane.

The sea-bird wheeling round it, with the din
of wings and winds and solitary cries,
Blinded and maddened by the light within,
Dashes himself against the glare, and dies.

A new Prometheus, chained upon the rock,
Still grasping in his hand the fire of love,
it does not hear the cry, nor heed the shock,
but hails the mariner with words of love.

"Sail on!" it says: "sail on, ye stately ships!
And with your floating bridge the ocean span;
Be mine to guard this light from all eclipse.
Be yours to bring man neared unto man.

Fees: There is a charge for admission.

Closest town: Portland.

For more information: Wadsworth-Longfellow House, 485 Congress Street, Portland, ME 04101. Phone (207) 879-0427. Maine Historical Society, 485 Congress Street, Portland, ME 04101. Phone (207) 774-1822.

VICTORIA MANSION

[Fig. 10(8)] This mansion, also known as the Morse-Libby House, is a wonderful example of an Italianate villa-style mansion. From ornately carved marble fireplaces to the painted murals and original elaborate furnishings, this home is a showplace of Victorian opulence. The decorative splendor reaches new heights at the Christmas season, when the mansion is full of holiday decorations and carolers in period costume perform. Enthusiastic guides give 45-minute tours every half hour.

The mansion was built in 1859 by Ruggles Sylvester Morse and is well-maintained today by the Victoria Society.

Directions: The Victoria Mansion is at 109 Danforth Street, between High and Park streets.

Facilities: Museum, gift shop.

Dates: Open May to mid-Oct. and during the Christmas season.

Fees: There is a charge for admission.

Closest town: Portland.

For more information: Victoria Mansion, 109 Danforth Street, Portland, ME 04101. Phone (207) 772-4841.

TATE HOUSE

[Fig. 10(9)] George Tate, a mast agent for the Royal Navy, built this elegant Georgian-style home in 1775. It's the only pre-Revolutionary War home in Portland open to the public. Highlights include its beautiful furnishing and an eighteenth century herb garden overlooking the Stroudwater River. The house is on the outskirts of Portland, near the Portland International Jetport.

Tate was an important man in Colonial times. This region's towering white pines were valued as masts for the British Navy. As masting agent, Tate oversaw their preparation and shipment to England. The home and its grounds are a significant display of Tate's prominence.

Directions: From downtown Portland, follow Congress Street, or ME 22, to Westbrook Street. The Tate House is at 1270 Westbrook Street.

Activities: Sight-seeing.

Facilities: Museum, garden.

Dates: Open June through Oct.

Fees: There is a charge for admission.

Closest town: Portland.

For more information: Tate House, 1270 Westbrook Street, PO Box 8800, Portland, ME 04102. Phone (207) 774-9781 or (207) 774-6177.

PORTLAND OBSERVATORY

[Fig. 10(10)] This 86-foot wooden tower was built in 1807 and is the only remaining signal tower on the East Coast. The octagonal tower was used to watch for incoming cargo ships. When a ship was spotted, the owner's flag was hoisted over the tower so preparations could be made to greet and unload the ship.

The view from the top of the observatory, reached by climbing 105 steps up a circular staircase, is tremendous. Unfortunately, the tower has been off limits since 1994 because of an infestation of wood-eating powder post beetles. If all goes well, it will be open to visitors again soon.

Directions: The Portland Observatory is at 138 Congress Street, in Portland's Munjoy Hill section.

For more information: Greater Portland Landmarks, 165 State Street, Portland, ME 04101. Phone (207) 775-5561.

MAINE NARROW GAUGE RAILROAD COMPANY AND MUSEUM

[Fig. 10(11)] Train buffs won't want to miss this museum, which features dozens of railroad cars that operated in Maine on narrow gauge, or 2-foot-wide, tracks. Most of these trains operated between the 1880s and the 1930s.

A highlight of the museum is a chance to take a 3-mile train ride along the waterfront, with views of lighthouses, Portland Harbor, and Casco Bay islands. The museum is housed in an old waterfront complex where trains were built more than a century ago.

Directions: Heading east on Fore Street out of the Old Port, the museum is on the right, about 0.2 mile past the India Street intersection. Turn into the 58 Fore Street complex; the museum is in the back.

Facilities: Museum, train rides.

Dates: The museum is open year-round. Train rides are offered year-round, except for Jan. through mid-Feb.

Fees: There is no admission charge for the museum. There is a charge for a train ride.

Closest town: Portland.

For more information: Maine Narrow Gauge Railroad Company and Museum, 58 Fore Street, Portland, ME 04104. Phone (207) 828-0814.

PORTLAND MUSEUM OF ART

[Fig. 10(12)] This downtown museum in an I.M. Pei-designed building houses an impressive permanent collection and displays interesting and varied rotating exhibits.

The museum has a fine collection of work by American painters, including some with Maine ties, like Winslow Homer, Edward Hopper, Andrew and Jamie Wyeth, and

Robert Indiana. The permanent collection also includes European artists, including Degas, Monet, Rodin, and Cassatt, an American who studied in Europe. A decorative arts collection features a large display of glassware and other items from the U.S. and Europe. The museum gift shop has some interesting items, and the café is open for lunch daily.

Directions: The Portland Museum of Art is at 7 Congress Square, at the intersection of Congress, High, and Free streets.

Facilities: Museum, shop, café.

Dates: Open daily, year-round.

Fees: With the exception of Friday nights, when admission is free, there is a charge.

Closest town: Portland.

For more information: Portland Museum of Art, 7 Congress Square, Portland, ME 04101. Phone (207) 775-6148.

CHILDREN'S MUSEUM OF MAINE

[Fig. 10(13)] This museum is a big hit with kids. It's full of hands-on exhibits for toddlers and older children. The museum's natural history displays are top-notch and use Maine settings to teach visitors about science topics. One exhibit takes kids into the Maine woods, where they can listen to the heartbeat of a hibernating bear. Another sinks to the depths of the sea, where kids can walk into the mouth of a life-sized humpback whale. Even parents will learn something here. Other exhibits allow exploration of a giant bird's nest, a space shuttle, a lobster boat, a fire engine, and a grocery store. For older kids, there are science and computer labs.

The Children's Museum of Maine also has a Camera Obscura room, one of only a handful in the United States. Using Renaissance-era technology, the camera obscura allows visitors to get a panoramic light image of the entire city from a room on the museum's third floor using a series of lenses for projection. The museum also has a shop and a playground.

Directions: The Children's Museum of Maine is on Free Street, near the intersection of Congress and High streets. It is next door to the Portland Museum of Art.

Facilities: Museum, shop.

Dates: Open year-round.

Fees: There is a charge for admission.

Closest town: Portland.

For more information: Children's Museum of Maine, 142 High Street, Portland, ME 04101. Phone (207) 828-1234.

PORTLAND PUBLIC MARKET

[Fig. 10(14)] Dozens of businesses sell fresh produce, organic poultry and meat, fish, just-baked pies and bread, flowers, dairy products, and other items at this airy, downtown market. Visitors can also buy prepared food to eat here or to go.

This market, which opened in the fall of 1998, was modeled after Seattle's Pike Market and has become a popular tourist destination, as well as a great place for locals to buy fresh groceries.

Directions: The Portland Public Market is on the corner of Preble Street and Cumberland Avenue, one block north of Congress Street. A parking garage across the street has an elevated walkway into the market and free parking for market shoppers.

Activities: Shopping, dining.

Facilities: Food booths, restaurants, restrooms.

Dates: Open year-round.

Fees: None.

Closest town: Portland.

For more information: Portland Public Market, 25 Preble Street, Portland, ME 04101. Phone (207) 228-2000.

SOUTHWORTH PLANETARIUM

[Fig. 10(15)] If you've ever wondered which constellation is which, or if you're interested in astronomy in general, don't miss the Southworth Planetarium at the University of Southern Maine. The planetarium puts on a series of astronomy shows and musical laser light shows. At the end of each show, the current night sky is projected on the planetarium's 30-foot dome and stars, constellations, and planets are identified.

The planetarium also has an exhibit area with multimedia displays on computer. The planetarium's Skywatch Hotline (phone 207-780-4719) gives callers the location of visible planets in the night sky, the rising times of the sun, and other astronomy information.

Directions: The Southworth Planetarium is in the Science Building on the Portland Campus of the University of Southern Maine. From Congress Street in downtown Portland, head west on Forest Avenue. Turn left on Falmouth Street. The Science Building will be on your left.

Activities: Stargazing.

Facilities: Planetarium, exhibits.

Dates: Open year-round.

Fees: There is a charge for the astronomy and laser light shows.

Closest town: Portland.

For more information: Southworth Planetarium, 96 Falmouth Street, Box 9300, Portland, ME 04104. Phone (207) 780-4249. Skywatch Hotline phone (207) 780-4719.

OSHER MAP LIBRARY

[Fig. 10(16)] This map library at the University of Southern Maine has an outstanding collection of 20,000 maps, from 1475 to the present. There are also explorers' narratives, including a 1494 printed and illustrated version of a 1493 letter from Christopher

Columbus describing his discoveries, 120 globes, and several early surveying instruments.

Some of the notable maps on display are a 1475 hand-colored woodcut of the Holy Land that is described as the first printed modern map, and a 1616 map of New England that includes the only known picture of Captain John Smith. The most talked-about map is one of three known copies of a 1775 map of the British colonies of North America that was used to negotiate the Treaty of Paris, which ended the Revolutionary War. It is widely described as the most important map in American history.

The maps tell an interesting story of how boundaries were viewed by various mapmakers over the years. For example, the colonies were described as New England, Nouvelle France, and Nieuw Nederlands, depending on the nationality of the map-maker. All the maps are of historic interest, but many can be viewed as beautiful works of art, as well, with their intricate, hand-colored line drawings and ornate decorative borders.

Directions: The Osher Map Library is on the ground floor of the Albert Brenner Glickman Family Library on the Portland campus of the University of Southern Maine. The library is on the corner of Forest Avenue and Bedford Street.

Dates: Open year-round.

Fees: None.

Closest town: Portland.

For more information: Osher Map Library, University of Southern Maine Library, 96 Falmouth Street, Portland, ME 04103. Phone (207) 780-4850.

FORE RIVER SANCTUARY

[Fig. 10(17)] You'll forget you are in a city once you head into this 85-acre nature preserve.

A 2-mile trail wanders across this Maine Audubon Society sanctuary. The blue-blazed trail, which was developed by the trail-building group Portland Trails, includes a boardwalk across a salt marsh and a bridge over the Fore River. It stops at a lovely spot, 25-foot Jewell Falls, Portland's only waterfall. A long, straight section of the trail follows the towpath of the old Cumberland and Oxford Canal, which was dug by hand in 1828 and ran 20 miles from Portland Harbor to Sebago Lake. Be very careful where the trail approaches and crosses an active railroad track.

Directions: There are trailheads at either end of the sanctuary trail. To enter at Rowe Avenue, drive west on Brighton Avenue, pass Capesic Street, and turn left onto Rowe Avenue. Park at the end of the road. The trailhead will be on your left.

To enter at Congress Street, drive west on Congress Street, then turn right on Frost Street. Take the first left into the Maine Orthopedic parking lot, where there is parking for hikers. The sidewalk leads to the trailhead.

Activities: Hiking, bird-watching.

Facilities: Trail with boardwalk.

Dates: Open year-round.

Closest town: Portland.

For more information: Maine Audubon Society, Gilsland Farm, PO Box 6009, 118 US Route 1, Falmouth, ME 04105. Phone (207) 781-6185.

Fore River Sanctuary Trail: 2 miles, one-way.

▓ BACK COVE

[Fig. 10] This large tidal basin on the northern edge of the Portland Peninsula is encircled by one of the city's most popular walking trails. The 3.5-mile Back Cove Trail is a magnet for strollers, joggers, and dog-walkers on pleasant days.

Much of the path runs along Baxter Boulevard. As it approaches a bridge crossing the mouth of the cove, don't be surprised if you smell baked beans. The tall brick chimneys nearby come out of the Burnham and Morrill factory. Inside, B&M Baked Beans are cooking in big brick ovens. This section of the trail is noisier than your average Maine coastal hike; there are six lanes of traffic on the adjacent highway. But the scenery—Back Cove on one side and Casco Bay on the other—is stunning. (Walkers are protected by cement barricades and tall chain link fences on this portion of the trail.)

The trees lining the Baxter Boulevard section of the cove are linden trees. With more than 300 of the trees, this is thought to be the biggest planting of the trees in New England. Linden trees were just beginning to bud along the boulevards of Europe when Americans entered World War I. The first 100 of the trees were gifts from an American Legion post as memorials to servicemen who died in the war. The lindens here have suffered from exposure to road salt, exhaust, and the soil they're planted in. But over the years veterans have replaced dead trees to continue the memorial.

The Back Cove is a great place for bird-watching. When the tide is low, nearly the entire cove is a mud flat. Bird watchers who walk around Back Cove after a high tide, when the exposed mud flats around the edges are visible, may see a variety of shore-birds, especially during the fall and spring migrations.

Back Cove is a good spot to learn how to differentiate the several types of gulls that frequent the area.

The easiest one to spot is the great black-backed gull (*Larus marinus*). At about 30 inches long, these gulls are much larger than the other gulls seen here, and as adults they have black backs and wings, white bodies, and yellow bills with a red dot near the tip. These gulls eat fish, shellfish, smaller birds, including ducks, and the chicks of other gulls. They can be seen here and all along the coast year-round.

Adult herring gulls (*Larus argentatus*) are about 25 inches long and have a gray swath across their backs and gray wings with black tips. Their yellow bills also have a red dot near the end. These gulls are commonly referred to as seagulls and they can be found year-round everywhere on the Maine coast, including in large numbers at landfills. Herring gulls often drop shellfish on sidewalks and parking lots to break the shell so they can eat the fish inside. The laughing gull (*Larus atricilla*) gets its name from its distinctive *ha-ha-ha-ha* call. It's about 15 inches long. In the summer, when the gull is occasionally spotted here, it has dark gray wings with black tips and a black head. In the winter, the black hood disappears. This gull's bill is red.

In late summer and fall, look for ring-billed gulls (*Larus delawarensis*), which have yellow bills with a black ring near the tip. Adults are about 19 inches long and have gray backs and wings. Their wingtips are black with white speckles.

Bonaparte's gulls (*Larus philadlephia*) are probably the smallest gulls you'll see on the Maine coast. They are about 12 inches long and have black heads in the summer; in the winter their heads turn white, with a black dot behind each eye. These small gulls have black bills and red legs and feet.

Gulls are easier to distinguish in adulthood, which is reached in 2 to 4 years, depending on the species. But they go through a series of seasonal molts and display various shades of tan and brown for their early years. Most good field guides include photos of juvenile and adult birds to help you figure out which gull you're watching.

If you can't find a specific gull in your field guide, don't forget to look at the terns, which are also members of the gull family.

Directions: Heading north on Forest Avenue, turn right on Baxter Boulevard, then take an immediate right on Preble Street Extension and park in the lot to your left.

Activities: Walking, biking, bird-watching.

Facilities: Trail.

Dates: Accessible year-round.

Closest town: Portland.

Back Cove Trail: 3.5-mile loop. Easy.

CASCO BAY ISLANDS

Early visitors called the islands in Casco Bay the Calendar Islands because there seemed to be an island for every day of the year. There may not be quite that many, but there are more than 100 islands in the bay, including several that are open to visitors and some that are quite easy to get to aboard passenger ferries.

Six islands are a ferry ride away from Portland Harbor. Four of them are part of the city of Portland. (Long Island seceded to become its own town in 1993, and Chebeague Island is part of the town of Cumberland.)

Casco Bay Lines runs regular ferries to Long and Great Chebeague islands and to Portland's four commuter islands: Peaks, Great Diamond, Little Diamond, and Cliff.

The ferry terminal operates much like a busy bus terminal, with passengers buying tickets at booths and standing in lines at various gates as upcoming departing and incoming boats are announced over a loudspeaker. If you're there in the morning, you'll see windswept-looking islanders getting off the ferry, travel mugs in hand, heading to their jobs or school on the mainland. Ride over the in the evening and you'll see the same crowd heading back to their island homes.

On a nice day or evening, the ferry ride is a lovely trip, even if you ride the boat right back to Portland. To get a real taste of the islands, get off and walk around or stay for lunch or dinner. Better yet, bring your bicycle. The islands offer some of the ingredients of great Maine cycling: little traffic and beautiful views. Casco Bay Lines charges a small fee to carry a bike on the ferry. It's possible to rent a bicycle on Peaks or Great Chebeague.

The Bicycle Transportation Alliance of Portland has prepared a brochure of bicycle routes on Peaks, Long, and Great Chebeague islands. Buy it through the mail from the alliance or at the Visitors Information Center in Portland.

Casco Bay Lines also offers special sight-seeing cruises. The mailboat cruise heads out to the farthest island, Cliff Island, stopping at four other islands, and takes four hours. The ferries also take special trips, including sunrise and sunset cruises, musical cruises with a cash bar, and trips to Bailey Island in the Harpswells (*see* page 115).

Directions: The Casco Bay Lines ferry terminal is on the eastern end of Commercial Street, the main street running along the Portland waterfront.

Activities: Boating, walking, bicycling.

Dates: The ferries run year-round.

Fees: There is a charge for riding the ferry.

Closest town: Portland.

For more information: Casco Bay Lines, PO Box 4656, Portland, ME 04101. Phone (207) 774-7871.

PEAKS ISLAND

[Fig. 9] Peaks Island is a 20-minute ferry ride from Portland. But once you get off the boat you'll find it hard to believe this quiet spot is that close to the mainland.

With about 1,000 year-round residents, Peaks is by far the most populous of the Portland islands. The population grows considerably during the summer rental season. The children attend an island school until fifth grade, then head to Portland for middle and high schools. Many Peaks residents commute on the ferry to jobs in Portland.

Peaks has a handful of restaurants, shops, and galleries, a grocer, a bike rental shop, and a first-rate sea kayaking school (*see* Maine Island Kayak Company, page 90).

It's a nice island to explore on foot or bicycle. Sticking to the roads near the shores, it's about 5 miles around. Beginning at the ferry terminal, walk up the hill to Island Avenue, the island's main street, and turn left. In a few blocks, turn right on Trefethen Avenue and head toward Seashore Avenue, which takes in a beautiful stretch of Peak's pretty and less inhabited eastern, or back, side.

Work your way back to the ferry landing, following the roads along the shore to Island Avenue.

If you want to rent a bike, stop at Brad's Recycled Bike Shop, next to Peaks Island Mercantile (where you can stock up on picnic fixings), on the corner of Central and Island avenues.

Directions: Casco Bay Lines runs at least 10 passenger ferries a day to Peaks Island, depending on the season. Begin at the Casco Bay Lines terminal on the eastern end of Commercial Street in Portland.

Activities: Walking, bicycling, sight-seeing.

Fees: There is a charge for the ferry ride to Peaks. The return trip is free.

Closest town: Portland.

For more information: Casco Bay Lines, PO Box 4656, Portland, ME 04101. Phone (207) 774-7871. Brad's Recycled Bike Shop, 115 Island Avenue, Peaks Island, ME 04106. Phone (207) 766-5631.

MAINE ISLAND KAYAK COMPANY

The Maine Island Kayak Company offers a wide variety of sea kayaking expeditions and classes for paddlers of all levels. Classes range from those for pure beginners to kayak instructor certification courses.

Explore the waters of Casco Bay in a half-day or full-day introduction to sea kayaking, or sign on for one of the longer trips, through Penobscot Bay, to Isle au Haut, or along the Down East coast. Other adventures take you far beyond New England, to the waters of Canada, Latin America, and the British Isles.

Directions: From the ferry landing, walk up the hill to Island Avenue and turn left. The Maine Island Kayak Company is down on the water to your left. If you're registered for a trip or class, a company guide will meet the ferry.

Closest town: Portland.

For more information: Maine Island Kayak Company, 70 Luther Street, Peaks Island, ME 04108. Phone (207) 766-2373.

DINING ON PEAKS ISLAND

Peaks Island has a handful of restaurants and places to buy lunch fixings. All of them are on Welch Street or Island Avenue, very near the ferry landing.

JONES LANDING. Welch Street, Peaks Island. This restaurant overlooking the ferry landing serves lunch and dinner. Check out the reggae music on a sunny Sunday afternoon. *Moderate.* *(207) 766-5542.*

PEAKS CAFÉ. Welch Street, Peaks Island. Here's the spot to visit for cappuccino and pastries. *Inexpensive.* *(207) 766-2479.*

GREAT DIAMOND ISLAND AND LITTLE DIAMOND ISLANDS

[Fig. 9] These Portland islands are connected by a sandbar at low tide. Both have sizeable summer communities and neighborhoods of weathered old coastal cottages.

Great Diamond Island was the site of Fort McKinley, a fort built in 1891 to protect

Portland Harbor and manned during the Spanish-American War and both World Wars. The fort was shut down in the 1940s, and its many buildings sat empty for decades. In recent years, developers renovated the complex and opened Diamond Cove, a summer resort. The old officers' quarters and barracks are now private homes. The Diamond's Edge Restaurant is in the old quartermaster's storehouse. There is also a gallery, summer theater, marina and store.

Directions: Casco Bay Lines runs ferries to Little Diamond Island, to the Great Diamond ferry landing, and to the Diamond Cove resort.

Fees: There is a charge for the ferry.

For more information: Diamond Cove, Great Diamond Island, Portland, ME 04109. Phone (207) 766-5804. Casco Bay Lines, PO Box 4656, Portland, ME 04101. Phone (207) 774-7871.

DINING ON GREAT DIAMOND ISLAND

The only restaurants on Great Diamond Island are at the Diamond Cove resort. High-speed ferries take diners to and from the resort a few times a night in the summer.

DIAMOND'S EDGE RESTAURANT. Diamond Cove, Great Diamond Island. This restaurant offers gourmet food in a casual setting. *Expensive. (207) 766-5850.*

STOWAWAYS' BAR AND GRILL. Diamond Cove, Great Diamond Island. Stowaways' is a beach-side bar and restaurant serving light food, grilled chicken, and lobster rolls. *Moderate. (207) 766-5850.*

LODGING ON GREAT DIAMOND ISLAND

DIAMOND COVE. Great Diamond Island. Rent a townhouse along the manicured parade grounds of the old Fort McKinley and have access to this resort's pool, beach, tennis, and other amenities. *Expensive. (207) 766-5804.*

LONG ISLAND

[Fig. 9, Fig. 11] Bring your bike to Long Island and spend an afternoon pedaling its perimeter. It's only a few miles around, but there are several places to stop and enjoy the scenery, which includes some sandy beaches. Pack a lunch or eat at a picnic table at The Spar, a casual spot near the town dock. The Spar also rents bicycles.

Directions: Casco Bay Lines runs ferries daily to Long Island. Start at the ferry terminal at the east end of Commercial Street in Portland.

Activities: Hiking, biking.

Fees: There is a charge for a ferry ride to Long Island. The return trip is free.

Closest town: Long Island.

For more information: The Spar Restaurant, Island Avenue, Long Island, ME 04050. Phone (207) 766-5985. Casco Bay Lines, PO Box 4656, Portland, ME 04101. Phone (207) 774-7871.

CLIFF ISLAND

[Fig. 11] The most remote of the Portland islands at 8 miles offshore, Cliff Island is a 90-minute ferry ride from Portland. This island has about 60 year-round residents. The summer population is about 400. In recent years, Cliff Island residents have conducted a national media campaign, trying to recruit more year-round families to their island.

Cliff Island is a hard one for visitors to explore. It has no public restrooms and no overnight accommodations, but there are a few miles of roads to cycle, a sandwich shop, and a market.

Directions: Casco Bay Lines runs ferries daily to Cliff Island. Start at the ferry terminal at the east end of Commercial Street in Portland.

Activities: Hiking, biking.

Fees: There is a charge for a ferry ride to Cliff Island. The return trip is free.

Closest town: Portland.

For more information: Casco Bay Lines, PO Box 4656, Portland, ME 04101. Phone (207) 774-7871.

MAINE ISLAND TRAIL

The Maine Island Trail is one trail in the state that can't be hiked. It's a 325-mile-long waterway for boats that includes 85 public and private islands and 13 shoreside parks, cottages, and campgrounds. It's quite popular with kayakers, but sailboats and motorboats can use the trail as well, and open canoes can be used on some portions of it. The Maine Island Trail begins in Casco Bay and winds its way all the way up the coast to the Machias area.

If you're an experienced boater interested in exploring this offshore trail, join the Maine Island Trail Association. Membership entitles you to a 250-page guidebook and provides permission for you to visit the privately owned islands on the trail.

Maine Island Trail Association members agree to a "leave no trace" eithic of land usage for these fragile islands. Keep in mind that damage to an island's thin soil or vegetation can take many years to repair. All waste—including solid human waste and toilet paper—should be carried off the islands. Cookstoves should be used instead of open fires. Below the high tide line, boats and foot traffic should stick to the beach and the rocks.

Anyone cruising the coast should steer clear of bird-nesting islands during the April 1 to mid-August nesting season. (These islands are not on the trail). Boaters should also avoid disturbing seals, especially calving seals in April, May, and June, who may abandon their pups if frightened away.

The state has 45 coastal islands that are available for public use. Information on them is included in the Maine Island Trail Association guidebook.

Directions: The Maine Island Trail begins in Casco Bay and continues more than 300 miles along the coast to the Machias area.

Activities: Boating, camping.

Fees: There is a charge for membership to the Maine Island Trail Association.

Closest town: Portland.

For more information: About volunteerism or the islands, Maine Island Trail Association, 41A Union Wharf, Portland, ME 04101. Phone (207) 761-8335. About membership, Maine Island Trail Association, PO Box C, Rockland, ME 04841. Phone (207) 596-6456. For a brochure on public islands, State Bureau of Parks and Lands, 22 State House Station, August, ME 04333. Phone (207) 287-3821.

L.L. BEAN

[Fig. 10(19)] While the giant in outdoor outfitters is based up the coast a bit in Freeport, L.L. Bean has a factory store in Portland that carries returned, refurbished, discontinued, and out-of-season items.

There are bargains to be had here, if you hit it on the right day. Just remember to check out the merchandise before you buy it; it may be embroidered with someone else's initials. This is one of three Bean discount factory stores in Maine. The other two are in Freeport and Ellsworth.

Directions: The L.L. Bean Factory Store is at 542 Congress Street. For easier parking, enter the back door on Free Street, down the block from the intersection of Free, High, and Congress streets (and the Portland Museum of Art). Parking is free at the garage across Free Street, if you get your ticket validated in L.L. Bean.

For more information: L.L. Bean, 542 Congress Street, Portland, ME 04101. Phone (207) 772-5100.

REPEAT PERFORMANCE

[Fig. 10(21)] Repeat Performance is a consignment store for quality outdoor gear and clothing. The prices are good on gently-used tents and other gear. The store also a good collection of factory seconds and closeouts.

Directions: Repeat Performance is at 311 Marginal Way in Portland. From Congress Street, head north on Forest Avenue just a few blocks. When you pass the main post office, look for Marginal Way on the right. Turn onto Marginal Way. Repeat Performance will be on your right in less than a mile. Next door is Play it Again Sports, which sells used sporting goods.

For more information: Repeat Performance, 311 Marginal Way, Portland, ME 04101. Phone (207) 879-1410.

THE MAINE ROCK GYM

[Fig. 10(20)] Brush up on your rock climbing skills at the Maine Rock Gym, which has indoor and outdoor climbing walls. The gym has more than 5,000 square feet of textured climbing surfaces, including a bouldering cave and a 25-foot horizontal roof. The handholds are moved regularly to keep things interesting.

Cormorants

If you see a black bird perched on a piling or buoy with its wings spread like a cloak held aloft, it's very likely a cormorant.

Both double-crested cormorants (*Phalacrocorax auritus*) and great cormorants (*Phalacrocorax carbo*) can be seen on the Maine coast, although the double-crested is much more common.

Unlike most diving seabirds, cormorants do not have enough oil in their outer feathers to keep them dry, so they must periodically find a perch and spread their wings to dry. Cormorants are terrific divers and swimmers and can dive 50 or more feet underwater for food.

The double-crested cormorant is named for two crests, or tufts, that are rarely noticeable on the bird's head. It's a common sight along the Maine coast in spring, summer, and fall and is about 32 inches long. Great cormorants are larger, about 36 inches long, with a white throat. More common on the Canadian coast, some great cormorants spend their winters on the Maine coast.

Directions: The Maine Rock Gym is at 127 Marginal Way. From Congress Street, head north on Forest Avenue, turning right on Marginal Way after the main post office. The Maine Rock Gym will be on your right.

Activities: Climbing.

Dates: Open year-round.

Fees: There is a charge for admission.

For more information: The Maine Rock Gym, 127 Marginal Way, Portland, ME 04101. Phone (207) 780-6370.

GALLERIES IN PORTLAND

Portland has a thriving arts scene, fed perhaps by the Maine College of Art, the downtown Arts District, the inspiring scenery or the casual lifestyle. There are many galleries in downtown Portland that show local artists and artists from farther up the coast. For contemporary Maine art, check out Greenhut Galleries on Middle Street in the Old Port and the Frost Gully Gallery at 411 Congress Street, among many others. The Maine College of Art has two galleries—the Institute of Contemporary Art and ArtWorks.

Directions: Greenhut Galleries is on Middle Street, at the top of the Old Port, between Market and Pearl streets. Frost Gully Gallery is at 411 Congress Street, just west of City Hall. The Maine College of Art is at 522 Congress Street, between Oak and Center streets.

For more information: Greenhut Galleries, 146 Middle Street, Portland, ME 04101. Phone (207) 772-2693. Frost Gully Gallery, 411 Congress Street, Portland, ME 04101. Phone (207) 773-2555. The Institute of Contemporary Art at Maine College of Art, 522 Congress Street, Portland, ME 04101. Phone (207) 879-5742, ext. 240.

BOATING OUT OF PORTLAND

Portland Harbor is a busy place year-round, with passenger ferries, oil tankers, lobster boats, and other vessels heading in and out to sea. In the summer there are hundreds of pleasure craft—cruise ships, party boats, nature cruises, yachts, and sailboats—giving the harbor an almost festive feel on sunny days. From Portland, you can catch a passenger ferry to a nearby island, eat brunch or dinner aboard an excursion boat, take a windy trip on a beautiful sailboat, or catch an overnight boat to Canada. While you're on the water, look for seabirds, seals, and even the occasional whale.

BAY VIEW CRUISES

The *Bay View Lady* is a 66-foot excursion boat that makes a variety of cruises daily in the summer. There's a lunchtime harbor cruise, "attitude adjustment" cruises at cocktail time, sunset cruises, seal-watching and island cruises, and a Portland Head-Light cruise. There are tables and windows on the lower deck that are perfect if you're sight-seeing with small children or want to grab lunch at the onboard snack bar. The view is great from the railed upper deck.

Directions: Cruises depart from Fisherman's Wharf at 184 Commercial Street on the waterfront.

Activities: Boating, seal and bird-watching, sight-seeing, dining.

Facilities: Restrooms, snack bar.

Dates: The *Bay View Lady* sails from May through Sept.

Fees: There is a charge for a cruise.

For more information: Bay View Cruises, 184 Commercial Street, Portland, ME 04101. (207) 761-0496.

OLDE PORT MARINER FLEET

The Olde Port Mariner Fleet takes passengers on harbor and seal cruises, whale watches, and on deep sea fishing expeditions. The fleet's *Casablanca* features dinner cruises.

Directions: The seal cruises, whale-watching trips, and deep sea fishing cruises leave from Long Wharf, at the bottom of Market Street on Commercial Street. The dinner cruises leave from the Custom House Wharf, also on Commercial Street, near the bottom of Pearl Street behind the U.S. Customs House.

Activities: Boating, sight-seeing, nature viewing, bird-watching, fishing, dining.

Facilities: Restrooms, some dining facilities.

Fees: There is a charge for a cruise.

For more information: Olde Port Mariner Fleet, Long Wharf, Portland, ME 04101. Phone (207) 775-0727.

THE *PALAWAN*

The *Palawan*, a vintage, 58-foot sailing sloop, takes passengers on half-day, full-day, and evening sails.

Directions: The *Palawan* leaves from the Custom House Wharf on Commercial Street, near the bottom of Pearl Street and behind the U.S. Customs House.

Activities: Sailing.

Dates: May through Nov., weather permitting.

Fees: There is a charge for sailing aboard the *Palawan*.

For more information: *Palawan*, PO Box 9715-240, Portland, ME 04104. Phone (207) 773-2163.

EAGLE TOURS

In the summer, Eagle Tours runs daily seal-watching cruises and Portland Head Light cruises. Its most notable trip is to Eagle Island, the former summer home of Adm. Robert Peary (*see* Eagle Island, page 115).

Directions: Eagle Tours is based on Long Wharf on Commercial Street, near the bottom of Market Street.

Activities: Boating, seal watching, sight-seeing.

Dates: Cruises run daily, from Memorial Day weekend to Columbus Day.

Fees: There is a charge for cruises.

For more information: Eagle Tours, 1 Long Wharf, Portland, ME 04101. Phone (207) 774-6498.

PRINCE OF FUNDY TOURS

Ride the *Scotia Prince* to Yarmouth, Nova Scotia, and back to Portland in 23 hours. This cruise ship and car ferry leaves Portland in the evening and arrives in Yarmouth 11 hours later. The ship stays in Nova Scotia for one hour before heading back to Portland. It will be dark for most of the trip to Canada. Watch for whales and seabirds during the return trip.

The ship has private cabins, restaurants, gambling casinos, lounges with floor shows, and plenty of windows and decks from which to enjoy the scenery.

This 23-hour cruise is called the Overnight Sensation. Visitors can also continue their vacation in Canada and ride back to Portland another day.

Remember this is an international cruise. Passengers must carry proof of citizenship—a valid passport or a birth certificate. Non-U.S. citizens must have a valid passport or a green card. Passengers may be asked to present their driver's licenses, although that is not a proof of citizenship.

Directions: The *Scotia Prince* departs from Portland's International Ferry Terminal, on the western end of Commercial Street near the base of the Casco Bay bridge to South Portland.

Activities: Boating, bird and whale watching, gambling.

Facilities: Private cabins, restaurants, casinos, lounges with floor shows, and shops on board.

Dates: The *Scotia Prince* cruises to Canada most days from early May to late Oct.

Fees: There is a charge for the cruise.

For more information: Prince of Fundy Cruises, International Ferry Terminal, 468 Commercial Street, Portland, ME 04101. Phone (207) 775-5616.

GOLFING IN GREATER PORTLAND

There are several 18-hole courses in greater Portland, including some that golfers rate as top-notch. Sable Oaks Golf Club in South Portland is probably the toughest course in the area. The Nonesuch River Golf Club in Scarborough is a new course that also has a golf school.

Directions: To reach Sable Oaks, take Exit 7 off I-95, turning right onto Maine Mall Road. At the next big intersection, turn left onto Running Hill Road. The Sable Oaks complex, which includes a Marriott Hotel, will be on your right.

To reach the Nonesuch River Golf Club, from I-295, take the Maine Mall Exit, before the tollbooth onto the Maine Turnpike. Bear left at the mall, then turn right onto Payne Road. At the fifth light, by Sam's Club, turn right onto ME 114. Nonesuch will be on your left in 0.5 mile.

Activities: Golfing.

For more information: Sable Oaks Golf Club, 505 Country Club Drive, South Portland, ME 04106. Phone (207) 775-6257. Nonesuch River Golf Club, 304 Gorham Road, Scarborough, ME 04074. Phone (207) 883-0007.

NIGHT LIFE IN PORTLAND

Portland has an active bar scene that is centered in the Old Port. It also has an impressive array of concerts and theater performances.

GRITTY MCDUFFS. 396 Fore Street, Portland. This Old Port brewpub has a good bar menu, as well as several varieties of its own brew on tap. *(207) 772-2739.*

THREE DOLLAR DEWEY'S. 241 Commercial Street, Portland. Regulars rub elbows with the tourists in this jam-packed night spot, which also serves a good lunch and dinner. *(207) 772-3310.*

KEYSTONE THEATER CAFÉ. 504 Congress Street, Portland. You can get drinks and dinner with your movie at this theater café. *(207) 871-5500.*

PORTLAND STAGE COMPANY. 25 Forest Avenue, Portland. This theater company puts on a few plays each year. *(207) 774-0465.*

DINING IN PORTLAND

Portland residents like to say there are more restaurants per person here than anywhere but San Francisco. That may or may not be true. But for a city of 65,000, Portland certainly has an abundance of great places to eat.

FORE STREET. 288 Fore Street, Portland. Seafood and meat entrées are simply but deliciously prepared, often in an apple wood-fired oven, at this popular gourmet restaurant with a harbor view. Try the mussels for an appetizer and the handmade chocolates for dessert. *Expensive. (207) 775-2717.*

PEPPERCLUB. 78 Middle Street, Portland. The inventive menu of veggies, seafood, and burgers changes nightly and is always interesting. *Moderate. 772-0531.*

AUBERGINE. 555 Congress Street, Portland. Aubergine is one of several bistro-style night spots in Portland. French food is the specialty here. *Moderate. (207) 874-0860.*

SAPPORO. Union Wharf, Commercial Street, Portland. This waterfront restaurant has a sushi bar and other Japanese food. *Moderate. (207) 772-1233.*

BECKY'S DINER. 390 Commercial Street, Portland. Becky's has been a Portland breakfast favorite for years. Now you can get dinner here, too. *Inexpensive.* (207) 773-7070.

Falmouth and Yarmouth Area

Mackworth Island near Falmouth is a 100-acre island that was given to the state by former Gov. Percival Baxter.

1. Gilsland Farm
2. Mill Creek Trail
3. Mill Creek Preserve
4. Foreside Preserve
5. Basket Island Preserve
6. Royal River Park
7. Winslow Memorial Park
8. Mast Landing Sanctuary
9. Wolfe's Neck Farm
10. Wolfe's Neck Woods State Park
11. Desert of Maine
12. Bradbury Mountain State Park
13. Joshua L. Chamberlain Museum
14. Bowdoin Pines
15. Peary-MacMillan Arctic Musuem
16. Thomas Point Beach
17. Cribstone Bridge
18. Land's End
19. The Maine Info. Center
20. DeLorme Mapping Co.
21. L.L. Bean

Lisbon Falls

95
201
9
ANDROSCOGGIN RIVER
196
Topsham
13
125
136
95
1
Brunswick
14 15 16

231
12
9
115
11
Freeport
21 8
ROYAL RIVER

MAQUOIT BAY
24
Birch Island
9 10
MIDDLE BAY
123
6 19
20
115
7
Harpswell Center
Cumberland Center
Yarmouth
Lower Goose Island
HARPSWELL SOUND

26
100
9
Cousins Island
Whaleboat Island
Orr's Island
Sturdivant Island
495
95
Basket Island
Great Chebeague Is.
17
Bailey Island
Falmouth
3
Ragged Island
2 4
5
18
1
Mackworth Island
PRESUMPSCOT RIVER
Long Island
Hope Island
Cliff Island
Eagle Island
N
Portland
Jewell Island
Ref: Delorme Maine Atlas & Gazetteer

LODGING IN PORTLAND

Portland has several large hotels, as well as a good supply of well-appointed inns and B&Bs.

THE POMEGRANATE INN. 49 Neal Street, Portland. This West End mansion is beautifully decorated with some funky but charming touches, *trompe l'oeil* walls, and a wonderful collection of sculpture and paintings. *Expensive. (207) 772-1006.*

THE INN ON CARLETON. 46 Carleton Street, Portland. This Victorian townhouse in the West End has period furnishings and Maine paintings in each room. Some shared baths. *Moderate. (207) 775-1910.*

PORTLAND SUMMER HOSTEL. 645 Congress Street, Portland. This hostel serves as a University of Southern Maine dormitory during the school year, so its very inexpensive rooms are only available from June 1 to August 25. Make your reservations far in advance by writing Portland Summer Hostel, care of HI-AYH, 1105 Commonwealth Avenue, Boston, MA 02215. *Inexpensive. Phone (207) 874-3281 (in season). Phone (617) 779-0900, ext. 16, (off-season).*

Falmouth and Yarmouth

These two waterfront towns north of Portland sit on the midshore of Casco Bay. Each has some interesting natural sites, as does the town of Cumberland, which lies between them. The Maine Audubon Society's headquarters at Gilsland Farm is here and is worth a stop any time of year. There are some interesting islands that are linked to the mainland with causeways, as well as some that take a bit more work to visit.

MACKWORTH ISLAND

[Fig. 11] Mackworth Island is a 100-acre island at the mouth of the Presumpscot River in Falmouth. It's connected to the mainland by causeway and ringed by a perimeter path that has nonstop ocean views. That beauty and accessibility make it a popular walking path for area families, dog-walkers, and tourists.

The island was given to the state by former Governor Percival Baxter. The interior of the island is the campus of the Gov. Baxter School for the Deaf. Visitors are asked to remain on the perimeter path and limit their use of the island to daylight hours.

The wide, 1.5-mile pathway has uninterrupted water views and a diverse forest. A high school biology class at the Baxter School catalogued the trees and put together a trail guide that identifies the 15 species of trees you'll encounter here. The guide starts with staghorn sumac (*Rhus tphina*) and shagbark hickory (*Carya ovata*) and concludes with sugar maple (*Acer saccharum*) and American beech (*Fagus grandifolia*).

Numbered signs correspond with the guides. Pick up a copy of *A Guide to the Trees of Mackworth Island* at the Maine Audubon Society's Gilsland Farm, which is just north of here on Route 1.

There are three spots on the trail where a side path provides beach access. If you're here at low tide, you can walk down and explore the intertidal zone. If you're here near a high tide, keep an eye out for birds feeding in the mud flats. There's also a spur heading inland on the northern end of the island. This leads to a pet cemetery, where Governor Baxter's horse and dogs are buried. The state maintains the cemetery at Baxter's request.

Directions: Heading north on Route 1, just north of Portland turn right on Andrews Avenue, following signs for the Governor Baxter School for the Deaf. Andrews Avenue will turn into the causeway that links Mackworth with the mainland. Cross the causeway and park in the visitor's lot by the gatehouse.

Activities: Hiking, bird-watching.

Facilities: Trail.

Dates: Open year-round, sunrise to sunset.

Fees: None.

Closest town: Falmouth.

For more information: State Bureau of Parks and Lands, 22 State House Station, Augusta, ME 04333. Phone (207) 287-3821.

Mackworth Island Trail: 1.5-mile loop.

GILSLAND FARM

[Fig. 11(1)] The headquarters of the Maine Audubon Society is at Gilsland Farm, a 65-acre wildlife sanctuary and environmental education center.

Gilsland Farm's 2.5 miles of nature trails encounter several habitats and can lead to some productive bird-watching spots. The 0.7-mile West Meadow Trail has two observation blinds overlooking the Presumpscot Estuary. Use the blinds to unobtrusively watch for migrating shorebirds and wintering waterfowl.

The Pond Meadow Trail, which is 0.6 mile, loops through a mixed forest before running by a pond where muskrats live. The North Meadow Trail encircles a meadow that is mowed late each summer and provides winter forage for Canada geese.

Gilsland Farm's Environmental Center is the scene of many natural history programs for people of all ages. There's also the Children's Discovery Center, a teachers' resource room, and The Nature Store, a great source of natural history books, bird-watching supplies, bird feeders, and other items.

Maine Audubon leads many natural history field trips around the state. There are also guided walks through the paths here at Gilsland Farm. Maine Audubon operates the Rare Bird Alert system in Maine. Its phone message, listing interesting bird sightings from around the state, can be heard at (207) 781-2332 and is updated weekly. Ask the people working at the front desk for any recent interesting bird or other wildlife sightings in the sanctuary.

Directions: Heading north on Route 1 in Falmouth, turn left into Gilsland Farm, which is just before the intersection of Route 1 and ME 88.

Activities: Walking, bird-watching.

Facilities: Trails, The Nature Store, children's displays.

Dates: Open year-round.

Fees: None.

Closest town: Falmouth.

For more information: Maine Audubon Society, Gilsland Farm, PO Box 6009, 118 Route 1, Falmouth, ME 04105. Phone (207) 781-6185.

West Meadow Trail: 0.7 mile loop.

Pond Meadow Trail: 0.6 mile loop.

North Meadow Trail: 1.2 mile loop.

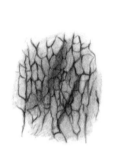 

SUGAR MAPLE
(Acer saccharum)

MILL CREEK TRAIL

[Fig. 11(2)] This is a short trail that heads through the woods to an old tidal mill, providing public access to Mill Creek and Mussel Cove, a large Casco Bay mud flat. The Mill Creek Preserve is up Mill Creek just a bit. At low tide, this mud flat is a popular spot with birds. Look for great blue heron (*Ardea herodias*).

This is one of the trails included in the Falmouth Conservation Commission's Falmouth Trail Guide. Pick it up at the nearby Maine Audubon Society's Nature Store at Gilsland Farm (*see* page 100).

Directions: Heading north on Route 1, turn right on ME 88, then turn right on Old Mill Road, which is immediately before Skillins Nursery. Drive to the end of Old Mill Road and park. The trail begins at the end of the road.

Activities: Walking, bird-watching.

Facilities: Trail.

Dates: Open year-round.

Fees: None

Closest town: Falmouth.

For more information: Falmouth Conservation Commission, 271 Falmouth Road, Falmouth, ME 04105.

MILL CREEK PRESERVE

[Fig. 11(3)] This Falmouth Conservation Trust preserve protects several acres of the salt marsh and land along Mill Creek, which runs into the Mussel Cove mud flats. Much of this marsh is covered with salt marsh hay (*Spartina patens*), which used to be farmed here. The salt marsh and mud flats here can provide some good bird-watching opportunities. Watch for great blue heron (*Ardea herodias*) and glossy ibis (*Plegadis falcinellis*), two species typically seen in coastal salt marshes.

GARTER SNAKE
(Thamnophis sirtalis)

There are no trails at this preserve but it is possible to walk on the upper edge of the marsh. It is also possible to canoe in Mill Creek, which is a tidal creek.

Directions: Heading north on Route 1 in Falmouth, turn right on ME 88. Drive about 1.5 miles, to the town pumping station on the left. Park there or along the road. Walk down the pumping station road to put in a canoe.

Facilities: None.

Activities: Bird-watching, canoeing.

Dates: Open year-round.

Fees: None.

Closest town: Falmouth.

For more information: The Nature Conservancy, Maine Chapter, Fort Andross, 14 Maine Street, Suite 401, Brunswick, ME 04011. Phone (207) 729-5181.

FORESIDE PRESERVE

[Fig. 11(4)] This 34-acre preserve sits in a swath of land between ME 99, or Foreside Road, and Mill Creek. A narrow strip of land separates it from The Nature Conservancy's Mill Creek Preserve.

Four color-blazed trails wander through the mixed forest here and total about 2 miles. There's a trail map on a sign at the trailhead. This is an easy place to keep your bearings, and it's not difficult to work your way to the Mill Creek floodplain.

If you're here in the spring, listen for warblers in the woods and look for wildflowers, especially Canada mayflower (*Maianthemum canadense*), tiny white flowers that grow in clusters above broad green leaves and look something like lily of the valley.

Directions: Heading north on Route 1 in Falmouth, turn right on ME 88, or Foreside Road. The dirt road leading into the preserve is on the right between two homes, directly opposite 177 Foreside Road. There is parking for a few cars in a lot down this road.

Activities: Walking, bird-watching.

Facilities: Trails.

Dates: Open year-round.

Fees: None.

Closest town: Falmouth.

For more information: Falmouth Conservation Commission, 271 Falmouth Road, Falmouth, ME 04105.

BASKET ISLAND PRESERVE

[Fig. 11(5)] Basket is a 9-acre island about 1.5 miles off the coast of Falmouth. A Cumberland Mainland and Island Trust preserve, it is also a popular island with boaters, so expect to find some picnickers here on nice days. There are two shell and gravel beaches where kayaks can be pulled up.

An out-of-control campfire destroyed the vegetation on a few acres in the island's center. You can see the recovery is well under way, although evidence of the fire is still visible. *A warning:* there is a lot of poison ivy on this island.

Directions: Boat to Basket Island from the town landing in Falmouth Foreside. Pull up on the beach at the northwest corner of the island. Larger boats can anchor offshore.

Activities: Boating, picnicking.

Facilities: None.

Dates: Open year-round.

Fees: None.

Closest town: Falmouth.

For more information: The Nature Conservancy, Maine Chapter, Fort Andross, 14 Maine Street, Suite 401, Brunswick, ME 04011. Phone (207) 729-5181.

ROYAL RIVER PARK

[Fig. 11(6)] This riverfront park in Yarmouth sits between two falls. There are picnic areas and a paved walkway along the river.

The Royal River is a popular canoeing spot. A 6-mile downstream paddle ends at Royal River Park, before the falls. The put-in is on Route 9, next to Gillespie Market.

Directions: The park is on East Elm Street in Yarmouth.

Activities: Walking, canoeing, picnicking.

Facilities: Picnic areas, footpath.

Dates: Open year-round.

Fees: None.

Closest town: Yarmouth.

For more information: Yarmouth Community Services, 52 School Street, Yarmouth, ME 04096.

DELORME MAPPING COMPANY

[Fig. 11(20)] It seems every parked car you see in Maine has a copy of the big, blue *Maine Atlas and Gazetteer* lying on a seat. This ubiquitous state atlas is published by DeLorme, a Yarmouth mapping company that produces maps, atlases, and software.

You can't miss the DeLorme building on Route 1 in Yarmouth. A 42-foot rotating and revolving globe fills the glass-encased lobby. This globe, built to one-millionth scale of Earth, is said to be the largest rotating globe in the world.

The DeLorme Map Store has a big selection of maps, software, natural history books, travel guides, GPS receivers, and other gadgets.

Directions: DeLorme is on Route 1 in Yarmouth.

Facilities: Store, restrooms.

Closest town: Yarmouth.

For more information: DeLorme Mapping Company, PO Box 298, Yarmouth, ME 04096. Phone (207) 846-7000.

THE MAINE INFORMATION CENTER

[Fig. 11(19)] This state information center has brochures on attractions, lodgings, and restaurants statewide. There are picnic areas, a dog-walking area, and restrooms.

Directions: The Maine Information Center is on Route 1 in Yarmouth. It is just north of Exit 17 off I-95.

Facilities: Tourist information, restrooms, vending machines, dog-walking area.

Dates: Open year-round.

Closest town: Yarmouth.

For more information: The Maine Information Center, Route 1, Yarmouth, ME 04096. Phone (207) 846-0833.

GREAT CHEBEAGUE ISLAND

[Fig. 11] Chebeague, as it's usually referred to, is the largest of the Casco Bay Islands at roughly 2 miles wide by 4 miles long. It's part of the town of Cumberland. While you can get here aboard a Casco Bay Lines ferry out of Portland, that ride takes about 1 hour. It's quicker to take the Chebeague Transportation Company ferry from Cousins Island in Yarmouth.

Like the other inhabited Casco Bay islands, Chebeague is mostly a summer community; but a few hundred people live here year-round. There are a few inns on the island, as well as a café, the 9-hole Great Chebeague Golf Club, and some beaches. Getting a car to Chebeague is complicated, so plan to bring your bicycle if you want to really explore the island. Bikes can be rented at Great Island Bike Rentals at the Sunset Bed and Breakfast. Maps of the island are available at the ferry terminals. When the tide is out, you can walk to the uninhabited, state-owned Little Chebeague Island from Great Chebeague. Keep an eye on your watch and don't stay more than an hour past low tide.

Directions: Parking for the ferry from Cousins Island can be tricky, especially in the summer. The parking lot that serves the ferry was at the center of a local dispute, so it would be a good idea to check with the Chebeague Transportation Company in advance about parking. To reach Cousins Island, from Main Street in Yarmouth, take Lafayette Street to a left on Princess Point Road. Turn left on Gilman Road and cross the causeway to Cousins Island.

Activities: Walking, biking, golfing.

Dates: The ferries run year-round.

Fees: There is a charge for the ferry.

Closest town: Cumberland.

For more information: Chebeague Transportation Company, Great Chebeague, ME 04017. Phone (207) 846-3700. Great Chebeague Golf Club, Great Chebeague, ME 04017. Phone (207) 846-9478.

DINING IN FALMOUTH AND YARMOUTH

EUROPEAN BAKERY AND TEA ROOM. 395 Route 1, Falmouth. The European Bakery is dominated by a long glass case chock-full of cookies, pastries, and other goodies. You can eat here or buy something sweet for later. *Inexpensive. (207) 781-3541.*

THE CANNERY. Lower Falls Landing, Yarmouth. This restaurant is one of several businesses in this refurbished sardine cannery overlooking the Royal River. The Cannery serves lunch and dinner from a well-rounded menu that is weighted toward seafood. *Moderate. (207) 846-1226.*

LODGING IN FALMOUTH AND YARMOUTH

Try out one of the inns on Chebeague for a longer look at island life.

CHEBEAGUE ISLAND INN. Chebeague Island. This three-story hotel is the last big, old inn in Casco Bay and doesn't appear to have changed too much since the 1920s. *Moderate to expensive. (207) 846-5155.*

Freeport

The coastal town of Freeport is most famous for its biggest business, outdoors outfitter L.L. Bean. The Bean retail store now serves as an anchor to a strip of factory outlets in downtown Freeport and, after Acadia National Park, is the second most visited tourist destination in Maine.

L.L. Bean is worth a stop, but there are some other places worth visiting in Freeport, including a peaceful bird sanctuary, a waterfront state park, and an organic farm operated by a nonprofit corporation to promote natural farming techniques. Freeport is the spot where Maine became a state. You can still eat in the tavern where the papers were signed to split from Massachusetts.

L.L. BEAN

[Fig. 11(21)] Millions of people visit the sprawling L.L Bean retail store in the center of Freeport every year. Even if you don't need a pair of Maine Hunting Shoes, a canvas bag, or a new backpack or canoe, there's plenty to look at here. Check out the indoor trout pond, an outdoor pond, and the little stone "mountain" in the shoe department for testing hiking boots. In L.L. Kids, a new children's store next door, there's an indoor climbing wall and more trout. Even if you're not shopping, most Bean employees are knowledgeable about the activities associated with their departments, which include fishing, hunting, paddling, cycling, skiing, and camping.

L.L. Bean is open 24 hours a day, seven days a week. The store isn't deserted in the middle of the night, although the shopping crowd is pretty thin at 2 a.m. While you're in town, check out the L.L. Bean factory store, for discounted items.

At its Outdoor Discover School, L.L. Bean offers classes in a variety of outdoor skills, including fly-fishing, shooting, wilderness skills, sea kayaking, canoeing, outdoor photography, and bicycling. Some classes are geared for children or families, but most of the students here are adults.

Directions: L.L. Bean is on Route 1 in the middle of Freeport. To reach the factory store, cross Route 1 in front of the main entrance and walk down the hill. The factory store is next to the big parking lots.

Closest town: Freeport.

For more information: L.L. Bean, 95 Main Street, Freeport, ME 04033. Phone (207) 865-4761.

THE OUTLETS

L.L. Bean isn't the only store in town. Drive into Freeport and you'll see that factory outlets have pretty much taken over the downtown area. There are bargains to be hunted down here, but don't be surprised if some stores' discounts are not terribly steep. There's a wide variety of stores, many of them selling clothing or accessories, including Donna Karan, Coach Leather, J. Crew, Brooks Brothers, The Gap, Banana Republic, Neiman Marcus, Reebok, Cole-Haan, and Benetton.

L.L. Bean doesn't have a monopoly on outdoor gear. Patagonia and North Face both have outlets here, as well.

Directions: Most of the outlets are on either Route 1 (Main Street) or Bow Street, which intersects with Route 1 in front of L.L. Bean.

WINSLOW MEMORIAL PARK

[Fig. 11(7)] This town park has a small tidal beach for swimming or launching a kayak. Try and use it at high tide; it's a big mud flat at low tide. There's also a big playground, a short nature trail, and 100 campsites. It's a pretty spot and a great place to wear out kids. There are no lifeguards.

Directions: Heading south on Route 1 from downtown Freeport, turn left on Staples Point Road and proceed to the park.

Activities: Nature walking, swimming, camping.

Facilities: Beach, nature trail, campsites with no hookups.

Dates: Open Memorial Day weekend through Sept.

Fees: There is an admission charge and a fee for camping.

Closest town: Freeport.

For more information: Winslow Memorial Park, Staples Point Road, Freeport, ME 04032. Phone (207) 865-4198.

MAST LANDING SANCTUARY

[Fig. 11(8)] This peaceful Maine Audubon Society bird sanctuary seems like it's on a different planet from the busy outlets of downtown Freeport. But it's barely a mile away from L.L. Bean. There are 3 miles of easy trails winding around this 140-acre sanctuary. Trail maps are available at the entrance. The 1.6-mile Loop Trail takes in a good sampling of the sanctuary's habitats and provides access to five short trails.

The Orchard and Deer Run trails are 0.5 mile long and run through an orchard and coniferous forest. The 0.3 mile Mill Stream Trail follows a stream along the eastern side of the sanctuary. The 0.25-mile Bench Loop Trail provides a view of the sanctuary's Hemlock Ravine. The 0.4-mile Estuary Trail loops through a coniferous forest.

In the summer, Maine Audubon operates a nature day camp here for children entering grades three to eight. All the camp's one- and two-week sessions include at least one overnight camping stay.

Directions: From Route 1 in Freeport, head east on Bow Street, which is across the street from L.L. Bean. In about 1 mile, turn left on Upper Mast Landing Road.

Activities: Hiking, nature-viewing, bird-watching.

Facilities: Trails.

Dates: Open year-round.

Fees: None.

Closest town: Freeport.

For more information: Maine Audubon Society, Gilsland Farm, PO Box 6009, 118 US Route 1, Falmouth, ME 04105. Phone (207) 781-6185.

WOLFE'S NECK FARM

[Fig. 11(9)] This organic farm on Casco Bay is open to the public as a demonstration farm and is known for its all natural beef, pork, and lamb. The best time to visit is for the Calf Watch in March and April. You can buy the farm's products in the farmhouse store. Wolfe's Neck also has a booth at the Portland Public Market (*see* page 84).

The farm has a winding trail system for hiking and cross-country skiing.

Wolfe's Neck Farm also operates a campground, Recompence Shore Campsites, with 100 wooded tent sites, many of them on the water.

The history of Wolfe's Neck Farm is a tale of the philanthropy and pioneering organic farming beliefs of Lawrence M.C. Smith and his wife, Eleanor Houston Smith, who purchased Wolfe's Neck and moved here from Philadelphia in the 1940s to begin an organic farming operation. Lawrence Smith died in 1975, and Eleanor Smith gave the farm to the University of Southern Maine in 1984, with the hope that it would become a demonstration model for alternative, all-natural agriculture techniques. Eleanor Smith died in 1987. In 1997, USM gave the farm to the nonprofit Wolfe's Neck Farm Foundation.

The farm wasn't the only object of the Smiths' generosity. The couple helped create nearby Wolfe's Neck Woods State Park and Popham Beach State Park in Phippsburg by buying the land before developers could and then selling it to the state for less than its appraised value. The Smiths donated the Mast Landing Bird Sanctuary to the Maine Audubon Society and gave the Percy and Small Shipyard to the Maine Maritime Museum in Bath.

Directions: From Route 1 in Freeport, take Bow Street (across from L.L. Bean) 2.25 miles to Wolfe's Neck Road. Turn right and drive 1.5 miles to Burnett Road. Turn left and you'll see the farm.

Activities: Hiking, cross-country skiing, camping.

Facilities: Trails, campsites for tents, camp store, farm store.

Dates: The farm is open year-round. The campground is open from mid-May to Oct.

Fees: None at the farm. There is a charge for camping.

Closest town: Freeport.

For more information: Wolfe's Neck Farm, 10 Burnett Road, Freeport, ME 04032. Phone (207) 865-4469. Recompence Shores Campsites, 10 Burnett Road, Freeport, ME 04032. Phone (207) 865-4469.

WOLFE'S NECK WOODS STATE PARK

[Fig. 11(10)] This lovely park is dedicated to nature study. A park naturalist puts on a range of nature programs year-round and offers guided tours of the trails.

Wolfe's Neck Woods has 5 miles of hiking trails that wander through the woods and along the shores of Casco Bay and the Haraseeket River. There are several interpretive signs pointing to natural sights along the way.

One point of interest is an unobtrusive overlook of Googins Island, a nesting sanctuary for osprey (*Pandion haliaetu*). If you hit this at the right time in the summer, you may see osprey fishing or flying to their nests with fish clutched in their talons. Googins Island is a nesting sanctuary that is closed to visitors.

Wolfe's Neck Woods has picnic areas, including some isolated spots with water views that would

OSPREY
(*Pandion haliaetus*)

cost you plenty in a restaurant.

Directions: From Route 1 in Freeport, follow Bow Street (across from L.L. Bean) 2.25 miles to a right turn at Wolfe's Neck Road. Drive another 2.25 miles to the park.

Activities: Hiking, nature study, birdwatching, picnicking.

Facilities: Trails, picnic areas, restroom, recreation field.

Dates: Open year-round.

Fees: There is a charge for admission.

Closest town: Freeport.

For more information: Wolfe's Neck Woods State Park, Wolfe's Neck Road, Freeport, ME 04032. Phone (207) 865-4465. Maine Bureau of Parks and Lands, 22 State House Station, August, ME 04333. Park phone (207) 865-4465.

THE DESERT OF MAINE

[Fig. 11(11)] The Desert of Maine is a huge sand dune resulting from the Ice Age, grazing sheep, and coastal winds.

The sand that makes up the dune was deposited during the last Ice Age. Soil and vegetation eventually covered the sand, but eighteenth century farming, especially overgrazing by sheep, exposed the sand. When the wind blew, a huge sand dune was built up over time.

The Desert of Maine is a tourist attraction, with kids' gem hunts in the sand, sand art exhibits, narrated coach tours, nature trails, a farm museum, and a gift shop. The Desert Dunes of Maine Campground is next door.

Directions: From I-95 heading north, take Exit 19, turning left onto Desert Road. The road ends at The Desert of Maine.

Activities: Sight-seeing.

Facilities: Trails, picnic area, gift shop, museum, campground.

Dates: Open from early May to mid-Oct.

Fees: There is a charge for admission.

Closest town: Freeport.

For more information: Desert of Maine, 95 Desert Road, Freeport, ME 04032. Phone (207) 865-6962.

Osprey

The osprey (*Pandion haliaetus*) population was devastated by DDT and other chemicals but has rebounded nicely since the pesticide was banned. The bird can now be seen all along the Maine coast, flying over the water with a fish grasped in its talons or standing over its massive stick nest atop a dead tree, channel marker, or platform.

An adult osprey can have a 5.5-foot wingspan. It has a white belly and face with a dark patch over its eyes and cheeks and a black back. While flying, it can be identified by the bend at the "elbow" of its wing.

Osprey eat only fish. They can be seen hovering over the water then diving, feet first, to grab the fish with their sharp talons. While flying, osprey like to carry their fish head first and will turn a fish around midair if it's caught the other way.

BRADBURY MOUNTAIN STATE PARK

[Fig. 11(12)] Six miles inland from Freeport, this state park in Pownal offers quiet woods for year-round use.

In the warmer months, the park is a nice spot for hiking, picnicking, and camping. There are 6 miles of hiking trails, including a 0.25-mile hike up the Summit Trail of Bradbury Mountain, where hikers will catch beautiful views of Casco Bay.

Thanks to its variety of eastern hardwood trees, this park is a beautiful spot for the fall foliage season. In the winter, the hiking trails are used by cross-country skiers and people on snowshoes.

There's a year-round camping area in a pine forest, and park rangers offer guided tours of the park year-round.

There's a variety of wildlife in Bradbury Mountain State Parks' forests. Songbirds and wild turkey (*Meleagris gallopavo*) can be heard in the woods. During the spring and fall, migrating hawks and eagles soar over the mountain. Moose (*Alces alces*), red fox (*Vulpes vulpes*), raccoon (*Procyon lotor*), and striped skunk (*Mephitis mephitis*) are among the mammals that live here.

Directions: From Route 1 in Freeport, near Exit 20 of I-95, head west on Pownal Road, then turn right on ME 9 to the park.

Activities: Hiking, cross-country-skiing, camping, picnicking, bird-watching, nature viewing.

Facilities: Trails, picnic areas and shelter, playground, ball field, campsites for tents and RVs (no hookups).

Dates: Open year-round.

Fees: There is an admission charge.

Closest town: Pownal.

For more information: Bradbury Mountain State Park, 528 Hallowell Road, Pownal, ME 04069. Phone (207) 688-4721.

RED FOX
(Vulpes vulpes)
Red foxes, which are not always red-colored, are distinguished from gray foxes by their white-tipped tail.

▨ CAMPING IN FREEPORT
There are campsites at Wolfe's Neck Farm (*see* page 107), at Winslow Park (*see* page 106), and at the Desert of Maine (*see* page 109) in Freeport and at Bradbury State Park in nearby Topsham.

BRADBURY STATE PARK. Six miles inland from Freeport in Pownal, this state park has rustic campsites, as well as picnic areas, a playground, and some easy hiking trails. *(207) 688-4712.*

▨ DINING IN FREEPORT
JAMESON TAVERN. 115 Main Street, Freeport. This is the tavern where Maine parted ways with Massachusetts in 1820. There's tavern fare in the bar and a huge menu in the dining room. *Inexpensive to moderate. (207) 865-4196.*

HARASEEKET LOBSTER AND LUNCH. Town Wharf, South Freeport. Go to the window and order a lobster or some fried food. Then sit on a picnic table and watch the boats come and go as you eat. *Inexpensive to moderate. (207) 865-4888.*

▨ LODGING IN FREEPORT
They may not outnumber the outlet stores, but Freeport has many B&Bs.

ATLANTIC SEAL BED & BREAKFAST. 25 Main Street, South Freeport. This B&B has beautiful harbor views. The owner also operates Atlantic Seal Cruises to Eagle Island. *Moderate. (207) 865-6112.*

THE HARASEEKET INN. 162 Maine Street, Freeport. This inn not far from downtown has 84 rooms and a dining room with delicious food. *Expensive. (207) 865-9377.*

Brunswick

Fans of Civil War-era history will want to stop in Brunswick, home of Civil War hero Joshua Chamberlain. The Joshua L. Chamberlain Museum has soared in popularity since he was depicted in the PBS miniseries *The Civil War* and in the movie *Gettysburg*. The author Harriet Beecher Stowe, whose *Uncle Tom's Cabin* helped solidify antislavery sentiments in the North, also lived in Brunswick. Her former home is now an inn.

Brunswick is also home to Bowdoin College, a small, private liberal arts school that houses a museum devoted to the arctic expeditions of Robert Peary and Donald MacMillan. Bowdoin is also the site of one of Maine's few old-growth forests.

Brunswick has a nice downtown, with some interesting shops and a great bookstore. Brunswick also has a major military installation, the Brunswick Naval Air Station. The base is home to a fleet of P-3 Orion surveillance planes, so don't be surprised if you see a small plane flying very fast overhead as you head up Route 1.

JOSHUA L. CHAMBERLAIN MUSEUM

[Fig. 11(13)] Joshua Chamberlain's time has come. Ever since his Civil War heroics and civility were depicted in a PBS series on the Civil War and in the movie *Gettysburg*, his former home in Brunswick has become a popular tourist destination, especially for Civil War fans. Chamberlain's wartime accomplishments included heroics in several battles and accepting General Lee's surrender at Appomatox.

Chamberlain, who was an instructor at Bowdoin before the war, returned home to Maine a hero. He was elected governor of Maine. He then served as president of Bowdoin for many years.

His former home has several rooms of Chamberlain exhibits, many of them focusing on the Civil War. The gift shop is full of Civil War items, as well.

Directions: The Joshua L. Chamberlain Museum is at 226 Maine Street, Brunswick's main street.

Activities: Sight-seeing.

Facilities: Partially restored home, gift shop.

Dates: Open Memorial Day weekend through Sept.

Fees: There is a charge for admission.

Closest town: Brunswick.

For more information: The Pejepscot Historical Society, 159 Park Row, Brunswick, ME 04011. Phone (207) 729-6606.

BOWDOIN PINES

[Fig. 11(14)] One of Maine's last remaining old-growth forests is on the campus of Bowdoin College. The 33-acre lot contains eastern white pines (*Pinus strobus*) that tower over other trees and a quiet loop trail. Some of these trees are 90 or more feet tall and more than 125 years old.

The forest was part of a 200-acre gift made by the town of Brunswick to Bowdoin College in 1791. The pines were included in the state's Register of Critical Areas in 1979. Bowdoin College uses the forest as a classroom for students studying biology and ecology.

Directions: The Bowdoin Pines are on either side of the Bath Road on the northeastern corner of the campus. From downtown Brunswick, take Maine Street south to Bath Road. Turn left and you'll see the pines on both sides of the road in two blocks.

Activities: Walking, viewing trees.

Facilities: Loop trail.

Dates: Accessible year-round.

Fees: None.

Closest town: Brunswick.

For more information: Bowdoin College Environmental Studies Program, 5010 College Station, Brunswick, ME 04011. Phone (207) 725-3629.

THE PEARY-MACMILLAN ARCTIC MUSEUM

[Fig. 11(15)] The Peary-MacMillan Arctic Museum, which is on the campus of Bowdoin College, honors the work of two Bowdoin alumni, Admirals Robert E. Peary of the class of 1877 and Donald B. MacMillan of the class of 1898.

In 1909, Peary became the first person to reach the North Pole. MacMillan was a crew member on that expedition. The three-room museum includes some fascinating artifacts from these two Arctic explorers' trips, including a dogsled and snowshoes. There are also Intuit-made tools, models of Peary's ship the *Roosevelt,* a kayak, and natural history specimens, including stuffed arctic birds and a polar bear.

Directions: The Peary-MacMillan Arctic Museum is on the first floor of Hubbard Hall, which is on the south side of the campus quad.

Activities: Sight-seeing.

Facilities: Museum, gift shop.

Dates: Open year-round.

Fees: None. Donations accepted.

Closest town: Brunswick.

For more information: The Peary-MacMillan Arctic Museum, Bowdoin College, 5010 College Station, Brunswick ME 04011. Phone (207) 725-3275.

THOMAS POINT BEACH

[Fig. 11(16)] This beach is a privately owned commercial park with a sandy, tidal beach. (Do your swimming at high tide or you'll be slogging through a mud flat.) There are campsites for tents and RVs, many pretty picnic areas, and a big playground.

This is the site of one of the Maine coast's major annual festivals: the Maine Arts Festival. Bluegrass festivals and kayak paddlefests are held here, as well.

Directions: From Cooks Corner in Brunswick, head south on Thomas Point Road. The beach will be on your left.

Activities: Swimming, picnicking, camping.

Facilities: Beach with changing rooms and life-guards, restrooms, picnic areas, campsites for tents and RVs. There are electric hookups, laundry, showers, and a dumping station.

Dates: Open Memorial Day weekend to Labor Day.

Fees: There is a charge for admission.

Closest town: Brunswick.

For more information: Thomas Point Beach, 29 Meadow Road, Brunswick, ME 04011. Phone (207) 725-6009.

STRIPED SKUNK
(*Mephitis mephitis*)

THE MAINE STATE MUSIC THEATER

This first-rate musical theater company puts on several programs each summer in the Pickard Theater at Bowdoin College. Tickets go fast, so call ahead and reserve one.

Directions: The Pickard Theater is on the Bowdoin College campus, inside Memorial Hall.

Dates: Performances are held from June through August.

Fees: There is a charge for admission.

Closest town: Brunswick.

For more information: Maine State Music Theater, 14 Maine Street, Suite 109, Brunswick, ME 04011. Phone (207) 725-8769.

DINING IN BRUNSWICK

Brunswick has some creative restaurants on Maine Street and two old-fashioned drive-ins (not drive-throughs!) on Bath Road.

FAT BOY DRIVE-IN. Bath Road, Brunswick. It's like something out of *American Grafitti*, complete with carhops, burgers, and fries. *Inexpensive. (207) 729-9431.*

SCARLET BEGONIA'S. 212 Maine Street, Brunswick. Pizza and Italian dominate the menu at this casual Maine Street spot. *Moderate. (207) 721-0403.*

LODGING IN BRUNSWICK

Brunswick has a variety of lodging choices, from big hotels and little motels to historic inns.

THE CAPTAIN DANIEL STONE INN. 10 Water Street, Brunswick. This old sea captain's house has a modern hotel attached. *Expensive. (207) 725-9898.*

BRUNSWICK B&B. 165 Park Row, Brunswick. This is a beautiful, intown mansion full of antiques and loaded with charm. *Moderate. (207) 729-4914.*

MINK
(Mustela vison)
Mink live in dens and eat muskrats, rabbits, mice, fish, snakes, frogs, and marsh-dwelling birds. Like skunks, they can emit a fetid odor which they use in marking their territory.

The Harpswells

The Harpswells is a peninsula that is more of an archipelago of causeway- and bridge-connected islands. There's Harpswell and Harpswell Neck to the west, Sebascodegan Island and Cundy's Harbor to the east, and Orr's Island and Bailey Island dangling down the middle. At the very tip of Bailey Island is windswept spot called, appropriately, Lands End.

Take a drive down these winding roads and you'll be rewarded with beautiful scenery, excellent bird-watching, and some very good lobster wharves.

CRIBSTONE BRIDGE

[Fig. 11(17)] The bridge that connects Orr's and Bailey islands is the only one of its type in the world. The large cement blocks here are laid honeycomb style, with no mortar or cement, to allow the tides to move in and out.

Directions: From Route 1 in Bath, follow ME 123 south into the Harpswells. Following the signs to Orr's Island, turn left on Mountain Road and then left on ME 24. You can't miss the bridge.

LAND'S END

[Fig. 11(18)] At the tip of Bailey Island is Land's End, a rocky, windswept point with a pretty park, a gift shop with every Maine souvenir imaginable, and stunningly beautiful water views. Be very careful on the rocks here. More than one person has been swept into the water by rogue waves.

Directions: From Route 1 in Brunswick, follow ME 24 south, across Orr's and Bailey islands to the very end of the road. There's a large parking lot to the right.

Activities: Sight-seeing.

Facilities: Footpaths, private gift shop.

Dates: Open year-round.

Fees: None.

Closest town: Bailey Island.

EAGLE ISLAND

[Fig. 11] This 17-acre island 3 miles off the coast of Harpswell was the much-loved summer home of North Pole explorer Adm. Robert E. Peary. Peary's heirs gave it to the state, and it looks much like it did before the explorer's death in 1920.

Peary spent much of his youth in Portland and grew to love Eagle Island as a teenager. Peary went on to buy the island and, eventually, to build a cottage that was perched on the rocky cliff and designed to feel like the pilot house of a large ship. Peary's library here has been restored, and his taxidermy bird collection is on display.

Leave time to wander the island. A network of nature trails loop through the hardwood and fir forests, along the shore and past the Peary family's old gardens, still

Admiral Robert Peary

In the early years of the twentieth century, two American explorers laid claim to discovering the North Pole. Dr. Frederick A. Cook and Adm. Robert E. Peary (1856-1920) both said they had reached the North Pole, in 1908 and 1909 respectively. They announced their rival claims within a week of each other and immediately began attacking the credibility of the other. Newspapers and exploration societies took sides, and the controversy became a national fixation.

The National Geographic Society backed Peary's claim, as did most of the scientific community. (Cook, after all, had been proven to lie about reaching the peak of Mount McKinley.) An exhaustively researched 1997 book, *Cook & Peary: The Polar Controversy, Resolved*, by Robert M. Bryce, concludes that neither man reached the North Pole.

Whether or not he reached the North Pole, Peary did receive the fame he was in search of when he mapped Greenland and explored the Arctic. He was raised near Portland and owned a summer home on Eagle Island in Casco Bay. The island is a state historic site. Peary's alma mater, Bowdoin College, has a museum devoted to Peary and another explorer, Donald B. MacMillan.

maintained by island caretakers.

Common eiders (*Somateria mollissima*) nest here, so some trails are closed for the nesting season, until mid-July.

There are moorings for private boats on the northwestern side of the island. If you don't have your own boat, you can get here on excursion boats out of Portland, Freeport, or Bailey Island.

In Portland, Eagle Tours operates excursion cruises to Eagle Island. In Freeport, Atlantic Seal Cruises heads to Eagle Island and throws a lobstering demonstration in, except on Sundays, when lobstering isn't allowed. Bring a lunch along, as there's no place to get food on Eagle Island.

Directions: Eagle Tours depart from Long Wharf on Commercial Street in Portland. Atlantic Seal Cruises leave from the Freeport Town Wharf in South Freeport.

Activities: Sight-seeing, boating, walking, bird-watching.

Facilities: Trails, historic home, restrooms.

Dates: The historic site is open daily in the summer and weekends in the early fall.

Fees: There is a charge for admission and for the boat ride.

Closest town: Harpswell, 3 miles.

For more information: Maine Bureau of Parks and Lands, 22 State House Station, Augusta, ME 04333. Friends of Eagle Island, RR1, Box 581, Orr's Island, ME 04066. Atlantic Seal Cruises, PO Box 146, South Freeport, ME 04078. Phone (207) 865-6112. Eagle Tours, The Coast Watch & Guiding Light Navigation Company, Inc., 74 Raydon Road Extension, York ME 03909. Phone (207) 774-6498.

DINING IN THE HARPSWELLS

Water views and seafood dominate the restaurant scene in the Harpswells.

COOK'S LOBSTER HOUSE. Route 24, Bailey Island. This big, comfortable seafood restaurant near the tip of Bailey Island has incredible views in every direction. *Moderate. (207) 833-2818.*

HOLBROOK'S LOBSTER WHARF. Cundy's Harbor. Watch a charming harbor in action as you eat lobster, fried fish, burgers, or hot dogs at this local institution. *Inexpensive. (207) 725-0708.*

LODGING IN THE HARPSWELLS

There are several good B&Bs and inns in the Harpswells. Just about all of them have water access or views.

HARPSWELL INN. 141 Lookout Point Road, South Harpswell. This comfortable inn used to be a shipyard cookhouse. It backs up to Middle Bay. *Moderate. (207) 833-5509.*

BAILEY ISLAND MOTEL. Route 24, Bailey Island. This nine-room motel is next to the Cribstone Bridge and is a stone's throw from the town landing. *Moderate. (207) 833-2886.*

Indian Pipe

Because it has no chlorophyll, the Indian pipe (*Monotropa uniflora*) plant's waxy stalk and single flower are a translucent white. It can be found growing on dark forest floors all along the Maine coast. Because of its ghostly appearance, it's one of the easiest plants to identify in the woods.

The Indian pipe is a saprophytic plant, meaning it gets nourishment from decaying organic matter, in this case, fungi that live on its roots.

Indian pipes turn black as they age or when picked.

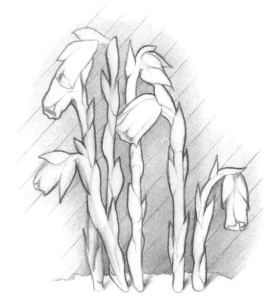

INDIAN PIPE
(*Monotropa uniflora*)

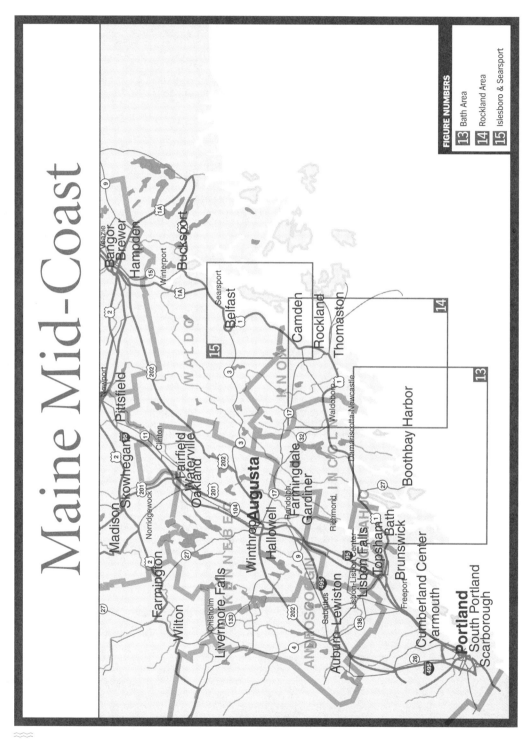

Mid-Coast Maine

The sweeping coastline of southern Maine gives way to a dramatically different landscape in Mid-Coast Maine. A series of peninsulas pointing into the Atlantic characterize this region. These bony fingers of land, bordered by tidal rivers and estuaries and spiked with tall firs and pines, are visited by an impressive variety of birds and sea life. They also appealed to early settlers and colonists, who used their protected harbors to build some of the biggest sailing ships of the seventeenth and eighteenth centuries.

Hundreds of islands speckle the water off the coast. Some are merely piles of granite rocks visible only at low tide while others are thickly covered with firs. Many provide important nesting spots for seabirds and should be admired from afar. Some have year-round populations and are an easy ferry ride away.

The peninsulas and islands are part of the Northeast's "drowned coast," a consequence

[*Above: The waterfront at Camden*]

of the Ice Age, when the state was covered by glaciers 1 mile or more thick. The weighty glaciers pressed down the land. When the ice melted, it ran into the depressed lowlands and the sea, raising the sea level by 400 feet. River valleys, scraped by the moving ice, became the bays and tidal rivers that now define the peninsulas. Hilltops became islands.

Evidence of the region's human history can be found all along this jagged section of the Maine coast. Native Americans lived along these peninsulas and feasted on their shores thousands of years ago. The remains of these feasts are visible today in piles of oyster shells on the river banks—garbage dumps of Indians known today as the Oyster Shell People that populated Maine's fertile riversides 2,000 years ago. The English founded their first colony in New England in 1607 on one of these peninsulas. The French and British fought over their claims here for 150 years. Several of the forts built to guard the entrances to the Mid-Coast's rivers still stand today. And Maine's largest private employer, Bath Iron Works, still builds ships here, on the same river where colonists launched the first North American-built ship.

The twists of geography make a trip down every peninsula a scenic drive. Even the locals don't tire of seeing stretches of water, which appear on either side of the road. After a high tide, the causeways over these tidal rivers can provide priceless views of great blue herons and other waders stalking their supper. And with few exceptions, the drive is something like a trip back in time. Weathered houses, picture book churches, general stores, and small community schools dot the roadsides. Unmanned fruit and vegetable stands include handwritten notes asking that customers leave the correct change in a cookie tin. And the only impatient drivers seem to have out-of-state plates.

One piece of advice to motorists exploring the Mid-Coast; the peninsulas make this region a beautiful one to explore by car. But they can also make a wrong turn very time consuming. Many a tourist has ended up at the end of the wrong peninsula and been frustrated to learn that while they can practically see their destination across the water, it will take another hour to drive up one finger of land and down another. So before turning south of Route 1, make sure you are heading down the right road.

The Bath Area

Shipbuilding was a vital industry for centuries in Maine, and villages up and down the coast saw their fortunes rise and fall with the prominence of wooden ships. The city of Bath offers an up-close look at both the history and current state of shipbuilding.

In the eighteenth and nineteenth centuries, shipbuilders were attracted to the deep water of the Kennebec River and to the towering pines that grew near its shores that were so suitable for masts of oceangoing vessels. By the 1850s, Maine ruled supreme in the shipbuilding industry. Shipyards dotted the Kennebec and other nearby rivers, and Bath was one of the nation's busiest ports. In 1909, the *Wyoming*, a 329-foot, six-masted sailing ship and the largest wooden ship built in America, was launched here.

Ships are still sliding into the deep waters of the Kennebec River. Driving into the city, it's impossible to miss the towering cranes and massive Aegis destroyers at Bath Iron Works, a defense contractor that's been building ships here for more than 100 years. BIW rarely opens the gates at its modern shipbuilding facility to the public, but its ships are easily visible from the street and nearby bridge.

BATH HISTORIC WALKING TOURS

[Fig. 13(1)] Bath's historic downtown district includes several old sea captains' homes (many recognizable by their rooftop widow's walks) including some that now serve as Bed-and-Breakfast inns. They are especially popular with antique hunters, drawn to Bath's antique shops and beautifully restored buildings. Sagadahoc Preservation, Inc. has prepared a map for self-guided walking and driving tours of the city. The tour features dozens of architecturally significant buildings, including some grand Italianate and Greek Revival homes built during the nineteenth-century heyday of shipbuilding in Bath. Very few pre-1750 homes remain. Most were destroyed in the French and Indian wars.

The tours begin at the Gothic Revival "Chocolate Church" that houses the Center for the Arts. Pick up a map at the Bath-Brunswick Chamber of Commerce.

Bath is a great place to spend a noisy, activity-filled Fourth of July. The city's three-day Bath Heritage Days celebration includes fireworks over the Kennebec River, history tours, and a fireman's bed race.

Directions: From Route 1, head North on Washington Street. Walking and driving tours begin at the brown "Chocolate Church" on the left.

Closest town: Bath.

For more information: Bath-Brunswick Chamber of Commerce, 45 Front Street, Bath, ME 04530. Phone (207) 443-9751.

SHELTER INSTITUTE

Visitors interested in home-building or carpentry should stop by the Shelter Institute, where thousands of people have learned how to build their own energy-efficient homes during courses that run from 1 to 15 weeks. Visitors are welcome at the institute and an adjoining shop of woodworking tools and books.

Closest town: Bath.

For more information: The Shelter Institute, 38 Center Street, Bath, ME 04530. Phone (207) 442-7938.

MAINE MARITIME MUSEUM

[Fig. 13(2)] Not far downriver from the modern destroyers at Bath Iron Works is the Maine Maritime Museum, where Maine's rich tradition of ship and boat building is displayed. The museum sits on the site of the old Percy & Small Shipyard, which

Bath Area/Phippsburg Peninsula

In 1909, the Wyoming, a 329-foot, six-masted sailing ship and the largest wooden ship built in America, was launched in Bath.

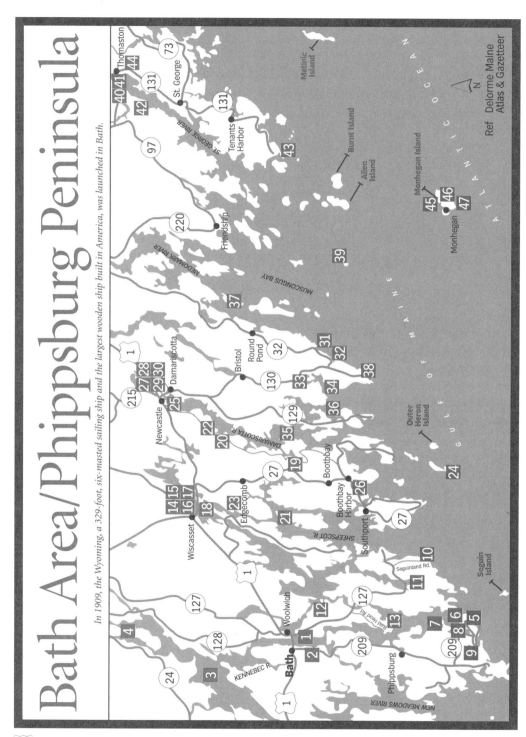

1 Bath Historic Walking Tours

2 Maine Maritime Museum

3 Merrymeeting Bay

4 Steve Powell WMA

5 Popham Beach State Park

6 Fort Popham

7 Popham Colony

8 Fort Baldwin

9 Morse Mountain Preserve

10 Reid State Park

11 Josephine Newman Wildlife Sanctuary

12 Montsweag Preserve

13 Bald Head Preserve

14 Castle Tucker

15 Nickels-Sortwell House

16 Musical Wonder House

17 Morris Farm in Wiscasset

18 Fort Edgecomb

19 Kenneth Stoddard Shell Museum

20 Ovens Mouth Preserve

21 Porter Preserve

22 Colby Wildlife Preserve

23 Singing Meadows

24 Damariscove Island

25 Dodge Point Preserve

26 Marine Resource Aquarium

27 Salt Bay

28 Salt Bay Preserve Heritage Trail

29 Damariscotta Mills Fish Ladder

30 Damariscotta Reversing Falls

31 Rachel Carson Salt Pond Preserve

32 LaVerna Preserve

33 Colonial Pemaquid

34 Pemaquid Beach Park

35 Menigawam Preserve

36 Witch Island Sanctuary

37 Hog Island Audubon Camp

38 Pemaquid Point

39 Eastern Egg Rock

40 Maine Watercraft Museum

41 Olson House

42 Georges River Scenic Byway and Bikeways

43 Marshall Point Lighthouse and Museum

44 Waldo Tyler WMA

45 Cathedral Woods Trail

46 Cliff Trail

47 Monhegan Light

Edwards Dam

Environmental history was made in July 1999, when workers started tearing down a 160-year-old dam on Maine's Kennebec River. The Edwards Dam isn't the first hydroelectric dam in the country to fall, but it's the first ordered removed by federal regulators when the owner wanted to keep it running. The Federal Energy Regulatory Commission made its historic decision in 1997, refusing to relicense the Edwards Dam under a 1986 law that requires the government to balance environmental protection and energy interests when considering licenses for generation facilities.

Conservationists say the removal of the Edwards Dam in Augusta, 40 miles upriver from the Kennebec's mouth to the Atlantic, will open up 17 miles of prime breeding habitat for several kinds of sea-run fish, which primarily live in the ocean but head up rivers to spawn in fresh water.

Several kinds of fish, including striped bass, shad, Atlantic sturgeon, shortnose sturgeon, blueback herring, Atlantic salmon, and rainbow smelt, could eventually flourish in the new breeding ground.

The removal of the 917-foot-long, 25-foot-high dam changed the water level, temperature and current in a long stretch of the Kennebec, and it could be years before the success of fish restoration projects can be judged. If the efforts are successful, the increased fish population will help boost an entire ecosystem, providing food for osprey, eagles, and other animals at the higher end of the coastal food chain.

built 41 four-, five- and six-masted schooners between 1894 and 1920. Several buildings remain as they appeared a century ago, and visitors can either use a museum map to guide themselves through the yard or take a one-hour guided tour.

There are also galleries of world-class marine art and artifacts related to Maine's 400-year maritime history. Expert and apprentice boatbuilders at a wooden boat shop, welcome questions as they work. A master model shipwright works on intricate small-scale ships near the museum's admissions desk.

There is also a building dedicated to the history of the lobstering industry in Maine. Here, visitors can sit aboard a lobster boat while watching a lobstering documentary written and narrated by E.B. White, and check out exhibits on lobster traps, boats, buoys, and canneries.

The museum has an impressive wooden boat collection that includes several working boats, which spend the warmer months floating at the dock or taking visitors on narrated tours of the river. The Maine Maritime Museum also offers specialty cruises, including trips to look at mid-coast lighthouses and fall foliage. Among the museum's craft is the 142-foot Grand Banks schooner *The Sherman Zwicker* and the *Chance*, a 31-foot Friendship sloop built in 1916. There are also moorings available for visitors arriving by boat.

The shipyard lawn is a pleasant picnic spot, weather permitting. Visitors can bring a picnic or hit the museum snack bar. For children, there is an outside play area with a nautical theme.

Directions: From Route 1, turn south on Washington Street. The museum is 1.6 miles south of BIW on the left.

Dates: Open daily except Thanksgiving, Christmas and New Year's Day.

Fees: There is a charge for admission.

Closest town: Bath.

For more information: Maine Maritime Museum, 243 Washington Street, Bath, ME 04530. Phone (207) 443-1316.

MERRYMEETING BAY

[Fig. 13(3)] Up the Kennebec River from Bath is Merrymeeting Bay, the largest tidal freshwater bay in New England and a favored spot of bird watchers and hunters. The 4,500-acre bay, named by settlers for the Indian gatherings held here centuries ago, is the confluence of six rivers—the Kennebec, Androscoggin, Cathance, Muddy, Abagaddasset, and Eastern.

Each spring and fall Merrymeeting Bay is a stopover for thousands of migrating geese and ducks on the Atlantic Flyway. Canada geese (*Branta canadensis*), snow geese (*Chen caerulescens*), green-winged teal (*Anas crecca*), blue-winged teal (*Anas discors*), and northern pintails (*Anas acuta*) are among the frequently seen migrants. Other ducks, including wood ducks (*Aix sponsa*) and hooded mergansers (*Lophodytes cucullatus*) nest along the bay. The tall, pale vegetation growing along the shores of Merrymeeting Bay is wild rice (*Zizania aquatica*). The rice, along with the nutrients carried into the bay with each tide, help Merrymeeting Bay sustain an impressive variety of wildlife.

Merrymeeting Bay's wildlife goes far beyond the avian visitors who stop each fall and spring for rest and sustenance. It's home to bald eagles and osprey, sturgeon and striped bass, beavers and otters. Getting a look at these inhabitants can be tricky. Most of the land surrounding the 4,500-acre bay is privately owned and posted against trespassing. But the roads encircling the bay give motorists several good vantage points for bird-watching. Bird watchers visiting for the fall migration should be aware that this is a very popular hunting spot.

WOOD DUCK
(Aix sposa)

Boating, both with paddles and motors, is permitted. But paddlers should be aware of the strong tidal currents here. Boaters can enter the bay at the town landing in Richmond.

The best way to experience Merrymeeting Bay is from Swan Island, site of the Steve Powell Wildlife Management Area (*see* below).

Directions: From Bath, take ME 128 north, following the Kennebec until it joins the bay to the left. From Brunswick, follow ME 24 out of town toward Bowdoinham and the bay will be to the right. To reach the Richmond boat launch, follow ME 24 into the town center, or take Exit 26 from I-95 and follow ME 197 into town.

Activities: Fishing, hunting, bird-watching.

For more information: Maine Department of Inland Fisheries and Wildlife, phone (207) 547-5300 for hunting and fishing season and license information. Friends of Merrymeeting Bay, Box 233, Richmond, ME 04357 for ecology information.

SWAN ISLAND AND THE STEVE POWELL WILDLIFE MANAGEMENT AREA

[Fig. 13(4)] With nesting bald eagles (*Haliaeetus leucocephalus*), a herd of white-tailed deer (*Odocoileus virginianus*), red squirrels (*Tamiasciurus hudsonicus*) wild turkeys (*Meleagris gallopavo*), ruffed grouse (*Bonasa umbelus*), and other birds and mammals, this 1,755-acre sanctuary at the head of Merrymeeting Bay is an ideal spot to catch a glimpse of wildlife. But a visit requires some planning.

The island may only be accessed from a state Inland Fisheries and Wildlife ferry, and reservations are required. There is a campground, also requiring reservations, with 10 Adirondack-style, three-sided shelters and a two-night limit. No vehicles, including bicycles, are allowed.

Visitors can explore the shore and hike on a gravel road that runs the length of the 4-mile-long island. There's also a 0.5-mile nature trail that loops around a field and a man-made pond, one of eight on the island. Look for wooden boxes nailed to trees several feet above the water. These nesting boxes are intended for wood ducks (*Aix sposa*). The colorful wood ducks, (the males can be easily identified by the laid-back, green crests on their heads) were nearly extinct in the 1930s. Restoration efforts, including the use of these nesting boxes, has helped the wood duck population rebound to abundance. Hundreds of ducklings are raised every year from the Swan Island nesting boxes. Other waterfowl, including hooded mergansers (*Lophodytes cucullatus*), make use of the boxes, as well.

The ponds and other wetlands on the island are home to ducks and wading birds. Deer and migrating geese frequent Swan Island's fields, which are maintained by the state. Small mammals—red squirrels, skunks, raccoons—live in the mixed forests. The fruit of the butternut and white oak trees is a favorite food for some of the forest dwellers.

Swan Island is a peaceful refuge for man and beast, but it once bustled with human activity. The island was called Perkins Township, in the eighteenth and nineteenth centuries. According to the state's guide to the island, the people of Perkins Township worked primarily in shipbuilding, ice cutting, fishing, and farming. But modern progress brought the demise of the island town. The arrival of iron-sided ships put an end to the shipyard. The invention of modern refrigeration made ice cutting obsolete. Pollution in the Kennebec damaged the fishery. By 1918, only the farmers were left. They gave up during the Depression, and the ferry service shut down in 1936, signaling an end of civilization here.

WHITE OAK
(Quercus alba)

Some of Perkins Township's buildings, including a 1758 Saltbox and an 1810 Federal-style home, still stand. The restored buildings are used by employees of the wildlife management area, either as homes or storage space, and visitors are given a detailed map of the area's buildings and foundations.

State wildlife officials, recognizing the island's ecological significance, bought nearly all of the land on the island in the 1940s and 1950s. The final piece of land, a family cemetery, was willed to the state in 1988. Stephen E. Powell was one of the first biologists to work at Swan Island. The wildlife management area was named in his honor after his death in 1971.

Directions: See directions to Richmond boat launch in Merrymeeting Bay (page 125).

Activities: Camping, hiking, bird-watching, wildlife observation and photography.

Fees: There is a charge for day use and for use of the campsites.

Closest town: Richmond.

For more information: Maine Department of Inland Fisheries and Wildlife, 270 Lyons Road, Sidney, ME 04330. General information: Phone (207) 287-8000. Reservations: Phone (207) 547-5322.

NIGHT LIFE IN BATH

Bath is a working city, not just a summer destination. Several downtown bars have music year-round, as does the Chocolate Church. In the summer, look for evening concerts at the downtown Library and Waterfront parks.

CENTER FOR THE ARTS AT THE CHOCOLATE CHURCH. 804 Washington Street, Bath. This big, brown church is the site of many concerts, plays and exhibits. *(207) 442-8455.*

HARBOR LIGHTS CAFÉ. 166 Front Street, Bath. This spot is open for lunch and dinner year-round and has live bands a few nights a week. *(207) 443-9883.*

DINING IN BATH

Bath has a variety of restaurants, many of which fill up on summer weekends, so reservations are advised. For seafood on a wharf or gourmet dining, head down some of the nearby peninsulas.

CENTER STREET GRAINERY. 36 Center Street, Bath. This health-food store also carries great baked goods, sandwiches, and soups that are perfect for taking out for a picnic. *Inexpensive. (207) 442-8012.*

KRISTINA'S RESTAURANT. 160 Center Street, Bath. Kristina's Restaurant and bakery attract loyal patrons from far and wide for breakfast, lunch, and dinner. *Moderate. (207) 442-8577.*

LODGING IN BATH

The innkeepers at Bath's many bed and breakfast inns take pride in their authentic décor.

THE INN AT BATH, 969 Washington Street, Bath. This antique-filled, in-town Greek Revival home has eight guest rooms, all with private baths and most with fireplaces. Two sets of rooms can be converted to suites for families. *Moderate to expensive, depending on the room. (207) 443-4294.*

THE FAIRHAVEN INN. North Bath Road, Bath. This 1790 colonial sits on 20 acres of woods and fields, which are available for hiking or cross-country skiing. Most of its nine rooms have private baths. *Moderate to expensive. (207) 443-4391.*

The Phippsburg Peninsula

The British began their colonization of New England in 1607 with a settlement at the mouth of the Kennebec. Their fort is long gone, but two other forts that did duty through several wars, protecting the shipping industries up the Kennebec, are available for exploration at the far reaches of the Phippsburg Peninsula.

This peninsula also has some sandy beaches, nature trails, and many spots to stop and admire the view. Most of these are accessed by the main highway running down the peninsula from Bath, ME 209. About 0.5 mile south of Bath on ME 209 is the Winnegance causeway. If you're here after a high tide, when food is most plentiful in the mud flats, pull over and look for feeding ducks and other birds. The General Store across the street can provide directions, coffee, or other provisions.

POPHAM BEACH STATE PARK

[Fig. 13(5)] This park's 3,600-yard sandy beach makes it a popular destination for locals and tourists in the summer. During the off-season, bird watchers and beach walkers pretty much have this scenic spot to themselves.

Along with its famous strip of sand, this park has a pitch pine (*Pinus rigida*) forest, a salt marsh where snowy egrets (*Egretta thula*) can sometimes be spotted, a tidal inlet at the mouth of the Morse River, and barrier dunes. At low tide, the expansive mud flats attract numerous shorebirds, and beachgoers can walk to an island. Piping plovers and least terns sometimes nest on the beach here. The Maine Audubon Society monitors the nests. For the protection of these endangered species, do not go near these nests.

Several islands are visible from the beach, including the five Heron Islands, which are a Nature Conservancy preserve and are home to nesting double-crested cormorants (*Phalacrocorax auritus*), black-backed gulls (*Laurs marinus*), and herring gulls (*Larus argentatus*). Also visible 6 miles out to sea is the Seguin Island Light, Maine's first island lighthouse. Its fixed, white light is visible for 18 miles. While the tower is only 53 feet high, the light was built on a hill, putting the beacon at 180 feet above the water and making it the highest beacon on the Maine coast.

The Kennebec River has become a popular striped bass fishing river. While anglers appear to have better luck from boats, some prefer to cast from the shore at Popham Beach. Striped bass (*Morone saxatilis*) were fished nearly to extinction a few decades ago, and strict regulations restored the population. There are still restrictions on when fishing is allowed and what size fish can be kept.

Swimming is allowed at Popham Beach, although the water is too cold for all but the hardiest of bathers.

Popham Beach is very popular on summer weekends, and many cars get turned away on sunny days. If the lot is full, don't be tempted to park along Route 209, where cars are routinely given hefty parking tickets.

Directions: From Bath, follow ME 209 to the park, which is well marked.

Activities: Swimming, bird-watching, fishing.

Facilities: Changing rooms, outside shower, restrooms, picnic spots, lifeguards, a ranger station at the entrance.

Dates: Open mid-Apr. through Oct., but gates are usually open year-round.

Fees: There is a fee charged for admission.

Closest town: Phippsburg.

For more information: Popham Beach State Park, Phippsburg, ME 04562. Phone (207) 389-1335. For fishing information, call the Maine Marine Resources Department. Phone (207) 633-9500.

FORT POPHAM

[Fig. 13(6)] This fort's strategic location allowed it to protect the Kennebec River shipbuilding industry during three wars. Construction started on the semicircular granite fort during the Civil War. The building was never completed, but it was modified and garrisoned during the Spanish-American War and again during World War I. Its granite arches and spiral staircases are open for exploration and provide panoramic views of the mouth of the Kennebec and Atkins Bay. The fort is open seasonally, although the grounds are accessible year-round. This is a great spot for bird-watching, picnicking, fishing and playing in the sand. Do not swim here; the current is quite strong.

Directions: From Bath or Popham Beach, continue down ME 209, which ends at Fort Popham.

Activities: Fishing, bird-watching, picnicking.

Dates: Open Memorial Day through September.

Closest town: Phippsburg.

For more information: Popham Beach State Park, Phippsburg, ME 04562. Phone (207) 389-1335.

POPHAM COLONY

[Fig. 13(7)] The British colonization of New England began in 1607 with the establishment of the Popham Colony in what is now Phippsburg, 13 years before the better-known Plymouth Colony was established in Massachusetts. The Popham Colony didn't last long. Those colonists that survived one Maine winter abandoned their new home and retreated to Great Britain in 1608. But they launched Maine's shipbuilding industry by building the 50-ton pinnace *Virginia*, which they sailed home to England. Little remains of that first colony, but it has been the site of some exciting archaeological exploration in the 1990s. Researchers, armed with a 1607 map, have unearthed part of the storehouse of the colony's Fort Saint George. The archaeologists return each summer to search for more artifacts and structures. The Field School program of the Friends of the Maine State Museum sponsors two one-week sessions with on-site archeology instruction and fieldwork.

Directions: From Popham Beach, continue about 1 mile down ME 209. Turn left on Fort Baldwin Road, and drive up a hill to the parking area and lawn.

Closest town: Phippsburg.

For more information: Friends of the Maine State Museum, 83 State House Station, Augusta, ME 04333. Phone (207) 287-2304.

FORT BALDWIN

[Fig. 13(8)] Up Sabino Hill from the Popham Colony site is Fort Baldwin, built in 1905 to take over the guard duties of the historic Fort Popham. The three batteries are tucked in a wooded area and have many nooks and crannies to explore. A six-story fire tower was built in 1942 and offers wonderful views of the coast.

Directions: From the parking area on Fort Baldwin Road (*see* Popham Colony directions above) walk up a 500-foot path to the fort.

For more information: Popham Beach State Park, Phippsburg, ME 04562. Phone (207) 389-1335.

MORSE MOUNTAIN PRESERVE

[Fig. 13(9)] This preserve is primarily a conservation and research area for Bates College, The Nature Conservancy, and the Maine Audubon Society and is a nesting spot for least terns (*Sterna antillarum*) and piping plovers (*Charadrius melodrus*). There is parking for a few visitors near the trailhead. A 2-mile trail wanders through a forest to the summit of Morse Mountain and on to Seawall Beach. The largest expanse of beach heather (*Hudsonia tomentosa*) in Maine grows in the barrier dune system here. The birds that nest on the beach are endangered species whose populations are being maintained only through intensive protection by conservation groups. Do not approach or linger near the nests or the fences that may surround them. These little birds lay their eggs directly on the sand, so be very careful where you step.

PORCUPINE
(*Erethizon dorsatum*)

Preserve rules prohibit visitors from using the beach above the high-tide line, where the terns and plovers raise their young. Keep in mind that this is not a recreational area and is not intended for sunbathing or picnicking.

Several long-term research projects are ongoing here. Scientists from Bates College and the University of Maine use the preserve to study how wind and water form dunes and beaches here. Biologists are also studying plant growth in the forest, the damage porcupines inflict on trees, and the population of fish in marsh canals. The undisturbed nature of this preserve also allows scientists to compare the survival of plant and animal species here with those in the nearby public parks. No dogs are allowed.

Directions: Drive south on ME 209 and continue south onto ME 216. The Morse Mountain Road and the parking area are about a mile down the road on the left. If the lot is full, try another day. Cars parked on the road will be ticketed.

Activities: Bird-watching, nature study, hiking.

Facilities: Trail.

Dates: Accessible year-round.

Fees: None.

Closest town: Phippsburg.

For more information: Morse Mountain Conservation Area. Care of Bates College, Lewiston, ME 04240. Phone (207) 786-6078. Or, The Nature Conservancy, Maine Chapter, Fort Andross, 14 Maine Street, Suite 401, Brunswick, ME 04011. Phone (207) 729-5181.

GOLF ON THE PHIPPSBURG PENINSULA

Sebasco Harbor Resort, Sebasco Estates. This scenic 9-hole course 12 miles south of Bath has two sets of tees. Pars are 33 and 31. It's one of the features at a sprawling old-style resort that also has a saltwater pool, tennis courts, and boat excursions for guests. The course is open to the public, space permitting.

For more information: Sebasco Harbor Resort, Route 217, Sebasco Estates, ME 04565. Phone (207) 389-9060.

CAMPING ON THE PHIPPSBURG PENINSULA

HERMIT ISLAND CAMPGROUND. Cross a causeway near the base of the peninsula to reach the Hermit Island Campground, a popular spot for tent campers. It has waterfront campsites, private sand beaches and warm water coves, small boat rentals, and daily guided cruises in a larger boat. Hermit Island is for tents, "pop-up" style trailers, and small pickup campers only; no motor homes or travel trailers are permitted.

Reservations for a week or longer are accepted the first business day in January with full payment within 30 days. Reservations for less than a week are accepted starting the first business day in March with full payment. No reservations are taken or are necessary after Labor Day.

Directions: From Bath, follow ME 209 and continue south on ME 216 to Hermit Road sign.

Fees: There is a fee charged for camping.

Closest town: Phippsburg.

For more information: Hermit Island, 42 Front Street, Bath, ME 04530. Phone (207) 443-2101.

DINING ON THE PHIPPSBURG PENINSULA

Whether you are in the market for takeout food or a sit-down dinner, you can count on a great view while dining on the Phippsburg Peninsula.

SPINNEY'S RESTAURANT. Popham Beach, Phippsburg. This beachside spot near Fort Popham has a takeout window and a dining room with ocean views. Serving three meals a day during the summer. *Inexpensive. (207) 389-2052*

LODGING ON THE PHIPPSBURG PENINSULA

Phippsburg has several B&Bs in historic buildings. It also has a resort with an old-fashioned feel.

POPHAM BEACH BED AND BREAKFAST. Popham Beach, Phippsburg. This B&B is a converted 1883 Coast Guard station. *Moderate to expensive, depending on the room. (207) 389-2409.*

SEBASCO HARBOR RESORT. Route 217, Sebasco Estates. This 600-acre resort has golf, swimming, boating, candlepin bowling, lobster bakes and other activities for guests. Its more than 90 rooms are in a variety of buildings, including cottages and an inn. *Moderate to expensive. (207) 389-1161.*

Georgetown Peninsula

Georgetown Peninsula dangles off the mainland between the Kennebec, Back, and Sheepscot rivers and is split nearly in two by long Robinhood Cove. It is actually a series of islands, with Arrowsic Island at the top and Georgetown at the bottom. Most visitors to this peninsula are headed for its enormously popular state park, or perhaps a gourmet restaurant or marina. But the Georgetown Peninsula is worthy of more exploration. Its lesser-known attractions include a first-rate nature sanctuary, an eagle roosting spot, mud flats frequented by all kinds of birds, and some scenic footpaths.

REID STATE PARK

[Fig. 13(10)] This park is very popular on warm summer days, so get here early or you won't get a parking space.

Its popularity is easy to explain. The park's 766 acres include two sandy beaches— Mile Beach and Half Mile Beach—rocky ledges, a tidal saltwater lagoon with water warm enough to loll in, sand dunes and salt marshes that attract all kinds of wildlife, and many tide pools with interesting sea life at low tide. While sunbathing is the main activity here in summer, cross-country skiers use the beach in the winter and bird watchers visit year-round.

The beaches here are nesting sites for piping plovers and least terns, which are monitored by Maine Audubon. Stay away from any fenced nesting areas. During the spring and fall migrations, look for the gull-like northern gannet (*Morus bassanus*) and hawks, including peregrine falcons (*Falco peregrinus.*) Wading birds, including great blue herons (*Ardea herodias*) and snowy egrets (*Ardea alba*) frequent the salt marshes. Look for them near shore after a high tide, standing nearly motionless until a fish or other prey gets too close, when these birds' heads can snap quickly into the water to catch their food.

Directions: From Route 1 in Woolwich, take ME 127 south for about 14 miles.

Activities: Swimming, bird-watching.

Facilities: Snack bar, bath houses with showers, restrooms, picnic tables with charcoal grills, ranger station at entrance.

Dates: Open year-round.

Fees: There is a charge for admission.

Closest town: Georgetown.

For more information: Reid State Park, Seguinland Road, Georgetown ME 04548. Phone (207) 371-2303.

⬚ JOSEPHINE NEWMAN WILDLIFE SANCTUARY

[Fig. 13(11)] Josephine Newman was a naturalist who spent most of her 90 years studying the varied habitats of her family's homestead on Robinhood Cove in Georgetown. When she died in 1968, she left 119 acres to the Maine Audubon Society. Visitors come to enjoy the quiet beauty or to learn about the flora and fauna that flourish in the sanctuary's forests, swamp, salt marsh, meadow, and coastline. Maine Audubon has prepared an impressive 59-page guide to the sanctuary, describing its habitats and inhabitants in great detail. It's not available at the sanctuary, however, so buy it ahead of time at the Maine Audubon Society store at Gilsland Farm in Falmouth.

TRAILS AT THE JOSEPHINE NEWMAN WILDLIFE SANCTUARY

The sanctuary has 2.5 miles of trails, divided into three blazed paths. Walking all three, with stops for exploring, can make for an interesting morning. Watch out for ticks in the high grass.

The blue-blazed Geology Trail is 0.6 mile long and takes visitors from a meadow, through mixed and conifer forests, past a cattail marsh, and on to Robinhood Cove and its reversing falls. Twenty numbered posts correspond with a self-guided nature tour in the Maine Audubon sanctuary guide. The red-blazed 1.25-mile Rocky End trail departs the Geology Trail to investigate a different portion of Robinhood Cove. The orange-blazed, 0.75-mile Horseshoe Trail leads to the ruins of a cabin on a ledge in the sanctuary's interior.

With its varied habitats, the sanctuary is an ideal spot to learn about coastal Maine wildlife. Its meadows and forests are home to white-tailed deer, woodchucks, foxes, and red, gray and northern flying squirrels. Many amphibians—including the American toad (*Bufo americanus*), spotted salamander (*Ambystoma maculatum*), and at least four types of frogs, live in its swamp or marsh. The bugs that hatch each spring in these wet areas feed a variety of birds, including redwing blackbirds and swallows. Osprey can often be seen diving for fish at Robinhood Cove. Some of the more common birds here are the ovenbird (*Seiurus aurocapillus*) and the black-throated green warbler (*Dendroica virens*). Listen for the ovenbird's distinctive *teacher-teacher-teacher* call as you walk through the forest.

Some of the best bird-watching at this sanctuary is at low tide at the mud flat, when sea and shorebirds come to feed on the worms, clams and other organisms live just below the silt surface.

Directions: From Route 1 in Woolwich, take ME 127 South for 9.1 miles to Georgetown. Look for the sanctuary sign on the right. Follow the entrance road to a small parking area.

Activities: Hiking, bird-watching.

Facilities: Trails.

Dates: Open dawn to dusk, year-round.

For more information: Maine Audubon Society, PO Box 6009, Falmouth, ME 04105. Phone (207) 781-2330.

MONTSWEAG PRESERVE

[Fig. 13(12)] The centerpiece of this 45-acre Chewonki Foundation preserve is its 1,500 feet of ledged shoreline along tidal Montsweag Brook. A 1.5-mile trail quickly descends from a dry forest of spruce, fir, birch, and maple, to a view of the brook's mud flats, across a salt marsh and alder swamp, and back into the woods. Wear waterproof shoes, as this hike can be wet. The trail is marked with blue blazes.

Directions: From Route 1 in Woolwich, head south on Montsweag Road. The trailhead is about 1.3 miles down the road on the left, marked with a blue blaze.

Activities: Hiking, nature-watching.

Facilities: Trail.

Dates: Open year-round.

Fees: None.

Closest town: Woolwich.

For more information: The Chewonki Foundation, 485 Chewonki Neck Road, Wiscasset, ME 04578. Phone (207) 882-7323.

BALD HEAD PRESERVE

[Fig. 13(13)] Eagles frequently roost in the pines at the top of the nearly 100-foot cliffs at Bald Head. The cliffs overlook the Back River, which separates Arrowsic and Georgetown. The 296-acre preserve also includes a salt marsh and wide mud flats. The cliffs can be observed from a canoe, which can be put in a small creek near the Arrowsic-Georgetown bridge at high tide. A woods road and a rough trail go into the preserve. The trail begins at the end of Bald Head Road. Veer left just after the woods road enters an old field area.

Please note that the land and cabin at the end of the peninsula are privately owned.

Directions: For the canoe put-in, from Route 1, take ME 127 to Arrowsic and turn right at the last road before the Arrowsic-Georgetown bridge. By land, in Arrowsic take a right on Steen Road and another right on Bald Head Road.

Activities: Paddling, bird-watching.

Facilities: Rough trail.

Dates: Open year-round.

Fees: None.

Closest town: Arrowsic.

BLACK-THROATED BLUE WARBLER
(Dendroica caerulescens)

For more information: The Nature Conservancy, Maine Chapter, Fort Andross, 14 Maine Street, Suite 401, Brunswick, ME 04011. Phone (207) 729-5181.

CAMPING ON THE GEORGETOWN PENINSULA

CAMP SEGUIN. Seguinland Road, Georgetown. This oceanfront campground has 30 sites and a tenting area, 20 amp hookups, a dump station, a store and a recreation hall and is 1 mile from Reid State Park. *(207) 371-2777.*

DINING ON THE GEORGETOWN PENINSULA

The Georgetown Peninsula has more than its fair share of good food. Dining choices include a gourmet restaurant considered one of the best in Maine and a lobster shack as authentic as they come.

ROBINHOOD FREE MEETINGHOUSE. Robinhood Road, Georgetown. The simplicity of the restored 1855 meetinghouse strikes a nice balance with a very long menu of gourmet dishes like artichoke strudel and Thai lobster. *Moderate to expensive. (207) 371-2188.*

FIVE ISLANDS LOBSTER COMPANY. Five Islands. Sit outside and watch the working boats bringing in their catch while you eat lobster and french fries at a picnic table. *Inexpensive to moderate. (207) 371-2950.*

LODGING ON THE GEORGETOWN PENINSULA

Gray Havens Inn. Seguinland Road, Georgetown. This classy, shingled inn sits on a cliff next to Reid State Park and has great water views from most rooms and its comfortable wraparound porch. *Expensive. (207) 371-2616.*

The Wiscasset Area

Historic homes and antique shops dominate the center of Wiscasset, which calls itself The Prettiest Village in Maine. In the late 1700s, Wiscasset was one of the busiest ports in New England. Its days as a busy seafaring town are long gone, but the homes built by wealthy sea captains and others remain. Some are open as museums, and others house antique shops.

Wiscasset is also home to Maine's only nuclear power plant. That plant, Maine Yankee, stopped operating and began the years-long process of decommissioning in 1997.

HISTORIC HOMES IN WISCASSET

The Society for the Preservation of New England Antiquities owns two of the many historic homes built when Wiscasset had a busy port.

CASTLE TUCKER

[Fig. 13(14)] This quirky brick mansion overlooking the harbor features an elliptical staircase and rooms full of Victorian furniture and marine art.

Directions: Castle Tucker is on the corner of Lee and High streets in Wiscasset.

Activities: Sight-seeing.

Facilities: Museum.

Dates: Open a few days a week for tours in the summer months.

Closest town: Wiscasset.

For more information: Castle Tucker, Lee Street at High Street, Wiscasset, ME 04578. Phone (207) 882-7364. Society for the Preservation of New England Antiquities, 141 Cambridge Street, Boston, MA 02114. Phone (617) 227-3956.

NICKELS-SORTWELL HOUSE

[Fig. 13(15)] This three-story Federal-style home was built for sea captain William Nickels but was turned into a hotel when the shipping industry hit hard times. In the late nineteenth century, Alvin Sortwell bought the home and restored it as a residence.

Just up Federal Street is The Old Lincoln Country Jail and Museum, where visitors can explore early nineteenth century cells and read the prisoners' graffiti.

Directions: The Nickels-Sortwell House is on Route 1 in Wiscasset.

Activities: Sight-seeing.

Facilities: Museum.

Dates: Open for tours a few days a week in the summer.

Fees: There is a charge for admission.

Closest town: Wiscasset.

For more information: Nickels-Sortwell House, 121 Main Street, Wiscasset, ME 04578. Phone (207) 882-6218. Society for the Preservation of New England Antiquities, 141 Cambridge Street, Boston, MA 02114. Phone (617) 227-3956.

MUSICAL WONDER HOUSE

[Fig. 13(16)] This Greek Revival house is now a museum with a mind-boggling array of music boxes, player pianos, and other musical machines.

Directions: The Musical Wonder House is on High Street in Wiscasset.

Activities: Sight-seeing.

Facilities: Museum.

Dates: Open Memorial Day weekend to mid-Oct.

Closest town: Wiscasset.

For more information: Musical Wonder House, 18 High Street, Wiscasset, ME 04578. Phone (207) 882-7163.

FEED THE BIRDS

Bird watchers will enjoy this store's selection of birdfeeders, birdseed, and natural history books. It's also a good spot to pick up some free advice and newsletters on local birding.

Directions: Feed The Birds is on Route 1 (Main Street) in the center of town.

For more information: Feed the Birds, Box 245, Wiscasset, ME 04578. (207) 882-8144.

MORRIS FARM

[Fig. 13(17)] The Morris Farm is operated by a local trust formed to save yet another Maine coast farm from falling to development. It's a working farm but also a community resource, offering educational programs, a summer camp, and a store that sells local farmers' produce.

The 50-acre farm has pastures and hay fields, a pond, a waterfall, and streams. There are organized tours, but the farm is also open for self-guided tours.

Directions: From Route 1 in Wiscasset, turn north on ME 27. Morris Farm is about 0.75 mile down the road.

Activities: Nature walking.

Facilities: Farm, trails, store.

Dates: Open year-round.

Fees: None.

Closest town: Wiscasset.

For more information: Morris Farm, Box 136, Wiscasset, ME 04578. Phone (207) 882-4080.

DINING IN WISCASSET

Wiscasset is blessed with some great takeout food and a town wharf with picnic tables, as well as some fine dining spots.

RED'S EATS. High Street, Wiscasset. This takeout stand sits next to the bridge over the Sheepscot River and has a handful of outside tables. There's often a line for Red's lobster rolls, onion rings and sandwiches. *Inexpensive. (207) 882-6128.*

TREAT'S. Main Street, Wiscasset. This is a gourmet takeout food and wine shop with great baked goods, fancy cheese, and imaginative soups and muffins. *Inexpensive. (207) 882-6192.*

LE GARAGE. Wiscasset. The dining room in this romantic spot is lit almost entirely by candles and features broad views of the harbor. Before dinner, check out the gift shop across the street in the old Customs House. *Moderate. (207) 882-5409.*

LODGING IN WISCASSET

Wiscasset has a few nice B&Bs in historic buildings.

THE MARSTON HOUSE B&B. Main Street. This B&B's two rooms are in a carriage house behind the Marston House antique shop. Check out the shop's collection of antique gardening tools and textiles. *Moderate. (207) 882-6010.*

SNOW SQUALL B&B. 5 Bradford Road. This B&B has several rooms and two suites, all of them named after Maine-built clipper ships. *Moderate to expensive. (207) 882-6892.*

Boothbay Peninsula

Boothbay Harbor is a bustling tourist magnet of shops and restaurants sitting on a picturesque harbor. There are plenty of interesting things to see in the area, even for those who don't like crowded sidewalks. The Boothbay Peninsula, which sits between the Sheepscot and Damariscotta rivers, is home to several nature preserves and a hands-on aquarium. It's also the jumping-off point for several nature cruises.

FORT EDGECOMB

[Fig. 13(18)] This octagonal blockhouse was built in 1808 and 1809 to protect what was then a very busy and important harbor in Wiscasset from possible British attack. It was garrisoned for the War of 1812 and again during the Civil War.

The two-story blockhouse sits on the shore of the Sheepscot River on Davis Island in a quiet 3-acre park. It's a great place to picnic and watch for harbor seals (*Phoca vitulina*). This is also a prime spot to watch for osprey (*Pandion haliaetus*), who nest on a nearby channel marker and trees. The birds can sometimes be seen flying with fish in their talons. The causeway near the park entrance is an area frequented by wading birds. Keep an eye out for them after a high tide.

Fort Edgecomb is also the site of several early American military and civilian reenactment exercises each summer. Call ahead for a schedule.

Directions: From Route 1 just across the river from Wiscasset, turn south on Eddy Road, (next to the hotel and restaurant) drive 0.5 mile to Fort Road.

Dates: Open Memorial Day to Labor Day. The grounds are accessible year-round.

Fees: There is a charge for admission.

Closest town: Edgecomb.

For more information: Fort Edgecomb, 66 Fort Road, Edgecomb, ME 04556. Phone (207) 882-7777. Off season, Maine Bureau of Parks and Lands, 22 State House Station, Augusta, ME 04333. Phone (207) 624-6080.

KENNETH STODDARD SHELL MUSEUM

[Fig. 13(19)] This shell museum is on the grounds of a tourist complex that includes miniature golf and an ice cream parlor. It's housed in a covered bridge and is clearly a labor of love for the sons of Kenneth Stoddard, an avid shell collector. Dozens of glass cases hold thousands of seashells, many from the Maine coast but many from all over the world, with typewritten information on each. If you've ever picked up a shell and wondered what it was, chances are you'll find your answer here.

Directions: From Route 1 in Edgecomb, head south on Route 27 until you see Hardwick Road and Dolphin Mini Golf on your left. The shell museum is behind the miniature golf course.

Dates: Daily through the summer.

Fees: No fee, although contributions are accepted.

Closest town: Boothbay.

For more information: Dolphin Mini Golf, Hardwick Road, Route 27, Box 452, Boothbay, ME 04537. Phone (207) 633-4828.

BOOTHBAY REGION LAND TRUST PRESERVES

Since 1980, the Boothbay Region Land Trust has preserved 788 acres of the Boothbay Peninsula, including islands, an old mill site, beaches, wetlands, and wildlife preserves. The preserves listed here are open for day use. Most include easy walking paths.

For more information: Boothbay Region Land Trust, 1 Oak Street, PO Box 183, Boothbay Harbor, ME 04538. Phone (207) 633-4818.

OVENS MOUTH PRESERVE

[Fig. 13(20)] This East Edgecomb preserve is composed of two smaller peninsulas reaching into a tidal basin near the center of the Boothbay Peninsula. There are 1.6 miles of trails to hike on the east peninsula and 3.1 miles of trails on the west peninsula. A footbridge joins the two peninsulas. All trails are blazed and travel along salt marshes and through pine forests. Wildflowers are common at Ovens Mouth. Look for pink lady's slipper (*Cypripedium acaule*) and bluebead lily (*Clintonia borealis*) in early summer in the forest. The lady's slipper is one of several orchids that grow in Maine's coastal forests and can be easily recognized by its inflated pouchlike lower petal. The bluebead lily is one of several lilies that grow in the Maine woods. It has small yellow-green flowers and blue berries, which are poisonous.

Directions: From the monument in Boothbay Center, drive north on ME 27 approximately 1.7 miles, take a left on Adams Pond Road. Bear right at the fork on to Dover Road and drive 2 miles. At the junction to Dover Road Extension, bear left to reach the west peninsula. Bear right to reach the east peninsula. There are parking areas on each peninsula.

PORTER PRESERVE

[Fig. 13(21)] This 19-acre preserve at the tip of Barters Island in Boothbay has a lovely 0.8-mile walk that begins in an old spruce and pine forest and wanders along a 0.5-mile of waterfront. There's also a sheltered cove with a sand beach that's a beautiful spot to sit and enjoy the view.

Directions: Driving south on Route 27, take a right at the monument in Boothbay Center onto Corey Lane. In 0.3 mile, bear right at the fork on Barters Island Road and travel 2.2 miles. Bear left on West Side Road; take a left on Kimbaltown Road. Proceed 0.5 mile and turn left at the fork onto a dirt road. The porter Preserve is 0.1 mile up the road on the right. There is a parking area on the right.

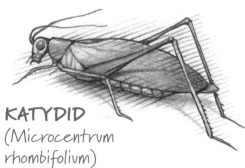

KATYDID
(Microcentrum
rhombifolium)

COLBY WILDLIFE PRESERVE

[Fig. 13(22)] This 12-acre preserve on Salt Marsh Cove in the Damariscotta River in East Edgecomb has a 0.6-mile loop hiking trail. When you're done exploring the preserve, drive up the River Road, a scenic stretch of highway that is a beautiful alternative to Route 27 for travelling from Boothbay to Newcastle and points east on Route 1.

Directions: From the monument in Boothbay Center, travel north on Route 27 for 2.9 miles to River Road. Turn right on River Road and travel 3.2 miles. The preserve is on your right.

SINGING MEADOWS

[Fig. 13(23)] This 16-acre meadow in Edgecomb was once part of an old salt water farm. There's a path through the meadow, which "sings" with the song of birds, crickets, grasshoppers, katydids and cicadas in the spring.

Directions: From Boothbay Center, travel north on Route 27 for 8 miles; turn left on Eddy Road and travel 0.5 mile to Cross Point Road. Turn left, and Singing Meadows is 0.3 mile on the right, after the Eddy School.

DAMARISCOVE ISLAND

[Fig. 13(24)] This island 7 miles south of Boothbay Harbor is a Nature Conservancy preserve and a National Historic Landmark. Its protected harbor and abundant natural resources in the surrounding waters have attracted visitors for hundreds of years. The Abenaki Indians, who called the island *Aquahega*, came to fish and collect. Early European colonists turned it into a major New World port in the 1600s. Damariscove Island was a farming and fishing community until the 1930s, when the last farm family left for the mainland and the U.S. Coast Guard decommissioned its station here. The island has returned to the wild, although signs of its old communities—some buildings and cellar holes—are still visible to hikers.

Today, Damariscove Island is an important nesting area for eiders (*Somateria mollissima*), with more than 500 pairs nesting here each summer. Black guillemots, great black-backed gulls, and herring gulls can also be seen in the summer, and snowy owls winter here. The northern portion of the 2-mile-long island is closed to visitors for the March 15 to August 15 nesting season. The Nature Conservancy has a dock on the harbor and provides brochures and a well-marked trail system.

The virtual lack of trees distinguishes Damariscove from other coastal Maine islands. Bayberry and steeplebush (*Spiraea tomentosa*)—named for their steeple-shaped pink flowers—are the most common plants. Stay on the trails or rocky shore to avoid trampling vegetation or encountering poison ivy.

The Nature Conservancy trail guide points out several interesting features, including a freshwater pond with a cranberry bog, a bayberry thicket that is home to nesting songbirds such as gray catbirds (*Dumetella carolinensis*) and the Bar Cove Beach, where salt-tolerant plants like wild radish and sea rockets grow.

Caretakers live in a small cabin near the dock in the summer. The only other structures on Damariscove Island are a natural and cultural history museum, a reconstructed Coast Guard lookout tower, two small buildings and the old Coast Guard station, which is privately owned.

You need a boat and the ability to navigate through some ledges to get to Damariscove Island. Please note that the harbor and pier are used by fishermen. Camping is not permitted but boats may anchor overnight in the protected harbor.

Directions: By boat, Damariscove Island is 7 miles south of Boothbay Harbor. Consult charts carefully to navigate through the ledges near the harbor and bring a dinghy for landing.

Facilities: Hiking trails.

Dates: Open year-round, but the northern portion of the island is closed to visitors for the Mar. 15 through Aug. 15 nesting season.

Fees: None.

Closest town: Boothbay Harbor, 7 miles.

For more information: The Nature Conservancy, Maine Chapter, Fort Andross, 14 Maine Street, Suite 401, Brunswick, ME 04011. Phone (207) 729-5181.

DODGE POINT PRESERVE

[Fig. 13(25)] The 506-acre Dodge Point Preserve sits near the top of the peninsula in Newcastle. It has more than 8,000 feet of frontage on the Damariscotta River with beaches popular for picnics and swimming. There is also striped bass, bluefish, and mackerel fishing. A well-maintained series of trails winds through a red pine forest for hiking and cross-country skiing.

Hunting is permitted here, but loaded firearms are not permitted on marked hiking trails and may not be discharged within 300 feet of trails or the parking area. This is State Reserved Land operated by the state Bureau of Public Lands with the help of the Damariscotta River Association.

Directions: From Route 1 in Newcastle, follow the River Road south for about 2.5 miles. Dodge Point will be on your left. There are trail maps at the entrance. Dodge Point can also be reached by boat. There is a public boat ramp 3 miles upriver of the property in the town of Damariscotta.

Activities: Hiking, boating, swimming, hunting, fishing, cross-country skiing.

Dates: Open year-round.

Fees: None.

Closest town: Newcastle, 2.5 miles.

For more information: Damariscotta River Association, PO Box 333, Belvedere Road, Damariscotta, ME 04543. Phone (207) 778-4111.

For hunting information, Maine Department of Inland Fisheries and Wildlife, Information Center, 284 State Street, 41 State House Station, Augusta ME 04333. Phone (207) 287-8000.

MARINE RESOURCES AQUARIUM

[Fig. 13(26)] This aquarium operated by the state Department of Marine Resources is small, but it provides a good close-up look at many kinds of fish that live off the coast of Maine. The most popular displays are several "touch tanks" that allow young and old to handle marine invertebrates, including scallops that clap like castanets when picked up, starfish, sea urchins, crabs, and squirting sea cucumbers. A large tank holds sharks and petting is allowed.

Directions: Follow ME 27 around the harbor to McKown Point. Signs point the way to the aquarium.

Activities: Viewing and handling sea life.

Facilities: Aquarium, shop.

Dates: Open Memorial Day to Columbus Day.

Fees: There is a charge for admission.

Closest town: West Boothbay Harbor.

For more information: Marine Resources Aquarium, McKown Point, West Boothbay Harbor, ME 04538. Phone (207) 633-9559.

GREEN SEA URCHIN
(Strongylocentrotus droebachiensis)

NATURE CRUISES

Several companies offer cruises that go in search of whales, puffins, and other wildlife. Others head for deep sea fishing grounds.

CAP'N FISH CRUISES. Wharf Street, Boothbay Harbor, has cruises for whale-watchers, seal-watchers and puffin-watchers. *(207) 633-3244.*

BALMY DAY CRUISES. Pier 8, Commercial Street, Boothbay Harbor, has nature cruises, harbor trips and a cruise to Monhegan Island. *(207) 633-2284.*

NIGHT LIFE ON THE BOOTHBAY PENINSULA

Most of the night life on this peninsula is found in Boothbay Harbor, which is hopping in the summer and slows down considerably during the cooler months.

GRAY'S WHARF. Pier One, Boothbay Harbor. This waterfront nightspot has dancing every night in the summer. There's also light food, video games and pool tables. *(207) 633-5629.*

CAROUSEL MUSIC THEATER. Route 27, Boothbay Harbor. This supper club is open nightly in the summer. *(207) 633-5297.*

DINING ON THE BOOTHBAY PENINSULA

Boothbay Harbor and the other towns on the peninsula are loaded with places to eat, from hot dog stands and lobster shacks to British-style tea rooms and gourmet dining rooms.

ROBINSON'S WHARF. Route 27, Southport Island. Lobster is the obvious specialty at this sprawling harborside wharf, but there's a variety of other takeout-style items. Try the grilled lobster sandwich. Eat inside or out. *Inexpensive. (207) 633-3830.*

🦞 LODGING ON THE BOOTHBAY PENINSULA

The peninsula has many big old inns and resorts that date back to the area's popularity with the "rusticators" in the late nineteenth century. Smaller B&Bs also dot the peninsula.

THE ALBONEGAN. Capitol Island. This old-fashioned waterfront inn has lots of return business. Spend an afternoon on its peaceful porch and an evening next to its big stone fireplace and you'll see why. *Moderate to expensive. (207) 633-2521.*

OCEAN POINT INN. East Boothbay. Only 15 minutes from Boothbay Harbor, this inn seems far removed from the hustle and bustle and has a beautiful ocean view. Its motel and cottages have fairly modern décor. *Moderate. (207) 633-4200.*

Pemaquid Peninsula

The jagged Pemaquid Peninsula begins in the calm waters of Salt Bay and ends in the dramatic surf at Pemaquid Point. It reaches down to the Gulf of Maine between Johns Bay and Muscongus Bay.

This peninsula has many natural sites but most visitors seem to drive directly to its most famous, Pemaquid Point. They are missing out on some wonderful bits of history and some beautiful spots to observe coastal plants and wildlife.

This region also has some charming little towns. The riverfront towns of Damariscotta and Newcastle sit at the top of the peninsula on Route 1. New Harbor is a lovely fishing village where visitors can eat a lobster or catch a boat for a puffin-watching trip.

🦞 SALT BAY

[Fig. 13(27)] The 2-square-mile bay at the head of the Damariscotta River estuary is a fascinating spot to explore both for its wildlife and its ancient history. Its mix of tidal salt marsh, mud flats, and eelgrass meadows create a rich habitat for birds and marine life.

The Salt Bay is prime bird-watching territory, both for migrants that come to feed in the spring and fall and for breeding birds that nest nearby. Look for the unmistakable hooded merganser (*Lophodytes cucullatus*), common goldeneye (*Bucphala clangula*), and other ducks during migration. Bald eagles, osprey, and American bittern nest nearby. The great blue heron can also be seen wading in the shallows. Pileated woodpeckers (*Dryocopus pileatus*) can be heard and seen in the woods. In the spring, young American eels or elvers (*Anguilla rostrata*) come here after a long journey from north of the West Indies. In May, the fish ladder between the bay and

Damariscotta Lake is alive with alewives heading to their spawning grounds.

The Damariscotta River Association headquarters is housed in the Salt Bay Farm Heritage Center, a 100-acre farm on the eastern shore of the bay. It's available for walking, bird-watching, cross-country skiing, or sledding. The association also sponsors bird walks and other activities, including an archeology field school, hawk watches, and canoe trips.

Directions: Heading north on Route 1 in Newcastle, turn left on Belvedere Road to the Salt Bay Farm.

Activities: Hiking, bird-watching, cross-country skiing, sledding.

Dates: Open year-round, daylight hours.

For more information: Damariscotta River Association, Belvedere Road, PO Box 333, Damariscotta, ME 04543. Phone (207) 563-1393.

SALT BAY PRESERVE HERITAGE TRAIL

[Fig. 13(28)] The Salt Bay Preserve Heritage Trail is a 3-mile-long path that heads across a small salt marsh and mud flat where Atlantic horseshoe crabs (*Limulus polyphemus*) and their cast-off shells can often be seen in the summer. It then takes in a beautiful stretch of the Salt Bay (there are several spots to relax on the rocks and watch for birds feasting or resting) before heading to an archaeological treasure, the Glidden Middens. The middens are ancient Indian oyster shell

Horseshoe Crabs

Horseshoe crabs (*Limulus polyphemus*) aren't crabs at all. They have their own class, Merostomata, and are more closely related to arachnids like ticks and spiders than crustaceans. Horseshoe crabs have a definite prehistoric look and are called living fossils because they have not evolved in hundreds of millions of years. Horseshoe crabs aren't dangerous and use their sharp-looking tails as rudders, not weapons. Horseshoe crabs are abundant along the middle Atlantic coast, where they crawl onto open beaches to mate. In Maine, the northern limit of their range, they are much less common and come ashore in only a handful of protected spots. At Salt Bay near Damariscotta, the horseshoe crabs can be seen every June, crawling into the intertidal mud flats to mate.

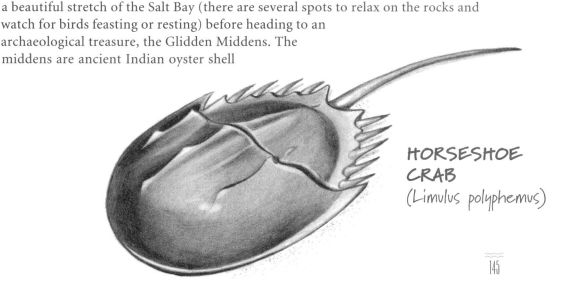

HORSESHOE CRAB
(Limulus polyphemus)

heaps built up over 1,500 years of feasts. The 30-foot-tall Glidden Middens are an impressive sight, especially considering that the white shells, some ground to dust and others still whole, date back 2,400 years. This midden and smaller oyster shell heaps found along the river's banks are included in the National Register of Historic Places and federal law protects them from any disturbance.

After the shell heaps, the trail concludes by winding through some woodlands and wetlands. This hike is easy and beautiful but it can be wet, especially at high tide when detours may be necessary. Waterproof shoes are recommended. This path crosses some private land, so stay on the trail.

Directions: From Route 1 in Damariscotta, head north on Mills Road, or ME 215, for about 1 mile. The Lincoln County Publishing Company, which permits hikers to use its parking lot, is on the left. Park on the far side of the lot, away from the buildings. Cross ME 215 to the marked trailhead and get a map.

For more information: Damariscotta River Association. Phone (207) 563-1393.

THE DAMARISCOTTA MILLS FISH LADDER

[Fig. 13(29)] The May spawning season for alewives (*Alosa pseudoharengus*) creates an unforgettable scene at the 50-foot fish ladder between Salt Bay and Damariscotta Lake. As the schools of silvery fish try to climb the series of steps to their spawning ground, scores of seagulls, ospreys, eagles, and even seals arrive to feast on the migrating alewives.

Directions: From Route 1 in Damariscotta, head north on ME 215 to Damariscotta Mills. The alewife ladder is behind an old fish-packing plant, near the intersection with Austin Road. Parking is available.

For more information: Damariscotta River Association. Phone (207) 563-1393.

DAMARISCOTTA REVERSING FALLS

[Fig. 13(30)] Reversing falls are phenomena caused by tides, typically at a narrow stretch in a tidal river. The Maine coast, with its many tidal rivers, has several reversing falls. At a reversing falls, river water runs toward the sea at low tide. As the tide rises, the seawater surges back up through the river narrows, working against the river flow and causing rapids and eddies. The calm time between the two tides is called slack tide. Reversing falls are a popular place for experienced kayak and canoe paddlers. Beginners shouldn't attempt to paddle in this or any reversing falls.

On the Damariscotta, the tides create a reversing falls at the narrows between the river and Salt Bay. Check a local paper or tide calendar to see when high tide will occur.

Directions: The reversing falls can be accessed by either the Route 1 bridge or ME 129-130 bridge over the Damariscotta River.

RACHEL CARSON SALT POND PRESERVE

[Fig. 13(31)] This preserve in New Harbor is dedicated to environmental pioneer Rachel Carson, who did research at this salt pond for her 1955 bestseller, *The Edge of the Sea.* Carson, whose later work, *Silent Spring,* helped spawn the modern environmental movement, was a founder of the Maine Chapter of The Nature Conservancy, which owns the preserve.

Most of the 78-acre preserve is on former farmland across ME 32 from the ocean. Old logging roads and walking trails wander through a hardwood and softwood forest.

But the highlight of the preserve is the 0.25-acre tidal pool on the shores of Muscongus Bay. This spacious tidal pool, when examined near low tide, is an ideal piece of Maine's rocky intertidal zone for amateur naturalists to explore. Mussels, crabs, periwinkles, and barnacles are often found here. Starfish and green sea urchins sometimes appear. Three easily distinguished types of seaweed—rock-weed, knotted wrack and Irish moss—can be studied up close.

But these typical inhabitants of tidal pools don't appear randomly within this or any other pool. They take their place in a layer of horizontal zones depending on how much dry air they can endure at low tide.

Explore the Salt Pond at low tide thinking of it in three distinct layers: the splash zone just above the high tide mark, the intertidal zone alternately exposed to air and submerged in salt water depending on the tide, and the subtidal zone that stays submerged.

The splash zone, which can be just one step away from dry land, tends to be marked with a black, slippery smudge. That black mark is blue-green algae, tiny plants that cluster together in colonies covered by a gelatinous film that prevents them from drying out. Only upon close inspection do these tiny creatures appear to be anything but a stain on the rocks. But they contain chlorophyll and produce

Rachel Carson

Rachel Carson's 1962 landmark book, *Silent Spring*, helped launch the environmental movement by alerting the nation to the dangers of pesticides.

Carson, a marine biologist who worked for the U.S. Fish and Wildlife Service, was already a popular and respected nature writer when *Silent Spring* was published. Her 1951 work, *The Sea Around Us*, was on the best-seller lists for more than a year and won a National Book Award.

Carson (1907-1964) had a summer home on Southport Island, near the end of the Boothbay Peninsula. It was there that she did much of the research for her 1955 book, *The Edge of the Sea*, exploring tide pools and salt ponds.

Today, a pool she used to visit in New Harbor is a Nature Conservancy preserve named in her honor. A national wildlife refuge along the southern Maine coast that provides important resting and feeding areas for birds migrating on the Atlantic flyway is also named for Carson.

Carson's last book, *The Sense of Wonder*, was published posthumously in 1965 and reissued in 1998. She wrote it as a magazine essay entitled *Helping Your Child to Wonder*, in which she urged parents to explore nature with their children.

Carson, who came under heavy criticism from the chemical industry over *Silent Spring*, died in 1964.

oxygen. The Salt Pond is home to three different kinds of periwinkle. One of these, the rough periwinkle (*Littorina saxatalis*) can endure long periods out of the water and can be seen here, where it crawls across the rocks, eating algae.

The intertidal zone, which is alternately exposed and submerged twice a day in the North Atlantic, is home to marine organisms that can survive in the open air for varying portions of the day. Here at the Salt Pond, that includes the common periwinkle (*Littorina littorea*), northern rock barnacles (*Balanus balanoides*), and blue mussels (*Mytilus edulids*).

Common periwinkles withstand time out of the water by sealing themselves to rocks with mucus during low tide to keep the inside of their shells moist. These little snails, which are smooth or finely ridged, are also equipped to breathe air for small amounts of time. They are the most common snails in New England and can be found by the scores all over the intertidal zone, here at the Salt Pond and all along the Maine coast.

The hard white bumps clustered on many of the rocks in the intertidal zone are northern rock barnacles. These white lumps are actually a system of shell-like plates that overlap to encase the barnacle in a hard little cone. At low tide, four plates close over the top like a trap door, shutting the dry air out. When the water again flows over the barnacle, the trap door opens and the barnacle's feathery legs dangle out, filtering food from the water. Once a barnacle has attached itself to a rock, it can't move. But every tide delivers a fresh supply of microorganisms for it to filter through and eat. It's easy to observe a barnacle open in shallow water, but keep in mind that the edges of its shell are sharp.

The blue mussel is one of a few bivalves that spend low tide lying out in the open instead of digging into the sand. Mussels tend to settle in clusters and attach themselves to rocks with a series of tough, hair-thin strings secreted from a gland. While their bond is not necessarily permanent, mussels, too, rely on the tide to deliver nourishment that they can filter from the water.

COMMON PERIWINKLE
(*Littorina littorea*)

The subtidal zone is home to animals that need to stay submerged, including a third type of periwinkle, the smooth periwinkle (*Littorina obtusata*). Green crabs (*Carcinus maenas*) are plentiful at Salt Pond, as are hermit crabs (*Pagurus longicarpus*). Green sea urchins (*Strongylocentrotus droebachiensis*) and northern sea stars (*Asterias vulgaris*) can be seen in this zone occasionally.

While some of the pool's inhabitants rely on the incoming tide for food, others prey on the marine life in the pool. Dog whelks (*Thais lapillus*), carnivorous snails slightly larger than periwinkles, drill holes in mussels, barnacles, and periwinkles. Starfish are predators of mussels. Occasionally one can be seen, its feet wrapped around each side of the mussel, slowly and patiently prying the shell open. Once the shell is open a crack, the starfish extends it stomach into the mussel shell to eat the mussel.

The periwinkles, mussels, and barnacles are permanent residents here. But often fish, which are typically here for the duration of the low tide, are washed in.

Most of the brownish green seaweed piled around the intertidal zone is rockweed (*Fucus vesiculosus*) and knotted wrack (*Ascophyllum nodosum*). The bulbs growing out of the seaweed's branches are actually air bladders that help the plant float at high tide and ensure it gets enough sun. At low tide, Irish moss (*Chondrus crispus*), a species of red algae, can be seen covering the lower rocks in the pool.

Since this is a nature preserve, please refrain from tossing rocks or collecting plants or shells. A list of this and other rules can be found at the registration box.

Directions: From Damariscotta, drive south on ME 130 for 10 miles to New Harbor. Turn left on ME 32 and continue about 1 mile to the salt pond. The sign for the preserve is on the right. Park along the side of the road. To prevent beach erosion, The Nature Conservancy asks that visitors use the steps by the registration box for beach access.

Activities: Hiking, tidal pool exploration.

Facilities: An interpretive brochure with a trail map is available at the registration box next to the preserve sign.

Dates: Open year round.

Fees: None.

Closest town: New Harbor.

For more information: The Nature Conservancy, Maine Chapter, Fort Andross, 14 Maine Street, Suite 401, Brunswick, ME 04011. Phone (207) 729-5181.

LAVERNA PRESERVE

[Fig. 13(32)] This Nature Conservancy preserve includes 3,600 feet of shoreline on Muscongus Bay. This stretch of rugged shoreline is remarkable for its diversity. There are some steep cliffs, a gravel beach and a dense spruce forest. In July and August, scan the damp spots here for the insectivorous plant sundew (*Drosera rotundifolia*) a small, white flower that traps insects on its sticky leaves and digests them.

Directions: The LaVerna is accessible only by boat (with some difficulty) until The Nature Conservancy arranges mainland access across private land from New Harbor. Check the status of access with The Nature Conservancy.

Activities: Birding, shoreline exploration.

Dates: Open year-round.

Fees: None.

Closest town: New Harbor.

For more information: The Nature Conservancy, Maine Chapter, Fort Andross, 14 Maine Street, Suite 401, Brunswick, ME 04011. Phone (207) 729-5181.

COLONIAL PEMAQUID

[Fig. 13(33)] This historic site on a point of land at the mouth of the Pemaquid River in Bristol offers archaeology and history lessons. Some of Maine's earlier European settlers lived here around 1625. Archaeological excavations have found 14 foundations of seventeenth and eighteenth century buildings. There are signs describing the digs and a museum of unearthed artifacts, including tools, coins, and pottery. There is also a 1908 reconstruction of the stone Fort William Henry, which the French and Indians destroyed in 1696.

After exploring the archeological site, the fort, and the museum, have a picnic on the grounds, which slope nicely down to Pemaquid Harbor.

Directions: From Route 1 in Damariscotta, follow ME 129 south for 4 miles, then take Route 130 to Colonial Pemaquid.

Dates: The museum, fort, and archeological sites are open Memorial Day to Labor Day. The grounds are accessible year-round.

Fees: There is a fee for admission.

Closest town: New Harbor.

For more information: Colonial Pemaquid, PO Box 117, New Harbor, ME 04554. Phone (207) 677-2423.

PEMAQUID BEACH PARK

[Fig. 13(34)] Cool off after a visit to Colonial Pemaquid with a stop at Pemaquid Beach. This 0.5-mile-long town beach is very popular, especially with families, so be prepared for crowds on warm days.

Directions: From Colonial Pemaquid, continue on Route 130 to the beach, which has a parking lot.

Activities: Swimming.

Facilities: Bathhouses, snack bar. No lifeguard.

Dates: Open summer days.

Fees: There is charge for admission.

Closest town: Pemaquid Beach.

For more information: Pemaquid Beach Park, Route 130, Pemaquid Beach, ME 04554. Phone (207) 677-2754.

MENIGAWAM PRESERVE

[Fig. 13(35)] It's called "Hodgdon's Island" on most maps. The locals call it "Stratton Island" for the Louisiana family that spent summers here for years before allowing it to return to nature and then donating it to The Damariscotta River Association, which calls it "Menigawam," the name the Strattons gave their cottage. Whatever it's called, this 30-acre wooded island in the Damariscotta River west of South Bristol is worth a visit, although visiting requires a boat. A walking trail follows the shore around the island, past an osprey nesting spot, and some small Indian oyster shell heaps left over from feasts centuries ago, to a cove popular with seals and a beach. The ruins of the Strattons' log cabin are dangerous and off-limits.

Directions: The best place to land a canoe, kayak, or other small boat is at Boat House Beach on the northeast corner of the island.

Activities: Hiking, bird-watching.

Dates: Open year-round, days only.

Fees: None.

Closest town: South Bristol.

For more information: Damariscotta River Association, PO Box 333, Damariscotta, ME 04543. Phone (207) 563-1393.

WITCH ISLAND SANCTUARY

[Fig. 13(36)] This 18-mile sanctuary about 0.25 mile off the coast of South Bristol is named for the "Witch of Wall Street," a resident in the late 1800s famous for her reported ability to foretell people's financial futures. There's a scenic shoreline trail and two beaches for swimming.

Directions: From Damariscotta, follow Route 129 to South Bristol. Park just past the drawbridge. You may put a small boat in at the town landing. Row under the bridge and head north past Gem Island to Witch Island. Plan on about 15 minutes of rowing.

Activities: Boating, swimming, picnicking.

Facilities: Trail, beaches.

Dates: Open year-round.

Fees: None.

Closest town: South Bristol.

For more information: Maine Audubon Society, 118 Route 1, Falmouth ME 04105. Phone (207) 781-2330.

Elvers

Every spring, tiny transparent eels called elvers make their way into the tidal rivers and estuaries of the East Coast.

These young American eels (*Anguilla rostratra*) have had a long trip. American eels spawn in the Sargasso Sea, north of the West Indies and 1,000 miles east of Florida. The larvae spend a year or longer drifting and swimming to feeding grounds in North America.

The 2- or 3-inch-long "glass eels" swim upriver to fresh water, where they may stay for 20 years and grow to be 3 feet long. They then swim downriver to the Atlantic and then back too the Sargasso Sea to spawn and die.

These eels are *catadromous* fish, meaning they spend most of their lives in rivers and head out to sea to spawn. Every other migratory fish in Maine is an *anadromous* fish, which lives in the ocean but spawns in rivers.

Elvers are in high demand in the Far East, where they are raised to adult size for the fine dining market.

When the market is right, the tiny glass eels can command hundreds of dollars a pound, making them the most valuable fish, per-pound, on the Maine coast.

A spirited and competitive fishing industry has grown around the tiny eels during the 1990s.

Elvers burrow into the mud during the day and migrate at night, so elver fishermen are most likely to be found tending their fine-mesh nets at night along many coastal rivers and streams in Maine.

HOG ISLAND AUDUBON CAMP

[Fig. 13(37)] The National Audubon Society operates an adult nature study camp here, with programs in field ornithology, ecology, nature study by kayak, and other topics. There is also a program for youths and occasional camp programs for families. Visitors are welcome to hike the trails on this 300-acre island, but there's no boat transportation provided for people not attending the camp. There is a dock near the north end of the island, and visitors should check in at the office there before roaming.

HOCKAMOCK TRAIL

The camp also has a more easily accessible 1-mile nature trail on the mainland. It's an easy walk through the woods, along the shore and through a meadow. Nature trail guides are provided at the National Audubon office.

Directions: From Route 1 in Waldoboro, take Route 32 south to Bremen. Take a right on Keene Neck road. The office and trailhead are on your right.

Activities: Hiking, bird-watching.

Facilities: Nature trail.

Dates: The ecology camp operates in the summer. The nature trail is open year-round.

Fees: None for nature trail.

Closest town: Bremen.

For more information: Audubon Ecology Camps and Workshops, National Audubon Society, 613 Riversville Road, Greenwich, CT 06831. Summers, phone (207) 529-5148. Off-season, phone (207) 529-5148.

DAMARISCOTTA-PEMAQUID RIVER CANOE TRAIL

Expert paddlers may contact Native Trails, an organization that identifies and maps old Indian canoe routes, for a map to this 40-mile trail that loops down and across the peninsula via the Damariscotta and Pemaquid rivers. Native Trails has also mapped an ancient canoe route from Penobscot Bay in Rockland to Merrymeeting Bay that it calls "Wawenock Ahwangan."

For more information: Native Trails, PO Box 240, Waldoboro, ME 04572. Phone (207) 832-5255.

PEMAQUID POINT

[Fig. 13(38)] This spectacular point, where the surf crashes onto the rocks beneath the scenic Pemaquid Lighthouse, is a magnet for tourists, who can often be seen scrambling down the rocks to photograph the lighthouse from its most dramatic angle. Use great caution when approaching the sea here, rogue waves have been known to pull sightseers into the surf. The 1827 lighthouse is not open to the public, but the former lighthouse keeper's house is the Fisherman's Museum, which is packed with exhibits on local mariners, the fishing industry, and the lighthouse's history.

The lighthouse offers an interesting sight for bird watchers: the mud nests of cliff swallows (*Hirundo pyrrhonota*) tucked under the eaves of the lighthouse tower. These birds, which summer here and winter in South America, build their nests out of mud pellets gathered from wetlands. Each gourdlike nest contains 1,000 or more pellets.

The geology at Pemaquid contributes to the drama of the point. The striped and sparkling layers of rock that seem to almost pour down into the surf are a form of bedrock typical of this region. The bedrock was formed about 400 million years ago when layers of sediment were folded and pressed by the clashing of continental plates. Some of the rock melted and flowed into cracks and crevices, creating dikes and sills of pegmatite granite.

The bedrock is exposed to view and open to examination on much of Maine's famed rocky coast, its layers giving out clues to the earth's history. Just a few feet inland, the bedrock is concealed by sediment and soil.

Directions: From Route 1 in Damariscotta, follow ME 130 south for about 15 miles to Pemaquid Point.

Activities: Sight-seeing.

Facilities: Scenic lookout, museum.

Dates: The museum is open from Memorial Day weekend until mid-Oct. The grounds are accessible year-round.

Fees: There is a charge for admission.

Closest town: New Harbor.

For more information: Fishermen's Museum, Pemaquid Lighthouse, New Harbor, ME 045554. Phone (207) 677-2494.

EASTERN EGG ROCK

[Fig. 13(39)] Puffins are something of an icon in Maine, adorning T-shirts, postcards and coffee mugs in souvenir shops up and down the coast. (Instead of posting a "No Smoking" sign, many businesses opt for a picture of a puffin with an X across it.) But while it is easy to find puffin-emblazoned souvenirs, seeing an actual puffin (*Fratercula artica*) takes some work.

This tiny island in Muscongus Bay is the easiest of the puffins' nesting islands to view. It's also the site of the first successful puffin restoration project. The National Audubon Society's Project Puffin transplanted puffin chicks from Newfoundland here in the 1970s. The puffins eventually started returning to Eastern Egg Rock to nest, and Project Puffin was a success.

Stephen W. Kress, the ornithologist behind Project Puffin, helped write a children's book on the restoration project entitled *Project Puffin: How We Brought Puffins to Egg Rock*. If you've got a child in your party, make sure to pick up a copy.

Puffins may be the stars of the show, but there are other birds nesting here, as well, including roseate terns (*Sterna dougallii*). All the birds must be admired from the boat, as landings are not permitted.

Directions: Two tour boat companies offer trips to Eastern Egg Rock. Hardy Boat Cruises of New Harbor, phone (207) 677-2026, and Atlantic Expeditions of Rockland, phone (207) 372-8621. The Maine Audubon Society usually sponsors a trip here each summer. Maine Audubon Society, PO Box 6009, Falmouth, ME 04105. Phone (207) 781-2330.

DINING ON OR NEAR THE PEMAQUID PENINSULA

From Damariscotta to Pemaquid Point, there's no shortage of good food, whether you are in the mood for fine dining or eating on a wharf.

PACO'S TACOS. Main Street, Damariscotta. This cozy downtown spot serves a wide variety of Mexican dishes for lunch and dinner every day but Sunday. *Inexpensive. (207) 563-5355.*

SHAW'S FISH & LOBSTER WHARF. Route 32, New Harbor. This wharf in a truly scenic working harbor has lobster and other items inside or out. *Inexpensive to moderate. (207) 677-2200.*

COVESIDE. Christmas Cove, Bristol. The Coveside, which also has a comfortable motel and an inn, caters to the yacht crowd and there are always world-class boats docked outside to admire. There's a bar plus a restaurant serving three meals a day of fish or other fare. *Moderate. Phone (207) 644-8282*

LODGING ON THE PEMAQUID PENINSULA

BRADLEY INN. Pemaquid Point Road, New Harbor. This comfortable Victorian inn has 12 guestrooms plus a dining room and pub popular with tourists and locals. *Moderate to expensive. Phone (207) 677-2105.*

YE OLDE FORTE CABINS. Pemaquid Beach. These cabins next to Fort William Henry have half-baths and shared shower rooms. *Moderate. Phone (207) 677-2261.*

Friendship Peninsula

This quiet peninsula juts into Muscongus Bay between the Medomak and Meduncook rivers and is dotted with beautiful coves and harbors that are home to many lobster boats. This peninsula is also popular with sea kayakers. At the peninsula's tip, the town of Friendship has a long history in sailing circles. It is the birthplace of the Friendship sloop, a single masted sailboat known for its seaworthiness. Friendship sloops were used by Maine fishermen in the late nineteenth century. Now they are a popular recreational sailboat. Reach the peninsula from the town of Waldoboro along Route 1. Waldoboro was once a busy shipbuilding town. The first five-masted schooner, the *Governor Ames*, was built here in 1884. Now Waldoboro is home to a variety of businesses, including the monthly newspaper *Maine Antiques Digest* and Borealis Breads, a bakery that sends delicious loaves to restaurants and shops up and down the coast. (The bakery also has a retail store, so stop by for some olive bread, rosemary focaccia, or other Borealis specialties.)

DINING ON THE FRIENDSHIP PENINSULA

One of the Maine coast's most famous restaurants isn't a lobster shack, it's a diner. That's just one of several interesting restaurants in and around Waldoboro.

MOODY'S DINER. Route 1, Waldoboro. Tourists and locals have been filling the booths and the counter of this Route 1 institution since the 1930s. There's some seafood on the menu, but many of Moody's patrons are looking for a break from lobster and prefer heaping plates of macaroni and cheese and other down-home dishes, to be followed by Moody's famous pies and thick milkshakes. *Inexpensive. Phone (207) 832-7785.*

PINE CONE CAFÉ. Friendship Street, Waldoboro. This casual gourmet spot has great vegetarian fare, soups, and seafood, as well as nice water views from the deck. *Inexpensive to moderate. (207) 832-6337.*

LODGING ON THE FRIENDSHIP PENINSULA

The Peninsula has several bed and breakfast inns, including some that cater to sea kayakers.

THE OUTSIDERS' INN B&B. Harbor Road, Friendship. This inn offers kayak rentals and lessons as well as rooms in a historic home. *Moderate. (207) 832-5197.*

FRIENDSHIP HARBOR HOUSE. This inn, operated by the people at the Maine Sport outdoors school just up the coast in Rockport, is billed as a kayaker's bed and breakfast. Kayak rentals and tours are available. *Moderate to expensive. (207) 832-7447.*

The Thomaston Area

Thomaston sits at the top of the Cushing and Saint George peninsulas, which lie on either side of the St. George River. Both peninsulas have sites worth exploring. The St. George peninsula is the departure point for boat trips to Monhegan, a mecca for birders and artists alike.

The town of Thomaston has a beautiful collection of historic homes, evidence of its prominence as a shipping center in the nineteenth century. It also has a 1930s reproduction of the home of General Henry Knox, President Washington's secretary of war.

Thomaston is also home to the Maine State Prison, which operates the Maine State Prison Store on Route 1, with a wide variety of inmate-made merchandise, mostly of wood. The showroom is worth a stop, especially if you're in the market for some plain pine furniture.

MAINE WATERCRAFT MUSEUM

[Fig. 13(40)] You can do more than look at classic wooden boats at this museum on the waterfront in Thomaston; you can rent them by the hour. There are 130 boats on display at this museum dedicated to honoring the art of Maine boat-making and restoring and preserving its boats. Among them are old Rangeley guide boats, birch-bark canoes, and classic mahogany outboard motorboats.

Directions: From Route 1 in Thomaston, follow Knox Street three blocks to the waterfront.

Dates: Open May to Oct. and by appointment.

Fees: There is a charge for admission.

Closest town: Thomaston.

For more information: Maine Watercraft Museum, 4 Knox Street Landing, Thomaston ME 04861. Phone (207) 354-0444.

OLSON HOUSE

[Fig. 13(41)] In "Christina's World," one of Andrew Wyeth's most famous paintings, Christina Olson sits in a golden field, leaning toward a weathered old farmhouse. Olson was a lifelong neighbor of Wyeth's wife in Cushing and was the subject of many Wyeth paintings. She spent most of her life in the house in that painting. Olson House is now open to the public, as part of the Farnsworth Art Museum in nearby Rockland. Wyeth fans headed to Rockland to see the extensive collection of the Wyeth Center at the Farnsworth will want to stop here and appreciate the quiet ruggedness of the landscape and the house, where Wyeth prints are hung in the bare rooms that inspired their originals. Some visitors are drawn to the field, where Wyeth's famous painting captured the disabled Christina pulling herself through the grass. Some people pose for photographs, while others set up easels to try the same vantage point as Wyeth.

Directions: From Route 1 in Thomaston, turn onto Wadsworth Street next to the Prison Store. Take a left at Fales & Son Store, and another left on Hathorn Point Road.

Dates: Open Memorial Day weekend to Columbus Day.

Fees: There is a charge for admission.

Closest town: Thomaston.

For more information: Farnsworth Art Museum, 352 Main Street, Rockland, ME 0484.1 Phone (207) 596-6457.

THE GEORGES RIVER SCENIC BYWAY AND BIKEWAYS

[Fig. 13(42)] The Georges River Land Trust has mapped a 50-mile scenic drive from inland Liberty along the St. George River to the tip of the St. George Peninsula in Port Clyde. Motorists can follow the river as it meanders into Thomaston and down the peninsula to Muscongus Bay.

The land trust also provides maps to suggested bike rides along lightly traveled roads in the St. George River watershed. The Headwaters Region and Middle Region routes have some steep hills and rough terrain and are best done on a mountain bike.

The Saltwater Region, which is south of Route 1 to the base of the Cushing Peninsula, has smaller hills and is a smoother ride but the road shoulders are narrow. Mileage for all three sections of the bikeway depends on the route you choose. An entire day could easily be spent pedaling the Saltwater Region.

For more information: The Georges River Land Trust, 328 Maine Street, Studio 206, Rockland, ME 04841. Phone (207) 594-5166. Maps are available at Chamber of Commerce offices in the area.

MARSHALL POINT LIGHTHOUSE MUSEUM

[Fig. 13(43)] It's not unusual to see photographers and painters on the lawn of the Marshall Point Lighthouse in Port Clyde. The simple white light tower sits against the beautiful background of Port Clyde Harbor, making for a lovely scene to capture on canvas or film. A museum in the lighthouse keeper's house contains local memorabilia. The grounds are open for picnics or sight-seeing.

Directions: Take ME 131 into Port Clyde. Follow signs to the lighthouse.

Dates: The museum is open May to Oct. Grounds accessible year-round.

Fees: None, contributions accepted.

Closest town: Port Clyde.

For more information: Marshall Point Lighthouse Museum, Marshall Point Road, PO Box 247, Port Clyde, ME 04855. Phone (207) 372-6450.

WALDO TYLER WILDLIFE MANAGEMENT AREA

[Fig. 13(44)] This tidal salt marsh on the Weskeag River in South Thomaston attracts many wading birds and ducks, but it takes some effort to see them. Like most state wildlife management areas, this 537-acre area has no trail system, and walking through the area is a bit tricky. Canoeing is allowed, but keep in mind that the Weskeag Marsh has strong tides. The tide is especially challenging at the nearby reversing falls in the center of South Thomaston.

Bird watchers should keep in mind that hunting and trapping are allowed here.

Directions: From Route 1 in Thomaston, head south on Buttermilk Lane, next to the Dragon Cement plant. Travel about 1 mile.

Activities: Bird-watching, canoeing, fishing, hunting, trapping.

Closest town: South Thomaston.

For more information: Maine Inland Fisheries and Wildlife, 41 State House Station, Augusta, ME 04333. Phone (207) 547-4165.

ART GALLERIES IN THE THOMASTON AREA

While Andrew Wyeth is undoubtedly this region's most famous painter, he is hardly the only artist to be inspired by the beauty of its land and sea. There are several galleries on the peninsula where artists' work can be admired or purchased. In South Thomaston, Art of the Sea, which is located in an old post office overlooking the reversing falls, specializes in marine art. It has an impressive collection of antique ship and boat models, as well as 10 rooms full of paintings, photos and sculpture related to the sea. Farther down the peninsula, the Port Clyde Arts and Crafts Society has a seasonal gallery for its 60 members.

Directions: From Route 1 in Thomaston, follow Buttermilk Lane south to South Thomaston. Turn right on ME73. Art of the Sea will be on the right. To go on to the Port Clyde Arts and Crafts Society, continue on ME73 to ME131. Head south for about 3.5 miles.

For more information: Art of the Sea. Phone *(207) 594-9396.* Port Clyde Arts and Crafts Society. Phone *(207) 372-0673.*

DINING IN THE THOMASTON AREA

THOMASTON CAFÉ AND BAKERY. 88 Maine Street, Thomaston. This casual breakfast and lunch spot is known for its fish cakes and fish chowder, as well as its imaginative vegetarian fare. *Inexpensive. (207) 354-8589.*

LODGING IN THE THOMASTON AREA

THE EAST WIND INN. Mechanic Street, Tenants Harbor. This elegant inn also has a public dining room specializing in seafood. Along with the inn, there's a cottage with three apartment-like suites. *Expensive. (207) 372-6366.*

THE CRAIGNAIR INN. Clark Island, Spruce Head. This former boarding house was built atop a granite ledge in 1928 to house workers from nearby granite quarries. Most of its simply furnished rooms have shared baths and great views. The former chapel is now an annex to the inn and has rooms with private baths. *Moderate. (207) 594-7644.*

Monhegan

[Fig. 13] Many first-time visitors to Monhegan spend their ferry ride back to the mainland figuring out how to return to this island that measures just 1.7 miles long and 0.5 mile wide. Visitors are attracted by the island's old-fashioned, simple feel (there are no cars and no streetlights, and fewer than 100 residents), its 17 miles of hiking trails, or the 600 kinds of wildflowers and 200 species of birds that have been identified here.

For some, it's just the way the light hits the island and its dark, hulking headlands that rise over the sea. Many painters, including some of America's most famous—Edward Hopper, Rockwell Kent, Robert Henri, George Bellows and Jamie Wyeth—have come to paint. That's not to mention the countless amateurs or not-yet-famous who can be seen carting easels or other art supplies off the ferry from Port Clyde or wandering the paths with sketchbooks in hand. The island remains an artists' colony in the summertime, and several artists usually open their studios to the public on any given day. (Check the bulletin board near the ferry landing for that day's schedule.)

Thanks to the foresight of some early conservationists, including Thomas Edison, son of the inventor, all development on Monhegan is clustered on the east side of the island. The rest of the island's 700 acres are preserved for those wishing to enjoy its natural beauty.

The summer boat schedule allows for day trips to Monhegan. But spend a night here to get the full flavor of the place. A few notes for visitors: If you're staying overnight, make reservations. There are only a handful of inns and B&Bs and camping is not allowed. Bring a flashlight; it gets dark at night, even if it's not foggy. Bring an extra sweater and a windbreaker. And bring long pants as protection against the deer ticks that carry Lyme disease.

Directions: Year-round ferry service is available from Port Clyde aboard the Monhegan-Thomaston Boat Line's *Laura B* or *Elizabeth Ann*. Reservations are recommended. Phone (207) 372-8848.

Seasonal ferry service is available from New Harbor aboard Hardy Boat Cruises, phone (207) 677-2026, and from Boothbay Harbor aboard Balmy Day Cruises, phone (207) 633-2284.

TRAILS ON MONHEGAN

Monhegan has 17 miles of trails that wander around its often dramatic coastline and across its quiet interior. A map is available at most island businesses. Note that the map does not give mileage and it is not to scale, so examine it carefully when planning your hike, especially if you are a day tripper and need to catch the boat back to Port Clyde.

Many of the trails intersect, so visitors can spend an hour or all day exploring this special place. The trails are numbered and marked with fairly inconspicuous signs nailed to trees.

CATHEDRAL WOODS TRAIL: [Fig. 13(45)] A good choice for the day tripper. This easy trail wanders through a forest of towering red spruce and is, indeed, as quiet as a church.

CLIFF TRAIL: [Fig. 13(46)] Try this only if you're spending the night. This strenuous trail winds around the perimeter of the island, crossing some beautiful but steep rocky headlands. Allow at least five hours for this trail.

OTHER TRAILS: The Cliff Trail can be reached (or departed) via a handful of much less strenuous trails, including the Whitehead Trail, Burnthead Trail, and Blackhead Trail. These three trails take a direct route across the island to some of Monhegan's most scenic vistas.

It's possible to take any of these trails, which are less than 0.5 mile each, to a section of the Cliff Trail, then use another easy trail to get back to the main road and Ferry Landing.

BIRDING ON MONHEGAN

Bird watchers flock to this island with the same reliability as the migrating birds. The appeal is obvious. Birders say they have seen 100 or more different kinds of birds in a single day on Monhegan. The island's isolated location makes it an inviting stop for all kinds of migrants in the spring and fall.

In one fall afternoon, a sharp-eyed visitor could hope to observe a wide variety of birds, including peregrine falcons (*Falco peregrinus*), and other hawks, several varieties of warbler, Eastern phoebes (*Sayomis phoebe*), cedar waxwings (*Bombycila cedrorum*), yellow-bellied sapsucker (*Psphyrapicus varius*), and dozens of others.

While not as busy as the height of the summer season, the spring and fall migration periods are a popular time for visiting Monhegan because of the wonderful bird-watching potential. Plan accordingly and make lodging reservations.

CEDAR WAXWING
(Bombycila cedrorum)

MONHEGAN LIGHT

[Fig. 13(47)] This 1824 granite lighthouse was automated in 1959. It sits on Monhegan's highest hill and has a beautiful view of the village, nearby Manana Island, and the open sea. The former keeper's house is now The Monhegan Museum, which has exhibits of local memorabilia and art.

Dates: The museum is open during the summer, 11:30 a.m. to 3:30 p.m.

Fees: None. Donations accepted.

For more information: Monhegan Museum, Phone (207) 596-7003.

DINING ON MONHEGAN

Monhegan is not overrun with restaurants, but there are a handful of spots where hikers can load up on provisions for a cliffside lunch.

THE PERIWINKLE. Monhegan. This restaurant has burgers, sandwiches, and ice cream and is open seasonally. *Inexpensive. (207) 594-5932.*

THE BARNACLE. Monhegan. This shop sells gourmet-style takeout, including delicious coffee, and is open seasonally. *Inexpensive. 596-0371.*

LODGING ON MONHEGAN

Camping is not allowed, so find a bed in one of the island's three inns or handful of B&Bs if you want to spend the night.

ISLAND INN. 10 Ocean Avenue, Monhegan. This classic inn has a great view of the harbor from its comfortable front porch and its dining room. There are 36 rooms, some with shared baths. Breakfast is included. *Expensive. (207) 596-0371.*

MONHEGAN HOUSE. 1 Main Street, Monhegan. This four-story inn has 32 rooms, shared baths and a popular café. *Moderate. (207) 594-7983.*

The Rockland Area

Many come to Rockland Harbor to catch a boat. Its busy ferry terminal is the departure site for rides to the popular island communities of Vinalhaven and North Haven and the more rustic Matinicus Island. Rockland Harbor is also home to a beautiful fleet of historic schooners and a large fleet of working fishing boats. But don't skip the rest of Rockland, the long-time commercial center of the Mid-Coast. There's a world-famous art museum, a very friendly downtown, and an opportunity to take a look at one of the most admired stretches of the Mid-Coast, Penobscot Bay.

Penobscot Bay is a giant indentation in Mid-Coast Maine, defined by the Saint George Peninsula to the west and The Blue Hill Peninsula and Deer Isle to the east. Its protected harbors and many islands make this a particularly appealing spot for boaters. Flocks of sea kayakers are a common site in Penobscot Bay in the summer.

Rockland has its most crowded weekend every August when thousands of people pour into town for the Maine Lobster Festival, a big party where Maine's most popular shellfish is feted and feasted upon.

▨ THE FARNSWORTH ART MUSEUM

[Fig. 14(1)] The Farnsworth is known for its collection of works by three generations of Wyeths: Jamie, Andrew, and N.C. This downtown museum also has an impressive collection of other nineteenth and twentieth century Maine-related works. The museum's Wyeth Center, housing Andrew and Betsy Wyeth's collection of Maine art, is in an adjacent church building. The Farnsworth Homestead, a faithfully preserved Victorian house, is next door.

Directions: 352 Main Street, Rockland.

Fees: There is a charge for admission.

Closest town: Rockland.

For more information: Farnsworth Art Museum, 352 Main Street, PO Box 46, Rockland, ME 04841. Phone (207) 596-6457.

▨ SHORE VILLAGE MUSEUM

[Fig. 14(2)] Lighthouse buffs won't want to miss the array of lighthouse and Coast Guard memorabilia at this downtown Rockland museum. With its flashing lights and working foghorns and bells, it's also popular with kids. Upstairs, there are Civil War artifacts and lots of local memorabilia.

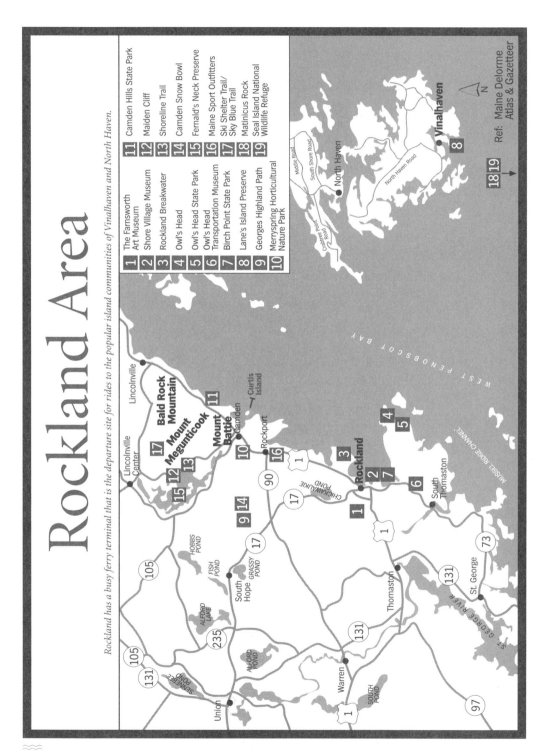

Rockland Area

Rockland has a busy ferry terminal that is the departure site for rides to the popular island communities of Vinalhaven and North Haven.

1	The Farnsworth Art Museum	11	Camden Hills State Park
2	Shore Village Museum	12	Maiden Cliff
3	Rockland Breakwater	13	Shoreline Trail
4	Owl's Head	14	Camden Snow Bowl
5	Owl's Head State Park	15	Fernald's Neck Preserve
6	Owl's Head Transportation Museum	16	Maine Sport Outfitters
7	Birch Point State Park	17	Ski Shelter Trail/ Sky Blue Trail
8	Lane's Island Preserve	18	Matinicus Rock
9	Georges Highland Path	19	Seal Island National Wildlife Refuge
10	Merryspring Horticultural Nature Park		

Ref: Maine Delorme Atlas & Gazetteer

Directions: From Route 1 in Rockland, head south on Limerock Street three blocks to 104 Limerock.

Dates: Open May 1 to Oct. 15 and by appointment.

Closest town: Rockland.

For more information: Shore Village Museum, 104 Limerock Street, Rockland, ME 04841. Phone (207) 594-0311.

SCHOONERS

The dress is casual, the food is great, and the scenery is truly unforgettable. Traditional sailing ships based in Rockland, Rockport, and Camden offer a variety of Maine coast cruises. The ships have varied accommodations and itineraries. They also have their own stories to tell, and most are on the National Register of Historic Places. These storied old schooners are a joy to see on the water. Every July, Rockland holds The Great Schooner Race, a good-natured but serious competition among these tall ships. Here are just a few of the dozen or so schooners based in Rockland.

The 132-foot *Victory Chimes*, which was built in 1900 to carry wood, is the last three-masted schooner on the East Coast. *(800) 745-5651.*

The 90-foot schooner yacht *Wendameen* fell into serious disrepair, but her captain restored her and launched her 57 years after she'd last set sail. The *Wendameen* takes passengers on one-night trips. *(207) 594-1751.*

The *Schooner Stephen Taber* is the oldest documented sailing vessel in continuous service in the U.S. *(800) 999-7352.*

J&E Riggin was built in 1927 for the oyster-dredging trade. *(800) 869-0604.*

Nathaniel Bowditch was built in 1922 as a racing yacht and served in the Coast Guard during World War II. *(207) 273-4062.*

ROCKLAND BREAKWATER

[Fig. 14(3)] If the idea of hiking out into the ocean sounds appealing, walk the length of the Rockland Breakwater. A walk along the granite breakwater to the lighthouse is a two-mile round trip. The breakwater was built to protect busy Rockland Harbor from rough seas, and it shouldn't be hiked in bad weather. The granite blocks can be slippery when wet and icy when cold. The breakwater gives walkers a great view of Rockland Harbor boat traffic, which is likely to include historic schooners, island ferries, classy yachts and fishing boats. This is also a popular fishing spot.

Directions: From Route 1 in Rockland, follow Waldo Avenue east for 0.5 mile to Samoset Road. Park at the end of the road. The trailhead is marked.

Closest town: Rockland.

OWL'S HEAD

[Fig. 14(4)] Owl's Head guards the southwestern entrance to Penobscot Bay with a lighthouse that sits on a high cliff. Owl's Head has two state parks and a transportation museum.

OWL'S HEAD STATE PARK

[Fig. 14(5)] The Owl's Head Lighthouse protects vessels entering Rockland Harbor on foggy days. On sunny days, the surrounding grounds are a wonderful spot for picnicking and watching the boat traffic heading into Rockland Harbor. The light-house is not quite 30 feet tall, but it sits on a rocky cliff and is visible 16 miles out to sea. There's a footpath from the lighthouse to the water, picnic tables and an outhouse.

Directions: From Route 1 just south of Rockland, turn east on North Shore Drive. Follow the signs to the park, turning left on Main Street and then left on Lighthouse Road.

Activities: Sight-seeing, picnicking and bird-watching.

Facilities: Trails, picnic areas, restrooms.

Dates: Accessible year-round.

Fees: None.

Closest town: Owl's Head.

For more information: Maine Bureau of Parks and Lands, 22 State House Station, Augusta, ME 04333. Phone (207) 287-3821.

OWL'S HEAD TRANSPORTATION MUSEUM

[Fig. 14(6)] This sprawling museum has a fascinating array of old airplanes, cars and motorcycles. There's an antique car auction every August. The museum's focus is "pioneer" vehicles built before 1920. Many of these old planes, cars, and other vehicles can be seen on the move during special events held regularly in the summer.

Directions: From Route 1 in Rockland, travel 2 miles south on Route 73.

Dates: Open year-round. Closed Thanksgiving, Christmas, and New Year's Day.

Fees: There is a charge for admission.

Closest town: Owl's Head.

For more information: Owl's Head Transportation Museum, PO Box 277, Owl's Head, ME 04854. Phone (207) 594-4418.

BIRCH POINT STATE PARK

[Fig. 14(7)] This park's sandy crescent-shaped beach, called Lucia Beach, allows swimming but has no lifeguards or facilities beyond outhouses. If the water is too cold for swimming, there are tide pools to explore.

Directions: From Route 1 in Rockland, follow ME73 south to North Shore Drive, turn left on Ash Point Drive, and then right on Dublin Road. Follow the signs to the park, turning left on Ballyhac Road and then bearing left to the park road.

Activities: Swimming, tide pool exploring.

Facilities: Outhouses.

Dates: Open year-round.

Fees: None.

Closest town: Owl's Head.

For more information: Bureau of Parks and Lands, 106 Hogan Road, Bangor, ME 04401. Phone (207) 941-4014.

▓ GOLF IN THE ROCKLAND AREA

THE SAMOSET. Warrenton Street, Rockport. This waterfront, par 70 course has spectacular ocean views.

For more information: The Samoset Resort, 220 Warrenton Street, Rockport, ME 04856. Phone (207) 282-5883.

▓ NIGHT LIFE IN THE ROCKLAND AREA

THE STRAND CINEMA. Main Street, Rockland. This two-screen, old-fashioned movie theater is a nostalgic change of pace for those accustomed to multiplexes, and it shows first-run movies. *(207) 594-7266.*

THE WATERWORKS PUB AND RESTAURANT. 5 Lindsey Street, Rockland. This nightspot features pub food and live music. *(207) 596-7950.*

▓ DINING IN THE ROCKLAND AREA

SECOND READ BOOKS AND COFFEE. 238 Main Street, Rockland. This spot near the Farnsworth museum complex offers fresh-baked goods, imaginative soups and sandwiches, as well as a good supply of used books and an Internet access terminal. *Inexpensive. Phone (207) 594-4123.*

CAFÉ MIRANDA. 15 Oak Street, Rockland. Reservations are recommended at this hotspot, which serves a festive mix of Italian, Cuban and seafood. *Moderate. Phone (207) 594-2034.*

▓ LODGING IN THE ROCKLAND AREA

THE SAMOSET RESORT. 220 Warrenton Street, Rockport. This modern resort has beautiful views, swimming pools, tennis courts, and one of the most revered golf courses in the state. *Expensive. Phone (207) 594-2511.*

THE OLD GRANITE INN. 546 Main Street, Rockland. This in-town inn was built in the early 1800s from blocks of local granite. *Moderate to expensive. Phone (207) 594-9036.*

Vinalhaven and North Haven

Catch the ferry in Rockland for the 1 hour, 15 minute ride to Vinalhaven or North Haven, islands about 13 miles out to sea.

▓ VINALHAVEN

[Fig. 14] This 9-mile-long island has a year-round community of about 1,200. It is also home to hundreds of lobster boats and is definitely a working island. Vinalhaven doesn't have all the amenities of some of Maine's more traditional tourist towns. But it's an interesting place to visit for the scenery, the harborside action, and the ferry ride from Rockland. Thanks to frequent ferries, visitors can come for a day or stay overnight. There is a business district near the harbor with several interesting shops and restaurants. If you plan an overnight stay, make reservations in advance.

Catch an early morning boat out of Rockland for a day trip to Vinalhaven, but keep an eye on your watch. The last ferry heads back to the mainland at 4:30, and spare beds are not easy to find in the summer. Also, getting a car onto the Vinalhaven ferry during the summer is a challenge, but a bicycle or a pair of sturdy shoes will do for a day of island exploring.

For more information: Maine State Ferry, phone (207) 596-2202. Vinalhaven Chamber of Commerce, Box 703, Vinalhaven, ME 04863.

QUARRIES

Vinalhaven had a bustling granite quarrying industry in the late 1800s. Vinalhaven granite can be seen in the columns at New York's Saint John the Divine Cathedral and at the Boston Fine Arts Museum. The granite industry is long gone, but two of the old quarries serve as popular swimming spots on hot summer days. Lawson's Quarry is on North Haven Road and Booth's Quarry is on Pequot Road. Both are within 1 mile or so of downtown and are marked with a sign. There are no lifeguards, restrooms, or changing areas.

Directions: From Main Street, head north on North Haven Road to Lawson's Quarry, or east on Pequot Road to Booth's Quarry.

For more information: Vinalhaven Community Council. Box 548, Vinalhaven, ME 04863.

LANE'S ISLAND PRESERVE

[Fig. 14(8)] This 45-acre island preserve is accessible over a causeway from Vinalhaven and is a 15-minute walk from the ferry landing. Several paths crisscross the interior, which is covered with low-lying shrubs and grass. Look for blueberry and rose bushes. There's a small cattail marsh known for nesting red-winged blackbirds (*Agelaius phoeniceus*) near the entrance and registration box. Look for asters, evening primrose, and three-toothed cinquefoil along its shore. Elsewhere, look for sandpipers, great blue herons and little green herons in the spring and summer. In the fall and winter, look for smaller hawks, like merlins (*Falco columbarius*) and kestrels (*Falco sparvarius.*) The preserve is managed by the town of Vinalhaven and a committee of local residents.

Directions: To reach the preserve from the ferry landing, bear right and go straight through town and turn right at the fountain. Pass the Armbrust Hill Town Park and cross the Indian Creek causeway. Continue 0.25 mile to The Nature Conservancy sign. Turn left and follow the road through the cattail marsh to the trails.

For more information: The Nature Conservancy, Maine Chapter, Fort Andross, 14 Maine Street, Suite 401, Brunswick, ME 04011. Phone (207) 729-5181.

OTHER PRESERVES

The Nature Conservancy has several other island preserves near Vinalhaven. They are only accessible by boat and have no trails. Most are fragile nesting environments for seabirds and are closed to visitors between February 15 and August 15. Still other preserves are open for exploration but shouldn't be taken on during a one-day trip.

BIG GARDEN AND BIG WHITE ISLANDS

Day visitors are welcome on Big Garden and Big White islands, which lie about two miles southeast of Vinalhaven, for shoreline exploration.

For more information: The Nature Conservancy, Maine Chapter, Fort Andross, 14 Maine Street, Suite 401, Brunswick, ME 04011. Phone (207) 729-5181.

VINALHAVEN LAND TRUST PRESERVES

The Vinalhaven Land Trust manages other preserves on Vinalhaven. They include Tip Toe Mountain, with an easy uphill hike, Middle Mountain and Perry Creek Preserve in the northwestern section of the island. These are several miles from the ferry landing, so plan accordingly if visiting for one day.

For more information: The Vinalhaven Land Trust, PO Box 268 Vinalhaven, ME 04863.

DINING ON VINALHAVEN:

THE HARBOR GAWKER. At the harbor, Vinalhaven. Great takeout crab rolls, chowder, and other fast seafood for eating on the nearby benches. *Inexpensive. (207) 863-9365.*

THE HAVEN. Main Street, Vinalhaven. A favorite gourmet restaurant for many residents and visitors. *Moderate. (207) 863-4969.*

LODGING ON VINALHAVEN

There are no campsites on Vinalhaven. There is one motel and a handful of B&Bs.

THE TIDEWATER MOTEL. Main Street, Vinalhaven. This motel is perched on the waterfront. The rooms are fairly generic, but the harbor view is extraordinary. *Moderate. (207) 863-4618.*

THE FOX ISLAND INN. Carver Street, Vinalhaven. Four rooms plus a suite, some with shared baths. *Moderate (207) 863-2122.*

NORTH HAVEN

[Fig. 14] North Haven is across a narrow causeway from Vinalhaven. But the two islands have a very different feel. North Haven has 350 year-round

BLUEBERRY
(Vaccinium sp.)

residents and a wealthy summer community. Residents appear to value their privacy. This island has even fewer beds for tourists than nearby Vinalhaven. The island is 9 miles long and 3 miles wide and can be explored by bicycle, despite a few hills. There's a charming downtown district with a handful of shops and galleries and the North Haven Golf Club at Waterman Cove. This course is open to the public during the summer. Phone (207) 867-2061 for more information.

Mullen's Head Park is a good destination for a bike ride from the ferry landing. There are picnic areas and footpaths. Take South Shore Road east from village.

For more information: North Haven town office, phone (207) 867-4433.

DINING ON NORTH HAVEN

North Haven has very few restaurants. Day trippers may want to grab some picnic fixings at Brown's Market on Main Street.

COOPER'S LANDING. Main Street, North Haven. This restaurant is open seasonally for lunch and dinner. *Moderate. (207) 867-2060*

LODGING ON NORTH HAVEN

There are no campsites on North Haven and very few spare beds, so either make reservations or plan on catching the boat back to the mainland.

PULPIT HARBOR INN. North Haven. This small B&B is about two miles from the ferry landing. *Moderate. (207) 867-2219.*

Matinicus Rock

[Fig. 14(18)] This mass of granite 22 miles off the coast in Penobscot is a nesting spot for Atlantic puffins (*Fratercula artica*). These quick-moving little birds with big, striped bills are appealing, but a boat trip to see them here should be undertaken only by those willing to stomach a few swells during what is typically a full day at sea. There is no landing on Matinicus Rock, but the puffins and other birds are usually visible from the tour boats as they circle the island.

Hunting for meat and feathers reduced Maine's once large puffin population to one nesting pair by the early 1900s. That pair, here on Matinicus Rock, was protected from hunters by a lighthouse keeper, and the colony eventually rebuilt itself. These days, more than 100 pairs of puffins nest on Matinicus Rock. (*See* Eastern Egg Rock page 153, for more on puffin restoration.)

Adult puffins arrive at Matinicus in April or May. Each pair raises one chick before August, then heads out to sea for the winter. June and July are good months to see the adult puffins carrying fish in their bills back to their chicks, which stay in burrowed nests.

While puffins are the stars of Matinicus Rock, they aren't the only interesting birds out here. The National Audubon Society is working to establish a common murre (*Uria aalge*) nesting population here. Also look for arctic and common terns, razorbill and black guillemot, and several types of gulls.

Directions: A few boats make regular excursions to Matinicus Rock. The Maine Audubon Society, Box 6009, Falmouth, ME 04105, phone (207) 781-2330, leads field trips every year. Atlantic Expeditions, phone (207) 372-8621, takes regular trips out of Rockland. Hardy Boat Cruises, Box 326, New Harbor, ME 04554, phone (207) 677-2026, takes occasional trips out of New Harbor.

ATLANTIC PUFFIN (*Fratercula artica*)

Puffins

Atlantic puffins (*Fratercula artica*) are often called clowns of the sea, thanks to their brightly-colored bills, stocky little bodies, white bellies and faces, and far from graceful gait. But the characteristics that make these seabirds appear somewhat comical serve them well in their ocean habitat.

Puffins spend most of their time at sea, coming ashore to treeless islands in April or May to mate and raise one chick. If the chick survives, it will return to the island in four or five years to breed. This breeding and nesting time is when puffins display their showy striped bills, color-rimmed eyes and white faces; after they head for the open sea in August, the adult puffins will lose their bright colors and their white face feathers will be replaced with dark. Like many other seabirds, puffins have black backs and white bellies—a color scheme that protects them from predators from above and below.

Puffins have a rolling walk, and they can sometimes be seen tumbling across the water or shore after landing from flight. Their wings are short and may beat 300 to 400 times per minute to get flying. Those powerful little wings are also designed for swimming, and puffins can "fly" underwater to dive for fish.

Atlantic puffins are not endangered; there are millions of them between Maine and Norway. Visitors to the Maine coast can see them on four islands—Matinicus Rock, Eastern Egg Rock and Seal Island off the Mid-Coast and Machias Seal Island off the far Down East coast. Machias Seal is the only island where visitors can get off a boat and view these birds from blinds. The puffin colonies on Eastern Egg and Seal Island are restored colonies (*see* 153); those on Machias Seal and Matinicus Rock are naturally occurring.

Biking and seeing the sights are popular activities around Camden.

SEAL ISLAND NATIONAL WILDLIFE REFUGE

[Fig. 14(19)] Some of the expeditions to Matinicus Rock will also circle the nearby Seal Island National Wildlife Refuge. This island is closed to all public use. Not only is it an important seabird nesting site, but it is also the site of unexploded ordnance left by the Navy during this island's days as a World War II bomb test site.

The National Audubon Society, U.S. Fish and Wildlife Service, and Canadian Wildlife Service have successfully restored the puffin and tern populations to Seal Island, which is now managed as a seabird sanctuary.

For more information: Seal Island National Wildlife Refuge, care of Petit Manan National Wildlife Refuge, Box 279, Milbridge, ME 04658. Phone (207) 546-2124

The Camden Area

Camden is an appealing tourist town with a picture-postcard harbor, mountains that seem to rise right out of the sea, and dozens of interesting shops and galleries. The sidewalks get a bit crowded in the summer, but you can lose the crowds by renting a kayak, hiking the Camden Hills, or checking out nearby Rockport or Lincolnville.

ROCKPORT

Rockport is decidedly more peaceful and a little more upscale than Camden. Rockport, too, has a picture-perfect harbor. The harbor-side Marine Park includes a statue of Andre the Seal, who delighted visitors with his antics in the harbor every summer for more than 20 years. Marine Park also has the remains of some nineteenth century lime kilns, reminders of a time when exporting lime for construction was a major industry here.

Rockport has attracted musicians, artists, and craftsmen for years. Today, some people come to study photography at the Maine Photographic Workshops or woodworking at the Center for Furniture Craftsmanship. Between the harbors of Rockport and Camden, look for a herd of distinctive black cattle with large white stripes around their middles. These are Belted Galloway cattle, or "Oreo cookie cows" as they are known locally, of Aldmere Farm, which imported the first herd of the cattle from Scotland to the U.S. in the 1950s.

MAINE SPORT OUTFITTERS

[Fig. 14(16)] A stop at this Route 1 business in Rockport is mandatory for outdoor enthusiasts planning to explore the region by kayak or bicycle. Maine Sport rents kayaks and bikes and leads kayak cruises that range from a few hours to several days. The "Harbor to Harbor" trip takes paddlers between Rockport and Camden. The sprawling store sells all sorts of gear, clothing, and equipment, and the staff is ready to discuss favorite routes. Maine Sport also operates an inn for kayakers in nearby Friendship.

Directions: On Route 1 in Rockport.

Closest town: Rockport.

For more information: Maine Sport Outfitters, Route 1, Box 956, Rockport, ME 04856. Phone (207) 236-8797 or (888) 236-8797.

GEORGES HIGHLAND PATH

[Fig. 14(9)] The Georges Highland Path is a hiking trail through the mountains of the Georges River watershed about 5 miles inland from Camden. Its 9 miles traverse portions of Ragged Mountain, Spruce Mountain, and Pleasant Mountain and there are some rugged spots. The path is split into three distinct sections and can be picked up in four spots: Thorndike Brook, the Yellow Gate at ME 17, Mount Pleasant Road, and Mount Pleasant Farm.

The path is blazed in blue and crosses private land. The Georges River Land Trust asks that you stay on the blazed trail. Also, bring a windbreaker and a sweater, as the highlands can be cool, even when it's warm at the coast. If you lose the trail, head downhill. The valleys have roads and houses.

TRAILS

Thorndike Brook Access Point to Mount Pleasant Farm Access Point. 9 miles. 5 to 7 hours. Moderate.

Thorndike Brook Access Point to Route 17 Yellow Gate. 4.9 miles. 3 to 5 hours. Moderate with steep sections.

Mount Pleasant Farm Access Point to Yellow Gate. 4.1 miles. 2.5 hours. Moderate.
Mount Pleasant Road north to Yellow Gate. 2.3 miles. 1.5 hours. Moderate
Mount Pleasant Road south to Mount Pleasant Farm Access Point. 1.8 miles.
1 to 1.5 hours. Moderate.

Directions: From Route 1 in Rockport, take ME 90 west 1 mile to ME 17. The
Yellow Gate access point is on ME 17 about 1 mile past ME 90 near Mirror Lake. To
reach the Thorndike Brook Access Point, continue on ME 17 another mile, turn right
on Hope Street and look for a parking area to the right in less than 1 mile. To reach
the Mt Pleasant Access Point, continue on ME 17 to Fogler Road, turn left at Fullers
Trading Post, then turn left again on Mount Pleasant Road. To reach the Mount
Pleasant Farm Access Point, continue on Fogler Road to the farm, where cars can be
parked to the left of the barn facing the mountain.

Activities: Hiking.
Facilities: Trails.
Dates: Accessible year-round.
Fees: None.
Closest town: Rockport, 1 to 2 miles.
For more information: Georges River Land Trust, 328 Main Street, Rockland,
ME 04841. Phone (207) 594-5166.

MAINE COAST ARTISTS

This gallery in an old firehouse showcases the work of some of Maine's best
contemporary artists, of both the famous and still emerging varieties. The nonprofit
cooperative organization holds several shows and workshops every year, along with a
popular auction every August. There is also a shop with unique handcrafted items.

For more information: Maine Coast Artists, 162 Russell Avenue, Rockland, ME
04841. Phone (207) 236-2875.

MERRYSPRING HORTICULTURAL NATURE PARK

[Fig. 14(10)] This peaceful spot on the southern edge of Camden is a must-see for
gardeners and amateur botanists. Its 66 acres include paths through woods and
wildflower fields and an arboretum with signs identifying many trees and plants.
There's also a large garden area with an herb garden, rose garden, rock garden and
annual and perennial borders that are bound to inspire home gardeners to dust off
their tools and get to work. A library in the preserve's Ross Center is loaded with texts
on horticulture. Merryspring also holds workshops, lectures, and plant sales.

Directions: From Route 1 in Camden, turn west on Conway Road.
Activities: Walking, studying plants.
Facilities: Trails, library.
Dates: Open year-round, dawn to dusk. Ross Center is open weekdays.
Fees: None. Contributions accepted.
Closest town: Camden.

For more information: Merryspring, PO Box 893, Camden, ME 04843. Phone (207) 236-2239.

CURTIS ISLAND

[Fig. 14] This small town-owned island at the entrance to Camden Harbor is accessible by kayak or other small boat. Look for loons (*Gavia immer*) and other waterfowl while paddling between the yachts and tall ships moored in the harbor. Land on the beach on the Camden side of the island and follow the walking path through the woods to the Curtis Island Light. Please respect the privacy of the residents of the keeper's house. Maine Sport Outfitters in Rockport leads kayak tours of Camden Harbor daily in the summer, weather permitting.

Directions: Accessible by boat, Curtis Island is the island with the lighthouse at the entrance to Camden Harbor.

Activities: Paddling, walking.

Facilities: Trail.

Dates: Open year-round.

Fees: None.

Closest town: Camden.

For more information: Camden town offices, 29 Elm Street, Camden, ME 04843. Phone (207) 236-3353. Maine Sport Outfitters, Route 1, Box 956, Rockport, ME 04856. Phone (207) 722-0826.

BOATS IN CAMDEN HARBOR

Camden is home port to several historic schooners, which take

WHITE-THROATED SPARROW
(Zonotrichia albicolis)

paying guests on cruises, usually of three to six days. Visitors in the mood for a shorter cruise can visit the harbor docks and find several schooners and even a converted lobster boat that take one- or two-hour trips around the harbor.

The *Lewis R. French,* an 1871 schooner, includes an island lobster bake on each cruise. Phone (800) 469-4635.

The *Roseway* was built as a private fishing yacht in 1925 and offers special sailing programs for teen-agers, as well as traditional tourist cruises. Phone (800) 255-4449.

CAMDEN HILLS STATE PARK

[Fig. 14(11)] The centerpiece of this park is Mount Battie and its views of Penobscot Bay. This is the view that inspired the poet Edna St. Vincent Millay to write her 1912 masterpiece *Renascense* and has inspired tourists to wax poetic ever since. But the rest of this park, with its rocky shore, 25 miles of hiking trails, and campsites, is worth exploring, too. Pick up a trail map at the park gate.

Directions: From Route 1 in Camden Village, head 2 miles north. The park entrance is on the West Side of Route 1.

Activities: Hiking, camping, cross-country skiing, snowmobiling.

Facilities: Park entrance station, picnic areas, outhouses, campsites with playground, bathrooms and showers.

Dates: May 15-Oct 15. Grounds are accessible year-round.

Fees: There is an entrance charge in the summer. There is also a charge for campsites.

Closest town: Camden.

For more information: Camden Hills State Park, 280 Belfast Road, Camden, ME 04843. (207) 236-0849. Campground phone (207) 236-3109.

HIKING IN CAMDEN HILLS STATE PARK

MOUNT BATTIE. [Fig. 14] On a clear day, the view from this 790-foot peak takes in many islands (identified on a series of panoramic signs), Camden Harbor, and a swath of sparkling sea. The 0.5-mile Mount Battie Trail to the summit is a moderate hike with some rocky, steep sections and takes about 45 minutes to ascend. The Mount Battie Auto Road allows a quick drive to the summit for tour buses and cars and is responsible for the crowds encountered at this spot during the summer. The lookout is much less crowded in early spring and late fall, when the road is closed. Mount Battie is topped by a 20-foot stone tower honoring veterans of World War I. Climb the circular stairs for an even better look around.

Mount Battie Trail: 0.5 mile. 45 minutes. Moderate.

MOUNT MEGUNTICOOK. [Fig. 14] With a 1,380-foot summit, Mount Megunticook is the highest point in the park. Its Ocean Lookout offers a panoramic view of the ocean and other Camden Hills and is a good hawk-watching spot in the fall. The summit is reached by taking the Nature Trail to the Megunticook Trail.

Nature Trail: 1.2 miles. 1 hour. Easy.

Megunticook Trail: 1 mile. 1 hour. Moderate.

BALD ROCK MOUNTAIN. [Fig. 14] This peak, also with spectacular ocean views, is reached via the steep Bald Rock Trail, which can be reached from the well-worn Ski Shelter Trail, 1.3 miles from its trailhead. (The Ski Shelter Trail is also known as the Snowmobile Trail.)

Bald Rock Trail: 0.5 mile. 30 minutes. Moderate.

Ski Shelter Trail: 5 miles. 3 hours. Easy. Provides access to several other inland trails.

SKI SHELTER TRAIL. [Fig. 14(17)] This former fire road, which is also known as the Snowmobile Trail, provides easy access from the Youngstown Road parking area to several trails and is popular for skiing and snowshoeing in the winter. Distances from Youngtown Road parking area to trails: Bald Rock Trail, 1.3 miles; Cameron Mountain Trail, 1.3 miles; Sky Blue Trail, 1.6 miles; Zeke's Trail, 2.5 miles; and Slope Trail, 3 miles.

Ski Shelter Trail: 3 miles. 2 hours. Easy to moderate.

SKY BLUE TRAIL. [Fig. 14(17)] This trail passes through blueberry clearings, a beech and maple forest and by some very large, very fragrant black spruce trees. It is reached by following the Ski Shelter trail for 1.6 miles and concludes near more trails.

Sky Blue Trail: 1.5 miles. 1 hour. Moderate.

SHORELINE TRAIL. [Fig. 14(13)] Most of the state park is to the west of Route 1, but across the highway is a picnic area and scenic walk along the rocky shore of Penobscot Bay.

Shoreline Trail: 0.3 miles. 15 minutes. Easy.

MAIDEN CLIFF. [Fig. 14(12)] This 800-foot cliff above Megunticook Lake offers beautiful inland views. A tall cross stands near the spot where an 11-year-old girl fell to her death in 1862 and should serve as a reminder to be careful when walking here. Maiden Cliff is outside of the park, on land owned by the town of Camden. The trail can be reached from the park.

Maiden Cliff Trail: 1 mile. 1 hour. Moderate.

OTHER TRAILS. Many of the trails winding through the Camden Hills intersect, providing varied scenery to hikers. For example, from the Mount Battie summit, hikers can follow the Tablelands Trail to the Ocean Lookout on Mount Megunticook. Or they can take the Ridge Trail from Ocean Lookout across the summit of Mount Megunticook to the Scenic Trail to the Maiden Cliff Trail.

Pick up a trail map at the park entrance to configure an interesting and scenic route. Some of the trails are suitable for cross-country skiing, and a local club grooms some trails for snowmobiling.

Tablelands Trail: 1.5 miles. 1.5 hours. Strenuous.

Ridge Trail: 2.5 miles. 2.5 hours. Moderate.

Scenic Trail: 0.8 mile. 45 minutes. Moderate.

CAMPING IN CAMDEN HILLS STATE PARK

The state park has 107 campsites for tents or trailers. There are restrooms, hot showers, shared water spigots, and a dumping station but no electrical hookups or individual water hookups. Reservations are strongly recommended in July and August. Minimum stay is 2 nights; maximum stay is 14 nights.

For reservations, call (800) 332-1501 within Maine and phone (207) 287-3824 from outside Maine. For information on mail registration, write Bureau of Parks and Lands, 22 State House Station, Augusta, ME 04333-0022. Reservations are accepted starting the first working day of January for the following summer.

CAMDEN SNOW BOWL

[Fig. 14(14)] This town-owned ski area on 1,300-foot Ragged Mountain lets skiers enjoy the view of Penobscot Bay and its islands from the slopes. There are nine alpine trails, from beginner to expert, served by two T-bars and a chairlift, and 20 miles of cross-country ski trails. The Snow Bowl also offers lessons and rentals.

The Snow Bowl also has a 400-foot toboggan chute with rentals and is the site of the annual U.S. toboggan championship.

Directions: From Route 1 in Camden, turn west on John Street.

Dates: Open as the snow permits. Toboggan chute is open weekends and holidays.

Fees: Lift ticket prices vary but are very reasonable. There is also a per-run charge for the toboggan chute.

For more information: Camden Snow Bowl Box 1207, Camden ME 04843. Phone (207) 236-3438.

FERNALD'S NECK PRESERVE

[Fig. 14(15)] This 318-acre Nature Conservancy preserve is on a peninsula pointing into Megunticook Lake. It's a peaceful spot with 5 miles of intersecting, blazed hiking trails. The preserve has more than 3 miles of lakeshore, 60-foot cliffs, and a bog. Take the blue- and red-blazed trails around the northern portion of the preserve to see the cliffs. The orange-blazed loop wanders by the Great Bog and passes several glacial erratics—large boulders carried great distances and then deposited by a glacier. One of these seemingly out-of-place boulders is known as Balancing Rock because it appears to be ready to roll over.

Most of these trails are relatively easy to walk, but they can get very muddy in the spring and some of the terrain is a bit rough.

Directions: From Route 1 in Camden, take ME 52 north. Bear left at the Y in the road and look for a road to the left marked Fire Road 50, directly across from highway marker 5016. Stay to the left at the next Y in the road onto a gravel road. (Park here if it is mud season.) Continue to a parking area next to the farmhouse at the end of the road. A small sign with The Nature Conservancy's oak leaf logo is posted next to a trail into the woods. Follow that trail to the registration box, where maps are available. Please note the time when the preserve and parking lot close or risk having your car locked in.

Activities: Hiking.

Facilities: None.

Dates: Open year-round.

Fees: None.

Closest town: Camden.

For more information: The Nature Conservancy, Maine Chapter, Fort Andross, 14 Maine Street, Suite 401, Brunswick, ME 04011. Phone (207) 729-5181

LINCOLNVILLE

Route 1 runs so close to the 850-yard Lincolnville Beach that from your car you can practically count the sunbathers jockeying for sand on a nice day. Sandy beaches are few and far between in this section of the Maine coast; however, many endure the crowds for a chance to sit on a beach. There's a small strip of craft and souvenir shops across Route 1 from the beach. Lincolnville Beach also has fishing boats for deep-sea fishing trips. And the car ferry leaves here for Islesboro.

KELMSCOTT FARM

A little farther inland is Kelmscott Farm, a nonprofit foundation and farm dedicated to preserving rare breeds of livestock. Visitors can admire the Gloucester Old Spots pigs, Cotswold sheep, Nigerian goats and other livestock, shop for woolen goods in the gift shop, and walk a nature trail.

Directions: From Camden, take ME 52 through Lincolnville Center, then 4.2 miles farther to Van Cycle Road and turn left at the Kelmscott Farm sign.

Dates: Open every day but Monday.

Fees: There is a charge for admission.

Closest town: Lincolnville.

For more information: Kelmscott Farm, RR2, Box 365, Lincolnville, ME 04849. Phone (207) 763-4088.

SEA KAYAKING IN THE CAMDEN AREA

It seems like one out of every three cars spotted in this region has a kayak or two strapped to its roof. Sea kayaking is very popular in coastal Maine, and the Camden area, with its protected harbors, is a great place to give it a try. Inexperienced paddlers shouldn't head out onto Penobscot Bay without a guide or some instruction.

Maine Sport, Rockport, takes kayakers on a variety of trips including many aimed at first-timers. Phone (207) 236-8797. **Ducktrap Sea Kayak Tours** in Lincolnville offers two-hour and half-day trips for people with no experience. Phone (207) 236-8608. **Mount Pleasant Canoe & Kayak**, West Rockport, offers day trips and inn-to-inn excursions. Phone (207) 785-4309.

CAMPING IN THE CAMDEN AREA

MEGUNTICOOK CAMPGROUND BY THE SEA. Route 1, Rockport. This campground has wooded sites for tents and RVs, 30-amp and cable hookups, cabin rentals, a heated pool, and kayak rentals. *594-2428.*

CAMDEN-ROCKPORT CAMPING. ME 90, West Rockport. Wilderness areas for tents plus water, sewer, electric, and cable hookups for RVs. *(207) 236-2498.*

NIGHT LIFE IN THE CAMDEN AREA

Camden is a hopping harbor town in the summer months.

CAMDEN CIVIC THEATER. Camden Opera House, Route 1, Camden. Look for dramas and musicals in the summer. *(207) 236-2281.*

BAYVIEW STREET CINEMA. 10 Bay View Street, Camden. This small theater shows art films. *(207) 236-8722*

SEA DOG TAVERN & BREWERY. 43 Mechanic Street, Camden. This brewpub is in an old woolen mill and overlooks a waterfall. *(207) 236-6863.*

Islesboro and Searsport Area

Islesboro has a working-class year-round community and an annual influx of wealthy summer residents.

Stockton Springs

203
131
7
137
141

Prospect Street

5 6
Searsport

Cape Jellison
7
175

Sears Island

PENOBSCOT RIVER

2
Belfast
BELFAST BAY

4

CROSS POND
3
3

166A
166

Castine

Belmont Road
52

TILDEN POND

Van Cycle Road

PITCHER POND
52

Northport

KNIGHT POND

North Islesboro

Back Road

Cape Rosier Road

173

Slab City Road

1

Islesboro

West Side Road

Islesboro Island

Lincolnville Center
235
173

Lincolnville
52

Main Road

1

MEGUNTICOOK LAKE
105

1

Camden

N

Ref: Delorme Maine Atlas & Gazetteer

1	Warren Island State Park
2	Audubon Expedition Institute
3	Lake Saint George State Park
4	Moose Point State Park
5	Penobscot Marine Museum
6	Bluejacket Shipcrafters
7	Fort Point State Park

🔲 DINING IN THE CAMDEN AREA

FRENCH & BRAWN MARKETPLACE. 1 Elm Street, Camden. This grocery store, with fresh soups, interesting sandwiches and a deli, is a great place to put together a picnic to enjoy while admiring the harbor right up the street. *Inexpensive. (207) 236-3361.*

THE WATERFRONT. Bayview Street, Camden. Seafood is the specialty at this local institution, which features a deck overlooking the harbor. *Moderate. (207) 236-3747.*

🔲 LODGING IN THE CAMDEN AREA

Camden, Rockport, and Lincolnville offer all kinds of lodging, from historic B&Bs and inns to modern motels and little tourist cabins.

OWL AND TURTLE GUEST ROOMS. 8 Bayview Street, Camden. These harbor-view rooms are right above the Owl and Turtle Bookshop. *Moderate. (207) 236-9014.*

NORUMBEGA. Route 1, Camden. The castle sitting on Route 1 at the top of Camden Harbor is actually an inn with beautiful rooms and gourmet food. *Very expensive. (207) 236-4646.*

Islesboro

Take a car ferry from Lincolnville Beach to the quiet summer resort community of Islesboro. The ferry lands at Grindle Point, where the lighthouse keeper's house is the town's Sailor's Memorial Museum with local maritime memorabilia. Like many Maine islands, Islesboro has a working-class year-round community and an annual influx of wealthy summer residents.

Some very wealthy folk have summer "cottages" here in the Dark Harbor section of the island. These mansions can't be seen from the road, although many can be admired from the sea. Islesboro has some shops and a handful of places to buy picnic fixings. There's also a beautiful town beach with picnic tables and lovely views at Islesboro's southern Pendleton Point.

The only inn is the casually elegant Dark Harbor House, which is expensive and books up well in advance. Unless you've got reservations there, make sure you don't miss the last boat back to the mainland.

Directions: Take the ferry out of Lincolnville Beach.

For more information: Islesboro town office, PO Box 76, Islesboro, ME 04848. Phone (207) 734-2253. Dark Harbor House, PO Box 185, Dark Harbor, Islesboro, ME 04848. Phone (207) 734-6669. Maine State Ferry Service, PO Box 214, Lincolnville, ME 04849. Phone (207) 789-5611.

Moose

If you visit Maine intent on seeing a moose, it's best to head inland where there is more of the animal's preferred swamp and pond habitat. But moose are spotted along the coast occasionally, even in the streets of Portland or wandering dangerously near the Maine Turnpike.

A full-grown moose (*Alces alces*) is about 7 feet high and 9 feet long and can weigh 1,400 pounds. Each year, the male moose grows a massive set of antlers, called a rack, that can be 5 or 6 feet across.

Maine's moose population has grown in recent years, to an estimated 35,000, probably because a spruce budworm infestation has killed trees, opening up more habitats for them inland. In response, Maine lawmakers have increased the number of the animals allowed to be killed during the annual moose hunt from 1,000 to 2,000. In 1999, the state was expected to increase the kill to 3,000 moose.

Every year, thousands of people pay to enter a lottery for the chance to bag a moose. Those whose names are selected get a license to shoot one moose. (Once a hunter has won a license, his or her odds of finding and shooting a moose are very high.)

There are about 600 car-moose accidents every year on Maine roadways, mostly in the spring when moose stand in roads to get away from bugs, or in the fall during mating season. Many people are injured and some are killed each year in those collisions.

MOOSE
(Alces alces)

WARREN ISLAND STATE PARK

[Fig. 15(1)] The state operates this 70-acre, spruce-covered island near Islesboro as a boaters' park. It's got picnic tables, sites for tent camping, and walking trails. There are also six moorings, a float, and a pier for boaters with large or small craft. The park recently started offering reservations for the campsites.

Directions: No public boats dock at Warren Island. It's about a 0.25-mile paddle from Islesboro.

Dates: Open Memorial Day weekend to Sept. 15.

Fees: There is a charge for day use and camping.

Closest town: Lincolnville, 0.25 mile.

For more information: Warren Island State Park, care of Camden Hills State Park, 280 Belfast Road, Camden, ME 04843. Phone (207) 691-1031 or (207) 236-0849.

For campsite reservations, call (800) 332-1501 within Maine and (207) 287-3824 from outside Maine. For information on mail registration, write Bureau of Parks and Lands, 22 State House Station, Augusta, ME 04333.

Belfast

Belfast, which was given its name in the mid-eighteenth century by Scotch-Irish settlers, has weathered the rise and fall of the shipbuilding industry and the subsequent rise and fall of the poultry processing industry. Since 1996, the credit card company MBNA has fueled the economy here. Belfast also has a healthy community of artists and back-to-the-land types. Its businesses include some "green" businesses specializing in environmentally sensitive products, two good bookstores, unique gift and clothing shops, a meditation center, and a spiritualist camp. Belfast feels a little more off the beaten path than some other coastal harbor towns because Route 1 bypasses it.

WALKING TOUR

The Belfast Chamber of Commerce provides maps for walking through Belfast's historic districts. There's also a footbridge over the Passagassawakeag River that is a popular spot for mackerel, bluefish, and striped bass fishing.

For more information: Belfast Area Chamber of Commerce, PO Box 58, Belfast, ME 04915. Phone (207) 338-5900.

AUDUBON EXPEDITION INSTITUTE

[Fig. 15(2)] This environmental education institute is associated with the National Audubon Society and Lesley College. It's based in Belfast but uses all of North America as its classroom.

Graduate and undergraduate students travel in customized school buses around regions of the U.S. and Canada, conducting research and studying ecology and other topics.

For more information: Audubon Expedition Institute, Box 365, Belfast, ME 04915. Phone (207) 338-5859.

LAKE SAINT GEORGE STATE PARK

[Fig. 15(3)] This park sits on the shore of a spring-fed lake about 15 miles inland from Belfast in Liberty. It has a swimming area with lifeguards, picnic tables, and 38 camping sites for tents and RVs. (A dumping station, showers, and restrooms are there, but no hookups.) Boats and canoes can be rented by the hour or the day. Fishing for brook trout, landlocked salmon, and other fish is a popular activity here.

There is a marked hiking trail across ME 3 from the lake. It's about 6 miles round-trip with a very steep incline at the start.

Directions: From Route 1 outside of Belfast, head west about 15 miles on ME 3 to Liberty.

Activities: Swimming, hiking, boating, camping, picnicking.

Facilities: Campsites with showers and restrooms, picnic tables, boat rentals and launch, entry station.

Fees: There is a charge for day use and camping.

Closest town: Liberty.

For more information: Lake St. George State Park, Route 3, RR1, Box 980, Liberty, ME 04949. Phone (207) 589-4255.

NIGHT LIFE IN THE BELFAST AREA

THE BLUE GOOSE. Route 1, Northport. This dance hall swings most weekends with contra dances, folk performances and other events. *(207) 338-3003.*

BELFAST BAY BREWING. 100 Searsport Avenue, Belfast. This brewpub has a restaurant and a pub. *(207) 338-4216.*

COLONIAL THEATER. 163 High Street, Belfast. This art deco gem shows first-run movies on two screens. *(207) 338-1930.*

DINING IN THE BELFAST AREA

A walk down Main Street will lead you past several restaurants, some specializing in down-home style food and others much more adventurous.

BELFAST CO-OP. 123 High Street, Belfast. This spot has a good assortment of healthy foods, a deli and a café. *Inexpensive. (207) 338-2532.*

DOS AMIGOS. 144 Bayside Road, Northport. For those who have had enough of New England fare, try the Mexican dishes at this spot just north of Belfast. *Moderate. (207) 338-5775.*

🕸 LODGING IN BELFAST

BELFAST BAY MEADOWS INN. 192 Northport Avenue, Belfast. This inn offers modern amenities like king-sized beds and TVs in a century-old inn. The complimentary breakfast offerings include lobster omelets and strawberry pancakes. *Moderate to expensive. (800) 335-2370.*

WONDERVIEW COTTAGES. US 1, Belfast. These 20 one- to three-bedroom tourist cottages all have screened porches, a view of Penobscot Bay, and access to a rocky beach. *Inexpensive to moderate. (207) 338-1455.*

Searsport

There is plenty of evidence of Searsport's history as an old seafaring town. In the late 1800s, more than 200 sea captains lived in Searsport, and many of their houses—some now doing duty as B&Bs—line the streets. The Penobscot Marine Museum has many artifacts of the local shipping and shipbuilding industries. Searsport's strip of antique stores and outside flea markets is appealing to antiques and bargain hunters.

🕸 MOOSE POINT STATE PARK

[Fig. 15(4)] This park between downtown Belfast and Searsport has a beautiful wide-open view of Penobscot Bay. There are picnic areas, outhouses, swings, and a footpath through the pines to tidal pools and a quiet point. There's a beach, but no swimming is allowed. With its spacious lawn, easy paths and scenic beach, this park is great spot to stop for a picnic and a walk.

Directions: On US 1 south of downtown Searsport.

Activities: Picnicking, walking, checking out tidal pools.

Facilities: Entry station, picnic areas, outhouses.

Dates: Open Memorial Day weekend to Oct. 1, but grounds accessible year-round.

Fees: There is a charge for admission.

Closest town: Searsport, 1 mile.

For more information: Moose Point State Park, Route 1, Searsport, ME 04974. Phone (207) 548-2882. Off season, Maine Bureau of Parks and Lands, 22 State House State, Augusta, ME 04333. Phone (207) 287-3821.

🕸 PENOBSCOT MARINE MUSEUM

[Fig. 15(5)] This museum uses a dozen historic buildings to guide visitors through the history of the marine industry of Maine, focusing on the Penobscot Bay region. There are historic boats and a faithfully restored and furnished sea captain's house. There are also displays of objects from the China trade that dominated the shipping industry in Searsport's late eighteenth century heyday, and a gallery that guides visitors through the evolution of seafaring vessels. A highlight of this museum is its galleries of world-class marine art and artifacts, including a gallery dedicated to the work of master marine painters Thomas and James Buttersworth.

An active Congregational Church on the museum grounds has Louis Comfort Tiffany windows. Children can play with the rigging on a ship mast in an outdoor play area.

Directions: Route 1 at the corner of Church Street in Searsport.

Dates: Open Memorial Day weekend to Columbus Day.

Fees: There is a fee charged for admission.

Closest town: Searsport.

For more information: Penobscot Marine Museum, PO Box 498, Searsport, ME 04974. Phone (207) 548-2529

BLUEJACKET SHIPCRAFTERS

[Fig. 15(6)] This Searsport business is known for manufacturing some of the finest model ship kits available. Most of Bluejacket's business is through the mail, but there is a showroom and retail store in its Searsport factory. The model ships on display include tiny re-creations of historic schooners, lobster boats, mahogany runabouts, and World War II destroyers.

Directions: Heading northeast out of Searsport on Route 1, look for Bluejacket in a gray building that looks like a miniature lighthouse.

For more information: Bluejacket Shipcrafters, PO Box 425, Stockton Springs, ME 04981. Phone (800) 448-5567.

FORT POINT STATE PARK

[Fig. 15(7)] Fort Point State Park in Stockton Springs sits on 154 acres at the tip of a peninsula in Penobscot Bay. A 200-foot pier welcomes boaters and is also a good fishing and bird-watching spot. The point is named for Fort Pownall, built in 1759 by the British to protect their territory during the French and Indian Wars. Only the earthworks remain today. The Fort Point Lighthouse guards the mouth of the Penobscot River here.

According to *A Birder's Guide to Maine*, Stockton Springs is "synonymous with ruddy ducks." These chunky, stiff-tailed sea ducks can often be found in rafts here in the fall. Red-tailed hawks (*Buteo jamaicensis*) may also be seen here.

Directions: From Route 1 in Stockton Springs, follow signs to Fort Point State Park. Bear right on Main Street, turn left on East Cape Road, then left again on Fort Point Road.

Activities: Fishing, picnicking, birding.

Dates: Officially open Memorial Day weekend to Labor Day, but the grounds accessible year-round.

Fees: There is a charge for admission.

Closest town: Stockton Springs.

For more information: Bureau of Parks and Lands, 106 Hogan Road, Bangor, ME 04401. Phone (207) 941-4014.

CAMPING IN SEARSPORT

Searsport Shores. Route 1, Searsport. This waterfront complex has 120 sites, including 40 designated for tents. It also has showers and toilets, 30-amp and water hookups for RVs, and a private beach. *Inexpensive. (207) 548-6059.*

DINING IN SEARSPORT

Searsport has fine dining and some good takeout food. Try a picnic at Moose Point State Park for lunch and dinner in an old sea captain's house.

JORDAN'S RESTAURANT. Route 1, Searsport. This local institution has eat-in or takeout food, including great french fries and shakes. *Inexpensive. (207) 548-2555.*

LIGHT'S DINER. Route 1, Searsport. This diner is attached to a funky 50s-style motel and serves lots of fried fish. *Inexpensive to moderate. (207) 548-2405.*

THE NICKERSON TAVERN. Route 1, Searsport. This is a gourmet restaurant in an old sea captain's house. *Moderate to expensive. (207) 548-2220.*

LODGING IN SEARSPORT

Searsport is loaded with old sea captain's homes now doing duty as B&B inns. For a brochure describing several, write the Searsport B&B Association, PO Box 787, Searsport, ME 04974. Searsport also has several motels and tourist cabins, for visitors who prefer cable TV to antique four-posters.

CAPTAIN A. V. NICKELS INN. Route 1, Searsport. This is a comfortable waterfront Victorian mansion with nine rooms, some of which share bathrooms. *Moderate. (207) 548-6691.*

WATCHTIDE. Route 1, Searsport. This big Victorian was once owned by General Henry Knox, George Washington's first secretary of war. It has beautiful views of Penobscot Bay and an interesting gift shop in the barn. *Moderate. (207) 548-6575.*

RED-TAILED HAWK
(Buteo jamaicensis)

Down East

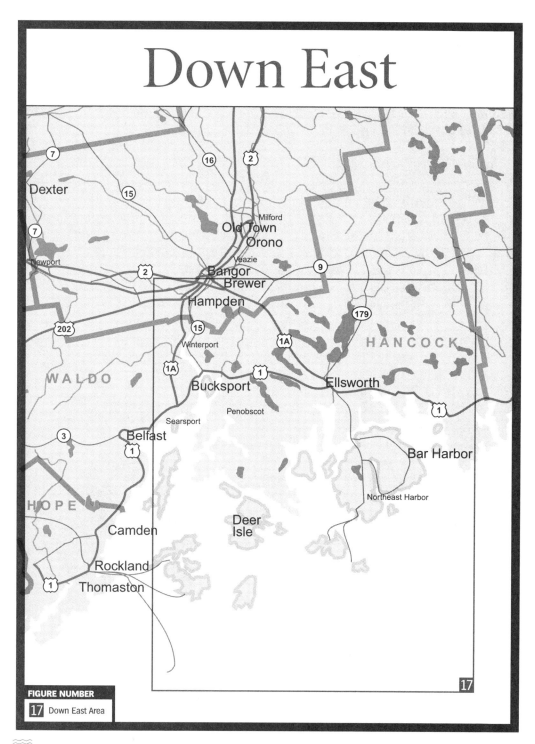

FIGURE NUMBER

17 Down East Area

Down East

There's no official boundary on the map stating where Mid-Coast Maine ends and Down East Maine begins. Outside of Maine, many people use the term Down East to refer to the entire state. Within Maine, however, Down East refers to Maine's easternmost coastal region, including the eastern portions of Hancock and Washington counties. Theories abound on the origins of the term Down East. The most likely has its roots in seafaring navigation; the prevailing winds on the Maine coast come from the southwest. Sailing downwind will take you Down East.

The most visited section of Down East Maine begins at the top of Penobscot Bay in the old seaport of Bucksport, which is overlooked by a historic fort and a modern paper mill, and continues on to Acadia National Park. To the east of Penobscot Bay, the Blue Hill Peninsula is a favorite destination for a diverse group of visitors. History buffs, classical music fans, bird watchers, kayakers, sailors, and anyone looking for a

[*Above: Schooner off Rockland Breakwater*]

scenic spot to spend a few hours or a few days will be rewarded by a trip down this long, winding crescent between the Penobscot and Blue Hill bays.

Keep your field guide on the front seat on a drive Down East. The numerous bays, coves, causeways, and estuaries that nudge in and meander across the land in this section of the Maine coast support an abundance of waterfowl.

Bucksport Area

At the mouth of the Penobscot River sits the town of Bucksport, a paper mill city with some interesting sites and the origin of one of the coast's most colorful local legends. The Penobscot riverfront is dominated by two local institutions, Fort Knox, one of New England's biggest forts, and a Champion International paper mill. Both are open for tours.

In 1764, the town was settled by Jonathan Buck. Buck is the subject of a local legend that is apparently fictional but provides an interesting explanation for the boot-shaped mark on his memorial stone. Buck, a Revolutionary War colonel, was rumored to have ordered the execution of a woman accused of witchcraft. As the tale goes, an outline of the woman's leg and foot appeared on a memorial near his grave. The granite monument, complete with the "witch's leg" outline, can be visited at Buck Cemetery. The real explanation for the boot on the monument is probably more mundane; it's thought to be caused by a flaw in the granite.

Admiral Robert Peary's Arctic exploration boat, the *Roosevelt*, was built on Verona Island, which sits in the Penobscot River between Bucksport and Prospect. The Peary ship was launched March 23, 1905.

A monument commemorating the *Roosevelt* is located in the park near the intersection of U.S. Route 1 and West Side Drive. Most businesses on Verona are located on the short stretch of US Route 1 between the Bucksport and Waldo-Hancock bridges.

▓ FORT KNOX

[Fig. 17(1)] The huge, granite Fort Knox sits at a narrows in the Penobscot River in Prospect, just before US Route 1 crosses the Penobscot into Bucksport. The fort was built between 1844 and 1869 and was strategically located to protect Bangor, at the time an important lumber-producing center, from the British. It was garrisoned during the Civil and Spanish-American wars, but it never came under attack. It was Maine's first granite fort and was used as a model for other forts in the state, including Fort Popham in Phippsburg, Fort Gorges in Casco Bay, and Fort Preble near Portland.

Today, Fort Knox, with its master granite work, long passageways, and many rooms, is fun to explore. A highlight for history buffs is its two enormous Rodman cannons, which could fire 300-pound shells as far as 2 miles. Tours of the fort are available in the summer. Fort Knox is also the site of many events, including concerts, Civil War re-enactments, concerts, and fencing demonstrations.

Directions: Fort Knox is on US Route 1, across the Penobscot River from Bucksport.

Activities: Picnicking, exploring the fort.

Dates: Open May through Oct.

Fees: There is a charge for admission.

Closest town: Bucksport.

For more information: Fort Knox State Historic Site, R.R. #1, Box 1316, Stockton Springs, ME 04981. Phone (207) 469-7719. Or the Friends of Fort Knox, phone (207) 469-6553.

CHAMPION INTERNATIONAL

[Fig. 17(2)] The Champion International paper mill makes 500,000 tons of lightweight coated paper a year for magazines and catalogs. To see how it's done, stop by for a tour. No children under 12 are allowed.

Directions: On Water Street, about 1 mile west of US Route 1.

Dates: Tours are held during the summer months, on Mondays, Wednesdays, and Fridays.

Fees: None.

Closest town: Bucksport.

For more information: Champion International, PO Box 1200, Bucksport, ME 04416. Phone (207) 469-1700.

H.O.M.E.

Joshua Chamberlain

Joshua L. Chamberlain (1828-1914) has always been a local hero in Maine. In recent years, the movie *Gettysburg* and the PBS documentary series *The Civil War* helped make him a well-known historic figure outside of his home state as well.

Chamberlain was born and raised in Brewer, Maine, and attended Bowdoin College in Brunswick and the Bangor Theological Seminary. He became a college professor but left a job teaching rhetoric at Bowdoin in 1862 to join the Union forces in the Civil War. He led the 20th Maine Voluntary Infantry Regiment through several battles and was credited with winning the decisive battle of Gettysburg at Little Round Top. Chamberlain, who rose through the ranks from lieutenant colonel to brigadier general, was later given the honor of accepting the official Confederate surrender at Appomattox. (Chamberlain's decision to have his men salute the surrendering Confederate soldiers as they marched by drew both praise and criticism in the North.) Chamberlain returned to Maine a hero. He served four, one-year terms as governor of Maine, and went on to become president of Bowdoin College.

[Fig. 17(3)] Just east of Bucksport in Orland is a colorful group of buildings set up like a small village. "This is h.o.m.e." says the sign hanging out front. The letters h.o.m.e. stand for Homeworkers Organized for More Employment. It was started in 1970 as a crafts cooperative but has grown into an interesting service organization and minicommunity that includes shelters, a food bank, a sawmill, a thrift store, an

Down East Area

Within Maine, Down East refers to Maine's easternmost coastal region.

Frankfort

46

5

ALAMOOSOOK LAKE

BRANCH POND

180 *GRAHAM LAKE* **179**

200

2 **Bucksport**

4

26

UNION RIVER **Ellsworth**

182

1A

3

Orland

3

27

1

1

Prospect

1

15

UPPER PATTEN POND

176

LOWER PATTEN POND

1

28

184

1

175

199

WIGHT POND

15

TODDY POND

3

Stockton Springs

Searsport

PENOBSCOT RIVER

Penobscot

172

230

Trenton

177

6 **7**

29 **30**

3

11 **12**

Blue Hill

31

Mount Desert Island

Bar Harbor

Castine

176

8

A C A D I A

13

16

172 **10**

9

Bartlett Island

N A T I O N A L

15

EAST PENOBSCOT BAY

14

Long Island

P A R K

102

Sedgwick

175

BLUE HILL BAY

Northeast Harbor

Islesboro Island

Southwest Harbor

3

Brooklin

15

17

Deer Isle

Sunshine Road

Deer Isle

20

JERICHO BAY

19 **18**

Stonington

Swans Island

Great Duck Island

North Haven

Marshall Island

Long Island

25

23

22

Vinalhaven Island

24

21

Vinalhaven

Isle au Haut

N

Ref: Delorme Maine Atlas & Gazetteer

1. Fort Knox
2. Champion International
3. h.o.m.e.
4. Craig Brook National Fish Hatchery
5. Great Pond Mountain Trail
6. Blue Hill
7. Blue Hill Trail
8. Parson Fisher House
9. The Phoenix Centre
10. Blue Hill Falls
11. Castine Walking Tour
12. Maine Maritime Academy and the *State of Maine*
13. Holbrook Island Sanctuary State Park
14. The Good Life Center
15. Goose Falls
16. Bagaduce Falls

17. WoodenBoat School
18. Crockett Cove Woods Preserve
19. Barred Island Preserve
20. Sunshine Campground
21. Western Head Trail
22. Cliff Trail
23. Goat Trail
24. Duck Harbor Trail
25. The Keeper's House
26. The Big Chicken Barn
27. Colonel Black Mansion
28. Birdsacre
29. Barcadia
30. Mount Desert Narrows Camping Resort
31. Kneisel Hall

education and day-care center, and a craft and produce store. Stop by and shop for organic vegetables or for crafts made by hundreds of Maine people.

Directions: h.o.m.e. is on Route 1 in Orland.

Dates. Open year-round.

Fees: None.

Closest town: Orland.

For more information: h.o.m.e., Box 10, Orland, ME 04472. Phone (207) 469-7961.

CRAIG BROOK NATIONAL FISH HATCHERY

[Fig. 17(4)] The U.S. Fish and Wildlife Service has raised Atlantic salmon for Maine rivers at the Craig Brook National Fish Hatchery in East Orland since 1871. The hatchery is not open to the public, but there is an Atlantic Salmon Museum with displays on the hatchery and salmon fishing. Visitors are welcome to use the hatchery's scenic grounds, which include picnic areas, a boat launch on the shores of Alamoosook Lake, and a nature path. The Great Pond Mountain trailhead is nearby.

Directions: From US Route 1 in Bucksport, drive 6 miles east to Fish Hatchery Road. To reach the Great Pond Mountain Trail, drive through the parking lot onto Don Fish Trail. The trailhead will be on the left in a little less than a mile. Park along the roadside. There are maps and brochures in a box at the trailhead.

Activities: Visiting the Atlantic Salmon Museum, picnicking, walking and hiking.

Facilities: Restrooms, picnic tables and grills, boat launch, interpretive nature path.

Dates: The visitor center and museum are open May through Oct. Grounds accessible year-round.

Fees: None.

Closest town: East Orland.

For more information: U.S. Fish and Wildlife Service, Craig Brook National Fish Hatchery, East Orland, ME 04431. Phone (207) 469-2803.

GREAT POND MOUNTAIN TRAIL

[Fig. 17(5)] On a clear day, the view from the top of 1,038-foot Great Pond Mountain takes in a beautiful swath of Maine, from the Camden Hills and Mount Desert Island on the coast to Mount Katahdin inland.

The trail is 2 miles long round trip, with some steep spots.

GOLF IN THE BUCKSPORT AREA
BUCKSPORT GOLF AND COUNTRY CLUB. This golf course is Maine's longest 9-hole course at 3,413 yards.

FRILLED SEA ANEMONE
(Metridium senile)

For more information: Bucksport Golf and Country Club. Duck Cove Road, Bucksport, ME 04416. Phone (207) 469-7612.

DINING IN THE BUCKSPORT AREA

Walk down Main Street and take your pick of ice cream, pizza, or dinner and a drink at MacLeod's.

MACLEOD'S. Main Street, Bucksport. This restaurant is a favorite among locals and travelers and serves basic dinner fare. *Moderate. (207) 469-3963.*

LODGING IN THE BUCKSPORT AREA

You can find a room with cable TV and AC, or one with antique furniture and a fireplace.

JED PROUTY MOTOR INN. Main Street, Bucksport. If you are in the mood for cable TV and other modern conveniences, this Best Western could be the place for you. *Moderate. (207) 469-3113.*

THE SIGN OF THE AMIABLE PIG. Castine Road, Orland. This inn, which is named after the weathervane atop its barn, is full of fireplaces, antiques, and Oriental rugs. *Moderate. (207) 469-2561.*

The Blue Hill Peninsula

The Blue Hill Peninsula is named for the lone 934-foot hill near its eastern shore and is the site of several small villages, each worthy of a visit. They include the quaint village of Castine and the casually elegant cultural center of Blue Hill. There is also the town of Brooklin, where E.B. White lived for many years and where *WoodenBoat Magazine* is published.

The small Cape Rosier Peninsula has a quiet nature sanctuary and the farm where Scott and Helen Nearing helped spawn a modern homesteading movement by living off the land and writing about their experiences. Many artists and craftspeople—including painters, potters, knitters, and a winemaker known for his hard apple cider—have settled here. Their work is available at galleries and businesses in the various peninsula towns.

A huge suspension bridge stretches off the base of the peninsula to Little Deer Isle, where motorists then drive over a narrow causeway to reach Deer Isle, a summer haven for artists, a year-round fishing community, and home to some interesting nature preserves. It is from the Deer Isle town of Stonington that you can catch the ferry to Isle au Haut, an isolated and lovely piece of Acadia National Park.

A number of tidal estuaries break into the land of the Blue Hill Peninsula, giving it a very craggy shoreline. These salt ponds and waterways make for some great bird-watching, especially during the spring and fall migrations.

BLUE HILL

[Fig. 17(6)] Blue Hill is the cultural and commercial center of the peninsula. It's the summer home of many musicians, some of whom perform at the Kneisel Hall Chamber Music School. There's a definite high-brow feeling to Blue Hill, where you'll find an exceptional community radio station (WERU, 89.9 FM), two good bookstores, several antique shops, art galleries, and good restaurants, and the Bagaduce Music Lending Library, which lends out scores and sheet music through the mail or in-person.

Blue Hill owes some of its cultural prosperity to the town's first cleric, Parson Jonathan Fisher. Fisher, who moved to Blue Hill in the 1790s and stayed until his death more than 50 years later, was something of a Colonial-era Renaissance man. He was an accomplished painter, builder, carpenter, inventor, and writer. He founded the Blue Hill Academy and built the Congregational parsonage that is now a museum showcasing his talents and contributions to Blue Hill.

BLUE HILL TRAIL

[Fig. 17(7)] At 934 feet, Blue Hill isn't high as mountains go. But it's the highest point in this area, so it offers some beautiful panoramic views on clear days. The fairly easy trail begins in an open field and travels through hardwood and spruce forests before concluding at the domed top of the hill. There's a fire tower for those who want to check out the view from a slightly higher vantage point. This is a popular hike on nice days, so expect to have some company atop the hill.

Directions: From US Route 1 in Orland, take ME 15, or the Blue Hill Road, south for 11 miles. Take a left on Mountain Road and look for the trailhead in 0.4 miles.

Trail: 2 miles (round-trip). Easy.

PARSON FISHER HOUSE

[Fig. 17(8)] This 1814 house, where Parson Jonathan Fisher raised nine children, is a good example of a Colonial family home. The house and much of its furnishings were built by Fisher. An addition houses a museum with some of Fisher's tools and bookbinding equipment.

Directions: From Blue Hill, head west on ME 15. The Parson Fisher House is just past the turnoff to South Blue Hill.

Dates: Open July through mid-Sept.

Fees: There is a charge for admission.

Closest town: Blue Hill.

For more information: The Jonathan Fisher Memorial Inc., PO Box 527, Blue Hill, ME 04614. Phone (207) 374-2459.

KNEISEL HALL

[Fig. 17(31)] This chamber music program has attracted world-class musicians to Blue Hill since it was started in 1922 by the noted Austrian violinist Franz Kneisel. Its instructors and students give regular concerts.

Directions: Kneisel Hall is on Pleasant Street in Blue Hill.

Dates: The various adult and youth programs take place in the summer months. Write for a schedule.

Fees: There is a charge for admission to the concerts.

Closest town: Blue Hill.

For more information: Kneisel Hall, PO Box 648, Blue Hill, ME 04614. Phone (207) 374-2811.

THE PHOENIX CENTRE

[Fig. 17(9)] This family-run center is near the Blue Hill Falls, a popular spot with kayakers. It offers a variety of sea kayak classes and trips, which last from a half day to several days. Canoe instructions are also available. The Phoenix Centre also has a Junior Guide program that teaches outdoor skills, including navigation, conservation, and first aid, to teenagers.

BLACK SPRUCE
(Picea mariana)
This evergreen is one of the most widely distributed conifers in North America, found from Alaska to Labrador.

Directions: The Phoenix Centre is on ME 175. If you're coming from Blue Hill, it's on the right, just after Salt Pond.

Closest town: Blue Hill.

For more information: The Phoenix Centre, Route 175, Blue Hill Falls, ME 04615. Phone (207) 374-2113.

BLUE HILL FALLS

[Fig. 17(10)] This reversing falls at the mouth of Salt Pond in Blue Hill Bay is popular with kayakers and canoeists because of its whitewater near high tide. Novice paddlers should not attempt this falls, as the current is quite strong. Park along ME 175 and watch for traffic while walking to the falls. On sunny days, the rocks along the river make a fine spot for bird-watching and picnicking.

Directions: From Blue Hill, follow ME 172/ME 175 south. The falls are near the bridge where ME175 heads to the left.

Activities: Paddling, bird-watching, picnicking.

NIGHT LIFE IN BLUE HILL

Blue Hill has an active year-round population. Many of their night-time activities revolve around music, but not solely chamber music.

THE LEFT BANK BAKERY AND CAFÉ. ME 182, Blue Hill. This popular spot offers good food all day. At night, it is accompanied by fine folk, jazz, and other music. Reservations are a good idea because many shows sell out. *Inexpensive to moderate. (207) 374-2201.*

DINING IN BLUE HILL

Blue Hill has several good restaurants. Most of them come with beautiful views as well as fine food.

JEAN-PAUL BISTRO. Main Street, Blue Hill. Jean-Paul offers breakfast, lunch, and tea. *Moderate. (207) 374-5852.*

FIREPOND. Main Street, Blue Hill. This restaurant sits on an old mill stream in the middle of the village and has excellent food. *Moderate to expensive. (207) 374-9970.*

LODGING IN BLUE HILL

Blue Hill has many fine inns, but don't arrive in the summer without a reservation.

BLUE HILL INN. Union Street, Blue Hill. This Federal-style inn is near the center of the village of Blue Hill and is full of antiques and fireplaces. Outside, there are gardens and an apple orchard. *Expensive. (800) 826-7415.*

JOHN PETERS INN. Peters Point, Blue Hill. This brick mansion sits on a beautiful point just outside the village of Blue Hill. Several of its rooms have fireplaces and decks. *Expensive. (207) 374-2116.*

HERITAGE MOTOR INN. Blue Hill. This is a plain motel with beautiful views. *Moderate. (207) 374-5646.*

Castine

With its stately white clapboard homes, elm-lined streets, and beautiful harbor, Castine could be a movie set for an all-American seaside village. Castine's history is as interesting as its scenery is beautiful. The British and the French battled over this town for much of the seventeenth and eighteenth centuries. (The Dutch held possession briefly, as well.)

The colonists suffered what some historians consider America's worst Naval defeat ever in 1779 when they failed to capture a poorly manned British fort. When more British troops arrived, the Americans, whose leaders included Commodore Dudley Saltonstall and Colonel Paul Revere, retreated upriver, scuttled their ships, and returned to Boston on foot. Castine remained a Tory community through the Revolutionary War.

Many British loyalists in New England settled here because they mistakenly believed that the Penobscot River would be the border between Maine and New

Castine's Elms

As you walk through the pretty village of Castine, stop and take a look at the trees that tower over the streets and sidewalks. Chances are you haven't seen streets lined with these oddly familiar trees in years.

They are American elms (*Ulmus americana*), which were killed by the tens of thousands from the 1930s to the 1970s across the country by elm bark beetles carrying the Dutch elm disease fungus.

A closer inspection of the Castine elms will reveal that each is tagged and numbered. It's part of Castine's aggressive campaign to see its elms survive. At the first sign of an infection, a tree is pruned and the diseased wood is promptly burned. Trees are also injected with a fungicide to kill any Dutch elm fungus. Trees that have been destroyed are replaced with new elms.

Castine launched its program to protect the village's elm trees decades ago, and was one of the first communities to inject trees with the fungicide. Vigilance on the part of citizens and village employees has made Castine's elm-saving campaign a success. While some trees have been lost, most have survived the blight that wiped out all the elms in neighboring towns.

Brunswick. When peace was declared at the end of the Revolutionary War, the loyalists learned that the New Brunswick border was set farther east at the St. Croix River. Many of them dismantled their homes, put them on barges, and moved to New Brunswick, where they established St. Andrews. Some of their Castine-built houses remain standing there today.

That wasn't the end of British occupation of Castine The British captured Castine's Fort George once again in 1812 but evacuated the next year, and Castine has been an American town ever since.

Castine is home to the Maine Maritime Academy and has many historic inns and interesting shops.

Directions: From Route 1 in Orland, head south on ME 175, then on ME 166 and ME 166A, into Castine. Follow Wadsworth Cove Road or State Street into the village.

CASTINE WALKING TOUR

[Fig. 17(11)] The best way to explore Castine and learn about its history is to stop in any downtown business and pick up a copy of a walking tour brochure prepared by the Castine Merchants Association. The walking tour can be completed in an hour or so, depending on how much time you spend at the historic markers along the way. It takes in Fort George, the Maine Maritime Academy; Dyce Head Lighthouse, which is now privately owned; archaeological excavations, and many beautiful and storied eighteenth and nineteenth century homes.

Directions: The brochure is available at many businesses on Main Street.

Closest town: Blue Hill.

For more information: Castine Merchants Association, PO Box 329, Castine, ME 04421.

MAINE MARITIME ACADEMY AND THE *STATE OF MAINE*

[Fig. 17(12)] The large, grassy campus overlooking the village of Castine is the Maine Maritime Academy, which offers undergraduate and graduate degrees in marine engineering, ocean studies, nautical science, and other fields. The academy is the source of the many young people in military-style uniforms you may encounter around town.

The Maine Maritime Academy's fleet includes nearly 100 boats, including the schooner *Bowdoin*, and the 500-foot training vessel *State of Maine*, which academy midshipmen take on cruises to ports all over the world. Students give tours of the *State of Maine*, a former Navy hydrographic vessel, on weekdays during the summer.

Directions: The Maine Maritime Academy is at the top of the hill in Castine and is bordered by Pleasant, Tarratine and Court streets. The *State of Maine*, when it is in port, docks at the Castine waterfront. For a schedule of *State of Maine* tours, ask at the dock or call the academy.

Closest town: Blue Hill.

For more information: Maine Maritime Academy, Castine, ME 04421. Phone (207) 326-4311.

GOLF IN CASTINE

THE CASTINE GOLF CLUB. Battle Avenue. This course's original nine holes were laid out in 1897, although the first five holes were moved from Fort George in 1918. The club also has clay tennis courts.

For more information: The Castine Golf Club. Battle Avenue, Castine, ME 04420. Phone (207) 326-8844.

DINING IN CASTINE

For a small town, Castine offers every kind of dining, from great takeout and casual waterfront fare to fine dining in some of the village's inns.

BAH'S BAKEHOUSE. Water Street, Castine. Great sandwiches, salads, and soups are available for eating in or out at this spot below the Village Inn. *Inexpensive (207) 326-9510.*

THE BREEZE. Town Dock, Castine. This tiny fast food snack bar sits right at the town dock. *Inexpensive. (207) 326-4032.*

DENNETT'S WHARF. Sea Street, Castine. You can't beat the view from this waterfront spot, which serves seafood and other fare. *Inexpensive to moderate. (207) 326-9045.*

▓ LODGING IN CASTINE

Several of Castine's historic buildings now house inns and B&Bs. If you're planning a summer visit, it's a good idea to make your reservations well in advance.

CASTINE INN. Main Street, Castine. This lovely, 1898 inn is a block from the harbor. Its dining room is open to the public. *Moderate to expensive. (207) 326-4365.*

THE PENTAGOET INN. Main Street, Castine. This elegant Victorian inn also opens its dining room to the public. *Moderate to expensive. (207) 326-8616.*

▓ HOLBROOK ISLAND SANCTUARY STATE PARK

[Fig. 17(13)] This sanctuary, which was donated to the state of Maine by longtime resident Anita Harris, has several habitats to explore on 1,350 acres of land. There is an island, upland forest, rocky shore, salt marsh, pond, and mud flats. The forest is home to deer, fox, muskrats, beaver, and porcupines. Harbor seals sometimes sun themselves on the ledges of Penobscot Bay. Holbrook Island is also a good bird-watching spot. Great blue herons (*Ardea herodias*) and ospreys (*Panion haliaetus*) are said to nest near the pond. There is a network of about 8 miles of old roads and trails for walking or cross-country skiing. The sanctuary has picnic areas, as well as a spot to launch a canoe or kayak.

While it's tempting to head right to the oceanfront of this sanctuary, the inland Fresh Pond and beaver flowage are interesting to explore. Reach the beaver flowage from the Lawrence Hill Road and look for beaver dams and lodges made from sticks and muskrat lodges made of cattails. In the summer months, look for water lilies in the pond, which is accessible from the Fresh Pond trail.

In the summer, Holbrook Island Sanctuary has a series of nature walks, including a late-night "owl prowl," that examine the preserve's wildflowers, birds, and habitats.

Directions: From ME 176 in Brooksville, go west on Cape Rosier Road, following signs to the sanctuary. The sanctuary headquarters has maps and nature walk information.

Activities: Hiking, picnicking, canoeing, kayaking, bird-watching, cross-country skiing.

Dates: Open year-round.

Fees: None.

Closest town: Harborside.

For more information: Holbrook Island Sanctuary, PO Box 280, Brooksville, ME 04617. Phone (207) 326-4012.

MAYAPPLE
(Podophyllum peltatum) Its immature fruits, seeds and other plant parts are poisonous.

GOOSE FALLS

[Fig. 17(15)] This reversing falls is at the inlet to the Goose Pond estuary. Like other reversing falls, the current runs out of the waterway at low tide and the ocean runs back into the estuary at high tide, creating rapids and eddies. Kayakers love reversing falls, but only experienced paddlers should try them.

Directions: From ME 176, go west on Cape Rosier Road, following it to a T in the road. Turn right at the Rosier Rainbow Grange Hall and drive for 2 miles before turning left on Harborside Road. Follow Harborside Road for about 1 mile. The falls occur at high tide at the entrance of the Goose Pond estuary, near the intersection of Harborside Road and Old Mine Road.

Activities: Paddling, sight-seeing.

Closest town: Harborside.

BAGADUCE FALLS

[Fig. 17(16)] Another reversing falls on the Blue Hill Peninsula is the Bagaduce Falls, between the Bagaduce estuary and Snow Cove. Like other reversing falls, the Bagaduce Falls comes alive at high tide, when water pours through a narrow channel, creating currents and eddies. Only the experienced should try paddling on reversing falls, as the currents can be deceptively strong.

Directions: The falls can be viewed near the ME 175/176 bridge over the Bagaduce River at North Brooksville.

Activities: Paddling, sight-seeing.

Closest town: North Brooksville.

WOODENBOAT SCHOOL

[Fig. 17(17)] The people who put out *WoodenBoat Magazine* offer classes at a 64-acre "saltwater campus" in the quaint town of Brooklin. More than 600 students attend the WoodenBoat School each year for courses in boatbuilding, seamanship, and related topics.

The WoodenBoat Store sells boatbuilding and woodworking tools, books, and videos. While you are in Brooklin, stop by the Friend Memorial Library, where the pretty Circle of Friends Garden is a memorial to E.B. and Katherine White, longtime Brooklin residents.

Directions: From downtown Brooklin, head about 1 mile down Naskeag Point Road.

Closest town: Brooklin.

For more information: WoodenBoat School, PO Box 78, Brooklin, ME 04616. Phone (207) 359-4651.

LITTLE BROWN BAT
(Myotis lucifugus)

Scott and Helen Nearing

Scott and Helen Nearing helped launch the modern "back-to-the-land" movement in the 1970s with a series of books on their success homesteading on simple farms in Vermont and Maine.

Scott Nearing (1883-1983) was a well-known social radical and peace activist before he and his wife, Helen, moved to the country after his views lost him two university positions. The Nearings spent decades living what they called "the good life," growing nearly everything they ate, eschewing all machinery but their cars, and leading physically active, vegetarian lives. At Forest Farm in Harborside, they built a stone house from rocks they found on the beach. They became heroes to environmentalists, vegetarians, pacifists, and a huge band of followers who left the cities to build their own solar-powered homes in the country. The Nearings wrote many books on their views and their life, and they allowed visitors to come to their farm and see homesteading in action. After Scott Nearing intentionally fasted to death in 1983 at age 100, his widow wrote *Leaving the Good Life*. She died in 1995 in a car crash near the Harborside farm at the age of 91. A trust now operates The Good Life Center at Forest Farm, and visitors are still welcome to come see the Nearing farm and learn about the couple's philosophy and lifestyle.

THE GOOD LIFE CENTER

[Fig. 17(14)] Helen and Scott Nearing sparked the modern homesteading movement when they moved back to the land, first in Vermont and then in Maine, and wrote a series of books about "the good life." Forest Farm, the Harborside farm where they spent their last four decades, is now open for tours and lectures on gardening and other issues related to living simply.

Directions: From ME 176, go west on Cape Rosier Road, following it to a T in the road. Turn right at the Rosier Rainbow Grange Hall and drive for 2 miles before turning left on Harborside Road. Follow Harborside Road for 2 miles. You'll see the ocean on your right. At the top of the hill, look for a mailbox on the left for the Nearing Good Life Center.

Activities: Sight-seeing, attending programs.

Facilities: Farm, museum, shop.

Dates: The center is usually open Thursday to Monday afternoons year-round, but it's a good idea to call ahead. Some programs are held in the evenings.

Closest town: Harborside.

For more information: The Good Life Center. Box 11, Harborside Road, Harborside, ME 04642. Phone (207) 326-8211. The Trust for Public Land. 33 Union Street, Boston, MA 02108. Phone (617) 367-6200.

▓ LODGING IN THE BROOKLIN/BROOKSVILLE AREA

You'll find several country inns and tourist cottages in this area.

EGGEMOGGIN REACH BED AND BREAKFAST. Winneganek Way, Brooksville. All the rooms at this B&B have wonderful water views. *Expensive. (207) 359-5073.*

OAKLAND HOUSE SEASIDE INN AND COTTAGES. Herrick Road, Sargentville. Many families return summer after summer to this resort, where they stay in cottages and eat in a main dining room. There is a private lake beach, hiking trails and plenty of activity. Cottages rent by the week. *Moderate. (207) 359-8521.*

HIRAM BLAKE CAMP. Harborside. Founded in 1916, this waterfront cottage colony has a group dining room with an added bonus—thousands of books to borrow. The resort also has hiking trails, rowboats, and other activities. Cottages rent by the week. *Moderate (207) 326-4951.*

Deer Isle

[Fig. 17] This island, which has been accessible by car since 1939, when a long, narrow suspension bridge was built over Eggemoggin Reach, includes the towns of Deer Isle and Stonington, as well as some smaller villages. Thanks to the nationally respected Haystack Mountain School of Crafts, many artists have settled on this 9-mile-long island. Their work is visible in galleries and shops all over the island, especially in the town of Deer Isle.

Stonington has the look and feel of a working waterfront and has a year-round fishing community. Like many other coastal communities, its history includes a strong ship-building and granite quarrying tradition. Deer Isle has some interesting nature preserves and other spots to admire the scenery. The Deer Isle Walking Trails Group has prepared a map that shows roads and trails good for hiking, cycling, and bird-watching. It's available at many island lodgings or from the trails group, for a charge. Thanks to the beautiful scenery and the calm, island-speckled waters of the Deer Island Thorofare just off its shore, Stonington has become one of the Maine coast's most popular jumping-off points for sea kayaking. There are many small islands that allow kayak landings and some calm coves in which to paddle and watch wildlife. Kayakers should join the Maine Island Trail Association (*see* page 92) to find out which islands are accessible. Or join an excursion hosted by a commercial kayak touring company (*see* Appendix E), several of which guide tours out of Stonington.

OLD MAN'S BEARD
(Usnea sp.)

Information: The Deer Isle Walking Trails Group. Phone (207) 367-2448. Island Heritage Trust, PO Box

369, Atlantic Avenue, Stonington, ME 04681. Phone (207) 367-6599. Maine Island Trail Association, PO Box C, Rockland, ME 04841. Phone (207) 761-8225.

CROCKETT COVE WOODS PRESERVE

[Fig. 17(18)] This 98-acre nature preserve, owned by The Nature Conservancy, is a good example of wet woodlands and has several varieties of lichens, moss, and other plants characteristic of this type of habitat. Among the network of footpaths in the preserve is a 0.25-mile interpretive nature trail with a very helpful brochure. The Crockett Cove Woods is a "fog forest," where fog carried in from the ocean by the wind clings to the trees. The ground, rocks, and trees are carpeted with a variety of flora that thrive in cool, moist conditions found in some of Maine's coastal forests. It's a good spot to learn to identify some mosses (green plants that multiply by spores) and lichens (communities of fungi and algae.)

The mosses and many of the other plants found here prefer or tolerate the acidic, nutrient-poor soil, which is a result of the region's granite bedrock.

The most common moss seen here is the Schreber's moss (*Pleurozium schreberi*), a feathery, relatively large moss at up to 4 inches long that lies in mats on the ground. Schreber's moss formerly was used to line fruit and vegetable boxes.

The small green plant that looks like a tiny pine tree seedling growing along the trail is not a seedling, it is hair-capped moss (*Polytricum juniperinum*), which can be seen growing in woods and other damp spots all over the coast of Maine. Its name—haircap—is in reference to its spore capsules, which grow on tall, woody red stems topped by a white spore.

Another distinctive plant here is the Staghorn clubmoss (*Lycopodium clavatum*), or ground pine, which looks like small pine boughs growing on the rocks. It has a distinctive stalk, which is topped by up to three yellowish spore cones. The yellow or red spongy moss growing near the bog is peat moss or sphagnum moss.

Several types of lichen can also be found here with the help of The Nature Conservancy's trail guide. Old man's beard lichen (*Usnea* sp) hangs from the trees. Reindeer lichen (*Cladina rangifera*) looks like 4-inch-tall silver trees.

The acidic soil here is low in nitrogen. At least two insectivorous plants, which trap and digest insects to supplement their nitrogen intake, grow here. The northern pitcher plant (*Sarracenia purpurea*) has reddish flowers that hang from the top of 20-inch stems

Hair-Capped Moss

It's easy to mistake hair-capped moss (*Polytricum juniperinum*) for a little pine or fir seedling. With its soft needles and erect posture, it looks like a tiny coniferous tree.

Hair-capped moss can be seen all along the Maine coast, especially on damp forest floors and along the edges of bogs. The term haircap refers to its spore capsules, which grow on a 9-inch red stem topped with a white spore.

and cup-shaped leaves that hold water. Insects become trapped in hairs on the leaves and drown in the water. Round-leaved sundew (*Drosera rotundifolia*) has tiny white flowers and traps insects on its sticky leaves.

Directions: Follow ME 15 south down the Deer Isle Peninsula, taking the right turn towards Sunset in Deer Isle Village. Three miles beyond the Sunset Post Office, turn right on Whitman Road. Turn right onto Fire Lane 88, where you will see The Nature Conservancy sign and registration box.

Activities: Walking, nature exploration, bird-watching.

Dates: Open year-round.

Closest town: Sunset, 3 miles.

For more information: The Nature Conservancy, Maine Chapter, Fort Andross, 14 Maine Street, Suite 401, Brunswick, ME 04011. Phone (207) 729-5181.

BARRED ISLAND PRESERVE

[Fig. 17(19)] This Nature Conservancy preserve includes an 11-acre island and a 40-acre mainland parcel on the southwestern shore of Deer Isle that are connected by a sand bar at low tide. It is not accessible at high tide, so check a local tide chart before scheduling a visit. Most of the preserve is covered with spruce and fir trees and shrubs. There is a main trail from the parking lot to the sandbar, but no trails on the island. There is an osprey (*Pandion haliaetus*) nest on the island's northwest corner. Visitors should give the nest wide berth by staying on the sandbar.

Frederick Law Olmsted, the landscape architect of New York's Central Park, owned Barred Island at the turn of the century. His grandniece, Carolyn Olmsted, gave the island to The Nature Conservancy. It is managed by Island Heritage Trust, a local land trust.

Directions: Heading south down Deer Isle on ME 15, take a right turn towards Sunset in Deer Isle Village. Then take a right on Goose Cove Road and follow this to The Nature Conservancy lot. If the lot is full, try again later as parking is not permitted on the road. There is a 1-mile moderately difficult walk to the island.

Activities: Hiking, shoreline exploration, bird-watching.

Closest town: Sunset.

For more information: The Nature Conservancy, Maine Chapter, Fort Andross, 14 Maine Street, Suite 401, Brunswick, ME 04011. Phone (207) 729-5181. Island Heritage Trust, PO Box 42, Deer Isle, ME 04627.

CAMPING ON DEER ISLE

Sunshine Campground. [Fig. 17(20)] This campground has RV electric hookups, a dump station, and tent sites. *(207) 348-6681.*

DINING ON DEER ISLE

Fishing is a big local industry on Deer Isle, so it's not surprising that many Deer Isle restaurants specialize in seafood. But you can get a good pizza here, too.

BAYVIEW RESTAURANT. Sea Breeze Avenue, Stonington. This comfortable spot serves local seafood and great fruit pie. *Inexpensive to moderate. (207) 367-2274.*

JOEY'S. Church Street, Deer Isle. Joey's specializes in pizza and sandwiches to eat in or take out. *Inexpensive. (207) 348-2911.*

LODGING ON DEER ISLE

Deer Isle lodging runs the gamut, from little B&Bs to larger inns. Most rooms seem to come with a view.

GOOSE COVE LODGE. Goose Cove Road, Sunset. This resort near the Barred Island Preserve is popular with outdoor explorers and families. Its lodge and cabins are comfortable and its dining room, which is open to the public, serves great food. *Moderate to expensive. (207) 348-2508.*

BURNT COVE BED AND BREAKFAST. Whitman Road, Stonington. Kayakers can launch their boats from this B&B's beach. *Moderate. (207) 367-2392.*

PILGRIM'S INN. Main Street, Deer Isle. This beautifully restored inn on a tidal cove has great views, wonderful food, private rooms and suites. *Expensive. (207) 348-6615.*

Island Pastures

Maine has several Sheep Islands, a few Hog Islands, and at least one Cow Island.

The names go back to an old coastal farming tradition: farmers ferrying their livestock out to island pastures where the only fence was the shoreline.

About a dozen Maine islands still have sheep grazing on them. The sheep keep vegetation low and views open, and it's said that the island air makes their wool especially warm.

Isle au Haut

[Fig. 17] Untouched by the tourism industry, this island 8 miles off the coast is a unique blend: part working fishing community, part summer home for the well-heeled, and part national parkland. In 1604, Samuel de Champlain named this "high island" rising out of Penobscot Bay Isle au Haut (pronounced Isle'-a-hoe or Eel'-a-hoe, depending on whom you ask). It is reached by a 45-minute ride aboard a mail-boat from Stonington.

Isle au Haut is a great destination, especially for hikers, birdwatchers, and naturalists. Fortunately, it is possible to make a day trip to Isle au Haut because overnight accommodations are limited. There's one inn and a handful of national park lean-tos, all of which require reservations, so plan ahead if you want to spend a night.

Day trippers should catch the first boat out to Isle au Haut, since the Park Service limits the number of daily visitors. During the summer months, a park ranger greets the boats that land at Duck Harbor with trail maps and other information. If you get off the boat at the town landing, take a right at the only road and you'll run into the ranger station.

Sixty-some people live year-round on Isle au Haut. Most of the adults fish for a living. The kids attend the one-room schoolhouse. After a day of hiking, visitors can walk through their small community, stopping in at the tiny post office and the general store.

BIRDING ON ISLE AU HAUT

A bird-watching trip to Isle au Haut begins on the mailboat. As the boat meanders its way through the dozens of islands that pepper Penobscot Bay, you will likely see lots of waterfowl, including common eiders (*Somateria mollissima*), common golden-eye (*Bucephala clangula*), and great cormorants (*Phalacrocorax carbo*). According to *A Birder's Guide to Maine*, Isle au Haut has the largest concentration of harlequin ducks in the western North Atlantic, with more than 150 birds, best seen from the eastern shore of Western Head, a rocky headland at the island's southwestern corner, during the winter and spring.

Directions: Take the Isle au Haut mailboat from the Isle au Haut Company Dock on Sea Breeze Avenue in Stonington.

Activities: Hiking, bird-watching, camping.

Facilities: Adirondack-style lean-tos for campers, ranger station, outhouse.

Fees: There is a charge to reserve a campsite on Isle au Haut, and a charge to ride the mailboat.

For more information: For boat information, Isle au Haut Company. Phone (207) 367-2093. To apply for a campsite reservation, write for a reservation form. Acadia National Park, Box 177, Bar Harbor, ME 04609. Phone (207) 288-3338.

HIKING ON ISLE AU HAUT

The National Park Service maintains about 18 miles of trails, many of which intersect, on Isle au Haut. Most of the trails run through the island's thickly wooded interior, but there are trails along the shoreline and cliffs as well. If you are only spending a day on the island, plan your hike carefully so that you make it back to the boat landing in time for your trip to the mainland.

One scenic hike for day trippers is to take Western Head Road from the Duck

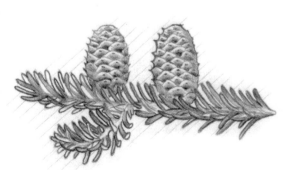

BALSAM FIR
(Abies balsamea)
This evergreen is a true fir species. True firs are identified by their twigs, which are smooth with slight depressions, unlike spruces, which have rough twigs.

Harbor Landing to the Western Head Trail and on to the Cliff and Goat trails, before heading back to the landing via the Duck Harbor Trail.

The Duck Harbor Trail [Fig. 17(24)] begins at the park ranger's station on the north end of the island. It connects with several other trails and the park campsites.

Western Head Trail: [Fig. 17(21)] 1.3 miles. Moderate with some rough terrain.

Cliff Trail: [Fig. 17(22)] 0.7 mile. Moderate with some rough terrain.

Goat Trail: [Fig. 17(23)] 2.1 miles. Moderate with some rough terrain.

Duck Harbor Trail: [Fig. 17(24)] 3.9 miles. Moderate with some rough terrain.

THE KEEPER'S HOUSE

[Fig. 17(25)] This inn is in the keeper's house of a working lighthouse. It has an abundance of beautiful scenery, gourmet food, and a one-of-a-kind location. The Keeper's House is a great base for a vacation exploring Isle au Haut, but many guests never leave the oceanfront grounds of the inn, where Adirondack chairs sit on the rocks next to the lighthouse. The inn has no electricity or telephone, but guests don't seem to miss either. In the evening you can read by gaslight or rest up for a day of hiking and biking with the inn's bicycles. Innkeepers Jeff and Judi Burke can provide directions to trails, sights, and swimming holes before sending you off with a healthy box lunch. To learn more about the Keeper's House, read Jeff Burke's book, *Island Lighthouse Inn, A Chronicle*. The nightly rates are expensive, but include three good meals.

Directions: Take the mailboat out of Stonington to Isle au Haut. Tell the captain where you are headed, and he'll drop you at the inn's dock. Reservations are required.

For more information: The Keeper's House. PO Box 26, Isle au Haut, ME 04645. Phone (207) 367-2261.

The Ellsworth Area

Too many visitors view Ellsworth as simply the last town to drive through before reaching Acadia National Park. But Ellsworth is worth a stop in itself. There's a first-class bird sanctuary, a beautifully preserved mansion, and, for bargain hunters, an L.L. Bean outlet. Ellsworth, once a busy shipbuilding town and still the government and business center of Hancock County, has a quaint downtown full of historic buildings.

THE BIG CHICKEN BARN

[Fig. 17(26)] In a state full of antique barns and used book barns, the Big Chicken Barn stands out. It has 21,000 square feet of antiques, books, and collectibles. The first floor is stocked by dozens of antique and collectible dealers. Upstairs, 9,000-square feet of used and antique books make this the biggest bookstore in Maine. Browsing is encouraged and the coffee is free.

Directions: The Big Chicken Barn is on the south side of Routes 1 and 3, between Bucksport and Ellsworth. It's 11 miles from Bucksport and 9 miles to Ellsworth.

Closest town: Ellsworth, 9 miles.

For more information: The Big Chicken Barn. Route 3, Box 150 A, Ellsworth, ME 04605. Phone (207) 667-7308.

COLONEL BLACK MANSION

[Fig. 17(27)] The descendants of Col. John Black, who built this Georgian mansion in the 1820's, donated it and all its contents to the county. It's chock-full of Black family antiques and interesting objects. The grounds include a beautiful garden and miles of walking or cross-country skiing trails. The carriage house contains a collection of carriages and sleighs.

Directions: The Colonel Black Mansion is on West Main Street, or ME 172, 0.25 mile west of Route 1.

Dates: Open June to mid-Oct.

Fees: There is a charge for admission.

For more information: Colonel Black Museum. PO Box 1478, Surry Road, Ellsworth, ME 04605. (207) 667-8671.

BIRDSACRE

[Fig. 17(28)] This 130-acre bird sanctuary was once the home of ornithologist Cordelia Stanwood (1865-1958). Her home, now the Stanwood Homestead Museum, is open to the public and has a nice collection of stuffed birds and eggs, as well as period furniture.

Miles of trails crisscross the grounds behind the house and wind past ponds and through woodlands. The color-blazed trails are easy to follow. There are picnic areas near Harriet's Pond near the rear of the sanctuary and next to McGinley Pond, close to the museum and parking area. Birdsacre is also an active rehabilitation center for injured birds, and there are always interesting birds, typically including some raptors and owls, in the tall pens and cages near the parking area. Some of these birds will eventually be returned to the wild. Volunteers for the Stanwood Wildlife Foundation operate the museum and sanctuary. Not surprisingly, many of these folks are avid birdwatchers, so if you're in the region to do some birding ask for some tips while you are here.

Directions: Birdsacre is on the west side of Route 3, between downtown Ellsworth and Mount Desert Island. It's easy to miss the entrance on this busy commercial strip. Look for the sign just north of the China Hill Restaurant.

Activities: Bird-watching, walking, picnicking, visiting the museum.

Dates: The sanctuary is open year-round, sunrise to sunset. The museum is open mid-May to Oct. It's a good idea to call ahead if you're planning to visit before Memorial Day or after Labor Day.

Fees: There is no charge for admission to the sanctuary, although donations are accepted. There is an admission charge for the museum.

For more information: Birdsacre, PO Box 485, Ellsworth, ME 04605. Phone (207) 667-8460.

DINING NEAR ELLSWORTH

This area of the Maine Coast is loaded with restaurants, from fast food joints to fine gourmet restaurants.

RIVERSIDE CAFÉ. 42 Main Street, Ellsworth. This breakfast and lunch spot in downtown Ellsworth looks like an old-fashioned luncheonette, but the food—interesting omelets and sandwiches—has been updated. It serves breakfast all day. *Inexpensive. (207) 667-7220.*

LE DOMAINE, Hancock. This French restaurant a few miles east of downtown Ellsworth is considered one of the best in Maine. Le Domaine also has an inn, where dinner is included in the room rate. *Expensive. (207) 422-3395.*

Trenton

Drivers bound for Mount Desert Island and Acadia National Park have to travel down Route 3 in Trenton, where there is a busy tourist strip of attractions. If you've got kids in the car, you may want to stop for a water slide or go-kart ride at Seacoast Fun Park. The Acadia Zoo has a petting zoo, an indoor rain forest and dozens of animals. Some, like the moose and white-tailed deer, are Maine natives. Others, including snow leopards, monkeys, and camels, are more exotic. Trenton also has two information centers stocked with brochures on the area. The Acadia Information Center is on the right, shortly before the Thompson Island bridge heading toward the park. The Mount Desert Island Regional Information Center is on Thompson Island. Both have phones, restrooms, and lots of information on area sites. If you are visiting Acadia National Park, make sure to stop at the park visitor center at Hull's Cove as well. (*See* page 217).

For more information: Seacoast Fun Park, phone (207) 667-3573. Acadia Zoo, phone (207) 667-3244. Acadia Information Center, phone (207) 667-8550. Mount Desert Island Regional Information Center, phone (207) 288-3411.

CAMPING NEAR TRENTON

Trenton has some modern campground facilities for RVs and tents. These have ocean views and provide shuttle bus service to Bar Harbor.

BARCADIA. [Fig. 17(29)] This campground has 200 sites for tents and RVs with hookups. *(207) 288-3520.*

MT. DESERT NARROWS CAMPING RESORT. [Fig. 17(30)] This resort, and its nearby sister campground, Narrows Too, have RV hookups and a heated swimming pool. *(207) 288-4782.*

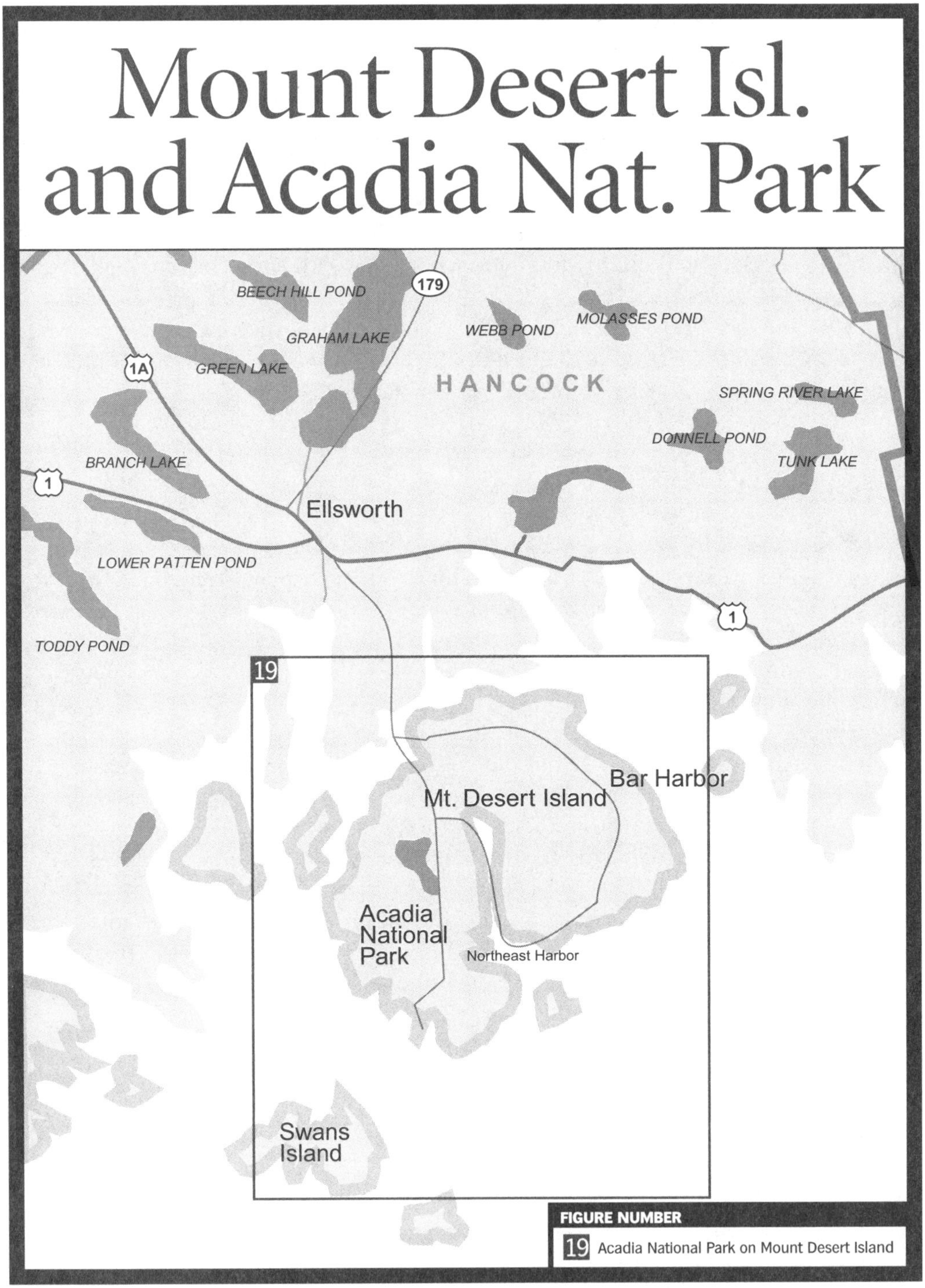

Mount Desert Isl. and Acadia Nat. Park

BEECH HILL POND

179

GRAHAM LAKE

WEBB POND

MOLASSES POND

1A

GREEN LAKE

HANCOCK

SPRING RIVER LAKE

DONNELL POND

TUNK LAKE

1

BRANCH LAKE

Ellsworth

LOWER PATTEN POND

1

TODDY POND

19

Bar Harbor

Mt. Desert Island

Acadia
National
Park

Northeast Harbor

Swans
Island

FIGURE NUMBER

19 Acadia National Park on Mount Desert Island

Mount Desert Island and Acadia National Park

Visitors to Acadia National Park [Figs. 18, 19] are hard pressed to pick out one favorite attraction of this 40,000-acre park. No one signature feature makes this a special place. Rather, it's the incredible variations in landscape that are the star of the show at Acadia.

The dramatic way the mountains rise from the ocean's shore, the towering firs that grow within reach of sea spray, the pink granite cliffs striped with black dikes, the fjord and lakes carved by a sheet of ice thousands of years ago—these features and others create a beautiful landscape that beckons to outdoor enthusiasts and other travelers.

Most of Acadia National Park is on Mount Desert Island, Maine's largest island at 108 square miles. (There are smaller pieces of the park much farther offshore on Isle au Haut and on Schoodic Point on the mainland.) The island's varied landscape provides habitats for a wide array of flora and fauna. Mount Desert Island is home to

[*Above: Visitors examine Thunder Hole on Acadia's Park Loop Road*]

more than 250 bird species, 50 kinds of mammals, and 1,000 plant species. Mount Desert is also the year-round home of about 10,000 people.

Evidence of the Ice Age is everywhere in the park. Look at a map, or at the large-scale topographic model of Mount Desert in Acadia's visitor center. All of the island's many lakes and ponds run north to south and are depressions left by the last glacier moving south more than 10,000 years ago. Other signs of the glacier's path are evident from a closer vantage point. Erratic boulders carried from miles away lie along several Acadia trails. And glacial abrasions and chatter marks—crescent-shaped fractures caused by glacial pressure—are visible on some of the rounded mountain summits and are etched into granite bedrock.

While ice played a major role in Mount Desert Island's ancient history, fire played a big part in its more recent past. In 1947, a two-week fire burned much of the eastern side of the island, destroying 18,000 acres, including 10,000 acres of Acadia National Park. The fire destroyed millions of dollars worth of property, including 67 huge "cottages" of wealthy summer people, 170 year-round homes, and five historic hotels The fire's path is still very obvious today because it wiped out the towering firs and spruces that cover the rest of Mount Desert Island. Today, sun-loving broadleaf trees—birch, aspen, maples, and others—have replaced the evergreens. As you hike through the woods in Acadia, the fire line can be startling as the path passes from the dark coniferous woods to the sun-dappled broadleaf forest. From one of Acadia's eastern mountaintops, look for a swath of paler green hardwood forest, next to the dark green, older evergreen forest, to see how widespread the destruction was.

Mount Desert's human history is as interesting as its natural history. Native Americans lived here for thousands of years. (The Abbe Museum in the park is dedicated to their history.) The island was "discovered" and named *l'Isle des Monts-deserts*, or island of barren mountains, in 1604 by the French explorer Samuel de Champlain. French Jesuits formed a small community here in 1613, but English soldiers destroyed the settlement shortly thereafter. Mount Desert was contested New World territory for more than a century, until colonists built the first permanent settlement in 1760.

In the mid-nineteenth century, "rusticators" came to Mount Desert to vacation. Among these early vacationers were Thomas Cole and Frederick Church, members of the Hudson River School of artists. Their paintings of the beautiful scenery attracted more visitors. By the end of the nineteenth century, Mount Desert Island soon became *the* place for America's wealthy to spend the summer. These rich and famous summer people built "cottages" of 50 or more rooms. The Rockefellers, the Vander-bilts, the Carnegies, and the Astors were among those who spent their summers here. One strip of oceanfront near Bar Harbor, the island's social center, became known as Millionaires' Row. While there are still some wealthy summer people on Mount Desert Island, the island never resumed its prominence as a summer resort for the moneyed after the 1947 fire destroyed most of its palatial estates.

Back in Mount Desert's heyday, some visitors spent their summers on sailboats, tennis courts, golf courses, and croquet fields. Others fell in love with the natural sites of the island. Some of these naturalists are responsible for the creative trail system that allows visitors today to walk beautifully carved granite steps and climb carefully-placed iron ladders as they hike the park. In the 1890s, individuals who financed path-building on Mount Desert Island could have a memorial path named for the person of their choice. The plaques memorializing these pathmakers, as they were called, can still be seen today along Acadia's trails. The New Deal's Civilian Conservation Corps came to Mount Desert Island during the Depression and refurbished old trails and built new ones.

Volunteer at Acadia

Many of Acadia National Park's historic trails were created by volunteer path builders. Today, volunteers still help maintain the network of trails and carriage roads through the park. Local residents, visiting school groups, and tourists who are just here for a few days all pitch in.

The park has an active, organized volunteer program. Volunteers meet three times a week. Typical assignments include cutting back brush or raking out drainage ditches. Some hiking may be involved.

If you decide to volunteer, bring gloves, a snack, and some water.

For more information: Acadia National Park Volunteer Coordinator, PO Box 177, Bar Harbor, ME 04609. Phone (207) 288-3934.

Today, there are 120 miles of hiking trails lacing Acadia National Park. Many are quite easy and take in beautiful strips of oceanfront or woods. Others, including the popular ladder trails up the park's cliffs, are strenuous and should not be undertaken by anyone even slightly afraid of heights. The trails in Acadia interconnect in such a way that energetic hikers can take in two or more mountaintops or lakefronts in a single day. Backcountry camping is not allowed in Acadia National Park, and hikers should plan their routes accordingly.

The spirit of conservation among some of the wealthy summer people is responsible for the creation of Acadia National Park. George Dorr of Boston, John D. Rockefeller Jr., and others, worried about the land's future, started working to preserve it, buying up pieces of property with an eye on future public use.

In 1916, Dorr presented the National Park Service with 5,000 acres of Mount Desert land. It was declared Sieur de Monts National Monument. In 1919, it was renamed Lafayette National Park, making it the first national park east of the Mississippi. In 1929, Acadia National Park was named. Dorr, who is known as the father of Acadia National Park, was also its first superintendent, holding the post from 1916 to 1944.

John D. Rockefeller Jr.'s contributions to the park were enormous. He donated one-third of Acadia's acreage to the park service. Rockefeller also designed and

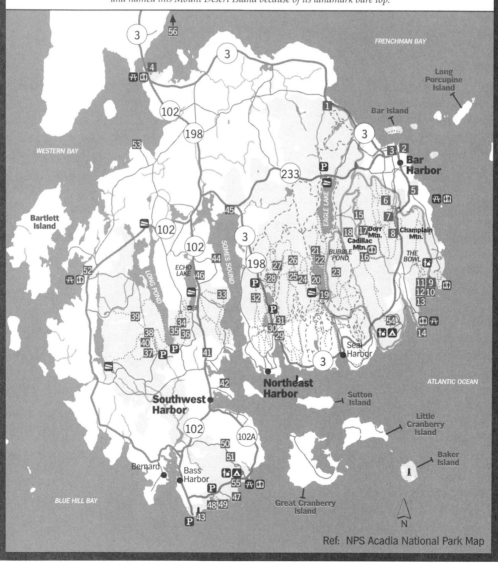

Acadia Nat. Park On Mt. Desert Island

French explorer Samuel Champlain sailed into the Frenchman Bay in 1604 and named this Mount Desert Island because of its landmark bare top.

Ref: NPS Acadia National Park Map

1	Hulls Cove Visitors Center
2	Bar Harbor Shore Path
3	Natural History Museum at the College of the Atlantic
4	Bar Harbor Oceanarium
5	Jackson Laboratory for Mammalian Research
6	Sieur de Monts Spring/Wild Gardens of Acadia
7	The Robert Abbe Museum
8	Precipice Trail
9	Sand Beach
10	Ocean Trail
11	Great Head, Beehive, and Bowl Trails
12	Thunder Hole
13	Gorham Mountain Trail
14	Otter Cliffs and Otter Point
15	Cadillac Summit Trail
16	Cadillac Mountain South Ridge Trail
17	Cadillac Mountain North Ridge Trail
18	Cadillac Mountain West Face Trail
19	Jordan Pond Nature Trail
20	Jordan Pond Shore Trail
21	Bubble Rock Trail to South Bubble
22	Bubble Rock Trail to North Bubble
23	Pemetic Mountain Trail
24	Penobscot Mountain Trail
25	Jordan Cliffs Trail
26	Sargent Mountain South Ridge Trail
27	Hadlock Brook Trail
28	Bald Peak
29	Asticou Azalea Gardens

30	Asticou Terraces and Thuya Garden and Lodge
31	Eliot Mountain Trail
32	Norumbega Mountain Trail
33	Acadia Mountain Trail
34	Canada Cliff Trail
35	Beech Mountain Trail
36	Valley and South Ridge Trails Loop
37	Perpendicular, Razorback, Bernard South Face and Sluiceway Trails
38	Mansell to Cold Brook Trail
39	Cold Brook Trail
40	Great Notch Trail
41	Wendell Gilley Museum of Bird Carving
42	Oceanarium Southwest Harbor
43	Bass Harbor Head Light
44	Somes Sound View Campground
45	Mount Desert Campground
46	Echo Lake Camp
47	Wonderland Trail
48	Ship Harbor
49	Ship Harbor Nature Trail
50	The Big Heath
51	The Hio Road
52	Pretty Marsh
53	Indian Point-Blagden Preserve
54	Blackwoods Campground
55	Seawall Campground
56	Lamoine State Park

Loop Road

The Carriage Roads

Trail

financed the historic carriage road system that makes the interior of Acadia National Park uniquely accessible to so many visitors.

The dramatic beauty of Acadia is no secret. More than 3 million people visit each year, making it one of the most-visited national parks in the country.

But many of those visitors see far too little of Acadia National Park and Mount Desert Island. They follow the park's auto loop road to some beautiful vistas. They drive up Cadillac Mountain, the highest mountain on the East Coast. They stop to eat at the Jordan Pond House. And then they head back to Bar Harbor with the crowds.

Admittedly, those tourists have seen some beautiful pieces of the Maine coast, but they have missed much more. That well-worn itinerary ignores the entire western side of Mount Desert, the Somes Sound fjord that splits the island, a handful of quaint villages, nature trails to quiet oceanfront points where seals sun on the rocks and seabirds dive for dinner, cobblestone beaches, several beautiful little islands accessible by public ferry, and more than a dozen other mountaintops that aren't nearly as crowded as Cadillac's. In sum, they've missed a lot of what makes Acadia National Park so special.

With some planning, a good pair of hiking shoes, and field guide or two in your pack, a trip to Acadia National Park can be a quiet journey of both natural and historic discovery.

Park Features

▒ THE CARRIAGE ROADS

One of the unique features of Acadia National Park is its 45-mile network of carriage roads, where visitors can walk, cycle, ride horse-drawn carriages, or cross-country ski through some very scenic territory on the eastern side of the park.

The roads were a gift from the philanthropist John D. Rockefeller Jr., a son of the founder of Standard Oil.

Rockefeller was one of many wealthy summer residents of Mount Desert Island in the early twentieth century. Over his objections, a ban on motor vehicles on Mount Desert Island was lifted in 1913. Rockefeller got to work designing a system of wide carriage roads that would remain free of automobiles and offer scenic views without disrupting the landscape.

These graceful roads wander up and down mountains, skirt lakes, and blend beautifully into the forested landscape. Pink granite coping stones, referred to by some as Rockefeller's teeth, serve as guardrails. Sixteen arched bridges, faced with hand-cut blocks of granite, show what an art stonecutting can be and are worth stopping to admire. Charming Tudor-style gate lodges sit at two entrances to the road system and look like something out of a fairy tale.

Rockefeller stayed committed to the carriage road system long after he'd donated the land to the park and paid to maintain the roads until his death in 1960.

The carriage roads can be walked, but many visitors prefer to cover more of the roads on bicycles, which can be rented at several island businesses. Pick up a map of the carriage road system before heading out. Many of the roads intersect, and loops of varying distances can be mapped out. Intersections are marked with numbered signposts. Keep a carriage road map with you to ensure you find your destination.

Horses are permitted on most of the carriage roads. The Wildwood Stable near Jordan Pond offers carriage rides to visitors. The stable also rents stalls to people vacationing with their horses. Horses are not for rent.

Remember that horses are powerful and somewhat unpredictable. If you run into a horse or horse-drawn carriage, stop and let it pass you.

Directions: The carriage road system can be accessed from six roadside locations: the Paradise Hill entrance is near the Hulls Cove Visitor Center; the Upper Hadlock entrance is near the Brown Mountain Gatehouse on the eastern side of ME 198; the Parkman Mountain entrance is about 2 miles south of the intersection of ME 198 and ME 233; the Jordan Pond entrance is at the gatehouse near the Jordan Pond Restaurant (park at the Jordan Pond parking area, not at the restaurant or the gatehouse); the Bubble Pond entrance is on the Park Loop Road; and the Eagle Lake entrance is on the north side of ME 233.

HULLS COVE VISITOR CENTER

[Fig. 19(1)] The Hulls Cove Visitor Center should be a first stop for every visitor to Acadia National Park. Here, you can pick up park maps and a copy of the monthly *Acadia Beaver Log*, a newsletter with a listing of naturalist programs, tide charts, sunrise/sunset tables, and other information that will come in handy.

Visitors can also speak with park rangers at the information desk. They can suggest hiking trails or activities geared to specific visitors' skills and interests and point toward productive bird-watching areas.

The Hulls Cove Visitor Center also has a large model of the park that gives a good preview of the landscape visitors will encounter. Often, a ranger will give a tour of the model, pointing out interesting spots.

Every 30 minutes, a 15-minute orientation film is shown in the theater here. It provides a good introduction to the park and has some beautiful footage.

The visitor center also has a well-stocked bookstore, where many commercial maps, hiking, biking, and paddling books, and field guides are available. The Park Service has some free maps and guides and sells inexpensive brochures to Acadia's self-guided nature trails and other areas.

Directions: Entering Mount Desert Island on ME 3, stay on ME 3 for 8 miles. The Hulls Cove Visitor Center is well marked.

Facilities: Information desk, restrooms, gift and bookshop, theater.

Dates: Open daily, May through Oct.

Fees: None.

Closest town: Bar Harbor, 2.5 miles.

For more information: Acadia National Park Headquarters, PO Box 177, Bar Harbor, ME 04609. Phone (207) 288-3338.

🏵 NATURALIST PROGRAMS

Park rangers offer a wide variety of nature programs for visitors. These vary as the seasons change but typically include narrated hikes, evening slide programs, and boat cruises. Special hikes are designed to examine geologic features, explore the shoreline, find beaver lodges, or learn about mosses, ferns, and fungi. Rangers set up stations to view peregrine falcons and count migrating hawks. Evening programs, which are usually held in the amphitheaters at the Seawall or Blackwoods campgrounds, examine the history of the park and look at plants, animals, and geology in Acadia.

For more information: Pick up a copy of the monthly *Acadia Beaver Log* at the visitor center. For general park information, phone (207) 288-3338.

Eastern Mount Desert Island

🏵 BAR HARBOR

At the turn of the century, Bar Harbor was a genteel summer community. But the Great Depression, the huge fire of 1947, and the establishment of the federal income tax all contributed to the end of an era for Bar Harbor as the playground for old money. But Bar Harbor has retained all of its old charm and is still very much a summer resort.

Many visitors pour through this little oceanfront town every summer. For some, it's a stop on the way to Acadia National Park. For others, Bar Harbor is a destination in itself. The streets are lined with shops: Some sell souvenirs and T-shirts, others sell interesting art and nice clothing. And there are numerous good restaurants and lovely inns. Many visitors maintain Bar Harbor as a base of operations for their trips into Acadia National Park. They can hike or bike all day, then sleep in a historic inn and have a cappuccino before heading out for another day of outdoor recreation.

Bar Harbor is busiest in July and August. September is also a nice time to visit; the crowds are smaller, the foliage is starting to turn, and temperatures tend to be warm during the day and refreshingly cool at night.

Acadia National Park is right next door, but Bar Harbor has several attractions worth visiting, too. They include a beautiful waterfront park, a natural history museum, an oceanarium, a shoreline path that wanders in front of some impressive

Beaver

The beaver (*Castor canadensis*) is the largest rodent in North America. As a species, beavers are quite resourceful. The dams that they build, with sticks and mud across a stream, create a habitat that is safe and nourishing for them.

The entrance to the beaver's dome-shaped lodge is underwater in the pond created by the dam. The pond also serves as cold-water storage space for winter food, and it promotes the growth of deciduous trees that make up most of a beaver's diet.

A beaver marks its territory by building a scent mound, a pile of mud upon which the beaver deposits a musky-smelling oil from its castor gland. Beavers use the oil from another gland, the anal gland, to waterproof their fur.

The beaver is equipped with sharp incisors that grow continuously, enabling it to gnaw down trees and eat branches. Its long, paddle-shaped tail is used as a rudder and as a warning device. If you startle a beaver in its pond, it will slap the surface with its tail to let other beavers know that there's danger nearby.

mansions, an island you can walk to when the tide is right, whale watch and nature cruises, and a world-renowned genetic research laboratory.

BEAVER
(Castor canadensis)

⬚ BAR ISLAND

[Fig. 19] Consult a tide chart and wear a watch when walking out to this lovely island just offshore from Bar Harbor. Bar Island is only accessible for an hour or so before and after low tide. That's when a wide gravel bar to the island is exposed.

The best part of this hike is the 0.5-mile walk out to the island. Keep an eye out for beds of mussels and other sea life that have been exposed by the tide. The abundance of food on the bar makes this a good bird-watching spot, especially in the off-season when other hikers are less likely to have chased off the birds.

The western side of the island is Acadia National Park land that seems far removed from the bustle of Bar Harbor. The eastern side is private land. Please respect the park boundary and the privacy of Bar Island's residents.

There is a path through the woods and along an old field on Bar Island, a remnant

Eelgrass

The bright-green ribbon-ike leaves of eelgrass (*Zostera marina*) can be seen growing near the banks of many tidal estuaries, rivers, and protected bays. The grass's dead leaves, which turn black, lie at the high tide mark on many beaches. Eelgrass is a flowering plant, not seaweed. Eelgrass tends to grow in shallow water, where it can get enough sun to survive, and it can flower and pollinate under water.

Eelgrass performs an important role in the coastal ecosystem, providing a habitat for striped bass, lobster, and many other marine animals. Canada geese feed on eelgrass, while many ducks forage for food in eelgrass beds.

Eelgrass also absorbs excess nutrients from the water and reduces erosion. While it seems to grow everywhere, eelgrass beds are still recovering from a disease that nearly destroyed all of the Atlantic beds in the 1930s. That "disease," which was then called the Wasting Disease, is still the subject of some debate on botanical circles. It could have been a disease, a mold or a temperature change. Now, eelgrass is threatened by water pollution, dredging and the development of structures like docks that block its sunlight.

of the island's past as a farming community. If you're curious about life on a small Maine island a century ago, Jack and Mary Jo Perkins have written and illustrated a book, *Parasols of Fern: A Book About Wonder*, based on the old diary of a child who lived here. The book is available at Bar Harbor bookstores.

Directions: From the Town Pier, walk 0.3 mile west on West Street to Bridge Street. The bar begins at the foot of Bridge Street.

BAR HARBOR SHORE PATH

[Fig. 19(2)] The Bar Harbor Shore Path provides an easy and very scenic stroll along the Bar Harbor waterfront. The 0.75-mile path begins at the eastern side of the Town Pier and passes the Bar Harbor Inn, a town park, and several lovely mansions. The crushed granite path is on private land, so please respect the residents' privacy. As you approach the end of the path, turn right onto a footpath into town, or turn around and follow the Shore Path along the waterfront.

Along the path, there are benches from which to enjoy the view, which includes the four Porcupine Islands: Sheep Porcupine Island, Burnt Porcupine Island, Bald Porcupine Island, and Long Porcupine Island. The easternmost of these islands is Long Porcupine Island, a nesting island for bald eagles and a Nature Conservancy Preserve.

Directions: The Shore Path begins at the eastern side of the Town Pier and is marked.

Closest town: Bar Harbor.

LONG PORCUPINE ISLAND

[Fig. 19] The easternmost of the Porcupine Islands in Frenchman Bay off Bar Harbor, Long Porcupine Island is an important nesting island for bald eagles (*Haliaeetus leucocephalus*). Several eagle chicks have hatched here since the island was donated to The Nature Conservancy in 1977. While it is open for part of the year, Long Porcupine Island is probably most easily enjoyed from afar. The 125-acre island has 100-foot granite cliffs and a very thick spruce forest that makes landing a boat and hiking difficult. The island is closed for the nesting season, from February 15 to August 15. Please don't disturb the bald eagles or black guillemots (*Cepphus grylle*) that nest here.

Directions: Long Porcupine Island is in Frenchman Bay, off Bar Harbor.
Dates: The island is closed during the February 15 to August 15 nesting season.
Closest town: Bar Harbor.
For more information: The Nature Conservancy, Maine Chapter, Fort Andross, 14 Maine Street, Suite 401, Brunswick, ME 04011. Phone (207) 729-5181.

NATURAL HISTORY MUSEUM AT COLLEGE OF THE ATLANTIC

[Fig. 19(3)] The College of the Atlantic is a four-year undergraduate college that specializes in human ecology and environmental studies. The school's oceanfront campus incorporates some of Bar Harbor's old cottages with newer shingled buildings. Students studying the environment use the Gulf of Maine as their laboratory. The school's Allied Whale Institute conducts a census of the whale population in the region, identifying whales by marks on their fins and tails.

The college's Natural History Museum is open to the public. It has interesting displays and dioramas on the wildlife and natural history of Mount Desert Island and the Gulf of Maine. A Discovery Room for kids features hands-on displays. Outside, there is a short nature trail.

Directions: College of the Atlantic is on ME 3 in Bar Harbor.
Dates: Open from mid-June to Labor Day.
Fees: There is a charge for admission.
Closest town: Bar Harbor.
For more information: Natural History Museum, College of the Atlantic. 105 Eden Street, Bar Harbor, ME 04609. Phone (207) 288-5015.

WHALE WATCHING

The Gulf of Maine is an important feeding ground for whales, and ferrying visitors out to see these sea mammals has become an industry in Bar Harbor.

Several companies offer whale-watching cruises out of Bar Harbor in the summer and fall. Depending on the cruise, the trip can last a couple of hours or all day. Some tour operators offer a money-back guarantee if you don't find a whale. Whale-watching cruises are also a good place to watch for seabirds, dolphins, and porpoises.

One frequently seen whale is the huge finback, or fin whale (*Balaenoptera physalus*), the second largest mammal on earth. Finback whales often grow to be 70 feet long and weigh 50 tons. They don't leap out of the water like some whales, but they can be spotted from a distance by their spouts, which can rise 20 feet in the air.

At 40 feet, the humpback whale (*Megaptera novaeangliae*) is smaller than the finback whale, but it delights whale watchers with its playful, acrobatic jumps, rolls, and splashes. There are an estimated 500 humpback whales in the Gulf of Maine. They migrate to the Caribbean in the winter to mate and give birth to calves before heading back to the Maine waters for the summer. Minke (pronounced minky) whales (*Balaenoptera acutorostrata*), which can be between 5 and 28 feet long, are also a common sight for whale watchers. While they aren't nearly as big as the other whales, they have been known to swim alongside whale-watching boats for an hour or more.

Closest town: Bar Harbor.

For more information: Bar Harbor Whale Watch Company, phone (207) 288-2386. Whale Watcher Inc., phone (207) 288-3322. Sea Bird Watcher Company, phone (207) 288-5033.

FERRY TO NOVA SCOTIA

The Cat is a high-speed, modern car ferry that crosses the Bay of Fundy to Yarmouth, Nova Scotia, in less than 3 hours at speeds of up to 55 miles per hour. While the scenery on the crossing tends to fly by at these speeds, the fast crossing does allow for convenient day trips to Nova Scotia and takes many hours off the drive to the Canadian maritimes. Aboard *The Cat*, there are bars, theaters, and a casino.

Directions: *The Cat* departs from the ferry terminal on Water Street in Bar Harbor. Bay Ferries has an office at 121 Eden Street in Bar Harbor.

Activities: Boating, dining, gambling.

Dates: *The Cat* operates daily in the summer. Call ahead.

Fees: There is a charge for riding *The Cat*.

Closest town: Bar Harbor.

For more information: Bay Ferries, 121 Eden Street, Bar Harbor, ME 04609. Phone (207) 288-3395.

BAR HARBOR OCEANARIUM

[Fig. 19(4)] This museum is especially popular with kids. It includes a marsh walk, a tank of harbor seals, a lobster hatchery, and several hands-on exhibits.

Directions: The Bar Harbor Oceanarium is 8 miles north of downtown Bar Harbor on ME 3.

Dates: The oceanarium is open from May through Oct.

Fees: There is a charge for admission. Discounts are available if you plan to visit the Oceanarium Southwest Harbor, too (*See* page 246).

Closest town: Bar Harbor.

For more information: Bar Harbor Oceanarium. (207) 288-5005.

JACKSON LABORATORY FOR MAMMALIAN RESEARCH

[Fig. 19(5)] The largest single employer on Mount Desert Island is the Jackson Laboratory, which was founded in 1929 and employs about 800 people. The lab is known for its genetic research and for its breeding of mice used to study diseases.

During most of the summer, the lab puts on a public program describing its work.

Directions: The Jackson Lab is 1.5 miles south of downtown Bar Harbor on ME 3.

Dates: The public program is held on Tuesdays and Thursday, from June through September.

Fees: None.

Closest town: Bar Harbor.

For more information: Jackson Laboratory. 600 Main Street, Bar Harbor, ME 04609. Phone (207) 288-3371.

NIGHT LIFE IN BAR HARBOR

Bar Harbor has several brewpubs and other night spots. It also has two movie theaters, including one where you get pizza with your flick.

LOMPOC CAFÉ AND BREW PUB. 32 Rodick Street, Bar Harbor. This pub serves lunch and dinner and has a beer garden and live entertainment in the summer. *(207) 288-9392.*

CARMEN VERANDAH. 119 Main Street, Bar Harbor. This nightclub above Rupunini Restaurant has pool, dancing, and live music. *(207) 288-2886.*

REEL PIZZA CINERAMA. 33 Kennebec Place, Bar Harbor. Sit in a comfortable arm chair for pizza and a movie at the Reel Pizza Cinerama. *(207) 288-3811.*

CRITERION THEATER. 35 Cottage Street, Bar Harbor. This gorgeous art deco theater plays first-run movies at night and adds a matinee on rainy days. *(207) 288-3441.*

DINING IN BAR HARBOR

Bar Harbor is full of good food, from creative vegetarian fare to gourmet dinners.

RUPININI. 119 Main Street, Bar Harbor. This local favorite has vegetarian offerings, burgers, and game. *Inexpensive to moderate. (207) 288-2886.*

THE READING ROOM. Newport Drive, Bar Harbor. Call in advance and reserve a table by the window at this former men's club in the Bar Harbor Inn. The curved windows have has wonderful views of Frenchman Bay and Bar Harbor's harbor. The Reading Room serves breakfast, lunch, and dinner. Reservations are recommended. *Moderate to expensive. (207) 288-3551.*

LODGING IN BAR HARBOR

There are plenty of beautiful rooms in downtown Bar Harbor's inns and bed and breakfasts, especially if money is no object. (The rates tend to drop right after Labor Day.) Make reservations in advance if you're planning on staying overnight in the summer. Many of the antique-filled mansion inns do not accept young children as

PILEATED WOODPECKER
(Dryocopus pileatus)

guests. If you are visiting with a family, think about staying in a housekeeping cottage or one of the family-oriented inns.

THE INN AT CANOE POINT. Route 3, Bar Harbor. This lovely Tudor-style waterfront inn is a few miles from the hustle and bustle of downtown Bar Harbor. *Expensive. (207) 288-9511.*

EDEN VILLAGE. Route 3, Bar Harbor. This is one of several colonies of tourist cabins outside of downtown Bar Harbor. *Moderate. (207) 288-4670.*

COVE FARM INN. Crooked Road, Bar Harbor. This family-friendly B&B is a short drive away from downtown Bar Harbor and Acadia National Park. The innkeepers have plenty of advice on exploring the area. *Moderate. (207) 288-5355.*

BAR HARBOR/MOUNT DESERT IS-LAND HOSTEL. Kennebec Street, Bar Harbor. You can't find a cheaper bed than at the hostel in the parish hall of St. Saviour's Episcopal Church. The hostel is accessible only at night. Write Box 32, Bar Harbor, ME 04609 for reservations. *Inexpensive. (207) 288-5587.*

Acadia National Park's Park Loop Road

Many visitors limit their view of Acadia National Park to vistas along the very popular and scenic Park Loop Road. The 27-mile drive provides a nice introduction to the park and is well worth taking. But don't make it your only look at the park.

Motorists can purchase a copy of the Park Loop Road self-guided tour at the Hulls Cove Visitor Center.

The tour has 15 stops, including some stunning overlooks of Frenchman Bay and some of the most popular attractions in the eastern side of the park, including Thunder Hole, Sand Beach, Otter Cliffs, the Jordan Pond House, and for a dramatic conclusion, the summit of Cadillac Mountain. Each stop has a parking area.

The Loop Road, which is well marked on park maps and signs, is busiest at the peak of the summer season. If you're here in July or August, try the tour early or late in the day to avoid crowds at the overlooks.

Directions: The Park Loop Road begins at the Hulls Cove Visitors Center.
Fees: There is a charge for the motorist guide to the Park Loop Road.

Sieur de Monts Spring

[Fig. 19(6)] Acadia National Park began on this tract of land at Sieur de Monts Spring. George B. Dorr, often called the father of the park, acquired land from donors surrounding this scenic spot in 1909 and gave it to the federal government in 1916 as part of Sieur de Monts National Monument, which eventually was renamed Lafayette National Park and then Acadia National Park. Dorr was the park's first superintendent.

The spring at Sieur de Monts can be seen through the glass enclosure of a protective Italian Renaissance-style well cover.

The Sieur de Monts Spring has a large parking area. From it, you can visit the spring, the Wild Gardens of Acadia, the Abbe Museum, and the Nature Center, a small museum with displays and literature on wildlife and natural resource research projects in Acadia National Park.

Keep your binoculars handy. This is a great place to watch for birds. *A Birder's Guide to Maine* rates it as one of the best bird-watching spots on Mount Desert, especially during the spring and fall migrations and nesting season.

In the mostly broadleaf forest here, look and listen for pileated woodpeckers (*Dryocopus pileatus*), flycatchers, warblers, and American woodcocks (*Scolopax minor*), whose noisy aerial courtship maneuvers are a harbinger of spring in Acadia National Park.

Several hiking trails, including some intersecting easy footpaths, are accessible near Sieur de Monts Spring. Look for a signpost behind the spring that points toward the trailheads.

The Dorr Mountain Trail is a steep trail up the east face of 1,270-foot Dorr Mountain (*see* page 227).

The Jesup Path is an easy trail that leads hikers through a birch grove and around a marsh. Keep an eye out for woodland birds here.

The Hemlock Trail crosses the Jesup Trail and meanders through a forest of tall hemlocks, coniferous trees that can be identified by their flat, flexible needles.

AMERICAN WOODCOCK
(Scolopax minor)

The Tarn Trail is a footpath along the western shore of The Tarn, a glacial pond just south of Sieur de Monts Spring on ME 3.

Directions: Follow the Park Loop Road to the Sieur de Monts Spring entrance.

Activities: Hiking, bird-watching.

Facilities: Nature Center, restrooms, trails, wild gardens of Acadia, the Abbe Museum.

Dates: The Nature Center is open from May through Sept.

Fees: None.

Closest town: Bar Harbor, 1.5 miles.

WILD GARDENS OF ACADIA

[Fig. 19(6)] Stop here early in your visit to acquaint yourself with the plants that you will see in the varied habitats that make up Mount Desert Island. This 0.75-acre garden is divided into 12 sections, each representing a habitat found on Mount Desert Island. The more than 400 species of plants grown here are labeled. A map is available at the garden entrance.

Among the habitats are deciduous and coniferous forests, where visitors can learn not only how to distinguish between the trees that grow in the park forests but also about the plants that grow beneath them. The seaside habitat contains sea lavender (*Limonium carolinianum*), beach pea (*Lathyrus japonicus*), beach grasses, and other plants that grow near the shore.

In the mountain section, look for the plants that can be found on Acadia's nearly bare mountaintops. These high-elevation plants include mountain sandwort, three-toothed cinquefoil, bluebell (*Campanula rotundifolioa*), and northern jack pine.

Heaths, another habitat type open for exploration in Acadia National Park, support numerous plants that thrive in acidic, low-nutrient soil, including rhodoras (*Rhododendron*), blueberry, huckleberry, and sweet gale. There are also sections representing the marsh, pond, bird thicket, damp thicket, meadow, and roadside habitats of the area.

The garden was started in 1961 by members of the Bar Harbor Garden Club and is maintained by volunteers. According to the Park Service, volunteers spend about 100 hours per week on the gardens in the summer. They use 900 pounds of compost each summer. Maintaining the beach habitat requires 105 pounds of seaweed, 30 gallons of seawater, and 50 gallons of sand each year.

Only native plants are included, so some plants that grow on Mount Desert in abundance but are not indigenous to the island are not represented here, including Rugosa rose, lupines, and purple loosestrife.

Directions: Follow the Park Loop Road to the Sieur de Monts Spring entrance.

Facilities: Footpaths, map and brochure.

Dates: Open daily year-round.

Fees: None, but contributions are requested for a copy of a map to the garden.

Closest town: Bar Harbor, 1.5 miles.

THE ROBERT ABBE MUSEUM

[Fig. 19(7)] The Abbe Museum is devoted to the history of Native Americans in Maine. Its displays include dioramas of early Native American settlements and exhibits on tools, pottery, and other artifacts. The museum also offers demonstrations and workshops in Native American basket weaving and other crafts, and sponsors an archeological field school in the fall.

The Abbe Museum was founded in 1928 by Dr. Robert Abbe, a New York surgeon who spent summers in Bar Harbor in the early twentieth century. Abbe was intrigued by the tools and other artifacts he found in ancient Indian shell heaps on Mount Desert Island and founded the museum as a way to preserve them and to teach others about the history of Mount Desert's earliest inhabitants.

Directions: Follow the Park Loop Road to the Sieur de Monts Spring parking area.

Facilities: Museum, gift shop.

Dates: Open mid-May through mid-Oct.

Fees: There is a charge for admission.

Closest town: Bar Harbor. 1.5 miles.

For more information: The Abbe Museum, Sieur de Monts Spring, PO Box 286, Bar Harbor, ME 04609. Phone (207) 288-3519.

DORR MOUNTAIN

[Fig. 19] At 1,270 feet, Dorr Mountain is Acadia National Park's third-highest peak. Several trails, all involving a steep hike, lead to the summit. Perhaps the most strenuous is the Ladder Trail, which climbs the mountain via hundreds of stone steps and some metal ladders. The Ladder Trail trailhead is on ME 3, just south of The Tarn, a glacial pond south of Sieur de Monts Spring.

The Dorr Mountain Trail, which can be reached from Sieur de Monts Spring, or from The Tarn or Ladder trails, includes a series of switchbacks through a broadleaf forest before giving way to a steep granite- stepped ascent.

For a longer, more gradual hike, take the Tarn Trail from the north end of the Tarn 1.4 miles to the Canon Brook trail, then another 0.6 mile to the Dorr Mountain South Ridge Trail. It's about 2 miles farther to the summit.

The Dorr Mountain summit has nice ocean views. The slightly higher mountain to the west is Cadillac Mountain, the highest point on the Atlantic coast.

From the summit, follow one of the routes back to the Tarn or Sieur de Monts Spring. Or, consult a park map and continue on to Cadillac Mountain, about 0.7 mile west, or Kebo Mountain, about 1.5 miles north.

Directions: Depending on your route, begin your hike at either the parking area of Sieur de Monts Spring or on ME 3, near the trailheads just north or south of The Tarn.

Dorr Mountain Trail: 1.5 miles to summit, a fairly steep hike.

Dorr Mountain Ladder Trail: 0.6 mile to summit, very steep ladder trail.

Dorr Mountain South Ridge Trail: 1.9 miles, moderately steep.

Champlain Mountain

[Fig. 19] Champlain Mountain is one of the best spots in Acadia National Park to get a glimpse of a peregrine falcon (*Falco peregrinus*). In 1991, a pair of peregrine falcons nested in the park for the first time in 35 years.

Peregrine falcons are known for their in-flight hunting ability. A peregrine can swoop down on its prey at speeds of 100 mph, knocking it to the ground. But these impressive birds were no match for the development and pollution of the 1950s and 1960s. Like other birds of prey, peregrines were very susceptible to the pesticide DDT, because they are so high on the food chain. The pesticide weakened the birds' eggs and eventually caused their reproductive systems to fail.

The peregrine falcon is considered one of the success stories of the federal Endangered Species Act, where it was listed as endangered in 1969. Thanks to a ban on DDT and the work of naturalists in Acadia National Park and other places, the falcons are breeding again. In 1997, there were 31 nesting pairs in New England.

In Acadia National Park, 22 chicks that were hatched in captivity were "hacked" or reintroduced to the wild from 1984 through 1986. When adult peregrines were seen coming to the park to nest, the hacking program was halted. After a few summers, the adults successfully raised chicks in nests in the park, and the peregrine falcon had made its comeback. In 1999, the falcon was taken off the endangered species list.

Bird watchers flock to the parking area of the Precipice Trail, which leads to the summit of Champlain Mountain, hoping to see the adult peregrine falcons or their young. Often, a park ranger will set up a telescope in the parking area in the morning for a falcon watch.

In March and April, adult peregrine falcons may be seen making aerial courtship maneuvers. In mid-April one bird will sit on the nest while the other perches nearby. The birds' chicks can be seen in July and August, practicing flying and exploring the area.

Directions: The Precipice Trail parking area is on the Park Loop Road, about 2.5 miles past the Sieur de Monts Spring entrance. It is well marked.

Closest town: Bar Harbor, 4 miles.

▨ PRECIPICE TRAIL

[Fig. 19(8)] One of Acadia's most challenging trails, the Precipice Trail, is not for children or anyone afraid of heights. It is more of a nontechnical climb than a hike: It ascends up the cliff and ledges, with iron ladders and handrails to help hikers scramble up the trail. Those

PEREGRINE FALCON
(*Falco peregrinus*)

that make the 0.8-mile climb are rewarded with beautiful views from the summit of Champlain Mountain. On a clear day, the summit provides views of Bar Harbor and Frenchman Bay, Schoodic Point and the open sea, and, inland, the other mountains of Mount Desert Island.

Don't take this hike in wet or icy weather, the terrain is too slippery. The Precipice Trail is usually closed from April through mid-August in order to protect nesting peregrine falcons and their chicks.

Take another trail down the mountain. The Precipice Trail is designed for heading up the mountain, not down it, and it's difficult for hikers to pass each other on its steep terrain.

A good alternate route down is the North Ridge Bear Brook Trail. Either stay on that trail to the Park Loop Road (you'll have to walk about 1.2 miles to your car if you parked at the Precipice parking area) or turn onto the East Face Trail to head back to the Precipice trailhead.

Champlain Mountain can also be reached from the Sieur de Monts Spring area by hiking the 2.5-mile Beachcroft Trail, which includes a beautifully crafted series of steps over the 731-foot Huguenot Head and is a strenuous hike because of the steep ascent.

Precipice Trail: 0.8 mile, one way.

Sand Beach

[Fig. 19(9)] If you've got your heart set on ocean swimming, this is the one place it is permitted in Acadia National Park. There are lifeguards and changing rooms to accommodate swimmers. But make sure to dip a toe before diving right in. The water temperature here in the summer is between 50 and 60 degrees Fahrenheit.

Sand Beach is one of only two sandy beaches in Acadia National Park. Scoop up a handful of the "sand" here and look closely; it's made mostly of finely crushed shells and sparkling quartz, a mineral component of granite, which makes up most of Mount Desert Island.

Winter storms will wash away a lot of the sand from this beach, but the currents will return it in the spring. Sand Beach sits at the edge of Newport Cove and is protected to the west by Great Head. It's a good jumping off point for some scenic oceanfront hikes.

Directions: Sand Beach is on the Park Loop Road. Take the first left after the fee collection station.

Activities: Swimming, hiking.

Facilities: Changing rooms, lifeguards.

Dates: Accessible year-round; lifeguards are on duty in the summer months.

Closest town: Bar Harbor, 5 miles.

For more information: Acadia National Park, PO Box 177, Bar Harbor, ME 04609. Phone (207) 288-3338.

HIKING NEAR SAND BEACH

The Ocean Trail, or Ocean Drive Trail as it is labeled on some maps, is a very easy 1.8-mile footpath that follows the water's edge to Otter Point, passing through a mixed forest and some Rugosa rose bushes, which are not indigenous to Mount Desert but grow plentifully here and in many other windy, salty spots. It begins near the stairs from the parking area at Sand Beach.

The Great Head Trail begins at the eastern end of the beach and takes hikers out to the 140-foot Great Head in a moderately easy loop. Look for the granite steps at the end of the beach. At the top of the steps, take a right and follow the trail, which has some rough footing.

PAPER BIRCH
(Betula papyrifera)
The bark from this tree was used by Indians to make lightweight canoes.

The Beehive Trail is a short but strenuous hike up the Beehive, a 520-foot, hive-shaped granite outcropping marked by pitch pines and mountain thickets. This hike shouldn't be undertaken by children or anyone afraid of heights. The steep 0.5-mile trail includes stepping stones and iron ladders and foot- and hand-rails, which are necessary to make the climb. To reach the Beehive, look for the Bowl trailhead across the Park Loop Road from the Sand Beach parking area. Follow the Bowl Trail 0.2 mile to the Beehive trailhead.

From the Beehive, follow the Bowl Trail to the Bowl, a small, round pond perfect for soaking hot, tired feet. Hikers who are not up to the climb of the Beehive can begin the Bowl Trail at its trailhead, 100 feet north of the Sand Beach parking area

Ocean Trail: [Fig. 19(10)] 1.6 miles one-way.
Great Head Trail: [Fig. 19(11)] 1.4 mile loop with some rough spots.
The Beehive Trail: [Fig. 19(11)] 0.8 miles round trip. Strenuous, ladder trail.
The Bowl Trail: [Fig. 19(11)] 1.4 miles round trip.

Thunder Hole

[Fig. 19(12)] Thunder Hole is a chasm named from the loud boom produced when ocean waves rush into a narrow crevice, trapping air that thunders against the rocks. A stairway leads down to a railed viewing area, which is a great place to watch and listen to this natural phenomenon.

Unfortunately, most summer visitors see Thunder Hole on calm days, when the sea sloshes unimpressively back and forth into the chasm. Visit Thunder Hole after a storm when the ocean is roiling to really hear the natural roar. Try to be here within two hours of a high tide.

Directions: The well-marked Thunder Hole parking area is on the Park Loop Road, about 0.9 mile past the Sand Beach parking area.

Facilities: Paved walkway and viewing area, gift shop, hiking trails.

Closest town: Bar Harbor, 6 miles.

HIKING NEAR THUNDER HOLE

The Ocean Trail that runs 1.6 miles between Sand Beach and Otter Point runs by Thunder Hole and can be picked up here. It's a popular, easy path, so try it early in the day to avoid the worst of the summer crowds.

The Gorham Mountain Trail [Fig. 19(13)] parking lot is less than 0.25 mile past Thunder Hole on the Park Loop Road. This moderately easy trail passes through a pitch pine forest before a fork in the trail. The two legs will rejoin in 0.5 miles. Head to the right to scramble over and under ledges and alongside ancient sea caves on the Cadillac Cliffs Trail. Rejoin the Gorham Mountain Trail to ascend up the open granite ledges that have spectacular views of the ocean, Porcupine Islands, Sand Beach, and Great Head. From the summit of 525-foot Gorham Mountain, either retrace your steps or continue north and hike to The Bowl (*see* opposite page).

Gorham Mountain Trail: 1.8 miles round-trip. Moderate, with some steep grades.

Otter Cliffs and Otter Point

[Fig. 19(14)] The Ocean Path and Park Loop Road both wind past the 110-foot Otter Cliffs. Offshore, a bell buoy marks the Spindle rock ledge. In 1604, the French explorer Samuel de Champlain sailed too close to shore while exploring here and hit the Spindle. He was forced into nearby Otter Cove for repairs, where he reportedly met friendly Penobscot Indians who guided him around the island, which he called *l'Isle des Monts-deserts* or the island of barren mountains. Otter Cliffs is a favorite spot for experienced rock climbers. Do not try and climb the cliffs unless you are a skilled rock climber. Outdoor schools on the island offer rock climbing courses and guided climbs. From the cliffs, walk 0.3 mile to Otter Point.

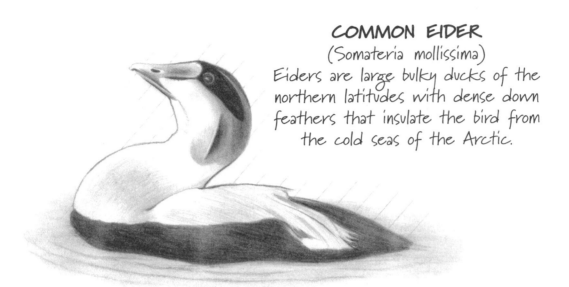

COMMON EIDER
(Somateria mollissima)
Eiders are large bulky ducks of the northern latitudes with dense down feathers that insulate the bird from the cold seas of the Arctic.

Otter Point is a great place to examine tide pools, so try and time this stop close to a low tide. The area between the high and low tide marks is called the intertidal zone. The rocky terrain here creates many large tide pools to explore. Look for barnacles, blue mussels, periwinkles, and green crabs here. Also look for limpets (*Notoacmaea testudinalis*), which have a 1-inch oval shell and cling to the rocks at low tide with a foot. (*See* pages 10-13 for more on exploring the intertidal zone.)

Bird watchers will want to scan the ocean here for seabirds, including black guillemots and common eiders. The common eider (*Somateria mollissima*) is North America's largest duck. The male eider is easy to identify by his snowy white neck, back, chest, and head, and black cap and wings. The female eider's brown feathers are much duller in comparison, but they serve her well as camouflage when she nests and raises her young near shore after her mate has gone to sea with the other male eiders. Eiders eat mussels and other shellfish, which they swallow whole and crush with powerful stomach muscles.

Eiders are best known for their eiderdown, the soft breast feathers used for stuffing pillows and comforters. The same insulating down enables them to live in cold ocean waters year-round. They were nearly hunted to extinction along the Maine Coast in the 1800s but have rebounded nicely.

Directions: Otter Cliffs and Otter Point are on the Park Loop Road. The Otter Cliffs parking area is about 0.7 mile past Thunder Hole. The Otter Point parking area is 0.3 miles past Otter Cliffs.

Closest town: Bar Harbor, about 7 miles.

Cadillac Mountain

[Fig. 19] At 1,530 feet, Cadillac Mountain is the highest point on the Atlantic coast and has beautiful views of the surrounding land and sea. It's a popular spot for watching both the sunrise and sunset. The summit can be reached by foot or by car, so be prepared for some company. The Cadillac Summit Trail is a paved 0.3-mile footpath that loops around the summit and has signs that identify the landmarks in every direction. Stay on the trail, as the subalpine vegetation growing off the trail is fragile.

In the fall, the park rangers and volunteers conduct a "hawkwatch" to count migrating raptors every day on the North Ridge Trail near the summit of Cadillac Mountain. In 1997, the hawkwatch counted 2,735 hawks and falcons. That included 1,179 sharp-shinned hawks (*Accipiter striatus*), 794 American kestrels (*Falco sparverius*), and 202 broad-winged hawks (*Buteo platypterus*). The hawkwatch is cancelled on rainy or foggy days. Otherwise, visitors should feel free to join in anytime between 9 a.m. and 2 p.m. daily.

Bring a jacket to Cadillac Mountain, where it is often windy and cooler than it is in lower spots in the park.

Directions: By car, the Cadillac Mountain Road is off the Park Loop Road, just south of the Cadillac Mountain Entrance to the park.

Activities: Hiking, bird-watching.

Facilities: Paved summit footpath, hiking trails, restrooms, gift shop.

Dates: Open year-round.

For more information: Acadia National Park, PO Box 177, Bar Harbor, ME 04609. Phone (207) 288-3338.

▒ HIKING ON CADILLAC MOUNTAIN

The easiest hike here is the Cadillac Summit Trail, a paved footpath that loops around the summit, beginning near the parking area. Several trails climb Cadillac Mountain. The most popular and scenic is the South Ridge Trail. This 3.7-mile trail starts about 100 feet south of the entrance to the Blackwoods Campground on ME 3 (*see* page 253).

The South Ridge Trail begins in a mixed forest but soon breaks out onto ledges with

AMERICAN KESTREL
(Falco sparverius)

jack pine; this is the 1947 fire line. Continue on to the Featherbed, a rush-filled glacial pond where rustic benches provide a good resting spot. Note the Pond and Canon Brook trails intersect with the South Ridge Trail here. The path gets steep and then offers even more panoramic views on its way to the summit.

The Cadillac North Ridge Trail begins on the Park Loop Road near the Cadillac Mountain entrance to the park. From the entrance, turn left onto the Park Loop Road (where the one-way section of the road begins). In about 0.6 miles, pull into the parking area on the north side of the road and look for the trailhead on the south side of the road. The 1.8-mile trail rises steadily across open ledges and through stands of evergreens. It offers good views of Bar Harbor.

The West Face Trail begins near the Bubble Pond parking area on the Park Loop Road and covers some very steep terrain before intersecting with the South Ridge trail near the Cadillac summit.

Cadillac Summit: [Fig. 19(15)] 0.3-mile loop from the parking lot. Easy.

Cadillac Mountain South Ridge: [Fig. 19(16)] 3.7 miles one-way. Strenuous and steep.

Cadillac Mountain North Ridge: [Fig. 19(17)] 2.2 miles one-way. Moderately steep.

Cadillac Mountain West Face: [Fig. 19(18)] 0.85 miles to South Ridge Trail. Strenuous and steep.

The Jordan Pond Area

Glaciers changed the face of Mount Desert Island. Twenty thousand years ago, the highlands here ran east to west. But as sheets of ice descended and then melted, they cut deep valleys that run north to south. Look at a map of the island and you'll see those north-south scrapes of long ago in a series of ponds, including Jordan Pond.

Travelers have been stopping at the Jordan Pond House at the south end of the pond since the turn of the century. The restaurant became known for its afternoon tea and popovers on the lawn, where the view takes in the pond, several mountains, and the rounded hills at the northern end of the lake called The Bubbles. Fortunately, this delicious afternoon tradition has survived, although the original restaurant burned down in 1979 and was rebuilt in 1982. But before filling up on popovers and jam, try one of the hikes that passes by Jordan Pond or explore the nearby carriage roads on foot, bicycle, or horse-drawn carriage. Swimming is not allowed in Jordan Pond, but canoeing and sailing are permitted. Fishing, typically for landlocked salmon and trout, is also allowed but a Maine fishing license is required.

Directions: The Jordan Pond parking area is on the Park Loop Road. Note that the restaurant parking area is for restaurant patrons. There is another, larger parking area just north of the restaurant lot.

Activities: Hiking, biking, riding in horse-drawn carriages, dining at the Jordan Pond House.

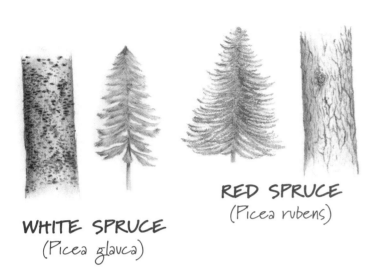

RED SPRUCE
(Picea rubens)

WHITE SPRUCE
(Picea glauca)

White Spruce or Red Spruce?

White spruce (*Picea glauca*) and red spruce (*Picea rubens*) can be found growing near each other on Mount Desert Island. The red spruce has rough, almost red bark, while the white spruce has smooth bark and a whitish cast to its trunk and needles.

The easiest way to tell these spruce trees apart is with your sense of smell. Crush a few needles between your fingers and sniff. If they smell like a skunk, the needles came from a white spruce, sometimes called a skunk spruce.

Facilities: Hiking trails, a nature path, carriage trails, a stable, restrooms, restaurant, and gift shop.

Dates: The Jordan Pond House is open daily from May through mid-Oct. for lunch, tea, and dinner. Wildwood Stables are open from mid-June through mid-Oct.

Closest town: Seal Harbor, 2 miles.

For more information: Jordan Pond House. Phone (207) 276-3316. Wildwood Stables. Box 241, Seal Harbor, ME 04676. Phone (207) 276-3622 in season. Phone (606) 356-7139 in the off-season.

HIKING NEAR JORDAN POND

JORDAN POND NATURE TRAIL. [Fig. 19(19)] The Jordan Pond Nature Trail is a very easy 1-mile loop. A trail brochure identifies some of the most common trees in this area, including the balsam fir, the red spruce, and the northern white cedar. The path wanders by a wetland before following the shore of Jordan Pond and heading back toward the Jordan Pond House and the trailhead.

Trail: An easy 1-mile loop.

JORDAN POND SHORE TRAIL. [Fig. 19(20)] The Jordan Pond Shore Trail is a 3.3-mile walk around the pond that can be started at the Jordan Pond parking area or The Bubbles parking area, north of Jordan Pond on the Park Loop Road. This trail is reasonably flat, but it has a few rocky spots on the western side of the pond.

Trail: A moderate 3.3-mile loop.

THE CARRIAGE ROADS NEAR JORDAN POND

The historic gate house just south of the Jordan Pond House is one of the most popular entrances to the carriage road system. The roads loop through the interior of the park, so it is best to get a carriage road map and devise a loop that suits your energy level and ability. If you are cycling and don't mind a steep hill, try riding up the west side of Jordan Pond and then either looping around Eagle Lake or Bubble Pond. Or cross the road from the Jordan Pond House, entering the carriage road system at the gate house. From here, you can ride past the Wildwood Stables to the carriage roads that circle Day Mountain. Make sure to bring a carriage road map, available at the Hulls Cove Visitor Center and at businesses in the Mount Desert Island villages, so you'll know which way to turn at the numbered road intersections.

BOATING ON JORDAN POND

There is a 10 horsepower limit on Jordan Pond. Most boaters seem to use canoes and kayaks. A boat launch is located at the far end of the Jordan Pond parking area.

HIKING AT THE BUBBLES AND BUBBLE POND

[Fig. 19(21), Fig. 19(22)] The two rounded peaks at the northern end of Jordan Pond are called The Bubbles. According to local legend, The Bubbles were originally called The Bubbies because of their resemblance to a woman's breasts, but their name was changed in the interest of propriety.

The Bubble Rock Trail is a moderate, yet occasionally steep, hike up either the 872-foot North Bubble or 766-foot South Bubble. The North Bubble leg of the trail is more rugged.

Bubble Rock, a large glacial erratic boulder, sits near the summit of the South Bubble, where a glacier deposited it more than 10,000 years ago. Many a hiker has had a photograph taken leaning against this boulder, which looks like it's about to roll down the mountain.

Nearby Bubble Pond is another pond created in a glacial gouge. Its parking area on the Park Loop Road provides access to the carriage road system and to the strenuous Pemetic Trail, which takes hikers through a spruce and fir forest and then up 1,248-foot Pemetic Mountain. The trailhead for the Cadillac Mountain West Face Trail also begins at the Bubble Pond parking area.

Swimming is not allowed in Bubble Pond, which serves as a drinking water reservoir. The pond is stocked with brook trout, and fishing is permitted with a Maine fishing license. Boating is allowed, but there is a ban on motors of more than 10 horsepower.

Directions: The Bubbles are reached from the Bubble Rock parking area on the Park Loop Road, about 1.8 miles north of the Jordan Pond House. The Bubble Pond parking area is another 1 mile north of the Bubble Rock parking area.

Activities: Hiking on trails, biking or walking the carriage roads, boating and fishing in Bubble Pond.

Bubble Rock Trail to South Bubble: Moderate. 1 mile round-trip.
Bubble Rock Trail to North Bubble: Moderate. 1 mile round-trip.
Pemetic Trail: Strenuous. 2.4 miles, round-trip.
Cadillac Mountain West Face Trail: Strenuous. 0.9 mile to Cadillac South Ridge Trail.

Eagle Lake

[Fig. 19] One of the more popular bike rides in Acadia is the 6-mile carriage road loop around Eagle Lake, the largest lake in the park. The scenery is beautiful: From every shore mountains provide a backdrop to the lake. Most of the road is flat, although there are a few hills to pedal. Make sure to bring a carriage road system map as you will face several intersections.

On the western shore of the lake is the trailhead for the Connors Nubble Trail, a short, 0.6-mile moderate hike that requires some scrambling to reach the 588-foot Connors Nubble.

Energetic cyclists can combine the Eagle Lake loop with rides on the carriage roads along Bubble Pond and Jordan Pond. If the Eagle Lake roads are too crowded and you aren't intimidated by some steep hills, try the quieter loop from the Eagle Lake parking area toward Aunt Betty Pond to the west.

For anglers, Eagle Lake is stocked with salmon, brook trout, and lake trout. There is a boat launch at the north end of the lake. Like Jordan and Bubble ponds, Eagle Lake has a 10 horsepower limit on boat motors. Canoes are the boat of choice here. Swimming is prohibited in Eagle Lake.

Directions: The Eagle Lake carriage road can be reached from the Eagle Lake parking area on ME 233, 2.3 miles west of ME 3. This ride could also be started from the Bubble Pond parking area.

Activities: Hiking on trails, walking or bicycling on carriage roads, boating, fishing.

Penobscot and Sargent Mountains

🕸 HIKING AT PENOBSCOT AND SARGENT MOUNTAINS

Among the regular hikers in Acadia National Park are a number of "peak baggers" who pride themselves on the number of mountains they have climbed. The park, with its relatively low mountains and web of interconnecting trails, is a good place to try the sport of peak bagging. Many of the mountains, including 1,194-foot Penobscot Mountain and 1,373-foot Sargent Mountain, lend themselves to this kind of hiking.

Visitors to Acadia National Park enjoy the view and sea breezes.

A network of trails runs through this section of the park, just to the west of Jordan Pond. The trail between Penobscot and Sargent mountains stops by a pond that is warm enough for cooling your feet or perhaps even taking a swim.

One route up Penobscot Mountain begins near the Jordan Pond House, where a footpath heads from the lawn to the Penobscot Mountain Trail. Take the Penobscot Mountain Trail, where switchbacks and some handrails and footbridges help hikers rapidly ascend the mountain, first through a mixed forest and then across open ledges to the barren summit. The summit has a nice vantage point on Mount Desert Island, taking in mountains, Jordan Pond, Frenchman Bay and the open ocean. An alternate route up Penobscot Mountain is the challenging Jordan Cliffs ladder trail. The Jordan Cliffs Trail trailhead is about 0.4 miles along the Penobscot Mountain Trail. (There are nesting peregrine falcons here, so this trail is often closed in the summer to protect the birds and their chicks.) Neither trail is recommended when conditions could be slippery.

From Penobscot Mountain, head north on the Sargent Mountain South Ridge Trail. Make sure to stop at the spring-fed Sargent Pond, a peaceful pond where trail crews have built some rustic benches. Continue on the South Ridge Trail about 1 mile to reach the Sargent Mountain summit.

An alternate route to the Sargent Mountain summit is the Hadlock Brook Trail, starting from the Parkman Mountain parking area near Northeast Harbor.

Once you've admired the stunning views from the Sargent Mountain summit, congratulate yourself for bagging the highest peak in Acadia that is not accessible by car. Retrace your steps to return to Jordan Pond, taking extra care on the steep sections of the trail.

Penobscot Mountain Trail: [Fig. 19(24)] Strenuous 1.5 miles to summit.

Jordan Cliffs Trail: [Fig. 19(25)] Strenuous ladder trail. 0.8 mile, one-way.

Sargent Mountain South Ridge Trail: [Fig. 19(26)] Moderate. 1.1 miles between Penobscot and Sargent mountains.

Hadlock Brook Trail: [Fig. 19(27)] Strenuous. 2 miles, one-way.

Parkman Mountain and Bald Peak

▓ HIKING AT PARKMAN MOUNTAIN AND BALD PEAK

[Fig. 19(28)] The views from 941-foot Parkman Mountain and 974-foot Bald Peak are not as stunning as from some of the other summits in Acadia. But when the crowds on some of the other mountain summits are getting to you, a quiet hike up Parkman or Bald Peak may be just what you are looking for.

Reach the 1-mile Parkman Mountain Trail from the Parkman Mountain parking area on the east side of ME 198, about 2.5 miles south of ME 233. Reach the 0.8, somewhat steep Bald Peak Trail by following the Hadlock Brook Trail, which begins on ME 198 just north of Hadlock Pond, for 0.3 miles, when the Bald Peak Trail heads to the left and climbs to the summit.

Parkman Mountain Trail: 1 mile one-way with a moderate climb over some ledges.

Bald Peak Trail: 0.8 mile with some steep sections.

Northeast Harbor

The seaside village of Northeast Harbor offers a genteel contrast to the wilds of Acadia. It is a chic community that caters to old money summer residents and well-heeled visitors.

Northeast Harbor is worth a stop to admire its beautiful seaside "cottages" and the yachts in its protected harbor and to window shop at the classy gift shops along Main Street. It also has some nice spots to eat and a beautiful inn. Gardeners (and others) will want to visit the two public gardens in Northeast Harbor.

Northeast Harbor is the jumping-off point for boat rides to Baker Island, Great Cranberry Island and Little Cranberry Island, which the locals call Islesford.

ASTICOU TERRACES AND THUYA GARDEN AND LODGE

[Fig. 19(30)] There are two very different gardens open to the public at the former summer home of Boston landscape architect Joseph Henry Curtis (1841-1928).

Asticou Terraces is named for the chief of the Penobscot Indians in the early 1600s when French settlers arrived on Mount Desert. Beds of native perennial plants are set in terraces up the western slope of Eliot Mountain and have a striking view of Northeast Harbor. Walk the paths here to reach Thuya Lodge and Gardens, Curtis' home and formal garden named for the area's abundant white cedars (*Thuya occidentalis*). Curtis created a trust for the gardens' future maintenance as a park.

At the top of the hill, Thuya Lodge has a horticultural library that is open to the public. Behind the lodge, carved wooden gates lead into the formal Thuya Garden, a peaceful spot to stroll, admire the flowers, or read by the reflecting pool.

Directions: Asticou Terraces is 0.5 mile south of the intersection of ME 198 and ME 3. Look for a small Asticou Terraces sign and a small parking area. To reach the Thuya Garden and Lodge without climbing the terraces, drive 0.2 miles south beyond the Asticou Terrace parking area and look for a small Thuya Garden sign, drive up the driveway and park.

Dates: Asticou Terrace and Thuya Gardens and Lodge are open July through Sept.

Fees: A donation is requested for admission.

Closest town: Northeast Harbor.

For more information: Thuya Garden and Lodge, Northeast Harbor, ME 04662. Phone (207) 276-5130.

ELIOT MOUNTAIN TRAIL

[Fig. 19(31)] Head out the back gate of Thuya Garden to climb the trail up Eliot Mountain. This trail scrambles up some granite ledges through a mixed forest to the tree-covered summit of 461-foot Eliot Mountain and a monument to Charles William Eliot, one of the founders of Acadia National Park. This trail is not in the park, so please respect private property by staying on the trail.

Trail: 1.4 miles round-trip.

ASTICOU AZALEA GARDENS

[Fig. 19(29)] Visit the Asticou Azalea Gardens in late May or June to see an explosion of color as dozens of varieties of azalea and rhododendron bloom at this Japanese-inspired garden. It has many Eastern elements, including a sand garden, stone bridges, and stone lanterns, that all seem to fit right in under the coastal pines.

Directions: The Asticou Azalea Gardens are 100 yards north of the intersection of ME 3 and ME 198.

Fees: None.

Dates: The garden is open from April through Oct.

Closest town: Northeast Harbor.

For more information: Asticou Azalea Gardens, ME 198, Northeast Harbor ME 04662.

▓ DINING IN NORTHEAST HARBOR

NORTHEAST HARBOR CAFÉ AND ICE CREAM PARLOR. Main Street, Northeast Harbor. This café has sandwiches, soup and great ice cream. Open for lunch and dinner. *Inexpensive. (207) 276-4151.*

REDFIELD'S. Main Street, Northeast Harbor. Reservations are required for dinner at this gourmet restaurant. *Moderate to expensive. (207) 276-5283.*

▓ LODGING IN NORTHEAST HARBOR

Northeast Harbor's lodgings tend to run toward casual elegance and high prices.

ASTICOU INN. Route 3, Northeast Harbor. This Victorian waterfront inn offers tennis, a pool, and elegant dining. *Expensive. (207) 276-3344.*

▓ ISLAND FERRIES FROM NORTHEAST HARBOR

During the summer, a park service naturalist leads a daily cruise from Northeast Harbor to Baker Island, a 123-acre uninhabited island 8 miles offshore that is part of Acadia National Park.

Private companies offer passenger service to Great Cranberry and Islesford, also known as Little Cranberry. Both islands have some year-round and seasonal residents and offer few tourist amenities. Great Cranberry has a grocery store and a gift shop. Little Cranberry has a restaurant and a gallery, as well as The Islesford Historical Museum. Highlights at the museum, which is operated by the park service, are displays on fishing and local history.

For more information: Consult the *Acadia Beaver Log* for information on park naturalist cruises. For ferry schedules to all three islands, call Beal and Bunker, Inc., phone (207) 244-3575 or the Islesford Ferry Company, phone (207) 276-3717.

Seal Harbor

Just a few miles east of Northeast Harbor is the exclusive village of Seal Harbor. Style queen Martha Stewart made headlines by buying a huge cottage, reportedly with its own English pub, here a few years back. And some of her neighbors' homes are said to be just as impressive.

For visitors, the highlight of Seal Harbor is its public town beach with restrooms, changing rooms, and a float for those willing to brave the cold water. There's also a lobster shack that offers ice cream and lemonade and other takeout-style fare on the nearby Seal Harbor Town Pier.

Directions: The beach and pier are off ME 3 in Seal Harbor.

Somes Sound Area

Somes Sound, the only fjord in the eastern United States, is another remnant of the Ice Age, when a glacier carved this 7-mile-long sea inlet that nearly cuts Mount Desert Island in two. The water in Somes Sound is 180 feet deep in spots. In the nineteenth century, ships sailed right up to the edge of the sound to collect fresh water from Man of War Brook.

The easiest way to get a good look at this fjord is to drive on Sargent Drive, a scenic auto road that runs up the eastern side of Somes Sound. RVs are prohibited from this road. A boat excursion out of Southwest Harbor or Northeast Harbor will provide a good view of Somes Sound's granite cliffs, and of the black basaltic dikes that run through them. The most dramatic views of Somes Sound are from the tops of Norumbega Mountain to the east or Acadia Mountain and Flying Mountain to the west.

Directions: From the east, reach Sargent Drive at the intersection of ME 3 and ME 198 in Northeast Harbor.

Closest towns: Northeast Harbor and Southwest Harbor.

HIKING NEAR SOMES SOUND

The Park Service classifies the hikes up both Norumbega and Acadia mountains as strenuous. They are not technically difficult, but they both involve some steep ascents and a bit of scrambling.

NORUMBEGA MOUNTAIN GOAT TRAIL

[Fig. 19(32)] To see Somes Sound from the east, head up the Goat Trail on 852-foot Norumbega Mountain. Find the trailhead north of Upper Hadlock Pond on ME 198. The hike is a steep and challenging 0.5 mile to the top. An easier descent is on the Norumbega Trail to Lower Hadlock Pond. Then follow the Hadlock Trail back to Upper Hadlock Pond.

Trail: A strenuous, 1-mile round-trip. Or make a 2.5-mile loop by hiking the Norumbega and Hadlock trails.

ACADIA MOUNTAIN TRAIL

[Fig. 19(33)] To hike 681-foot Acadia Mountain, begin at the trailhead across ME 102 from the Acadia Mountain parking area. The trail crosses the Man of War Fire Road, then begins with a steep ascent on switchbacks and stone steps through tall white pines (*Pinus strobus*) and spruces. The climb is more gradual, moving through clusters of pitch pines and across ledges. At 0.6 mile, you reach the west peak of Acadia Mountain, with a view of Echo Lake to the west. Follow the trail across a ridge—the only east-to-west ridge on any of Acadia's mountains—to the 646-foot east summit, where the view of Somes Sound is unbeatable. Follow the trail's steep descent, the toughest part of this hike. The trail crosses a bridge over Man of War Brook and intersects with the Man of War Fire Road, which you can follow back to the beginning of the Acadia Mountain Trail for a 2.5-mile loop.

Trail: Strenuous. 2.5 miles, including a loop onto the Man of War Fire Road.

Western Mount Desert Island

ECHO LAKE

[Fig. 19] Most of 237-acre Echo Lake is bordered by private land. The southern end of the lake is in Acadia, and the Park Service maintains a swimming beach there.

Echo Lake is the only freshwater lake in the park where swimming is permitted. On hot summer days the parking lot fills up early.

There is a boat launch at Ike's Point on the southeastern shore. Echo Lake has a 10 horsepower limit on boats. Anglers can fish for brook trout. A Maine fishing license is required.

Not far from the Echo Lake Beach is Beech Mountain, where there are several interesting trails, including a ladder trail that scales Beech Cliff.

Directions: Echo Lake Beach is on ME 102. From the northern end of Mount Desert Island, follow ME 102 south to a sign that says Acadia National Park Echo Lake Entrance. The parking area for Ike's Point is just north of the Echo Lake Beach parking area.

Activities: Swimming, boating, fishing, and hiking.

Facilities: Lifeguards, dressing rooms, restrooms.

Dates: Accessible year-round, facilities available only in the summer months.

Fees: None.

Closest town: Southwest Harbor, 1.8 miles.

For more information: Acadia National Park, PO Box 177, Bar Harbor, ME 04608. (207) 288-3338.

HIKING NEAR ECHO LAKE

The 839-foot Beech Mountain gets its name from the towering beech trees (*Fagus grandifolia*) that grow near its base and lower slopes. These gray-barked trees have prickly burred fruit that split in the fall to release small brown beechnuts, a favorite food of squirrels.

Beech Mountain looks down at Echo Lake to the east and Long Pond to the west. It is accessible from a number of interconnecting trails. As is the case with many Mount Desert Island mountain hikes, the shortest way up is also the most challenging.

BEECH CLIFF TRAIL

[Fig. 19(34)] The Canada Cliff Trail is a very strenuous ladder trail and should not be undertaken by young children or anyone afraid of heights. The trail switchbacks up the cliff, providing hikers with handrails and iron ladders. Once they've scaled the cliff, hikers can continue on to other Beech Mountain trails to visit the summit and its fire tower. The trailhead for the Beech Cliff Trail is near the Echo Lake Beach parking area.

Trail: 0.9 mile one-way, steep.

BEECH MOUNTAIN TRAIL

[Fig. 19(35)] The Beech Mountain Trail is reached from the Beech Mountain parking area. It's a steady 0.6-mile climb to the summit. To reach the trailhead, heading north on ME 102 along Eagle Lake, turn left on Beech Hill Cross Roads just north of the lake. Bear left on Beech Hill Road and follow it to the end and the Beech Mountain Parking area.

Trail: 0.6 mile one-way. Strenuous and steep trail.

VALLEY AND SOUTH RIDGE TRAILS LOOP

[Fig. 19(36)] For those wishing a longer hike through the forest before reaching Beech Mountain, try hiking the Valley Trail up the mountain. For an alternate route back to Long Pond, take the South Ridge Trail for the descent. The trail begins at the parking area near the southern end of Long Pond. Heading north out of Southwest Harbor on ME 102, turn left on Seal Cove Road and then right on Long Pond Road to the parking area.

Trail: A moderate, 3-mile trip.

⊞ HIKING AT WESTERN MOUNTAIN: MANSELL MOUNTAIN, BERNARD MOUNTAIN, AND KNIGHT NUBBLE

The two highest summits in this region of Mount Desert are 949-foot Mansell Mountain and 1,071-foot Bernard Mountain. These two peaks, along with the smaller Knight Nubble between them, make up what is known as Western Mountain. Their tree-covered summits don't offer the views found on Mount Desert Island's eastern summits although Mansell does provide a view of Long Pond. But there are interesting trails here that don't typically attract the crowds that some of the eastern mountains do. A network of trails here can be reached from the south from the parking area at the base of Long Pond, or from the Gilley Field parking area off the Western Mountain Road. The Western Mountain area can be approached from the north by following a trail that begins on the Long Pond Fire Road. Driving north on ME 102 out of Southwest Harbor, turn left on Seal Cove Road. The Long Pond Road and the Western Mountain Road will be on the right. To reach Gilley Field, turn right on the Western Mountain Road, then bear right at the fork.

In a national park full of interesting man-made trails, the Perpendicular Trail [Fig. 19(37)] up Mansell Mountain stands out. This 1930s-era trail includes a long winding stairway created by stonecutters. The stairs are steep, as is the rest of this hike. You'll need to use the iron handrails and climb a ladder to reach the 949-foot summit. Unlike most of Acadia's ladder trails, this one attracts few hikers. Reach the Perpendicular Trail from the parking lot at the southern end of Long Pond.

Two other trails—Mansell Mountain Trail and Razorback Trail [Fig. 19(37)] — also take a steep route up Mansell Mountain, although these trails aren't as unique in their construction as the Perpendicular Trail. Take either of these trails down, turning left on the Cold Brook Trail [Fig. 19(39)], an easy path that connects several trails in this section of the park, to get back to Long Pond.

To hike Bernard Mountain, begin at the gravel parking area at Mill Field off the Western Mountain Road. Take the Bernard Mount South Face Trail 1.7 miles to the forested summit. Head east to find the Sluiceway Trail, which provides a more direct and steep descent down Bernard Mountain to Mill Field.

Perpendicular Trail: [Fig. 19(37)] A strenuous ladder trail, 1.2 miles one-way.

Razorback Trail: [Fig. 19(37)] A strenuous ascent, 1 mile, one-way.

Bernard South Face Trail: [Fig. 19(37)] A somewhat steep walk, 1.7 miles to summit.

Sluiceway Trail: [Fig. 19(37)] A steep ascent of 1.1 miles.

Southwest Harbor

The town of Southwest Harbor is the commercial center of the western side of Mount Desert Island, but don't go looking for the hubbub of Bar Harbor. This is the quiet side of the island.

There are several spots worth visiting in Southwest Harbor, including an impressive museum dedicated to the art of bird carving, an oceanarium, and a scenic lighthouse. Southwest Harbor has a first-rate kids' bookstore at Oz Books, while nearby Somesville has Port in a Storm Bookstore, which has reading material for everyone, including a good selection of natural history books.

If you are a sailor, stop by The Hinckley Company, builder of some of the finest yachts made today. If the high-priced boats are out of your range, The Hinckley Store sells smaller items with the distinctive H logo.

There are several inns, two private campgrounds, and a National Park Service campground nearby. All in all, Southwest Harbor is a good base of operations for exploring the less congested western side of Mount Desert Island.

WENDELL GILLEY MUSEUM OF BIRD CARVING

[Fig. 19(41)] Wendell Gilley was a master bird carver who lived in Southwest Harbor until his death in 1983. This museum showcases hundreds of his intricately carved life-sized birds, from tiny songbirds to large raptors.

There are also rotating exhibits of world-class nature art, carving demonstrations, and a gift shop full of bird-carving and bird-watching supplies.

The Wendell Gilley Museum holds regular classes and workshops on bird carving and has a carver in residence.

Directions: The Wendell Gilley Museum is north of Southwest Harbor on ME 102, a block north of the Great Harbor Marina.

Facilities: Museum.

Activities: Browsing, watching bird-carving.

Dates: The museum is open every day but Monday, June through Oct. It is open Friday through Sunday in May, Nov. and Dec., and open by appointment Jan. to Apr. Classes and special events are held year-round.

Fees: There is a charge for admission.

Closest town: Southwest Harbor.

For more information: Wendell Gilley Museum, PO Box 254, Southwest Harbor, ME 04679. Phone (207) 244-7555.

OCEANARIUM SOUTHWEST HARBOR

[Fig. 19(42)] For most children and some adults, the highlight of this small oceanarium is the touch-tank, where visitors can pick up sea cucumbers, scallops, and other sea creatures. Other features include 20 tanks of sea life from the coast of Maine, a fishing gallery explaining the history and present state of the fishing industry, and exhibits on tides, seaweed, seagulls, and other marine topics.

Directions: Heading south on ME 102 in Southwest Harbor, turn left on Clark Point Road. The oceanarium will be on the right, next door to the Coast Guard Station.

Activities: Looking at and touching sea life, exploring gallery.

Facilities: Touch tanks, exhibits.

Dates: Open every day but Sunday, from mid-May to late Oct.

Fees: There is a charge for admission. There is a discount for people visiting this oceanarium and the Bar Harbor Oceanarium (*see* page 222).

Closest town: Southwest Harbor.

For more information: Oceanarium Southwest Harbor. Clark Point Road, Southwest Harbor, ME 04679. Phone (207) 244-7330.

BASS HARBOR HEAD LIGHT

[Fig. 19(43)] This lighthouse on the southern tip of western Mount Desert Island may look familiar. Thanks to its scenic location it appears on many Maine postcards and calendars. The lighthouse was built in 1858, and it still marks the entrance to Blue Hill Bay and Bass Harbor for mariners by flashing a red light every four seconds. To visit, park at the lighthouse lot and walk down a steep walkway. The lighthouse is automated. Please respect the privacy of the keeper's house residents.

Directions: Take ME 102 south to ME 102A into Bass Harbor. Go straight ahead down Lighthouse Road to the parking lot.

Closest town: Bass Harbor.

CAMPING NEAR SOUTHWEST HARBOR

Acadia National Park's Seawall Campground is nearby (*see* page 253). There are also some commercial campgrounds. Backcountry camping is not allowed in Acadia National Park. The Appalachian Mountain Club operates a very popular camp on Echo Lake.

SOMES SOUND VIEW CAMPGROUND. Hall Quarry Road, Mount Desert. [Fig. 19(44)] This campground has sites for tents and RV sites with electrical and water hookups. *(207) 244-3890.*

MOUNT DESERT CAMPGROUND. Route 198, Somesville. [Fig. 19(45)] This campground has sites for tents and RVs, some with hookups. *(207) 244-3710.*

ECHO LAKE CAMP. [Fig. 19(46)] This Appalachian Mountain Club camp has tents with beds and bedding, a group dining room and recreation hall, boats to take out on the lake and daily and evening programs. AMC accepts reservations by mail starting April 1. For more information, write AMC, 5 Joy Street, Boston, ME 02215.

▓ DINING IN SOUTHWEST HARBOR

You expect good seafood in Southwest Harbor, but the great Mexican food may come as a surprise.

BURDOCK'S NATURAL FOODS. Main Street, Southwest Harbor. Stock up on picnic supplies or trail mix at Burdock's. *Inexpensive. (207) 244-0108.*

LITTLE NOTCH CAFÉ. Main Street, Southwest Harbor. Stop here for great pizza, soup, and desserts. *Inexpensive. (207) 244-3357.*

RESTAURANT XYZ. Shore Road, Manset. This Mexican restaurant specializes in dinner dishes from Xalapa, Yacaan, and Zacatecas. *Moderate. (207) 244-5221.*

▓ LODGING IN SOUTHWEST HARBOR

Southwest Harbor has a big, classy hotel and several cozy B&Bs.

THE CLAREMONT. Claremont Road, Southwest Harbor. This grand old inn overlooks Somes Sound and holds the annual Claremont Croquet Classic. Jackets are required at dinner in the dining room, which is open to the public. Lunch is more casual in the waterfront Boat House, also open to the public. *Expensive. (207) 244-5036.*

THE INN AT SOUTHWEST. Main Street, Southwest Harbor. This Victorian "cottage" has nine rooms, all with private baths, and many with harbor views. *Moderate. (207) 244-3835.*

Seawall

The Seawall picnic area is a nice spot to take a break after a visit to the nearby Big Heath, Ship Harbor Nature Trail, or Wonderland Trail. There are picnic tables under the tall spruces and a cobblestone beach to explore. The view includes Great Cranberry Island and the open sea, and even though the scenery is lovely, there usually aren't too many visitors. Try birding at Seawall in the early morning, when nesting and migrant warblers can be heard in the forest and seabirds can be seen from the rocks.

Directions: Heading south on ME 102 in Southwest Harbor, bear left at ME 102A. The Seawall picnic area will be on your left.

Activities: Bird-watching, picnicking, beach exploring.

Facilities: Picnic areas, restrooms.

Closest town: Southwest Harbor, 4 miles.

Wonderland Trail

[Fig. 19(47)] The Wonderland trail is an easy walk that winds through the woods to the ocean. While there is less than a mile between the roadside trailhead and the shore, the trail takes in a nice mix of the scenery typical of Acadia National Park.

The 0.7-mile trail starts in a mixed forest of deciduous and coniferous trees, and leads hikers past some lichen-covered rocks and pitch pines to a grove of spruces that grow along the ledges above the shore. The trail reaches its beautiful and dramatic conclusion at the shoreline, where huge granite blocks tumble to the sea.

At low tide, wander along the rocks here to see what sea life is either living or trapped in the many tide pools.

Wonderland is a good place to watch and listen for some of the more than 20 species of warblers that nest in Acadia National Park. Black-throated green warblers (*Dendroica virens*) have yellow faces and olive green patches on their heads and backs. Their distinctive buzz-like song sounds like a "zee zee zoo zee" coming from the tree tops.

GRAY JAY
(*Perisoreus canandensis*)
Gray Jays are familiar camp visitors and will steal scraps of food from campers.

The boreal chickadee (*Parus hudsonicus*) is primarily a bird of the Canadian spruce forest, but its range descends into a few northern New England forests. While you are likely to see many black-capped chickadees (*Parus atricapillus*) in the park and the rest of Maine, the boreal chickadee is more elusive. But if you are keeping a life list of birds, this is a good spot to keep your eyes and ears peeled for this addition. The boreal chickadee is brown with a darker crown and back. Like the ubiquitous black-capped chickadee, its call is a "chick-a-dee" song, but it's slower and has a bit of a buzz to it.

Directions: Heading south out of Southwest Harbor on ME 102, bear left onto ME 102A. Wonderland is about 1 mile past the Seawall Campground on the left. There is a parking area at the trailhead.

Trail: 1.4 miles round-trip. This trail takes approximately 1.5 hours to hike.

Closest town: Southwest Harbor, 4.6 miles.

Ship Harbor

[Fig. 19(48)] Take this easy hike early in your visit for a good introduction to the natural sites of Acadia National Park. A brochure prepared by Eastern National explains various bits of natural history along this route, which makes an elongated figure eight through the woods to the shore.

The Ship Harbor Nature Trail [Fig. 19(49)] begins in an old apple orchard, a relic of this land's days as farmland, before quickly descending into a forest of tall red spruce (*Picea rubens*) and white spruce (*Picea glauca*).

The trail passes through an open rocky outcrop, where lichen can be seen growing on the boulders. The trail then heads through some tamarack trees (*Larix laricina*). The tamarack, which is also known as the larch tree, is one of the only coniferous trees to drop its needles in the fall.

The trail emerges from the forest at an open headland of pink granite bedrock. It's possible to carefully work your way down to the water and, at low tide, examine the tide pools.

As the trail loops back inland, it runs along the edge of the harbor where, depending on the tide, the water can be 8 inches or 8 feet deep. The harbor turns to mud flat and finally to salt marsh as the trail continues back to the trailhead.

With its nice variety of habitats, the 1.3-mile Ship Harbor Nature Trail can be a satisfying spot to look for birds. The boreal spruce forest attracts several kinds of warblers and purple finches (*Carpodacus purpureus*).

The spruce forest on western Mount Desert Island is the best place to look for northern bird species whose southern range drops into northern New England. They include the boreal chickadee (*Parus hudsonicus*), spruce grouse (*Dendragapus canadensis*), and gray jay (*Perisoreus canandensis*).

Also watch for sea ducks, including buffleheads (*Bucephala albeola*) and oldsquaw (*Clangula hyemalis*), in the harbor, especially in the fall and winter.

The mud flat and marsh at the top of the harbor are feeding places for seabirds, including gulls, who will arrive after a high tide looking for sea worms, clams and other food.

Directions: From Southwest Harbor, head south on ME 102 and bear left on ME 102A. The Ship Harbor Nature Trail parking area is a little more than 4 miles from the turn, and about 0.25 mile past Wonderland.

Remember to pick up a trail map, either at the Hulls Cove Visitor Center or from the trailhead.

Closest town: Southwest Harbor, 4.8 miles.

Trail: 1.3 miles. This trail takes approximately 1.5 hours to hike.

The Big Heath

[Fig. 19(50)] The Big Heath is a freshwater peat bog, also known as the Seawall Bog, near the southwestern tip of Mount Desert. Its damp environs host a number of bog plants, which typically require few nutrients and tolerate highly acidic soil. Peat bogs like this one are often found atop granite bedrock, which contributes to the acidic nature of the soil. Plants typical of peat bogs that can be seen here include sphagnum mosses (*Sphagnum species*), the insectivorous northern pitcher plant (*Sarracenia purpurea*), and bog-loving orchids, including the rose pogonia (*Pogonia ophioglossoides*) and grass pink (*Calopogon pulchellus*). The forest includes Atlantic white cedar (*Chamaecyparis thyoides*) *and* the tamarack (*Larix laricina*), both trees that tolerate boggy conditions well. There was no fire damage on this side of Mount Desert Island in 1947, so the forest is considerably older than those in eastern sections that were burned.

The Big Heath is home to warblers, including the buzzing palm warbler (*Dendroica palmarum*), Wilson's warbler (*Wilsonia pusilla*), and Canada warbler (*Wilsonia canadensis*). The best bird-watching here may be in spring, when the warblers' spring colors and a field guide make their identification easier, especially for novices. In the fall, many of these little birds look muddy brown and will be harder to differentiate.

Tour the Big Heath from the Hio Road, a fire road closed to motor vehicles that is a nice route to walk or bike ride. The Hio Road was one of the Civilian Conservation Corps projects done in the park in the 1930s. Reach the Hio Road from the back of Loop C in the park's Seawall Campground. The 2-mile fire road concludes at ME 102, which can be busy, especially in the summer. Returning to the campground along The Hio Road makes it easy to continue your day on the Wonderland or Ship Harbor trails.

Directions: Heading south on ME 102 in Southwest Harbor, bear left at ME 102A. The Seawall campground will be on your right. Follow the signs to the back of Loop C to reach The Hio Road.

Closest town: Southwest Harbor, 4 miles.

NORTHERN PITCHER PLANT
(Sarracenia purpurea)

Swans Island

Swans Island is a 12-square-mile island populated mostly by fishermen and summer residents. It may be reached by a 40-minute ferry ride out of Bass Harbor. Swans Island has a handful of restaurants but little more to offer in the way of tourist amenities. It is a nice destination for a day trip, particularly with a bicycle. Either pack a lunch or buy picnic fixings at the general store in Minturn, one of three small villages on Swans Island.

A day spent with a bicycle here could include a stop at the Swans Island Museum, the square Hockamock Head Light, Fine Sand Beach, and a granite quarry that has been turned into a swimming hole. Also plan an afternoon stop at Atlantic Blanket Company, where Maine sheep wool is woven into luxuriously soft Swans Island Blankets.

Those spending the day on foot will probably want to shrink their island agenda to include a trip to just the general store and quarry or just the Atlantic Blanket Company and the beach. Make sure to leave enough time to catch the return boat back to Bass Harbor. Camping is not permitted on Swans Island, and spare beds are hard to find. As you ride the ferry to and from Swans Island (or any of the ferry-connected islands off Mount Desert Island), keep an eye out for seabirds, especially double-crested cormorants (*Phalacrocorax auritus*), seagulls, and black guillemots (*Cepphuys grylle*).

Directions: The car ferry to Swans Island departs from Bass Harbor. The ferry terminal has detailed island maps for hikers and bikers.

Activities: Walking, biking, swimming, and picnicking.

Closest town: Swans Island.

For more information: The Maine State Ferry Service, PO Box 114, Bass Harbor, ME 04653. Phone (207) 244-3254. Atlantic Blanket Company, Swans Island, ME 04685. Phone (207) 526-4492.

Pretty Marsh

[Fig. 19(52)] The park service maintains a picnic area at Pretty Marsh Harbor. There are picnic tables and restrooms and a beautiful view out toward Bartlett Island.

It's also the jumping off point for a scenic bike ride on one of the fire roads built by the Civilian Conservation Corps, the Long Pond Fire Road. Keep in mind that motor vehicles are allowed on this road, which has two good-sized hills. At the top of the second hill, about 3 miles into the ride, stop at the Pine Hill parking area and look across the fire road for the cedar post marking the Pine Hill Trail, also known as the Western Trail. This connects with the trails that climb the Western Mountain, which is made up of three summits—Bernard Mountain, Mansell Mountain, and Knight Nubble (*see* page 244).

Continue on the Long Pond Fire Road until it loops back to ME 102. Pedal about 1 mile north to return to the Pretty Marsh picnic area and create a 5-mile loop.

Directions: The Pretty Marsh picnic area is on ME 102 on the western shore of Mount Desert Island and is marked with a sign.

Activities: Picnicking, biking, hiking.

Facilities: Picnic tables, restrooms.

Closest town: Bernard, 6 miles.

Indian Point-Blagden Preserve

[Fig. 19(53)] This Nature Conservancy preserve on the western shore of Mount Desert Island has 110 acres of mature forest and nearly 0.25 mile of shoreline. It supports an impressive array of birds. A checklist available at the entrance lists more than 125 species of birds that have been spotted there. At least 12 species of warblers and six kinds of woodpeckers nest here. From the parking area, hike the 1.2 mile-Big Wood Trail through the woods, keeping an ear tuned for bird calls and an eye out for white-tailed deer (*Odocoileus virginianus*). In the sky you may see osprey (*Pandion haliaetus*) and bald eagles (*Halaeetus leucocephalus*).

The Blagden Preserve is bordered on either side by private land. Please stay on the trails and respect preserve boundaries.

Directions: From the causeway onto Mount Desert Island, bear right at the fork in the road, following ME 102/108 toward Somesville. In 1.8 miles, turn right on Indian Point Road. In 1.7 miles, bear right at the fork. The preserve entrance is 200 yards away on the right. There is a sign and parking area. Please register at the entrance.

Activities: Hiking, bird-watching.

Facilities: Trail, map and brochures.

Dates: Open year-round.

Closest town: Thompson Island causeway, 4 miles.

For more information: The Nature Conservancy, Maine Chapter, Fort Andross, 14 Maine Street, Suite 401, Brunswick, ME 04011. Phone (207) 729-5181. Or Blagden Preserve Steward, RR1, Box 7060, Bar Harbor, ME 04609.

Camping in Acadia National Park

Backcountry camping is not allowed in Acadia National Park. There are two Park Service campgrounds in Acadia: Blackwoods on the east side of Mount Desert and Seawall on the west side. These campgrounds have sites for tents and trailers up to 35 feet. There are no hookups. Each site has a picnic table and grill. There are restrooms and cold water faucets nearby. Both sites have amphitheaters, where park rangers hold evening programs on natural and cultural history in the park. Both campgrounds have two-week limits for campers. A private concessionaire runs a camp store and hot showers within 0.25 mile of each campground.

THE BLACKWOODS CAMPGROUND

[Fig. 19(54)] This campground is open year-round. Reservations are required from June 15 to Sept. 15. During the off-season, sites are provided on a first-come, first-served basis.

Directions: The Blackwoods Campground is about 5 miles south of Bar Harbor on Route 3.

Facilities: Campsites, picnic tables, restrooms, fire rings, cold water faucets. No hookups. Privately run camp stores and hot showers nearby.

Dates: Open year-round.

Fees: There is a charge for camping.

For more information: For reservations, call Biospherics, phone (800) 365-2267.

SEAWALL CAMPGROUND

[Fig. 19(55)] The Seawall Campground accepts campers on a first-come, first-served basis from late May through September.

Directions: The Seawall Campground is about 4 miles south of Southwest Harbor on Route 102A.

Facilities: Campsites, picnic tables, restrooms, cold water faucets, fire rings. No hookups.

Dates: Open late May through Sept.

Fees: There is a charge for camping.

For more information: No reservations are accepted. Acadia National Park, PO Box 177, Bar Harbor, ME 04609. Phone (207) 288-3338.

GOLFING ON MOUNT DESERT ISLAND

KEBO VALLEY CLUB. This 1891 golf course near downtown Bar Harbor is one of the oldest in Maine. It's a very scenic and popular 18-hole, par-70 course, so call ahead for a tee time.

For more information: Kebo Valley Club, Route 3, Bar Harbor, ME 04609. Phone (207) 288-3000.

NORTHEAST HARBOR GOLF CLUB. Northeast Harbor has a par-69, 5,300-yard course.

For more information: Northeast Harbor Golf Club, PO Box 647, Northeast Harbor, ME 04662. Phone (207) 276-5335.

CAUSEWAY CLUB. This Southwest Harbor course is par 65 for 4,700 yards.

For more information: Causeway Club, Fernald Point Road, Southwest Harbor, ME 04679. Phone (207) 244-3780.

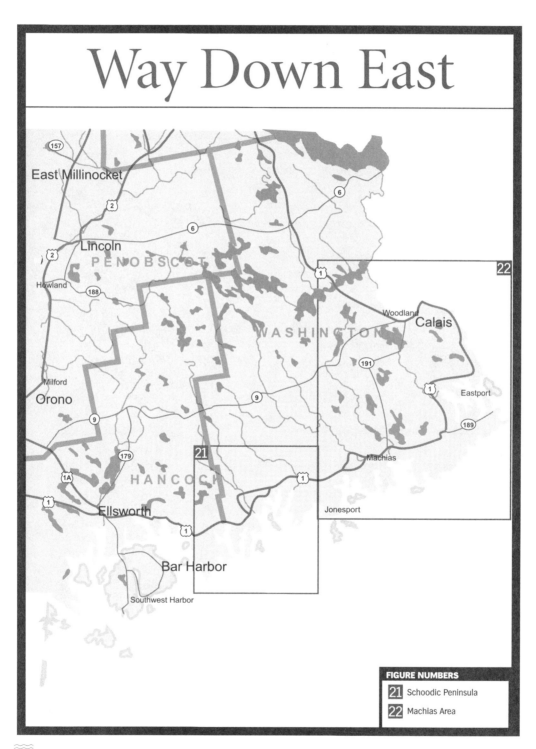

Way Down East

157

East Millinocket

2

6

Lincoln

6

2

PENOBSCOT

1

Howland

188

22

Woodland

Calais

WASHINGTON

Milford

191

Orono

9

1

Eastport

9

189

179

21

1A

HANCOCK

Machias

1

1

Ellsworth

Jonesport

1

Bar Harbor

Southwest Harbor

FIGURE NUMBERS

21 Schoodic Peninsula

22 Machias Area

Way Down East

I f you're an early riser, you can sip your coffee and be among the first people in the country to see the sun rise while visiting this, the northeast corner of Maine. For that reason, some call this section of Maine the Sunrise Coast. Others call it the Bold Coast for the bold and dramatic headlands and cliffs found here. Still others refer to the far reaches of Maine as the foggy coast for reasons that will become obvious to any visitor.

This region begins where the typical tourist track drops off. While tourist amenities become fewer and farther between, the absence of crowds and the rich scenery make this a wonderful region to explore.

The region is known for its dramatic tides, which can reach as high as 28 feet in the far corner of the state. The landscape here includes forests, blueberry barrens, giant peat bogs, rocky shorelines, and steep headlands.

[*Above: West Quoddy Head Lighthouse*]

The farthest reaches of the Maine coast have incredible wildlife-watching opportunities. Seals and whales can be seen from rocky points. Puffins and terns viewed can be viewed on an offshore island. The region is considered a stronghold for bald eagles, which winter around Cobscook Bay. And a national wildlife refuge near the Canadian border is the first stop on the Atlantic Flyway and a major staging area for migratory waterfowl and shorebirds.

Eastern Hancock County

Pity the millions of tourists who surge onto Mount Desert Island every summer but never think to ride another hour or two up the coast. They miss out on some spectacular scenery and serious wilderness open for exploring.

LAMOINE STATE PARK

[Fig. 19(56)] When the campgrounds on busy Mount Desert Island fill up, in-the-know campers head to nearby Lamoine State Park, just a few miles east on the mainland.

This 55-acre state park has a beautiful view across Eastern Bay to Mount Desert Island. Several of its 61 campsites have ocean views, and all are an easy stroll away from the shore. There is a boat launch, a pier for saltwater fishing, a playground, and picnic areas for day visitors or campers.

Directions: From ME 3 in Ellsworth, take ME 184 southeast 8 miles to the state park.

Activities: Picnicking, camping, fishing, and boating.

Facilities: Picnic tables, fishing pier, boat launch, playground, restrooms, campsites for tents and RVs, (no hookups), showers, and restrooms.

Dates: Open May 15 to Oct. 15.

Fees: There is a charge for admission and for camping.

Closest town: Lamoine.

For more information: Lamoine State Park. Route 184, Lamoine, ME 04605. Phone (207) 667-4778. Off-season, Maine Bureau of Parks and Land, 22 State House Station, Augusta, ME 04333. Phone (207) 941-4014.

DONNELL POND PUBLIC RESERVED LAND

[Fig. 21(1)] Nearly one-half million acres of wild land in Maine are managed as state public reserved land. Recreational and timber uses co-exist on much of this land, and visitors can find some very remote spots to camp, hike, and fish in the area. While most of the public reserved land is inland, a handful of large areas are on the eastern coast of the state.

The Donnell Pond Public Reserved Land unit's 14,000 acres include miles of shorefront on Donnell Pond, Tunk Lake, and Spring River Lake. Schoodic Beach, on the southeastern shore of Donnell Pond, is a popular swimming and sunning spot. Campsites on the lakefronts are accessible by foot or water. Three mountains in the area—Schoodic, Black, and Caribou—offer panoramic views to hikers. With an early start, an energetic hiker can take in two or three of these peaks. Hikers may want to avoid the area during hunting season, as it is popular with deer, bear, and moose hunters.

Directions: Donnell Pond Public Reserved Land is 12 miles east of Ellsworth, off ME 182 or ME 183.

Activities: Hiking, camping, boating, swimming, fishing, hunting.

Facilities: Backcountry campsites.

Dates: Open year-round.

Fees: None.

Closest town: Sullivan, 3 miles.

For more information: Maine Bureau of Parks and Lands, 22 State House Station, Augusta, ME 04333. Phone (207) 287-3821.

BLACK MOUNTAIN TRAIL
[Fig. 21(2)] The hike up 1,094-foot Black Mountain wanders through spruce and oak forests and takes in some impressive granite ledges. The trail is marked with stone cairns and is steep at times.

Trail: Moderate. 2.2 miles round-trip.

Directions: From Route 1 in Ellsworth, take ME 183 east for 4.5 miles, cross the old railroad tracks and turn left on Fire Road 34K. The trailhead is 2.5 miles up the fire road and is marked with stone cairns.

SCHOODIC MOUNTAIN TRAIL
[Fig. 21(3)] The hike up 1,069-foot Schoodic Mountain is the most popular in the Donnell Pond area, perhaps because it offers such beautiful views of Cadillac and the other Mount Desert Island peaks. Hikers travel through mixed forests and along some blueberry fields before climbing some steep ledges. The windy summit has a radio tower.

Trail: Easy, with a few steep sections. 6 miles round-trip.

Directions: From Route 1 in Sullivan, drive north on ME 200 for about 3.75 miles to East Franklin. You will see two bridges. Park north of the second bridge. The Schoodic Mountain trail begins between the two bridges, heading east.

CATHERINE MOUNTAIN
[Fig. 21] The trail up 942-foot Catherine Mountain is an easy hike through woods and along ledges.

Trail: Easy. 1.5 miles.

Directions: From Franklin, drive east on ME 182. Look for a turnoff on the right, directly after Fox Pond, and park. Look for an unmarked trail into the woods.

Schoodic Peninsula

Some call this section of Maine the Sunrise Coast because you can be among the first in the country to see the sun rise.

1	Donnell Pond Public Reserved Land
2	Black Mountain Trail
3	Schoodic Mountain Trail
4	Catherine Mountain Trail
5	Acadia National Park's Schoodic Section
6	Oceanwood Campground
7	Humboldt Field Research Station
8	Petit Manan NWR
9	Upper Birch Island Preserve
10	Pineo Ridge
11	The Great Heath
12	McClellan Town Park
13	Pleasant River Salmon Fry Hatchery and Wild Salmon Resource Center

Ref: Delorme Maine Atlas & Gazetteer

N

The Schoodic Peninsula

This peninsula, which is often overlooked by summer visitors, includes some picturesque seaside communities—Winter Harbor, Prospect Harbor, and Corea— and 2,000 acres of Acadia National Park.

▓ ACADIA NATIONAL PARK'S SCHOODIC SECTION

[Fig. 21(5)] This 2,000-acre parcel is the only piece of Acadia National Park that is on the mainland. A 6-mile, one-way road loops through the national parkland, taking in some stunning views. There are several spots to pull over and enjoy the scenery, as well as picnic areas and some hiking trails. The highlight of the peninsula is Schoodic Point, where waves crash against the pink granite shore at high tide. Visitors should also try hiking one of the trails to Schoodic Head, the highest point on the peninsula at 440 feet, for a beautiful view of Mount Desert Island and Frenchman Bay.

The trails here wander through a classic coastal Maine forest. Cool, moist air often leaves fog clinging to the northern white cedar and jack pines here and helps support the haircap moss, reindeer moss, and antler lichen that grow profusely along boulders and rotting logs.

Begin a visit to the peninsula at the Frazier Point Picnic Area, which has restrooms, picnic tables, and a parking area. Mosquito Harbor, to the north of the point, is a good spot to look for sea ducks and loons.

Leave your car here if you plan to cycle the Schoodic Point Park Loop Road. The road, which is a scenic trip for motorists or cyclists, becomes one-way at the picnic area.

Follow the Schoodic Park Loop Road 2.9 miles to a fork and head right past a U.S. Navy installation to Schoodic Point. Visitors who arrive at high tide, especially on a stormy day, are in for a show as the waves crash onto the rocky pink granite shore. Lower tides expose some tide pools for exploration. Be very careful on the rocks here, especially with children, and look out for rogue waves. This can be a great place to watch for seabirds, especially during the spring and fall migrations. Scan the offshore sky for northern gannets (*Morus bassanus*), identifiable by

LABRADOR TEA
(*Ledum groenlandicum*)
These members of the acid-tolerant heath family have thick, leathery leaves and five-petaled white flowers.

CHIMNEY SWIFT
(Chaetura pelagica)
This species makes nests in hollow trees, chimneys, wells, and barns. Chimney swifts are the most widespread swift in America. They winter in the upper Amazon rain forest.

their missile-like dives into the sea.

The wide black stripes in the pink bedrock are basaltic dikes. Both the granite and the dikes are the result of volcanic activity hundreds of millions of years ago.

Back on the Park Loop Road, pull in to the Blueberry Hill parking area and head into the interior of the peninsula on the 1-mile Anvil Trail. Hikers travel through a coastal "fog forest" to the 180-foot Anvil headland and then climb a twisting, wooded trail to Schoodic Head. On a clear day, the view here takes in the mountains of Mount Desert Island.

You'll see a fair amount of jack pines (*Pinus banksiana*), which are at the southern end of their range here. Identify them by their stubborn gray cones, which will remain on branches for years after the branches have died.

For some variety, follow the 1.75-mile Schoodic Head Trail for your return trip. The trailhead is just west of the Blueberry Hill parking area.

Directions: From Route 1 in Gouldsboro, head south on ME 186 for about 9 miles and turn right on Moore Road. The park entrance is 1.3 miles ahead and is well marked.

Activities: Hiking, bird-watching, scenic driving, picnicking.
Facilities: Picnic area, restrooms, trails.
Dates: Open year-round.
Fees: None.
For more information: Acadia National Park. P.O. Box 177, Bar Harbor, ME 04609. Phone (207) 288-3338.

PADDLING AROUND THE SCHOODIC PENINSULA
Two Schoodic Peninsula businesses will take visitors out in sea kayaks.
MOOSELOOK GUIDE SERVICE. Mooselook Guide Service in Gouldsboro offers three-hour kayak trips, with instruction, every morning and evening in the summer,

weather permitting. Mooselook also rents kayaks, canoes, and mountain bikes.

For more information: Mooselook Guide Service, HC35, Box 246, Gouldsboro, ME 04607. Phone (207) 963-7720.

SCHOODIC TOURS. Schoodic Tours in Corea offers kayak tours and ecology walking tours. It also rents kayaks and mountain bikes.

For more information: Schoodic Tours. General Delivery, Corea, ME 04624 (in the summer), or 7 Pinewood Street, Orono, ME 04473 (in the winter). Phone (207) 963-7958 in the summer and (207) 866-4717 in the winter.

GOLF ON THE SCHOODIC PENINSULA

GRINDSTONE NECK GOLF COURSE. This 9-hole, par 36 public course in Winter Harbor has some lovely ocean views.

For more information: Grindstone Neck Golf Course, Grindstone Ave., Winter Harbor, ME 04693. Phone (207) 963-7760.

CAMPING ON THE SCHOODIC PENINSULA

No camping is allowed in the Schoodic section of Acadia National Park, but there is at least one private campground on the peninsula.

OCEAN WOOD CAMPGROUND. Birch Harbor. [Fig. 21(6)] This campground has 70 campsites, including some wilderness, oceanfront sites. Some hookups. *(207) 963-7194.*

DINING ON THE SCHOODIC PENINSULA

You can opt for fine dining or down-home Down East fare on the Schoodic Peninsula. Don't forget about picnicking on the rocks at Schoodic Point.

FISHERMAN'S INN. 7 Newman Street, Winter Harbor. This restaurant specializes in seafood, Italian food, and chargrilled beef. *Moderate. (207) 963-5585.*

CHASE'S RESTAURANT. 193 Main Street, Winter Harbor. The chowder, fried fish and other basic fare attract locals and visitors alike to Chase's booths and counter for three meals a day. *Inexpensive. (207) 963-7171.*

LODGING ON THE SCHOODIC PENINSULA

There are several B&Bs and inns on the peninsula, including some geared toward outdoor explorers.

OCEANSIDE MEADOWS INN. Route 195, Prospect Harbor. The innkeepers at this 1860s waterfront inn have degrees in geography, marine biology, and ecotoxicology, and they use a 200-acre nature preserve to share their knowledge. The property includes a marsh, tidal pools, and a sand beach. *Moderate. (207) 963-5557.*

THE BLACK DUCK INN ON COREA HARBOR. Crowley Island Road, Corea. This white clapboard inn sits on 12 acres, including rocky outcrops, a tidal bay and salt marsh, and nature trails. There are single rooms in the inn and waterfront cottages. *Moderate.* (207) 963-2689.

Steuben to Addison

Washington County begins here in Steuben, with the first of several jagged and naturally rich peninsulas dangling into the Gulf of Maine. Route 1 meanders through a series of coastal communities, including Steuben, Milbridge, and Cherryfield. You don't have to stray very far from Route 1 to see a variety of undisturbed natural sites: botanically rich peat bogs (including the state's largest), a nationally important wildlife preserve, a first-rate glacial delta, and offshore islands where thousands of birds nest each summer. If you are an architecture fan, stop in Cherryfield and pick up a map of its National Historic District at a local business. Dozens of architecturally impressive buildings are highlighted.

HUMBOLDT FIELD RESEARCH INSTITUTE

[Fig. 21(7)] Every summer, natural history students and professionals come to Steuben to attend weeklong field seminars and workshops on specialized topics at the Humboldt Field Research Institute at Eagle Hill. The instructors are national authorities in their fields. The students range from amateur naturalists to graduate students and professionals. Dozens of advanced classes are held on very specialized topics, including aquatic etymology, geomorphology, and forest ecology. The institute publishes a peer-reviewed natural history journal, *Northeastern Naturalist.*

For more information: Humboldt Field Research Institute, PO Box 9, Dyer Bay Road, Steuben, ME 04680. Phone (207) 546-2821.

PETIT MANAN NATIONAL WILDLIFE REFUGE

[Fig. 21(8)] This 6,000-plus-acre wildlife refuge provides important habitat for nesting and migrating birds. The refuge includes 10 miles of shoreline on Petit Manan Point, 570 acres on Gouldsboro Point, 628 acres in the town of Milbridge, and 31 offshore islands.

On the mainland portion of the refuge, a variety of habitats—spruce, hardwood, and jack pine forests, peat bogs, hayfields, marshes, beaches, and rocky shoreline—have attracted more than 300 species of birds.

These birds aren't here by accident. The land here is intensely managed to provide the habitats necessary for a number of species. For example, blueberry barrens are periodically burned and hayfields are mowed to open land for courting woodcock (*Scolopax minor*), a member of the sandpiper family, and to provide food for songbirds.

Three freshwater impoundments have been built to attract breeding and migrating waterfowl. Thousands of black ducks (*Anas rubripes*) make use of the resulting wetlands every fall.

Refuge workers have boosted the badly depleted tern population on Petit Manan Island and several other islands by luring them with tern decoys and recorded tern calls. Atlantic puffins were also attracted to Seal Island and returned naturally to Petit

Manan Island. (The birds nesting on Petit Manan Island can be seen from some of the tour boats operating out of Bar Harbor.) Petit Manan is also the site of Maine's second tallest lighthouse, the 123-foot, granite Petit Manan Light, which can be seen 2 miles off Petit Manan Point on clear days.

The national wildlife refuge has two interpretive trails. The Birch Point Trail heads through blueberry fields and a spruce forest to Birch Point on the western shore of the peninsula. The John Hollingsworth Memorial Trail, also called the Shore Trail, heads to the eastern shore. From there, you may walk along the shore to Petit Manan Point.

Directions: From Route 1 between Steuben and Milbridge, head 5.7 miles south on Pigeon Hill Road to the refuge parking area.

Activities: Bird-watching, hiking, shoreline exploration.

Facilities: Parking lots and informational kiosk.

Dates: Open year-round. Seabird nesting islands closed April 1 to Aug. 1.

Fees: None.

Closest town: Steuben, 6 miles.

For more information: Petit Manan National Wildlife Refuge, PO Box 279, Milbridge, ME 04658. Phone (207) 546-2124.

KELP
(*Laminaria agardhii*)
Kelps are the most conspicuous group of brown seaweeds in North America. Kelps have a cylindrical stem and a specialized holdfast that attaches to rocks or other objects.

UPPER BIRCH ISLAND PRESERVE

[Fig. 21(9)] This sheltered island in the Pleasant River near the Addison Peninsula has been a nesting spot for great blue herons for more than 30 years. In 1983, 80 nests were counted in the 60 trees in the island's spruce forest. A pair of bald eagles has also nested here. The ledges off the shore of Upper Birch Island are popular with harbor seals.

Most of the island has steep shores. The southern end has a gravel beach. There are no trails, but it is possible to explore the shoreline after landing a boat. Like many other nesting islands, Upper Birch Island is closed for the February 15 to August 15

Wild Maine Blueberries

Maine is the country's largest blueberry-producing state, but the blueberries grown here are different than those found nearly anywhere else.

Wild Maine blueberries, or lowbush blueberries (*Vaccinium angustifolium*), are smaller than the blueberries grown elsewhere in the United States. They are sweet with a bit of tartness, and their fans insist they make the best blueberry pie. While you can buy them fresh in Maine markets, or from pickup trucks along the side of Route 1, lowbush blueberries are mostly used in processed foods, like boxed muffin mixes and cereals.

Most of Maine's commercial blueberries are grown in Washington County in rocky fields called barrens left by glaciers. Most of the berries are picked the same way they've been harvested for more than a century, with a fine-toothed blueberry rake. Thousands of migrant workers and local people looking to pick up extra cash perform the back-breaking job of raking the 3-inch-high bushes, pulling the berries from the leaves and pouring them into buckets.

Lowbush blueberry bushes have tiny white flowers, which if pollinated will produce berries. Blueberry growers help this process along by trucking in millions of bees each spring.

The bushes on commercial blueberry barrens are usually kept pruned low to the ground—often by burning. The bushes you'll find along the carriage roads at Acadia National Park or on the trails up coastal mountains can grow to be 1 foot or more tall. It is permitted to pick and eat ripe berries in the parks. Do not pick or eat berries on commercial barrens. The barrens are private property and the berries may have been treated with an herbicide.

nesting season. Please don't disturb the eagles or herons, either by approaching their nests or lingering offshore.

Directions: Upper Birch Island is between Ripley Neck and the Addison Peninsula in the Pleasant River.

Activities: Bird-watching, shoreline exploration.

Dates: Upper Birch Island is closed to the public during the Feb. 15 to Aug. 15 nesting season.

Closest town: South Addison, 1 mile.

For more information: The Nature Conservancy, Maine Chapter, Fort Andross. 14 Maine Street, Suite 401, Brunswick, ME 04011. Phone (207) 729-5181.

PINEO RIDGE

[Fig. 21(10)] If you are interested in glacial geology, take a drive or walk along the Pineo Ridge, a world-class example of a glacial delta. The Pineo Ridge is a series of deltas and moraines—ridges of sand, rocks, and sediment left behind by glaciers—

from the last Ice Age, approximately 16,000 years ago. Back then, the delta was under 400 to 500 feet of sea water as the sheet of ice melted and flooded the landscape here. The coast, freed of its burden of heavy ice, then gradually rose again to its original level. Now, the delta is miles of flat blueberry barrens, marked by boulders and small ponds called kettleholes, formed by melting blocks of ice. Parallel ridges and wave-cut cliffs can be seen along the gentle slopes of the delta.

This is wild Maine blueberry country, and the blueberry barrens are private, commercially harvested blueberry fields, so don't walk on the fields or pick the berries. You can walk on the gravel roads that traverse the blueberry barrens. Do not visit in May or June, when swarms of honeybees are released to pollinate the blueberry bushes. (Roadside signs warn of the dangers of exploring the area during pollination season.) If you see a fire, chances are it was intentionally set. The blueberry bushes are very resistant to fire, so every few years the fields are burned to rid them of other plants.

Blueberry barrens can be good bird-watching territory. Birders report seeing warblers and upland sandpipers (*Bartramia longicauda*) in the barrens here.

Directions: From Route 1 in Cherryfield, take ME 183 north 1.3 miles to a fork in the road. Turn right on the unmarked Ridge Road. Follow it for about 5 miles, bear left at the next fork, and park off the road. A U.S.Geological Survey topographic map would be helpful in identifying the glacial formations.

Activities: Bird-watching, walking, geologic exploration.

Dates: Accessible year-round, but should be avoided in May and June when bees are used to pollinate the blueberries.

Closest town: Cherryfield, 6 miles.

THE GREAT HEATH

[Fig. 21(11)] At 6,000-plus acres, the Great Heath is Maine's largest peat bog. Much of the heath is part of the state's system of Public Reserved Land and is open for recreational use. The best way to explore this giant peat bog is from a canoe in the Pleasant River, which bisects the heath.

The Great Heath has typical peat bog vegetation—scrubby, low-lying bushes like sheep laurel (*Kalmia angustifolia*), sphagnum mosses, a variety of pink orchids, and insectivorous pitcher plants and sundew. Yellow-bellied flycatchers (*Empidonax flaviventris*), Lincoln's sparrows (*Melospiza lincolnii*), and other songbirds rustle through the thicket-like vegetation. Ducks, hawks, osprey, and owls have also been recorded here.

The Great Heath is a series of raised bogs that have merged together or coalesced. The elevated areas of the bog are above the water table, so anything growing there must get its moisture from precipitation. The cool, damp atmosphere of Down East Maine helps support the vegetation that tolerates this habitat.

Directions: From Route 1 in Cherryfield, take ME 183 north 1.3 miles to a fork in the road. Turn right on the unmarked Ridge Road. Drive nearly 5 miles (the road will become a dirt road) and turn right onto another dirt road. Take the first dirt road on the left to reach the Pleasant River. (There are several spots to put in a canoe on the Pleasant River. Consult a local map or the Bureau of Parks and Lands for more ideas.)

Activities: Canoeing, bird-watching.

Fees: None.

Closest town: Cherryfield, 6 miles.

For more information: Maine Bureau of Parks and Lands, 22 State House Station, Augusta, ME 04333. Phone (207) 287-3821.

CAMPING BETWEEN STEUBEN AND ADDISON

MCCLELLAN TOWN PARK. [Fig. 21(12)] This park in Milbridge has a few tent sites, picnic areas, and restrooms. Call the town office for information. *(207) 546-2422.*

DINING BETWEEN STEUBEN AND ADDISON

THE KITCHEN GARDEN RESTAURANT. Village Road, Steuben. The gardens surrounding this historic house are as impressive as its delicious, organic dinners. *Moderate. (207) 546-2708.*

RED BARN RESTAURANT AND MOTEL. Main Street, Milbridge. This comfortable restaurant serves three meals a day. *Inexpensive to moderate. (207) 546-7721.*

LODGING BETWEEN STEUBEN AND ADDISON

An Addison B&B provides a different kind of hiking partner.

PLEASANT BAY BED & BREAKFAST AND LLAMA KEEP. West Side Road, Addison. This B&B is on a 110-acre, waterfront llama farm. You can walk 3 miles of trails—with or without a llama. *Moderate. (207) 483-4490.*

The Jonesport Area

PLEASANT RIVER SALMON FRY HATCHERY AND WILD SALMON RESOURCE CENTER

[Fig. 21(13)] This Columbia Falls hatchery raises up to 200,000 salmon fry a year for stocking in Down East Maine rivers. The adjacent resource center has tanks of salmon and volunteers to describe the work being done to restore the wild population of Atlantic sea-run salmon in local rivers.

Directions: The hatchery and resource center are on Main Street in Columbia Falls, right next to the river.

Dates: Open weekdays during the summer and sporadically the rest of the year.

Fees: None.

Closest town: Columbia Falls.

For more information: Pleasant River Salmon Fry Hatchery, PO Box 201, Columbia Falls, ME 04623. Phone (207) 483-4336.

BEALS ISLAND REGIONAL SHELLFISH HATCHERY

[Fig. 22(16)] This hatchery provides tiny clams for flats up and down the coast of Maine. It includes an education center with displays on aquaculture and the clamming industry and tours of the hatchery.

Directions: From Route 1 between Columbia Falls and Jonesboro, take ME 187 south to Jonesport, and cross the bridge to Beals Island. Turn left after the bridge.

Dates: Open to the public daily during the summer.

Fees: None.

Closest town: Beals Island.

For more information: Beals Island Regional Shellfish Hatchery, Beals Island, ME 04611. Phone (207) 497-5769.

GREAT WASS ISLAND PRESERVE

[Fig. 22(1)] Great Wass Island is the anchor of the 50-island Great Wass Archipelago and projects farther out to sea than any other land mass in eastern Maine. A bridge and causeway connect the island to the mainland.

This 1,570-acre Nature Conservancy preserve is an ecological treasure. The Gulf of Maine and the Bay of Fundy meet here, and the mixing currents create a cool, moist, and often very foggy climate that is hospitable to a remarkable selection of wildlife and unusual plants.

The island includes a spruce forest, a large jack pine forest, and extensive peat bogs, or heaths. The moist, acidic soil of the peat bogs provides the perfect habitat for sphagnum mosses and several varieties of orchids, including the striking dragon's mouth orchid (*Arethusa bulbosa*). This bright pink orchid, which resembles a long-tongued dragon, blooms for less than a week in early June. Another rare plant found here is the baked-apple berry (*Rubus chamaemorus*), a subarctic relative of the raspberry that produces one golden berry. Insectivorous plants—pitcher plants and sundews—that can get nutrients from the insects they digest, thrive here, as well.

Several rare but hardy plants thrive on its wind-battered headlands. Beachhead iris (*Iris hookeri*), marsh felwort (*Lomatagonium rotatum*), and bird's eye primrose (*Primula laurentiana*) are all subarctic species that tolerate the rough conditions of the Great Wass shore.

Osprey (*Pandion haliaetus*) nest on Great Wass, and bald eagles (*Haliaeetus leucocephalus*) nest nearby. The peat bog is home to nesting palm warblers (*Dendroica palmarum*), boreal chickadees (*Paris hudsonicus*), and spruce grouse (*Canachites canadensis*).

The island's marshlands are frequented by great blue herons (*Ardea herodias*), sandpipers, and other shorebirds. Offshore, look for rafts of common eiders (*Somitaria mollissima*). Harbor seals (*Phoca vitulina*) can sometimes be seen sunning themselves on offshore ledges.

Because of the fragile landscape here, most of the island is off-limits to visitors. Rough weather conditions and terrain on the island make it a difficult one to explore.

Two paths head from The Nature Conservancy parking lot to the shoreline. (Make sure to pick up a trail map at the parking area.) It's possible to walk along the shore between the two trails, returning by the same route, to make a 5.5-mile hike, and to walk along the rocky shore to the southern end of the island. That will add another 9 miles, round trip, from the shore end of the Cape Point Trail. Please refrain from continuing along the shore to the eastern shore of the island. It is a long, very difficult hike and there is private property to respect. Please stay on the trails or the rocky shoreline. The Nature Conservancy warns visitors that the trails are very rough and will take longer than expected to hike. Make sure to wear sturdy shoes and be prepared for cold, wet conditions.

The 1.5-mile Mud Hole Trail follows the northern shoreline of the island to Mud Hole Point. The 2-mile Little Cape Point Trail heads across the interior of Great Wass, wandering through spruce and jack pines before offering a good look at a peat bog via a "bog bridge" and continuing on to the island's Cape Cove. Leave yourself a good five hours to walk the 5.5-mile loop.

Directions: From Route 1 in Jonesboro, take ME 187 to Jonesport, crossing the bridge over the Moosabec Reach to Beals. Drive through Beals to Great Wass Island. Veering right, follow the road about 3 miles to Black Duck Cove, where there is a Nature Conservancy parking area on the left. This is a sensitive preserve, and The Nature Conservancy doesn't want too many visitors at any given time. If the parking area is full, try another day.

Activities: Hiking, bird-watching.

Facilities: Trails.

Dates: Open year-round.

Fees: None.

Closest town: Beals, 3 miles.

For more information: The Nature Conservancy, Maine Chapter, Fort Andross. 14 Maine Street, Suite 401, Brunswick, ME 04011. Phone (207) 729-5181.

NATURE CRUISES OUT OF JONESPORT

If you want to see a puffin up close, get aboard a boat with Captains Barna and John Norton out of Jonesport. Every summer morning, weather permitting, the Nortons head for Machias Seal Island, the only puffin colony island where landings are permitted (*see* Machias Seal Island, page 273).

Also out of Jonesport, Captain Laura Fish's Island Cruises takes passengers on cruises around nearby islands, including Great Wass and Mistake islands, both Nature Conservancy preserves. Customized cruises are available.

For more information: Captain Barna Norton, RR1, Box 990, Jonesport, ME 04649. Phone (207) 497-5933. Captain Laura Fish, Kelley's Point Road, RR1, Box 1360, Jonesport, ME 04649. Phone (207) 497-3064.

CAMPING IN JONESPORT

JONESPORT CAMPGROUND. [Fig. 22(2)] The town-operated Jonesport Campground has water views, outhouses, and some electrical hookups. Sites go on a first-come, first-served basis. *(207) 497-5926.*

DINING IN THE JONESPORT AREA

You can rub elbows with the locals at a lunch counter or enjoy an ocean view at restaurants in Jonesport.

TALL BARNEY'S RESTAURANT. Main Street, Jonesport. Lobstermen frequent this spot next to the bridge to Beals Island for basic down-home food, including some

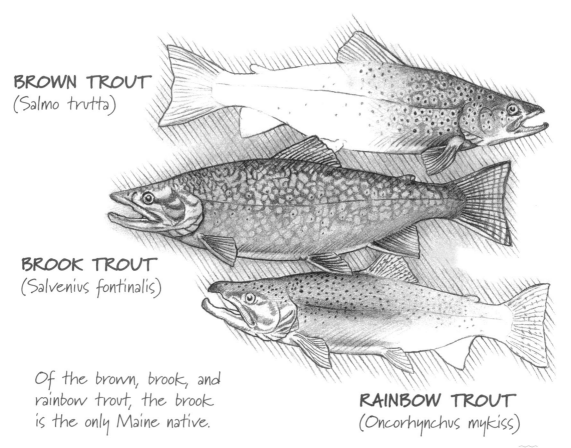

BROWN TROUT
(Salmo trutta)

BROOK TROUT
(Salvenius fontinalis)

RAINBOW TROUT
(Oncorhynchus mykiss)

Of the brown, brook, and rainbow trout, the brook is the only Maine native.

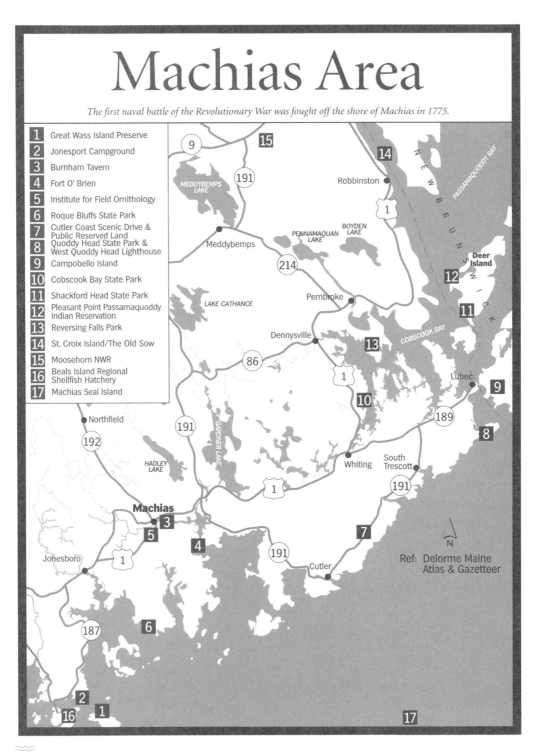

Machias Area

The first naval battle of the Revolutionary War was fought off the shore of Machias in 1775.

1. Great Wass Island Preserve
2. Jonesport Campground
3. Burnham Tavern
4. Fort O' Brien
5. Institute for Field Ornithology
6. Roque Bluffs State Park
7. Cutler Coast Scenic Drive & Public Reserved Land
8. Quoddy Head State Park & West Quoddy Head Lighthouse
9. Campobello Island
10. Cobscook Bay State Park
11. Shackford Head State Park
12. Pleasant Point Passamaquoddy Indian Reservation
13. Reversing Falls Park
14. St. Croix Island/The Old Sow
15. Moosehorn NWR
16. Beals Island Regional Shellfish Hatchery
17. Machias Seal Island

Ref: Delorme Maine Atlas & Gazetteer

great chowder. (Don't sit at the big center table unless you are a regular.) *Inexpensive.* *(207) 497-2403.*

HARBOR HOUSE CAFÉ. Sawyer Square, Jonesport. This seasonal cafe offers lobster and great coffee inside or outside. The Harbor House also has B&B rooms year-round and an antique store. *Moderate. (207) 497-5417.*

LODGING IN THE JONESPORT AREA

B&B inns dominate the lodging choice in this section of the coast.

TOOTSIE'S BED & BREAKFAST. Trynor Square, Jonesport. This Victorian B&B has water views and is open year-round. *Inexpensive. (207) 497-5414.*

The Machias and Machias Bay Area

The first naval battle of the Revolutionary War was fought just off the shore of Machias in 1775, when colonists captured the British schooner *Margaretta*. Machias takes its Colonial history seriously. The tavern where colonists plotted their battle has been preserved, as have many other historic buildings and sites. Machias is the also the site of a respected summer ornithology institute, at the University of Maine at Machias. Many tourists ignore Machias, but it's a good jumping-off spot for scenic drives down the Starboard Peninsula or up the beautiful Cutler coast.

BURNHAM TAVERN

[Fig. 22(3)] This 1770 tavern appears much as it did in 1775 when patriot Jeremiah O'Brien and a band of colonists planned their assault on the *Margaretta* in what was the first naval battle of the Revolutionary War. Items from the original tavern and from the *Margaretta* are on display. Upstairs there are displays of period furniture, tools, and other historic items. The gambrel-roofed, yellow tavern is the oldest building in eastern Maine. The Daughters of the American Revolution restored it in the early 1900s and give tours.

Machias means "bad little falls" in Micmac. After touring the tavern, visitors should walk next door to The Bad Little Falls Park. There, pedestrians can walk on a suspension bridge over a waterfall.

Directions: The Burnham Tavern is in the middle of Machias, just north of the Machias River on ME 192.

Dates: The museum is open weekdays from mid-June through September and by appointment.

Fees: There is a charge for admission.

Closest town: Machias.

For more information: The Burnham Tavern. Main Street, Machias, ME 04654. Phone (207) 255-4432.

FORT O'BRIEN

[Fig. 22(4)] This fort was built in 1775 to protect the busy logging center of Machias. The British destroyed it the same year. It was rebuilt in 1777, only to be destroyed again by the British in 1814. Now, earthworks that were refortified during the Civil War are all that remain. It is a State Historic Site and a scenic spot for a picnic, with a view of Machias Bay and its islands.

Directions: Fort O'Brien is on ME 92, about 5 miles east of Machias.

Activities: Sight-seeing, picnicking.

Facilities: Picnic area.

Dates: The site is open Memorial Day to Labor Day.

Fees: None.

Closest town: Machias, 5 miles.

For more information: Fort O'Brien, Maine Bureau of Parks and Land, 22 State House Station, Augusta, ME 04333. Phone (207) 941-4014.

INSTITUTE FOR FIELD ORNITHOLOGY

[Fig. 22(5)] This nonprofit program at the University of Maine at Machias holds yearly seminars on shorebirds, migration, and other topics, in Maine, New Brunswick, New Jersey, and elsewhere. Most of the programs focus on field identification. Amateurs and seasoned birders are welcome. The institute also holds a summer camp program for teenagers in cooperation with the American Birding Association.

For more information: The Institute for Field Ornithology, University of Maine at Machias, 9 O'Brien Avenue, Machias, ME 04654. Phone (207) 255-1289.

ROQUE BLUFFS STATE PARK

[Fig. 22(6)] This 274-acre state park overlooking Englishman Bay offers saltwater and freshwater swimming. The saltwater swimming is at a scenic, 1-mile-long pebble beach, but the water is extremely cold in these parts. The water in a large freshwater pond feels quite warm in comparison and is popular with children. There are picnic areas with grills, changing areas, restrooms, and a playground.

Directions: From Route 1 in Machias, drive 6 miles south on Roque Bluffs Road.

Activities: Swimming, walking, picnicking.

Facilities: Picnic areas, changing areas, restrooms, and playground.

Dates: Open May 15 through Sept. 20.

Fees: There is a charge for admission.

Closest town: Roque Bluffs.

For more information: Roque Bluffs State Park, Roque Bluffs Road, Roque Bluffs, ME 04648. Phone (207) 255-3475, in season, and (207) 941-4014, off-season.

CUTLER COAST SCENIC DRIVE AND PUBLIC RESERVED LAND

[Fig. 22(7)] One of the most beautiful drives along the Maine coast begins in East

Machias on ME 191 and follows the Bold Coast for 27 miles to West Lubec. In Cutler, a spectacular piece of land has been preserved for public use. The Cutler Coast Unit of Public Reserved Land is a 2,200-acre parcel with a 5.4-mile loop trail through the woods, a bog, and meadows, and along the steep cliffs. There are three tent campsites off the trail.

The dramatic scenery along this trail makes it a nice hike for anyone, but birders will find it particularly satisfying. According to the book *A Birder's Guide to Maine*, 190 species have been reported here, including bald eagles, peregrine falcons, and six owl species. As you scan the ocean along the cliffs, keep an eye out for whales, as well as seabirds.

Directions: From East Machias, follow ME 191 through the village of Cutler. Continue about 3.5 miles on ME 191 to a small parking area with a sign next to a meadow on the east side of the road. The trailhead is at the parking lot.

Activities: Hiking, camping, bird-watching.

Facilities: Trail, three primitive campsites, no fires permitted.

Dates: Open year-round.

Fees: None.

Closest town: Cutler, 3.5 miles.

For more information: Maine Bureau of Public Lands, Eastern Regional Office, Airport Road, PO Box 415, Old Town, ME 04468. Phone (207) 827-5936.

Leach's Storm Petrels

These sparrowlike seabirds are near the southern end of their range on the Maine coast.

Thousands of Leach's storm petrels (*Oceanodroma leucorhoa*) nest on Maine islands. But sightings of these 9-inch birds are very rare because they spend most of their time well out to sea. They come ashore only to nest and then are nocturnal. Leach's storm petrels lay one egg in a burrow in the ground.

The Leach's storm petrel is all black with a white rump. It has a forked tail.

A similar species, the Wilson's storm petrel (*Oceanites oceanicus*), can sometimes be seen on the offshore Maine waters. At about 7 inches, it's slightly smaller than the Leach's storm petrel and does not have a forked tail.

MACHIAS SEAL ISLAND

[Fig. 22(17)] This treeless, 15-acre island is the best place off the Maine coast to get an up-close look at puffins, terns and other seabirds. It is the only island with a puffin colony where landings are permitted. Blinds allow visitors to watch and photograph the birds from an unforgettably close vantagepoint.

Machias Seal Island is the subject of some international dispute. The United States and Canada both claim ownership to the island. Canada operates a lighthouse here, and Canadian Wildlife officials protect the birds and limit the number of visitors. While the two nations disagree on who owns the island, their dispute has remained amicable. Both countries declined to take the case to the World Court at The Hague several years ago.

Two Maine coast captains take visitors out to Machias Seal Island. Advance reservations are essential. (It's a good idea to book your trip early in your visit. If bad weather cancels the trip, you have time to try again.)

Unlike some of the islands off the Maine coast where puffins have been reintroduced by humans, Machias Seal Island has a naturally occurring puffin colony. That makes puffins seen here "countable" under the rules of the American Birding Association. The colony on Matinicus Rock is also naturally occurring or wild.

Thousands of puffins return to Machias Seal Island from the open North Atlantic every May to nest in burrows. Other species on Machias Seal Island are endangered razorbill auks (*Alca torda*), arctic terns (*Sterna paradisea*), common terns (*Sterna hirundo*), and common murre (*Uria aalge*). Familiarize yourself with these birds before your excursion, and bring your field guide along.

A visit to Machias Seal Island is unforgettable for seasoned or novice birdwatchers. As the boat approaches the island, visitors can see and hear thousands of birds calling, swimming, and diving for food. Once on shore (a bit of a tricky undertaking since there is no dock), visitors can walk on wooden boardwalks and paths across the island to the blinds. Watch every step you take, as tern eggs and chicks are often on the path. You can't miss the adult terns, which dive at visitors. Tour operators suggest wearing a hat for protection against "guano bombs." The blinds have become part of the scenery for the puffins, which perch atop them and roam around them. The blinds have sliding window covers on each side. Open only one side at a time to avoid detection. The ride out to Machias Seal Island takes about one and one-half hours. A typical visit on the island lasts between 45 minutes and three hours. Make sure to bring rain gear, sturdy waterproof shoes, warm clothing, and plenty of film.

Directions: Two Maine companies—one in Jonesport, the other in Cutler—take visitors to Machias Seal Island. You need a permit to visit. (Both companies also offer other nature cruises.)

Activities: Bird-watching.

Facilities: The boats have restrooms. The island has boardwalks and bird blinds.

Dates: Weather permitting, boats head to Machias Seal Island daily, roughly from Memorial Day through Aug.

Fees: There is a charge for the boat ride.

For more information: Captains Barna B. and John E. Norton, RR1, Box 990, Jonesport, ME 04649. Phone (207) 497-5933. Or, Bold Coast Charter Company, Captain Andrew Patterson, PO Box 364, Cutler, ME. Phone (207) 259-4484.

DINING IN THE MACHIAS AREA

You can have lunch with a llama or eat gourmet food in the book-lined dining room of a 1776 Cape-style home in this region. There are also some good pizza and sandwich spots.

LLAMA LUNCH HIKES. West Kennebec Road, Machias. Call Steeplebush Farm ahead of time to arrange a lunch and a nature hike with a llama. *Inexpensive to moderate. (207) 255-4244.*

MICMAC FARM. Route 92, Machiasport. This restaurant in a historic home has a handful of well-prepared entrées, candlelight dining, fireplaces, and water views. *Moderate. (207) 255-3008.*

LODGING IN THE MACHIAS AREA

From motel to mansion, there's lodging of every sort in the Machias area.

THE RIVERSIDE INN. Route 1, East Machias. This restored Victorian mansion also has a gourmet restaurant. *Moderate. (207) 255-4134.*

MACHIAS MOTOR INN. 26 East Main Street, Machias. This motel has decks overlooking the tidal Machias River and a heated indoor pool. *Moderate. (207) 255-4861.*

Cobscook and Passamaquoddy Bays

Maine's easternmost communities are clustered around these two sprawling bays near the Canadian border. The region is known for its dramatic and powerful tides. High tide can reach 28 feet here. The nutrient-rich mud flats and marshes left by these tides attract large flocks of birds, especially migrants preparing to head south in the fall. The region is also known for its healthy bald eagle population.

There are several parks in easternmost Maine, including a national refuge for migratory waterfowl, the island where FDR spent many summers, and a picnic spot with a great view of the churning, tide-fed currents in a reversing falls.

The city of Eastport and town of Lubec are the commercial centers of this region. While only a couple miles apart by water, they're a good 40-mile drive apart.

QUODDY HEAD STATE PARK AND WEST QUODDY HEAD LIGHTHOUSE

[Fig. 22(8)] Many of the visitors to Quoddy Head State Park come to admire the West Quoddy Head Lighthouse, the only red-and-white-striped lighthouse in Maine. The lighthouse sits on the easternmost point of land in the United States. (East Quoddy Head Lighthouse is across the channel in New Brunswick, Canada.)

The 481-acre state park also has beautiful views across the Grand Manan Channel and into lower Passamaquoddy Bay, where harbor seals and whales can sometimes be spotted. This state park is a microcosm of the eastern Maine coast.

There's a raised peat bog, a dense spruce forest, and volcanic rock cliffs that rise 200 feet above the surf. All are accessible by footpaths, and the fragile peat bog can be viewed from a boardwalk. Another trail leads to Gulliver's Hole, a foaming sea pocket visible from a high overlook.

The variety of habitats makes this park a great spot for birdwatchers, who scan the woods and peat bog for boreal species and the seas for seabirds, including kittiwakes (*Rissatridactyla*) and oldsquaw (*Clangula hyemalis*).

The park has picnic tables with priceless ocean views, so bring a lunch along when visiting. The adjacent Quoddy Head Light is operated by the U.S. Coast Guard. The grounds are open to the public, but the lighthouse is not. A footpath connects the park and the lighthouse grounds.

Directions: From ME 189 in Lubec, head south on South Lubec Road. Following the signs to the state park, turn left on West Quoddy Head Road.

Activities: Hiking, picnicking, bird-watching.

Facilities: Trails, picnic areas, restrooms.

Dates: Open May 15 through Oct. 15, but visitors may walk past the closed gates and explore the grounds during the off-season.

Fees: There is a charge for admission.

For more information: Quoddy Head State Park, West Quoddy Head Road, Lubec, ME 04652. Phone (207) 733-0911. Off-season, phone (207) 941-4014.

CAMPOBELLO ISLAND

[Fig. 22(9)] Campobello Island is Canadian soil, but it is the site of a U.S.-Canadian international park and is easily accessible from Maine via a bridge from Lubec. It is a site of considerable historic and natural interest, so any visitor who makes it to far eastern Maine should include a trip to Campobello.

The Roosevelt Campobello International Park is a 2,800-acre park named for Franklin Delano Roosevelt, who spent many summers enjoying the natural wonders of the island. He was just 1 year old when his father bought land and an unfinished summer home on Campobello in 1883. Eventually, the family bought an 18-bedroom "cottage," which is now open to the public. FDR spent many summers on Campobello sailing, hiking, horseback riding, and reading in the family cottage. Then in 1921 Roosevelt was struck with polio while visiting the island. While his wife, Eleanor Roosevelt, and their children, including one who was born here, continued to visit, FDR didn't make it back for 12 years. His remaining visits were as the president of the United States. The U.S. and Canadian governments formed the international park in 1964 as a memorial to Roosevelt and to the cooperation between the two countries. It is overseen by a joint commission with equal representation from the U.S. and Canada, and it claims to be the only international park of its type in the world.

Begin a visit to Campobello at the visitor's center, where displays and a movie tell the history of the Roosevelt family and Campobello. Pick up a map of the park's 8.4 miles of roads and 8.5 miles of walking trails.

The barn-red shingled cottage where Franklin and Eleanor Roosevelt spent their summers is open for tours and offers a vivid glimpse of how the Roosevelts spent their time here. One room is now a museum containing a display of photographs from

Roosevelt's four terms in office, as well as various furnishings and artifacts from his family's summers here. The rest of the house remains as the family used it. Wicker chairs, hand-hooked rugs, and other furnishings give the home a relaxed but elegant feel. Outside, footpaths wander by gardens and to a handful of other attractive cottages, which are used by the park's conference program. One floor of the Hubbard Cottage is open for tours when it isn't occupied by conference participants.

The international park at Campobello includes 2,800 acres of preserved natural land, including miles of beautiful seacoast. Scenic roads circle the park, and several short paths (most less than 1 mile) intersect with the roads to take visitors farther into the natural area. Several locations are highlighted on the park map. Most have picnic facilities and interpretive signs. Upper Duck Pond and Lower Duck Pond are protected saltwater coves popular with migratory waterfowl and shorebirds. There is easy access to island beaches at Con Robinson's Point, Liberty Point, and Fox Farm. Eagle Hill Bog can be viewed from a boardwalk. Friar's Head, an easy 0.7-mile walk from the visitor's center, is one of several spots with observation decks.

Remember when visiting Campobello that upon crossing the bridge you are on Atlantic time, one hour later than Eastern Standard Time. Camping is not allowed in the international park, but it is allowed at the adjacent Herring Cove Provincial Park.

Directions: From ME 189 in Lubec, cross the FDR International Bridge to Campobello Island. Be prepared for a customs stop. The park is 1.5 miles past the bridge on Campobello.

Activities: Visiting the cottage, scenic driving, hiking.

Facilities: Visitors center, trails, picnic areas, restrooms.

Dates: Open Memorial Day weekend to Columbus Day.

PIPSISSEWA
(Chimaphila umbellata)
The plant's name comes from the Cree Indians, who called them "pipsisikweu," which means "it breaks into small pieces," because they used the leaves as medicine for treatment of kidney stones and gallstones.

Fees: None.

Closest town: Lubec, 1.5 miles.

For more information: Roosevelt Campobello International Park, PO Box 129, Lubec, ME 04652. Phone (506) 752-2922. Herring Cove Provincial Park. Phone (506) 752-2396.

COBSCOOK BAY STATE PARK

[Fig. 22(10)] Cobscook Bay State Park is part of the Moosehorn National Wildlife Refuge, part of a chain of migratory bird refuges that begin here and stretch to Florida (*see* page 280). *Cobscook* is an Indian word meaning boiling tides, and the 24-foot rushing tides are a big attraction here.

There are several ways to enjoy the scenery at this 888-acre, oceanfront park in Dennysville. There are nature-walking trails that are groomed for cross-country skiing in the winter, picnic areas, and several campsites, including many that are in secluded oceanfront spots.

Cobscook Bay is one of the best spots in Maine to watch for bald eagles (*Haliaetus leucocephalus*). This region is a wintering area for these birds, which are listed as threatened federally and by the state. Bald eagles mate for life, and they return to their nests each year. Do not linger near a bald eagle's nest; the birds are not tolerant of human disturbance and can be scared from their nests permanently.

Directions: Cobscook Bay State Park is off Route 1, about 4.5 miles north of Whiting.

Activities: Camping, hiking, boating, skiing, bird-watching.

Facilities: Tent and RV campsites (no hookups), running water and showers, picnic areas, restrooms, and trails.

Dates: The park is open year-round. The campsites are available from May 15 to Oct. 15.

Fees: There is a charge for admission and for camping.

For more information: Cobscook Bay State Park, RR1, Box 127, Dennysville, ME 04628. Phone (207) 726-4412.

SHACKFORD HEAD STATE PARK

[Fig. 22(11)] This 90-acre peninsula near Eastport has an easy, 0.5-mile path through the woods to Shackford Head, where the view takes in nearby salmon aquaculture pens, as well as Lubec and Campobello across Cobscook Bay.

Fish farming has become a vital business in Maine, bringing in more than $40 million in sales revenue annually. The coast of Down East Maine is perfect for salmon fishing operations like the one seen here because of the strong tides and currents, good water quality, and water temperatures between 32 and 55 degrees Fahrenheit. Fish farmers lease the land and water for fish pens from the state.

Directions: From Route 1 in Perry, take ME 190 to Broad Cove Road on the right.

Or from Eastport, take Broad Cove Road west out of town. Follow signs to the park. The trail to Shackford Head begins at the parking lot.

Activities: Hiking, bird-watching.

Facilities: Trail, restrooms.

Dates: Open year-round.

Fees: None.

Closest town: Eastport.

For more information: Shackford Head State Park, Maine Bureau of Parks and Lands, 22 State House Station, Augusta, ME 04333. Phone (207) 941-4014.

PLEASANT POINT PASSAMAQUODDY INDIAN RESERVATION

[Fig. 22(12)] About 600 members of the Passamaquoddy Indian tribe live on the reservation at Pleasant Point. Another 550 live 50 miles inland at the Indian Township Reservation. The Waponahki Museum on the Pleasant Point Reservation is dedicated to preserving the Passamaquoddy language, history, and culture. Some Passamaquoddy Indians make finely crafted baskets, jewelry and carved items that can be found in galleries and stores on the reservation and in nearby towns.

Directions: The reservation is on ME 190, 7 miles north of Eastport.

Dates: The museum is open by appointment.

Fees: Donations are accepted.

Closest town: Perry.

For more information: Waponahki Museum. PO Box 295, Perry, ME 04667. Phone (207) 853-4001.

REVERSING FALLS PARK

[Fig. 22(13)] Pack a picnic and enjoy the show of the rushing currents and whirlpools fed by the strong tides at the town-owned Reversing Falls Park in Pembroke. A channel between the tip of a mainland peninsula and Falls Island creates the reversing falls, where water literally roars in and out at high and low tides. There's plenty of coastline to explore here and an easy 0.8-mile nature trail along a protected cove. Keep an eye out for osprey and bald eagles. Also watch for harbor seals playing in the currents or sunning on ledges.

Directions: Heading north on Route 1 from Dennysville into Pembroke, turn right into Pembroke at the Triangle Grocery Store, and then turn right at the Odd Fellow Hall onto Leighton Neck Road. Take the third right onto a road marked with a Reversing Falls sign. Drive down a hill and turn left onto a gravel road in about 1.5 miles. Follow that road 2 miles to the park.

Activities: Picnicking, hiking, wildlife watching.

Facilities: Trail, restrooms, picnic areas.

Dates: Open year-round.

Fees: None.

THE OLD SOW

[Fig. 22(14)] The Old Sow is the largest tidal whirlpool in the Northern Hemisphere. At an estimated 50 feet across, it can put on quite a show of swirling currents and jetties at each incoming and outgoing tide. The Old Sow is between Deer Island, New Brunswick, and Maine's Moose Island, so it's only visible from a boat.

Some of the charter boats and ferries in the area will sail by the Old Sow if asked. Harris Whale Watching takes whale watchers out daily in the summer.

For more information: Harris Whale Watching, 24 Harris Point Road, Moose Island, Eastport, ME 04631. Phone (207) 853-4303.

ST. CROIX ISLAND

[Fig. 22(14)] A small island in the St. Croix River is a little-known but historic spot in the history of the settlement of North America. In 1604, the island became the first attempt at a European settlement in this region of North America. A small band of French colonists, led by Sieur de Monts and Samuel de Champlain, landed here in 1604, intending to build a settlement. It was a bitterly cold winter, and several members of the French party died. The survivors left within months, headed to more hospitable conditions in what is now Nova Scotia.

The island, an International Historic Site overseen by the U.S. and Canada, isn't accessible from land. There is a historic marker and picnic area with a view of the island at a rest stop on Route 1 about half-way between Robbinston and Calais.

Directions: Heading north on Route 1 from Robbinston toward Calais, look for the observation area on the right as you approach Red Beach.

Activities: Sight-seeing.

Facilities: On the mainland, shelter with interpretive signs, picnic tables, and restrooms.

Dates: Open year-round.

Fees: None.

Closest town: Calais, 6 miles.

For more information: Superintendent, Saint Croix Island International Historic Site, care of Acadia National Park, PO Box 177, Bar Harbor, ME 04609. Phone (207) 288-3338.

MOOSEHORN NATIONAL WILDLIFE REFUGE

[Fig. 22(15)] The Moosehorn National Wildlife Refuge is the northernmost in a chain of Atlantic Flyway refuges for migratory birds that runs between Maine and Florida. It has two sections, the 7,200-acre Edmunds Unit adjacent to Cobscook Bay and the 17,200-acre Baring Division south of Calais that includes Cobscook Bay State Park (*see* page 278).

Portions of the refuge are intensely managed by the U.S. Fish and Wildlife Service, which creates clearings to promote the breeding of the American woodcock (*Philohela minor*). These shy birds live in alders by day and clearings at night. In the past, the clearings needed by the woodcock, and many other bird and mammal species, were created by forest fires and farming. Today, refuge managers use clear-cutting and controlled burns to achieve the same result. The most exciting time to see a woodcock is in early April and May when the male performs dramatic aerial courtship flights, spiraling hundreds of feet into the air before diving to the ground and warbling to his mate. For a chance to see this springtime ritual, ask at the refuge office for directions to where the woodcocks have been courting. Plan to watch unobtrusively from the side of a clearing at dusk.

Visitors are occasionally allowed to accompany wildlife biologists on woodcock-banding trips in the refuge. Call ahead of time to ask about such a trip.

The refuge is also a great place to see many other bird species, especially during the spring and fall migration. At least three pairs of bald eagles nest here. Check out the area around the Magurrewock Marsh near Route 1 at the Baring Division and around the Dennys Bay coast of the Edmunds Unit for eagles. Canada geese, common loons, and several kinds of ducks can often be seen in the refuge's wetlands.

Large and small mammals also live in the refuge. Black bears (*Ursus americanus*), moose (*Alces alces*), and white-tailed deer (*Odocoileus virginianus*) are among the larger mammals. Black bears can sometimes be seen searching for food in old apple orchards and blueberry fields, or wandering along the old roads that cross the refuge.

Moosehorn has more than 50 miles of roads that are open to hikers, cross-country skiers, and snowmobilers, but not to motor vehicles. There is also a short nature trail next to the refuge headquarters.

Hikers should be aware that much of the Moosehorn National Wildlife Refuge is open to deer hunters during the rifle season and trappers in the fall. Blaze orange clothing should be worn.

BLACK BEAR
(Ursus americanus)
At birth, a bear weighs only half a pound, but will grow to 300 pounds when mature.

Directions: From Calais, head west on Route 1 for 3.5 miles. Turn left on Charlotte Road. In 2.5 miles, turn right on the refuge road to reach the refuge headquarters.

Activities: Bird-watching, hiking, cross-country skiing, bicycling, summer interpretive programs.

Facilities: Headquarters has bird lists, maps, and restrooms.

Dates: The refuge is open year-round.

Fees: None.

Closest town: Calais, 6 miles.

For more information: Moosehorn National Wildlife Refuge, RR1, Box 202, Suite 1, Baring, ME 04694. Phone (207) 454-7161.

DINING IN LUBEC AND EASTPORT

Seafood is the specialty just about everywhere in this region.

HOME PORT INN. 45 Main Street, Lubec. This inn has a popular restaurant that specializes is innovative fish dishes. *Moderate. (207) 733-2077.*

EASTPORT LOBSTER AND FISH HOUSE. 167 Water Street, Eastport. The bar and dining room here have water views. *Moderate. (207) 853-6006.*

WA-CO DINER. Bank Square, Eastport. Breakfast begins at 6 a.m., and the bar is open until midnight on weekends at this booth-and-counter-style diner. *Inexpensive. (207) 853-4046.*

LODGING IN LUBEC AND EASTPORT

Several historic homes in Lubec and Eastport now serve as B&Bs.

PEACOCK HOUSE BED AND BREAKFAST. 27 Summer Street, Lubec. This antique-filled B&B is in an old sea captain's house. *Moderate. (207) 733-2403.*

MOTEL EAST. 23 Water Street, Eastport. This motel has a cable TV and a great view of Passamaquoddy Bay. *Moderate. (207) 853-4747.*

Appendices

A. When in Maine…

These are things to keep in mind while traveling in Maine. There are exceptions to some of these items, and new laws take effect every year. Please check with authorities for up-to-date, pertinent information.

Taxes: Maine has a 7 percent tax on all lodging, restaurant, and bar bills. This so-called hospitality tax is not usually included in advertised rates. Maine's sales tax is 5.5 percent.

Smoking: Smoking is banned in all Maine restaurants, so don't look for the smoking section.

Helmets: Adults are not required to wear helmets on motorcycles or bicycles in Maine. Children are required to wear helmets on motorcycles and bicycles.

Rules of the road: Maine requires all occupants of a car to wear a seatbelt, and young children must be in safety seats. State law prohibits anyone under the age of 19 from riding in the bed of a pickup truck.

Park bargain: Admission fees to the state parks can add up if you plan to visit a few parks or are traveling with several people. The state offers an inexpensive annual vehicle pass that can be purchased at any state park and pays for itself quickly.

Fishing: A fishing permit is not required for saltwater fishing. A permit is required for fishing in fresh water. A license is required to set a lobster trap. Tampering with someone else's trap carries a hefty fine.

Long distance: Maine has one area code, 207. It is not necessary to dial 1 before calling anywhere within the state, but many in-state calls are long-distance, toll calls.

Holiday: Maine and Massachusetts are the only states to recognize Patriots' Day on April 19. Government offices and some financial institutions are closed.

World Wide Web: Maine's Tourism Department has a web site that includes many activities and places to eat and drink. Find it at www.visitmaine.com

B. Maine Books and References

Acadia's Biking Guide and Carriage Road Handbook by Tom St. Germain, Parkman Publications, Bar Harbor, ME 1997.

Activity Guide to Acadia National Park by Meg Scheid and Carol Peterson, Eastern National, Bar Harbor, ME 1997.

AMC Guide to Mount Desert Island and Acadia National Park compiled by the Appalachian Mountain Club, field guide by Chris Elfring, Appalachian Mountain Club Books, Boston, MA 1993.

Biking on Mount Desert Island by Audrey Minutolo, Down East Books, Camden, ME 1996.

A Birder's Guide to Maine by Elizabeth C. Pierson, Jan Erik Pierson, and Peter D. Vickery, Down East Books, Camden, ME 1996.

The Coast of Maine Book by Rick Ackermann and Kathryn Buxton, Berkshire House Publishers, Lee, MA 1996.

A Complete Guide to Maine's Orchids by Philip E. Keenan, DeLorme Mapping, Yarmouth, ME 1983.

The Edge of the Sea by Rachel Carson, Mariner Books, Boston, MA 1998.

Glaciers and Granite, A Guide to Maine's Landscape and Geology by David L. Kendall, North Country Press, Unity, ME 1993.

Hiking Maine by Tom Seymour, Falcon Press, Helena, MT 1995.

Hiking on Mount Desert Island by Earl D. Brechlin, Down East Books, Camden, ME 1996.

Hot Showers: Maine Coast Lodgings for Kayakers and Sailors by Lee Bumsted, Audenreed Press, Brunswick, ME 1997.

Lighthouses: A Guide to Coastal and Offshore Guardians by Barbara Feller-Roth, DeLorme Mapping Company, Yarmouth, ME 1988.

Maine: An Explorers Guide by Christina Tree and Elizabeth Roundy, The Countryman Press, Woodstock, VT 1997.

The Maine Atlas and Gazetteer, DeLorme Mapping, Yarmouth, ME 1998.

Maine Forever: A Guide to Nature Conservancy Preserves in Maine by Ruth Ann Hill, Maine Chapter, The Nature Conservancy, Brunswick, ME 1989.

Maine Handbook by Kathleen M. Brandes, Moon Publications, Chico, CA 1998.

Maine Lighthouses, A Pictorial Guide by Courtney Thompson, CatNap Publications, Mount Desert, ME 1998.

Maine's Natural Heritage by Dean Bennett, Down East Books, Camden, ME 1988.

National Audubon Society Field Guide to New England by Peter Alden and Brian Cassie, Alfred A. Knopf, Inc., New York, NY 1998.

The Nature of North America by David Rockwell, The Berkley Publishing Group, New York, NY 1998.

Nature Walks in Southern Maine by Jan M. Collins and Joseph E. McCarthy, Appalachian Mountain Club Books, Boston, MA 1996.

The Northeast Coast by Maitland A. Edey and the editors of Time-Life Books, Time-Life Books, New York, NY 1973.

Roadside Geology of Maine by D.W. Caldwell, Mountain Press, Missoula, MT 1998.

The Seaside Naturalist by Deborah A. Coulombe, Prentice Hall, Englewood Cliffs, NJ 1984.

The Sense of Wonder by Rachel Carson, Harper Collins, New York, NY 1998.

Walking the Maine Coast by John Gibson, Down East Books, Camden, ME 1991.

Wildflowers: A Guide to Some of Maine's Most Beautiful Flora by Barbara Feller-Roth, DeLorme Mapping, Yarmouth, ME 1983.

C. Conservation and Historic Preservation Organizations

Maine Audubon Society, 118 Route 1, PO Box 6009, Falmouth, ME 04105. Phone (207) 781-2330. Web site www.maineaudubon.org

Maine Coast Heritage Trust, 169 Park Row, Brunswick, ME 04011. Phone (207) 729-7366. Web site home.acadia.net/userpages/mchtme/index.html

Maine Historical Society, The Center for Maine History, 485 Congress Street, Portland, ME 04101. Phone (207) 774-1822. Web site www.mainehistory.org

The Nature Conservancy, Maine Chapter, Fort Andross, 14 Maine Street, Suite 401, Brunswick, ME 04011. Phone (207) 729-5181. Web site www.tnc.org/infield/State/Maine/

National Audubon Society, PO Box 524, Dover-Foxcroft, ME 04426. Phone (207) 564-7946.

Natural Resources Council of Maine, 271 State Street, Augusta ME 04330. Phone (207) 622-3101.

D. Lighthouses on the Maine Coast

Maine's jagged rocky coast can be hazardous to mariners. More than 70 lighthouses have been built along the coast and its islands to warn ships of dangerous points and mark the entrances to harbors. These sentinels of the Maine coast have in some cases outlived their usefulness and could be replaced by cheaper but less charming aluminum poles with solar panels and plastic lamps. In 1999, the Coast Guard, finding it hard to justify the cost of maintaining the dozens of lighthouses along the Maine Coast, transferred ownership of 28 lighthouses to nonprofit groups and local governments. The new owners will maintain these historic and beautiful structures, while the Coast Guard will continue to maintain their lights, foghorns, and other navigational aids. Coast Guard officials hope the Maine Lights program, enacted by Congress in 1996, will catch on throughout the country.

Some people collect lighthouse sightings the way birders keep bird lists and peak-bagging hikers collect mountain summits. Some of Maine's lighthouses are on islands well out to sea, but many are easily reached by car or public ferry. The lighthouses have all been automated, and many of the keepers' houses are now private homes, so please respect the privacy of residents while admiring the lighthouses. Several Maine lighthouses are accessible by car, some are located within parks, and some of them have museums. One, on Isle au Haut, has an inn in its keeper's house. Here, listed by region, are some of the lighthouses that are either accessible by car or ferry or can be easily viewed from shore:

SOUTHERN COAST

Cape Neddick Light, York

This scenic lighthouse, which is often called Nubble Light, is easily visible from the town of York's Sohier Park (*see* page 35).

CASCO BAY

Cape Elizabeth Light, Cape Elizabeth

This light and the nearby state park are still known as Two Lights (*see* page 68), even though a second light here was removed in 1924. This light and keeper's house, which were captured in an Edward Hopper painting, are on private property but can be seen from Two Lights State Park.

Portland Head Light, Cape Elizabeth

Maine's first lighthouse, Portland Head Light was commissioned by President George Washington and built in 1791. There's a museum and the Fort Williams Park here (*see* page 67).

Spring Point Light, South Portland

This lighthouse at the end of a breakwater marks a ledge at the entrance to Portland Harbor (*see* page 70). It's easily accessible from the grounds of Southern Maine Technical College. The Portland Harbor Museum is nearby.

Bug Light, South Portland

This small lighthouse sits at the end of a breakwater on the southern side of the entrance to Portland Harbor. There's a park on the grounds (*see* page 71).

MID-COAST

Burnt Island Light, Southport

This 1821 light, which guards the west entrance to Boothbay Harbor, is easily visible from shore and is a popular picnic spot with boaters.

Pemaquid Light, Bristol

This 1827 lighthouse sits on a dramatic point. The keeper's house is now a museum on the local fishing industry and the lighthouse (*see* Pemaquid Point, page 152).

Fort Point Light, Stockton Springs

This lighthouse, which guards the mouth of the Penobscot River, is on the grounds of Fort Point State Park (*see* page 184).

Marshall Point Light, Port Clyde

Marshall Point Light sits on a beautiful point and has the Marshall Point Lighthouse Museum in its keeper's house (*see* page 157).

Owl's Head Light, Owls Head

Owl's Head Light is the centerpiece of Owl's Head State Park (*see* page 164).

Rockland Breakwater Light

This lighthouse sits at the end of a 0.8-mile jetty. Visitors can walk out to the light and its brick keeper's house (*see* Rockland Breakwater, page 163).

Monhegan Light

The keeper's house at this granite lighthouse is now a local museum. Reach Monhegan on boats from Port Clyde, New Harbor, or Boothbay Harbor, and walk to the lighthouse (*see* page 160).

DOWN EAST

Browns Head Light

This lighthouse on the island of Vinalhaven (*see* page 165) is about 6 miles on a rocky road from the ferry landing.

Grindle Point Light

Take the ferry from Lincolnville to Islesboro (*see* page 179) to see this 1851 lighthouse, which is near the island ferry dock.

Dyce Head Light, Castine

A trail leads to this lighthouse from the village of Castine. The keeper's house is a private residence (*see* page 197).

Isle au Haut Light

The keeper's house at this lighthouse is the Keeper's House Inn (*see* page 207). To visit, take the mailboat from Stonington and walk about 1 mile to the lighthouse.

MOUNT DESERT ISLAND

Bass Harbor Head Light, Tremont.

There's a parking area and pathway down to the Bass Harbor Head Light (*see* page 246) on the southwestern shore of Mount Desert Island, but the view is best from the water.

Hockamock Head Light

To see the square Hockamock Light (*see* page 251), take the Swans Island ferry out of Bass Harbor, then ride a bike about 4 miles to the light.

Baker Island Light

The Islesford ferry from Northeast Harbor takes visitors to Baker Island. Acadia National Park sponsors occasional naturalist walks to the lighthouse (*see* page 241).

WAY DOWN EAST

Prospect Harbor Light

This 1850 lighthouse sits on the grounds of a Naval facility but can easily be seen from the road or from across the harbor.

West Quoddy Head Light, Lubec

This is Maine's only red-and-white-striped lighthouse and sits on the easternmost point of the continental United States. It's accessible from Quoddy Head State Park (*see* page 275).

E. Web Sites on the Maine Coast

Acadia National Park: www.nps.gov/acad/
Bigelow Laboratory for Ocean Sciences: www.bigelow.org
Gulf of Maine Aquarium: http://octopus.gma.org/
The Lobster Institute at the University of Maine: www.lobster.um.maine.edu/lobster
Maine Audubon Society: www.maineaudubon.org
Maine Birding: www.mainebirding.net
Maine Bureau of Parks and Land: www.state.me.us/doc/prkslnds/prkslnds.htm
Maine Department of Inland Fisheries and Wildlife: http://janus.state.me.us/ifw/
    homepage.htm
Maine Geologic Survey: http://web.ddp.state.me.us/doc/nrimc/mgs/mgs.htm
Maine Guides Online: www.maineguides.com
Maine Island Trail Association: www.mita.org
Maine Department of Marine Resources: www.state.me.us/dmr/homepage.htm
Maine Natural Resources Information and Mapping Center: http://web.ddp.state.me.us/
    doc/nrimc/nrimc.htm
Maine Office of Tourism: www.visitmaine.com
Maine Professional Guides Association: www.maineguides.org
The Nature Conservancy, Maine Chapter: www.tnc.org/infield/State/Maine/index.html
Roosevelt Campobello International Park: www.fdr.net
USGS Woods Hole Field Center: http://woodshole.er.usgs.gov/

F. Workshops, Camps, and Courses

If you're interested in learning more about birds or other natural features on the Maine coast, there are a few schools that offer serious classes on natural history topics.

AUDUBON ECOLOGY CAMP

The National Audubon Society operates an adult nature study camp on Hog Island in Muscongus Bay. Topics include field ornithology, ecology, and nature study by kayak. There is also a youth program and some family programs.

For more information: Audubon Ecology Camps and Workshops, National Audubon Society, 613 Riversville Road, Greenwich, CT 06831. In the summer, write Audubon Ecology Camp, Keene Neck Road, Medomak, ME 04551. Phone (207) 529-5148.

THE CHEWONKI FOUNDATION

The Chewonki Foundation offers wilderness trips for adults, families, and teenagers, a Maine Coast Semester that focuses on environmental topics for high school juniors, and a summer camp for boys.

For more information: The Chewonki Foundation, 485 Chewonki Neck Road, Wiscasset, ME 04578. Phone (207) 882-7323.

HUMBOLDT FIELD RESEARCH INSTITUTE

This nonprofit research institute holds weeklong seminars and workshops on specialized natural history topics that attract amateur and professional naturalists. The institute publishes a peer-reviewed natural history journal, *Northeastern Naturalist.*

For more information: Humboldt Field Research Institute, PO Box 9, Dyer Bay Road, Steuben, ME 04680. Phone (207) 546-2821.

INSTITUTE FOR FIELD ORNITHOLOGY

This nonprofit program at the University of Maine at Machias holds yearly seminars on a variety of birding topics for beginning and expert bird watchers.

For more information: The Institute for Field Ornithology. University of Maine at Machias. 9 O'Brien Ave., Machias, ME 04654. Phone (207) 255-1289.

SHOALS MARINE LABORATORY

This marine science research station on Appledore Island in the Isles of Shoals offers a series of weeklong adult education courses on topics like plant ecology, island birds, and marine mammals. The laboratory, which is operated by Cornell University and the University of New Hampshire, also offers undergraduate for-credit courses.

For more information: Shoals Marine Laboratory, GH14 Stimson Hall, Cornell University, Ithaca, NY 14883. Phone (607) 255-3717.

G. Special Events, Fairs, and Festivals

Summers along the Maine coast are jam-packed with festivals, fairs, and lobster boat races. Things tend to slow down a bit in the winter months.

FEBRUARY

U.S. National Toboggan Championships, Camden—This toboggan race raises money for the Camden Snow Bowl and draws hundreds of teams, some serious and many light-hearted. Phone (207) 236-3438.

MARCH

Portland Flower Show, Portland—This huge horticultural show arrives just as Mainers are ready for spring. Phone (207) 775-4403.

Saints and Spirits Weekend, Camden—This weekend celebrating the Camden region's microbreweries and pubs features live entertainment and takes place the weekend before or after St. Patrick's Day. Phone (207) 236-4404.

Maine Boatbuilders Show, Portland—This annual event features more than 200 exhibitors, including more than 90 boatbuilders. Phone (207) 774-1067.

APRIL

Fishermen's Festival, Boothbay Harbor—This Boothbay Harbor festival celebrates fishermen. Highlights include a lobster crate race, fish chowder contest, the crowning of Miss Shrimp Princess, a memorial service for fishermen lost at sea, a blessing of the fleet and a boat parade. Phone (207) 633-2353.

MAY

Memorial Day—Many Maine coast communities observe Memorial Day with parades and other ceremonies. Try the Wiscasset parade for a nice small-town observance. Phone (207) 882-8205.

JUNE

Old Port Festival, Portland—This one-day street fair in Portland's Old Port begins with a parade and features many food vendors, performers, and sidewalk sales. Phone (207) 797-5982.

LaKermesse, Biddeford—This huge festival celebrates the Franco-American heritage of Biddeford. Phone (207) 282-1567.

Beachfest, Old Orchard Beach—This annual festival includes sandcastle-building contests and other beach activities. Phone (800) 365-9386.

Coastal Arts and Heritage Week, Camden—This is a weeklong program of cultural activities and events. Phone (207) 236-4404.

JULY

Fourth of July—Many Maine towns have fireworks displays over the ocean on the Fourth of July. Portland, Bath, and Bar Harbor are popular places to celebrate Independence Day. Phone (207) 772-5800, (207) 725-8797, or (207) 288-5103.

Rockland Schooner Days, Rockland—Highlights of this Rockland festival that honors Maine's fleet of historic schooners includes a parade of the beautiful ships, a fireworks display, kayak races and more. Phone (207) 596-0376.

Annual Native American Festival, Bar Harbor—This festival at Bar Harbor's College of the Atlantic includes the Maine Indian Basketmakers Alliance sale, craft demonstrations, storytelling, drumming, singing, and dancing. Phone (207) 288-3519.

North Atlantic Blues Festival, Rockland—This two-day festival draws top blues performers to Rockland's Harbor Park. Phone (207) 596-6055.

Ethno Pops Concert, Ogunquit—This annual music event highlights a different type of music each year. Phone (207) 646-6170.

Seaside Festival, Kittery—This annual festival at Kittery's Fort Foster feature food, entertainment, and craft booths. Phone (207) 439-3800.

Yarmouth Clam Festival, Yarmouth—This busy festival features a parade, entertainment, and lots of food (including clams, of course). Phone, (207) 846-3984.

Belfast Bay Festival, Belfast—This waterfront festival is more than 50 years old and includes a carnival and chicken barbecue. Phone (207) 338-5900.

AUGUST

Lobster Festival, Rockland—This is a huge celebration of Maine's favorite crustacean. It features exhibits, crafts, ship tours and lots of lobster. Phone (207) 596-0376.

The Maine Festival, Brunswick—This four-day festival at Thomas Point Beach in Brunswick celebrates Maine's art and artists and includes a juried craft and art fair, seven performances and lots of food. Phone (207) 772-9012.

Annual Indian Ceremonial Days, Eastport—This event at the Pleasant Point Reservation includes Native American ceremonies, crafts, dances, and food. Phone, (207) 853-4644.

Annual Sidewalk Art Show, Ogunquit—An impressive sidewalk art show in an historic artists' colony. Phone (207) 646-2939.

Lobster Festival, Winter Harbor—Highlights of this festival on the Schoodic Peninsula include lobster boat races, a marine trade show, a blueberry pancake breakfast, a fish chowder luncheon, and a lobster dinner. Phone (207) 963-7658.

Wild Blueberry Festival, Machias—Maine Wild Blueberries are celebrated with a parade, performances, a craft fair, a baking contest, and a blueberry pie-eating contest. Phone (207) 255-6665.

SEPTEMBER

Blue Hill Fair, Blue Hill—Highlights at the Labor Day Weekend Blue Hill Fair include sheep dog trials, livestock shows, and agricultural and arts and crafts exhibits. Phone (207) 374-3701.

Thomas Point Beach Bluegrass Festival, Brunswick—This Labor Day weekend bluegrass festival draws nationally acclaimed performers. Phone (207) 725-6009.

Windjammer Weekend, Camden—This Labor Day weekend festival celebrates the windjammer industry with live music, demonstrations, fireworks, and the Schooner Bum Talent Show. Phone (207) 236-4404.

Capriccio, Ogunquit—This annual 10-day festival celebrates the arts with theater, music, storytelling, poetry readings, fashion shows, ballet, and other performances. Phone (207) 646-6170.

Eastport Salmon Festival, Eastport—This festival features boat tours, a fishing derby, a farmers' market, arts and crafts displays, and plenty of salmon. Phone, (207) 853-4644.

OCTOBER

"Chowdah" Challenge, Freeport—Chefs put their seafood chowder recipes to the test in this annual competition. Attendees get to judge the entries. Phone (207) 865-1212.

Festival of Scarecrows, Rockland—Creatively made scarecrows pop up all over town during the fall festival, which includes contests, a farmers' market, and other events. Phone (207) 596-6457.

MDI Lions Club Acadia Triathlon, Mount Desert Island—Competitors in this annual race on Mount Desert Island tackle a 26-mile triathlon course on foot, bicycle, and canoe. Phone (207) 288-3511.

NOVEMBER

Many Maine coast communities have holiday light displays in November and December. One lovely lit-up spot this time of year is Nubble Lighthouse in York. While you're here, check out the holiday lights in York Village and York Beach. Phone (207) 363-1040.

DECEMBER

Holiday celebrations continue through December in many Maine coast communities.

Christmas Prelude, Kennebunkport—The Christmas Prelude includes wonderful decorations, including a tree adorned with local lobstermen's buoys. Santa arrives here, as he does in many harbor towns, in a lobster boat. Phone (207) 967-0857.

New Year's Portland, Portland—Portland welcomes in the New Year in a big way, with a variety of New Year's Eve musical performances, dances, films and other events and fireworks over the harbor at midnight. Phone (207) 772-9012.

RUBY-THROATED HUMMINGBIRD

(Archilochus colubris)
Hummingbirds have the unique ability among birds to fly backwards or straight up or down. The ruby-throated is the only hummingbird seen over most of the eastern U.S.

H. Outfitters, Suppliers, & Boat Charters

The following outfitters, guides, suppliers, and boat charters are listed alphabetically by city.

Maine Saltwater Outfitters and Guide Service, 836 West Alan Road, Alna, ME 04535. Phone (207) 882-8392. Saltwater fly-fishing trips.

Acadia Bike & Canoe, 48 Cottage Street, Bar Harbor, ME 04609. Phone (207) 288-0342. Bike, canoe, and kayak rentals, tours.

Acadia Outfitters, 106 Cottage Street, Bar Harbor, ME 04609. Phone (207) 288-8118. Kayak tours.

Bar Harbor Whale Watch Company, Route 3, Bar Harbor, ME 04609. Phone (207) 288-2386. Whale-watch cruises.

Coastal Kayaking Tours and Acadia Bike, 48 Cottage Street, Bar Harbor, ME 04609. Phone (207) 288-9606. Kayak and bike rentals and tours.

Down East Nature Tours, PO Box 521, Bar Harbor, ME 04609. Phone (207) 288-8128. Nature and bird-watching tours.

National Park Sea Kayak Tours, 39 Cottage Street, Bar Harbor, ME 04609. Phone (207) 288-0342. Sea kayak tours.

Sea Bird Watcher Company, 52 West Street, Bar Harbor, ME 04609. Phone (207) 288-5033. Bird- and whale-watching cruises.

Whale Watcher Inc., 1 West Street, Bar Harbor, ME 04609. Phone (207) 288-3322. Whale-watching cruises.

Sea Escape, Captain Les McNelly, PO Box 7, Bailey Island, ME 04003. Phone (207) 833-5531. Fly-fishing, island and seal watch cruises. Boat to Eagle Island.

Coastal Maine Outfitters, RR 4, Box 4140, Belfast, ME 04915. Phone (207) 722-3218. Hunting lodge and guides for grouse, woodcock, puddle and sea duck hunting.

Pro Fish n' Sea, Captain Roger Provencher, 139 Cleaves Street, Biddeford, ME 04005. Phone (207) 284-8068. Fishing charters for mackerel, stripers, bluefish, groundfish, sharks, tuna.

The Phoenix Centre, Route 175, Blue Hill Falls, ME 04615. Phone (207) 374-2113. Sea kayak instruction and tours, canoe instruction, junior guide program on outdoor skills.

Pine Island, Captain A.J. Campbell, PO Box 66, Boothbay, ME 04527. Phone (207) 63305143. Charter fishing for sharks, striped bass, bluefish.

Balmy Day Cruises, Pier 8, Commercial Street, Boothbay Harbor, 04538. Phone (207) 633-2284. Nature cruises, harbor cruises, Monhegan trip.

Bingo, Captain Jeff Ritter, PO Box 463, Boothbay Harbor, ME 04538. Phone (207) 633-3775. Fishing charters for cod, pollock, haddock, cusk.

Cap'n Fish Cruises, Wharf Street, Boothbay Harbor, ME 04538. Phone (207) 633-3244. Whale-watching, seal watching, puffin watching, and other nature cruises.

Tidal Transit Ocean Kayaking Company, PO Box 743, Boothbay Harbor, ME 04538. Phone (207) 633-7140. Sea kayak sales, rentals, instruction, and tours.

Maine Coast Experience, HCR 64, Box 380, Brooklin, ME 04616. Phone (207) 359-5057. Sea kayaking, whale-watching, island hiking, oceanfront resort.

Center Street Cycles, 11 Center Street, Brunswick, ME 04011. Phone (207) 729-5309. Sales and rentals of bikes, local cycling advice.

Wild Irish, Captain Pat Keliher, 141 Harding Road, Brunswick, ME 04011. Phone (207) 846-1015. Fly-fishing for striped bass.

Narraguagus Guide Service, Captain Tom Carter, RR 1 Box 263CC, Cherryfield, ME 04622. Phone (207) 546-3735. Fishing charters for striped bass.

Bold Coast Charter Company, Captain Andrew Patterson, PO Box 364, Cutler, ME 04626. Phone (207) 259-4484. Nature cruises, bird-watching trips, puffin trips to Machias Seal Island.

Granite Island Guide Service, RR 1, Box 610A, Deer Isle, ME 04627. Phone (207) 348-2668. Kayaking, hiking, and camping trips, duck hunting guide.

Harris Whale Watching, Harris Point Road, Eastport, ME 04631. Phone (207) 853-4303. Whale-watching cruises.

***Charger*, Captain George Warren**, 567 Boothbay Road, Edgecomb, ME 04556. Phone (207) 557-2628 (day), (207) 882-9309 (night). Charter fishing, sail and power boat rentals.

Cadillac Mountain Sports, 34 High Street, Ellsworth, ME 04605. Phone (207) 667-7819. And 26 Cottage Street, Bar Harbor, ME 04609. Phone (207) 288-4532. Outdoor gear and clothing.

L.L. Bean Factory Store, High Street, Ellsworth, ME 04605. Phone (207) 667-7753. Discounted outdoor equipment and clothing.

L.L. Bean, Route 1, Freeport, ME 04033. Phone (207) 865-4761. Outdoor equipment and clothing, Outdoor Discovery Schools on many activities, including kayaking, canoeing, fly-fishing, wilderness skills, bicycling, wing shooting, and outdoor photography.

Maine Waters, 14 Sandy Beach Road, Freeport, ME 04032. Phone (207) 865-9337. Kayaking lessons and guides.

Patagonia, 9 Bow Street, Freeport, ME 04032. Phone (207) 865-0506. Outdoor clothing, including some deeply discounted items.

Seaspray Kayaking, 78 Desert Road, Freeport, ME 04032. Phone (888) 349-7772. Sea kayak sales, instruction, and trips.

Son Rae Charters, Matt Reed, HC 33 Box 10A, Georgetown, ME 04548. Phone (207) 371-2813. Fishing charters, kayak trips.

Captain Barna Norton, RR 1, Box 990, Jonesport, ME 04649. Phone (207) 497-5933. Puffin cruises to Machias Seal Island.

Captain Laura Fish, Kelley's Point Road, RR 1, Box 1360, Jonesport, ME 04649. Phone (207) 497-3064. Nature cruises, custom cruises.

Cape-able Bike Shop, Arundel Drive, Kennebunkport, ME 04046. Phone (207) 967-4382. Bicycle sales and rentals, local cycling advice.

Indian Whale Watch, PO Box 2672, Ocean Avenue, Kennebunkport, ME, 04046. Phone (207) 967-5912. Whale-watching cruises.

Nautilus Whale Watch, PO Box 2775, Kennebunkport, ME 04046. Phone (207) 967-0707. Whale-watching cruises.

Kittery Trading Post, 301 US Route 1, Kittery, ME 03904. Phone (207) 439-2700. Outdoor equipment and clothing. Kayak lessons and seminars on outdoor activities.

Seafari Charters, 7 Island Avenue, Kittery, ME 03904. Phone (207) 439-5068. Fishing, whale-watching, and scuba diving charters.

Ducktrap Sea Kayaking, Route 1, Lincolnville Beach, ME 04849. Phone (207) 236-8608. Kayak instruction and trips.

Captain Chester "Skid" Rowe, Box 784, Litchfield, ME 04350. Phone (800) 472-2036. Fly-fishing cruises for striped bass, bluefish.

DDiving, PO Box 157, Milo, ME 04463. Phone (800) 828-1102. Scuba diving lessons and tours.

Hardy Boat Cruises, Shaw's Lobster Wharf, Route 32, New Harbor, ME 04554. Phone (207) 677-2026. Puffin and seal-watching cruises, trips to Monhegan.

Pteropod, **Captain Robert Pratt**, Maine Marine Consultants, 58 East Neck Road, Nobleboro, ME 04555. Phone (207) 691-7245. Fishing and sailing trips.

Captain Satch and Sons, 793 Morrills Mill Road, North Berwick, ME 03901. Phone (207) 324-9655. Charter fishing for striped bass, mackerel, bluefish. Also shorter family cruises to view seals and lobstering and to try fishing.

North Creek Guide Service, 74 Summit Terrace, North Yarmouth, ME 04097. Phone (207) 829-6792. Hunting and fishing guide.

Northeast Antlers, 551 Atlantic Highway, Northport, ME 04849. Phone (800) 558-7658. Fly-fishing instruction and trips.

Bunny Clark, PO Box 837, Ogunquit, ME 03907. Phone (207) 646-2214. Deep-sea fishing and sight-seeing cruises.

Finestkind Cruises, PO Box 1828, Ogunquit, ME 03907. Phone (207) 646-5227. Lobstering, sight-seeing, and lighthouse cruises.

The Deborah Ann, **Captain Mark Young**, Perkins Cove, Ogunquit, ME 03907. Phone (207) 361-9501. Whale-watching cruises.

Ugly Anne, **Ken Young Sr.**, PO Box 863, Ogunquit, ME 03907. Phone (207)-646-7202. Groundfish cruises and charters.

H2Outfitters, PO Box 72, Orr's Island, ME 04066. Phone (207) 833-5257. Sea kayak instruction and trips.

Maine Island Kayak Co., 70 Luther Street, Peaks Island, ME 04108. Phone (800) 796-2373. Sea kayaking instruction and trips.

Tidal Trails Eco-Tours, PO Box 321, Pembroke, ME 04666. Phone (207) 726-4799. Sea kayaking, canoeing, mountain biking, hiking, charter boats, cottages.

Kennebec Charters, 12 Bayledges Road, Phippsburg, ME 04562. Phone (207) 389-1883. Fishing charters, lighthouse cruises to Seguin Light.

Bay View Cruises, 184 Commercial Street, Portland, ME 04101. Phone (207) 761-0496. Excursion cruises, including seal-watching and lighthouse cruises.

Calendar Islands Guide Service, PO Box 10513, Portland, ME 04104. Phone (207) 829-4578. Fly-fishing guide on coastal rivers.

Eagle Tours, 1 Long Wharf, Portland, ME 04101. Phone (207) 774-6498. Seal-watching and lighthouse cruises, trips to Eagle Island.

Forest City Mountain Bike Guides, PO Box 16038, Portland, ME 04101. Phone (207) 879-2512. Guided bike/walk tours of greater Portland.

Go Fish, **Captain Ben Garfield**, PO Box 10541, Portland, ME 04104. Phone (207) 799-1339. Fishing charters for striped bass, bluefish, shark, mackerel.

L.L. Bean Factory Store, 542 Congress Street, Portland, ME 04101. Phone (207) 772-5100. Discounted outdoor equipment and clothing.

Repeat Performance, 311 Marginal Way, Portland, ME 04101. Phone (207) 879-1410. Sales of consigned outdoor gear and clothing and factory overstocks and seconds.

Province Mountain Outfitters, Captain Robin Thayer, 13 Church Street, Richmond, ME 04357. Phone (207) 737-4695. Fly-fishing instruction and trips for women only.

Every Place Wild, PO Box 866, Rockport, ME 04856. Phone (207) 236-2177. Guide for canoeing, kayaking, fishing, hiking, and camping.

Maine Sport Outfitters, US Route 1, PO Box 956, Rockport, ME 04856. Phone (207) 236-8797. Sales and rentals of outdoor equipment and clothing, sea kayaking trips and lessons, guided fishing trips.

Trina Lyn Sportfishing Charter, Captain Todd Stewart, PO Box 431, Saco, ME 04072. Phone (207) 284-2352. Sport-fishing charters.

Penobscot Bay Outfitters, 118 Nickerson Road, Searsport, ME 04974-3937. Phone (888) Sea-Duck. Sea duck hunting guides.

Happy Hooker II, **Captain Jerry Sullivan**, RR 1, Box 842, South Harpswell, ME 04079. Phone (207) 833-5447. Offshore fishing for cod, bluefish, sharks, tuna, and inshore fly-fishing for striped bass and bluefish.

Eastern Mountain Sports, Maine Mall, South Portland, ME 04106. Phone (207) 772-3776. Outdoor clothing and gear, including camping supplies.

Maine Fishing and Diving Charters, 175 Harriet Street, South Portland, ME 04106. Phone (207) 767-0796. Sea fishing and diving charters.

Mansell Boat Company, Shore Road, Southwest Harbor, ME 04679. Phone (207) 244-5625. Sailboat and powerboat rentals and sailing lessons.

Olde Port Mariner Fleet, 634 Cape Road, Standish, ME 04084. Phone (207) 642-3270. Whale-watching, fishing, island/seal trip, lighthouses cruises.

Maine Sea Ducks, 18 Pine Street, Thomaston, ME 04861. Phone (207) 354-6520. Hunting and fishing guides.

Obsession Sportfishing Charters, 4 Patricia Drive, Topsham, ME 04086. Phone (207) 729-3997. Light tackle and fly-fishing charters.

Georges River Outfitters, 1384 Atlantic Highway, Warren, ME 04864. Phone (207) 273-3818. Guides for fishing and hunting.

Maine Outdoors Expeditions, 156 Come Spring Lane, Warren, ME 04864. Phone (207) 273-2840. Canoeing, camping, fishing, hiking.

Mount Pleasant Canoe & Kayak, PO Box 86, West Rockport, ME 04685. Phone (207) 785-4309. Canoe and kayak sales, rentals, instruction, and trips.

Chewonki Foundation, RR 2, Box 1200, Wiscasset, ME 04578. Phone (207) 882-7323. Wilderness trips including sea kayaking, lake and river canoeing, hiking, camping, and backcountry skiing.

Bath Cycle & Ski, Route 1, Woolwich, ME 04579. Bike and ski sales and rentals, local cycling advice.

Women Backcountry Guided Adventures, 26 Bates Street, Yarmouth, ME 04096. Phone (207) 846-3036. Hiking, camping, and backpacking trips for women.

Mainely Fishing, Captain Richard C. Witham, 41 Emus Way, York, ME 03909. Phone (207) 363-6526. Fishing charters for groundfish, bluefish, striped bass, sharks. Scenic tours.

Rip Tide Charters, 1 Georgia Street, York, ME 03909. Phone (207) 363-2536. Fly-fishing and light tackle charters.

Harbor Adventures, PO Box 345, York Harbor, ME 03911. Phone (207) 363-8466. Sea kayak instruction and trips.

Shearwater Charters, PO Box 472, York Harbor, ME 03911. Phone (207) 363-5324. Fly-fishing instruction and charters, specializing in striped bass.

I. Glossary

Acidic—Characterized by an excess of hydrogen ions; typically detrimental to soil fertility or lake inhabitants.

Amphipod—A crustacean of the order Amphipod including the sand fleas and beach hoppers. There are 3,000 species of amphipods.

Anadromous—Migrating from sea water into fresh water to spawn, as salmon or shad.

Arthropod—Invertebrate animals with jointed legs, segmented body, and exoskeleton, including crustaceans.

Basalt—Dark, fine-grained igneous rock common in dikes and lava flows.

Bivalve—The class of mollusks with two-part shells, including mussels and clams.

Bog—Peat-dominated wetland, generally acidic, poor in nutrients.

Boreal—Descriptive of a northern coniferous forest and its inhabitants.

Brackish—Salty, but less so than sea water.

Coniferous—Cone-bearing trees; evergreens or softwoods.

Continental drift—Theory that the continental land masses drift across the earth as the earth's plates move and interact in a process called Plate Tectonics.

Crustaceans—Animals that wear segmented shells and have segmented legs are arthropods, such as insects and crustaceans. Crustaceans are arthropods that live in the water and breathe by gills, such as lobsters, barnacles, crabs, and shrimps.

Deciduous—Trees that lose their leaves in winter; hardwoods.

Detritus—Decomposed plant and animal matter that has been worked to sediment size through the action of water and sand.

Diatoms—One-celled algae with cell walls of silica that make up the first links in the aquatic food chain.

Ebb tide—The movement of the tidal current away from shore; a decrease in the height of the tide.

Ecosystem—A biological community existing in a specific physical environment.

Estuary—Brackish-water areas influenced by the tides and located where the mouth of a river meets the sea.

Exoskeleton—An external skeleton, such as the shell of a mollusk or arthropod.

Gneiss—Banded metamorphic rock. (Pronounced "nice.")

Habitat—Where an animal lives; its natural home.

Headland—A rocky promontory sticking out from the coast.

Inlet—An opening through which ocean waters enter and leave an enclosed body of water, such as a sound, bay, or marsh.

Intertidal zone—The zone along the shore between high and low tide marks.

Littoral—Pertaining to the seashore, especially the intertidal area.

Metamorphic—Rocks formed from other rocks under intense pressure and temperature, typically due to mountain building.

Monadnock—A hill or mountain of resistant rock that stands above the surrounding low-lying area.

Neap tide—Lowest range of the tide, occurring at the first and last quarter of the moon.

Orogeny—Mountain-building event.

Pangea—Supercontinent formed from Laurentia and Gondwana about 350 million years ago.

Pelagic—The division of the ocean that includes the whole mass of water; it is divided into the neritic zone (water depth 0-600 feet) and the oceanic zone (water deeper than 600 feet).

Phytoplankton—Plant plankton.

Plankton—Aquatic organisms that float at the mercy of the currents or have limited swimming abilities.

Quartzite—Metamorphic rock formed from sedimentary rocks, typically sandstone in which the main element is quartz.

Salt marsh—An area of soft, wet land periodically flooded by salt water.

Schist—Layered metamorphic rock formed from shales and characterized by parallel layers of platy minerals, such as mica.

Sedimentary—Rocks formed when sediments—sand, mud, plant material, sea shells—are deposited in a place and accumulate over millions of years.

Shale—Sedimentary rock composed of clay, mud, and silt grains which easily splits into layers.

Spring tide—Tide of maximum range occurring at the new and full moon.

Striae—Parallel scratches or grooves in a rock outcrop, cut by the sandpaper-like passage of a grit-filled glacier.

Till—Salt, sand, gravel, and boulders frozen into or on top of a glacier that are left as an unsorted mixture on the earth after the ice melts.

Understory—Shrubs and nonwoody plants that live underneath trees in a forest.

Zooplankton—Animal plankton.

Index